peripateticus non ut philosophus ... homo.

cxxiiii

Marsilius ficinus laurentio medici v. magnanimo.
Oliverium ardoinum, insignem peripateticum commendare
et non mediocriter, ni aristoteles sineret, cum et plurimum
commendarem. Si aristoteles quam pecuniam felicitati
necessariam iudicavit, libros suos absque nummis
componere potuisset, et aristotelicus iste aristo
telica sine nummis posset interpretari. Intelli
gis quo quid velit. Oliverius peripateticus est, non
cynicus. At non est indigens philosophi hec appetere.
Sit ita sane. Verum non ut philosophus est, hec postu
lat, sed ut homo. Utrum vero philosophi sit, pecu
niam petere, postquam confessus disputabimus. Vale.
Salutat te Laurentius boninconstrus miniatensis,
poeta astronomicus, astronomusque poeticus.

Neque amor sine religione neque religio sine amore lau
datur.

xxv

Marsilius ficinus philippo cortonio lucensi. Mitto
ad te amorem quem promiseram. Mitto et religionem.
ut agnoscas et amorem meum religiosum esse,
et religionem amatoriam. Sane ita natura compara
tum est, ut neque amor honestus sit, nisi religio
sus. neque religio vera nisi amore suscepta.
Salutat te angelus manettus, Iannotii oratoris
filius, paternae virtutis heres.

THE LETTERS OF MARSILIO FICINO

Volume 11

(*Liber XII*)

The Letters of
MARSILIO FICINO

Translated from the Latin by members of the Language
Department of the School of Philosophy and Economic Science, London

VOLUME 11

being a translation of
Liber XII

SHEPHEARD-WALWYN

This translation first published in 2020 by
Shepheard-Walwyn (Publishers) Ltd
107 Parkway House, Sheen Lane,
London SW14 8LS
www.shepheard-walwyn.co.uk

Publisher's Note:

The beehive motif shown on the title page appears on a number of Ficino Manuscripts which were illuminated for Lorenzo de' Medici's library. The end-papers show two pages in Ficino's own hand from a manuscript containing Book 1 of his *Letters*. This is now in the Biblioteca Nazionale Centrale, Florence (Cod. Naz. II IX 2)

British Library Cataloguing in Publication Data
A catalogue record for this book
is available from the British Library

ISBN: 9780856835193

Typeset by RefineCatch Limited, Bungay, Suffolk
Printed and bound through
s|s|media limited, Rickmansworth, Hertfordshire

THIS VOLUME IS DEDICATED TO
MICHAEL J.B. ALLEN
FOR MANY YEARS OF FRIENDSHIP
AND ENCOURAGEMENT

Contents

Acknowledgements

The translators are grateful to Durham University Library Archives and Special Collections for generously allowing the translators to use their copy of the Venice edition of Ficino's *Epistolae* with its valuable annotations. This is once again reproduced as the Latin text.

Thanks go to the Bayerische Staatsbibliothek, Munich, for kindly supplying a copy of manuscript, MS Lat. 10781 and thereby providing another version of the text for letters 1 to 5 and the basis for Appendices A and B, the early text of *De sole*.

Thanks are also due to the Württembergische Landesbibliothek of Stuttgart for permission to use as the jacket illustration a page from their manuscript of *De comparatione solis ad deum*, HB XV 65, fol. 7r. Acknowledgements for other illustrations are due to the Alamy Photo Library, Chris Rees, Gabinetto Fotografico delle Gallerie degli Uffizi, Ministero per i beni e le attività culturali e per il turismo, Musée de Condé, Museo di San Marco, Photo Scala, and the Royal Collection Trust.

The translators wish to express their gratitude for suggestions and help from a number of scholars on individual points: their indebtedness to these and the wider community of scholars is partly discharged through the Notes and Bibliography, but on difficult points of astrology, thanks go to Charles Burnett as well as to Geoffrey Pearce, who once again gave his careful consideration to the astrological passages. In addition, special thanks are due to our publisher, Anthony Werner, for his constant support and encouragement.

Letter Titles

Prohœmium Marsilii Ficini in duodecimum epistolarum librum ad Hieronymum Rossium dilectissimum suum
The preface of Marsilio Ficino to the twelfth book of his letters, dedicated to his beloved Girolamo Rossi

1 Nullus mala penitus et curas extirpare potest
No one is able to eradicate evils and cares completely

2 Solem non esse adorandum tanquam rerum omnium auctorem
The Sun should not be worshipped as the maker of all things

3 Copula philosophiae cum legibus, quod felix et nobilis sit philosophus
The bond between philosophy and the law; the happiness and nobility of the philosopher

4 Cur semper eadem & antiqua tractem
Why I keep coming back to the same ancient themes

5 Similitudo Mercurii cum Saturno
Mercury's similarity to Saturn

6 Apologia in librum suum de sole & lumine
Defence of his book on the Sun and Light

7 Saepe in coelestibus gemini sunt. Item soles duo
There are often twins among the heavenly beings; there are also two Suns

8 In librum de sole dono missum
My book 'On the Sun', sent as a gift

9 Amor ipse Deus amantem redamari iubet
Love, which is itself God, decrees that the lover is loved in return

My book on the Sun; also the star of the Magi at this solemn feast of the Epiphany

22 Pro Bacchi dono. Item Evangelicum illud: ex aqua vinum factum
In return for a gift of Bacchus, and the Gospel account of wine made from water

23 Pro libro de vita iterum imprimendo. Item auspicium de amicitia immortale
In support of the reprinting of my book 'On Life'; also a sign of immortal friendship

24 Commendatio brevis in causa iusta
A brief commendation in a just cause

25 Plato multa Christianis consentanea dixit. Platonici multi Christiana sunt imitati
Plato said many things that are consistent with Christian teachings; many followers of Plato seem to have adopted Christian teachings

26 Semper aliquid agendum, et quoad fieri potest, in eodem perseverandum
There is always something to be done and it should be persevered with as far as is possible

27 Sapientes filii sunt Minervae: haec Philosophiam parit: Philosophia philosophos
The wise are the children of Minerva: she gives birth to Philosophy and Philosophy gives birth to philosophers

28 Pro libro de sole
My book 'On the Sun'

29 Pro libro de Sole
My book 'On the Sun'

30 Quid sentiat de astrologia
My view of astrology

31 Pro libro de sole
My book 'On the Sun'

Appendix Letters

A *Exhortation to lead a moral, contemplative and religious life* (1492, based on chapter 26 of *De vita*, I, 1489)

B *De sole* (early version, 1492)

C Bindaccio Ricasoli to Gregorio Scuto, letter added to *De sole*

D Marsilio Ficino to Jacopo Volaterra, letter accompanying a copy of *De sole* (1496)

E Jacopo Volaterra to Marsilio Ficino, in reply

F Marsilio Ficino to Germain de Ganay, on the death of Giovanni Pico della Mirandola (1495)

G Dedication of Athenagoras translation to Germain de Ganay (after 1494, published 1498)

H1 Marsilio Ficino to Germain de Ganay with Orphic material (1496)

H2 Extract from an earlier Hymn of Orpheus, sent to Cosimo de' Medici (1462)

I Marsilio Ficino to Gianfrancesco Pico della Mirandola (1495)

J *Privilegium,* allowing publication of the Letters (1495)

K Letter from Piero Dovizi to Marsilio Ficino (1495)

L Marsilio Ficino to Paolo Orlandini (1496)

M Robert Gaguin to Marsilio Ficino (1496)

N Marsilio Ficino to Aldus Manutius (1497)

O Egidio da Viterbo to Marsilio Ficino (1497)

List of Illustrations

Introduction

Ficino's twelfth book of Letters marks the completion of his letter compilation. It has a distinctive character that reflects the political situation of the time. The purpose of this introduction is therefore to present the circumstances in which the twelfth book was written, which calls for a review of its contents, a brief overview of the momentous changes that were taking place in Florence at the time, and an account of its actual publication.

But first a word about our own edition: though this current volume presents the twelfth and final book in Ficino's collection, it is the eleventh in our series. It will be followed by a translation of the second book, omitted earlier on the grounds that it is not so much a collection of letters as a gathering of nine short Platonic treatises. This will complete our edition of *The Letters of Marsilio Ficino* as he published them. Some further items that were not included by him in the published collection have been incorporated as Appendix material in this as in our other volumes. In the present book, that includes not only letters but also important documents such as Ficino's Will and his defence of his and the city's response to Savonarola.

The content of the Letters of this book

The De sole letters

More than half of the letters in this book have some connection with Ficino's short work, *De sole*, on the Sun. This began as an extended letter to Count Eberhard V of Württemberg, contained within the original version of Book XI and completed during 1492. The dedicatory preface was retained in the later printed version of Book XI (Letter 33), but most of the rest, which we have in the early manuscript, was removed from the Letters collection because by the time the latter was printed *De sole* had already been published. The early version, preserved in the manuscript Mo2, is presented here in translation for the first time as Appendix B. Soon after being sent to Count Eberhard, it was expanded, paired with another work on light, and published as *De sole et lumine*, printed by Antonio Miscomini in Florence on 31st January, 1493. However, the preface from Book XI and the final chapter, which fell into Book XII by the time the arrangement of these last two books was finalised, were both retained in the Letters collection, as were the two letters about it that were included in the first and subsequent printed versions of *De sole et lumine* (Letters 6 and 7 in this book).

Ficino gave away many copies of *De sole et lumine*, which was printed simply and unadorned, in a slim volume amounting to only 73 pages. Some copies were probably given in person, for example to Giovanni di Stefano (Letter 36), while others were sent with accompanying letters of which we can count at least 22 in this volume. They were sent to Rome, Milan, Venice, France, Germany and Poland. In fact, he says he has been 'taking care for a long time now that my books on the Sun and Light might be in the hands of all my friends.'

This small work was designed to be accessible. Basing it on Plato's use of the Sun as the visible representative of the Good or the One in the creation, Ficino develops the comparison of the Sun to God on many levels. Although he includes a certain amount of astronomical and astrological material, the real intent of the work is to direct the mind to higher things. The significance of the Sun, and its worthiness to be the subject of reflection for men of philosophy and religion alike, is summed up in a letter to Francesco Soderini, Bishop of Volterra (Letter 19). There he points out three ways in which the Sun performs wonders: at the earthly level, in the heavens and above the heavens:

> beneath the heavens, in spring and summer, it quickens so many things that seemed dead throughout the winter; in the heavens it illumines, measures and controls all the heavenly bodies; and above the heavens, all that is invisible not just to our eyes but to our minds also, the Sun renders visible, so to speak, by reminding us, through marvellous displays of the heavenly bodies, to contemplate all that is above the heavens.

Similarly in Letter 30, to Poliziano, who had criticised his interest in such questionable subjects, he states clearly and categorically, 'I am not teaching astronomy so much as pursuing moral allegories through astronomy and searching for means of rising up to the divine.'

The other letters

Another major theme continued in this volume is the prevalence of evil in the world and how to deal with it (Letter 1), as well as the many evils being unleashed through the deteriorating political situation (Letters 37, 38 and 40). The first of this striking trio is the address composed for the French King Charles VIII on his arrival in Florence (Letter 37). Bowing to the inevitable, it welcomes the king as a peacemaker and restorer of religion, referring to his onward mission not just to restore French rule over the kingdom of Naples, but also to regain the kingdom of Jerusalem from Muslim rule in order to re-establish Christian ownership of pilgrimage sites in the Holy Land. To our modern ears, this letter reads as obsequious flattery, but it followed well-known formulae for appeals of a similar nature, several of which relate to the march of Charles VIII through the Italian peninsula. In recent studies of the literature generated by that event, it is generally agreed that Ficino's stands out as eloquent and well-reasoned – though there is no agreement on whether it was ever formally presented to the King in person.

Letters 38 and 42 are both addressed to Giovanni Cavalcanti, with whom Ficino enjoyed a long and close friendship, although their careers drew them in different directions. The first of these two letters reviews traditional arguments for the existence of Divine Providence, despite the presence of abundant evils in the world. He urges a long view, accepting that we cannot always see the reasons for things, and advocating faith in the curative possibilities of adversity. It is in his review of Platonic and Christian teachings on these themes that he mentions the recent prophecies of Savonarola. The way in which he does so has sometimes been taken as a firm endorsement of the Dominican monk, whom he calls 'a man distinguished in holiness and wisdom'. Yet it is possible to read even here some reservations, as it is God's mercy rather than the new leader who is credited with the city's reprieve from destruction. In Letter 40, written only eight days later, he speaks of enemies of God in such a way that it is hard not to think he still has Savonarola in mind. His opposition becomes apparent in the *Apologia* he wrote after Savonarola's execution in 1498 (Appendix Q), when he felt obliged to make a clear stand, and this is discussed in the notes there.

Under the general topic of the redress of evils come two letters that are appeals for justice to be done (Letters 24 and 32), though in neither case do we have particulars of what was at issue. It is of note that when Ficino does send a gift to the judge whose leniency he is invoking, it is entirely separate from the request, and after it (Letter 33).

Ficino continues to have in mind the care of individuals who have sought his guidance in their philosophic studies. These include the German lawyer, Martin Prenninger, with whom he discusses the inner connections of law, wisdom, and that inner light that signifies both happiness and an enduring nobility (Letter 3). With Filippo Buonaccorsi (Callimachus), who was still employed at the Polish court, he reflects on different kinds of movement. With a young nobleman from Rimini, Ramberto Malatesta, he again links inner light and wisdom, stressing the need for wisdom to accompany power (Letter 17) as well as musing on the nature of friendship (Letter 18). Another young man who found his way to Ficino at this time was Francesco Cattani da Diacceto, who was to become his successor. Two letters written to him in this volume address topics of fundamental importance: Letter 1, already mentioned, is on evils, and Letter 14 sets out unambiguously the qualities that are required for a follower of Platonic wisdom: an ability to use one's intellectual gifts in the pursuit of higher knowledge, a firm basis in religion, and the power of eloquence to express what one learns or observes. By higher knowledge, he is referring to the Platonic ideas which exist on a higher level of reality than instantiations of species derived from them in the natural world, which form the main emphasis of Aristotelian science.

In a few letters Ficino speaks of the way in which he works. In Letter 4 he admits to Filippo Valori, then ambassador to the Pope, that he constantly returns to the same themes. In Letter 15, a further confession to him betrays a moment of doubt as to whether he is actually achieving anything. However, in Letter 26, to Callimachus, after an opening reflection on the necessity of movement and action, these iterations are described in a more positive manner, as a progression:

> For what is Marsilio doing today? What he did yesterday. What will he do tomorrow? Again, what he is doing today. As you see,

within the walls of the academy I always revolve around the same point again and again. But what I have been doing while circling thus for so long, and have done over and over again and am now putting together anew, you will understand from the titles of my books, a list of which I am sending you to read, together with my book on the Sun, so that through the brilliant testimony of this Phoebean gift our friendship may shine out for present and future generations.

Thus what characterises the letters of this book is Ficino's concern to make sure that his urgent message for the welfare of society was disseminated in the widest possible way, in the hope that it might bring about a change of heart and of action. Awareness that old age was creeping up on him (in Letter 22 he thanks his physician, Mazzingo, for a gift of wine which will 'comfort me in my old age') and that his eyesight was failing could only have added to that sense of urgency, but the main driver perhaps lay in the dramatic changes he had seen in the life of the city during the previous few years, and a sense of the need for people to reassess their priorities and put first things first.

The historical background

The dates of the letters in this book run from late September 1492 to December 1494. On 8th April, 1492, Lorenzo de' Medici had died, leaving a vacuum of effective leadership in Florence, since his son Piero, who took over his father's role as leading citizen, showed little aptitude in handling what was a very tricky situation. Internally, Florence was already riven with political tensions. Lorenzo had made many enemies through treating the revenues of the state as if they were his own and through dispossessing, or attempting to dispossess, some of his enemies. Meanwhile relations between Florence and other states were fast deteriorating. On 25th January, 1494, King Ferrante of Naples, with whom Lorenzo had reached an understanding, also died, leaving a highly unpopular successor. The Duke of Milan was encouraging the French King to march on Italy and make good his claim to the kingdom of Naples, and some leading Neapolitans had gone to join the French cause, leaving the kingdom of Naples in a state of deep division. For the French army to reach Naples it had to pass through Florentine territory. This was scarcely in the city's interest and there were deep disagreements about how to handle the situation. Piero took charge but was unable to form new alliances and when the French king, Charles VIII, marched into Tuscany, Piero was panicked into making far more concessions than his fellow citizens considered reasonable: he had handed over the key fortresses of Sarzana and Pietrasanta as well as the ports of Pisa and Livorno. As a result, amidst rioting and disorder in the streets, he was driven from the city.

During this period, Ficino also suffered personal losses. Quite apart from the loss of Medici patronage, which by now was a mixed blessing, he also lost good friends. Angelo Poliziano died on 24th September, 1494. Three weeks later, Giovanni Pico della Mirandola lay sick and dying as Charles VIII entered the city. In fact, the king, remembering Pico from his days in Paris, sent a kind letter and two physicians to attend him, from his personal train. But to no avail. Pico died on 17th November. There was little time for mourning as negotiations continued with the French, and Ficino played some minor role in these. He certainly visited the French camp on a number of occasions, as we see from Letters 39, 41 and 42, and he was taking advantage of the opportunity to interest members of the French court in the study of Plato. In Letters 27 and 35 he had arranged to send several books to Germain de Ganay in Paris, and in Letter 34, he had sent *De sole* to the French ambassador, Jean Matheron. Later letters from the time of the French presence in the city and after (Letters 39, 41, 42 and Appendices F, G and H) mention further books for the French court, while Appendix M shows the strength of that connection, which proved to be most fruitful as humanist scholars at the French court became enthusiasts for Ficino's writings, ensuring their wide dissemination during the sixteenth century.

In a further personal loss, Filippo Valori, who had been a most generous patron and friend to Ficino from the mid-1480s, died on 29th November, 1494, while on an ambassadorial mission to Naples. He was not yet forty years old.

These losses all came at a time of public distress and increasing dissension, with the rise of hostile factions. A central figure in the polarisation of opinion within the city was undoubtedly Girolamo Savonarola. Much has been written about this radical reformer, who was invited to Florence at the insistence of Pico della Mirandola and through the influence of Lorenzo de' Medici, for he had already been sent away from Florence in 1488 by his own Vicar General as an unsuitable teacher for the novices at San Marco. However, by 1490, when he returned, his style had changed and the growing popularity of his rousing sermons led to his election as prior of the monastery. By 1492, he was gaining in political influence, attacking corruption in the city government but also attacking lovers of philosophy. His was a harsh and rigorous kind of devotion that brooked no compromise. His sermons were apocalyptic, and when the French King arrived at the gates of the city this seemed to justify his direst prophecies of divine retribution for the city's sins.

When the leading members of the Medici family fled the city in November, Florence was left without a head. The sympathies of the junior branch of the Medici family, that is, the children of Pierfrancesco de' Medici, who later shed the name Medici and became known as Popolani, lay with the French. Although there were many able Florentines in government posts, some of the best were away on diplomatic missions connected with the looming wars, and some were persuaded that a more republican, less oligarchic, form of government might be a better way forward. Some families, like the Valori, were so disappointed in Piero de' Medici that they transferred their allegiance to Savonarola, who consequently had sufficient moral authority to be chosen as head of the diplomatic missions sent to negotiate with the French. In some ways this marks the height of his power and popularity. Ficino and others were content to serve under him on those missions.

However, by 1495 Savonarola had formed bands of *Fanciulli* (boys' brigades) to enforce puritanical codes of dress and conduct. Different factions began to emerge and the rivalries between them intensified. The followers of Savonarola were known as *Piagnoni* (wailers or whiners), no doubt named by their opponents for their lamentations over the current state of affairs. The more politically active among the followers of the Friar were called the *Frateschi*. Ranged against them were the so-called *Arrabbiati* (rabid, mad dogs) along with a fairly aggressive band of young aristocrats, the *Compagnacci*, who flaunted their privileged lifestyle in a series of extravagant banquets. Loyal supporters of the now exiled Medici were known as the *Primati* (princes and magnates). Some Medicean supporters felt sympathetic to the Savonarolan camp and were known as *Bigi* (Greys), as distinct from the *Bianchi* (Whites), who were firm republican Savonarolans. The *Bigi* were probably included among the *Tiepidi* (lukewarms) whom Savonarola constantly harangued. All these factions made trouble for one another in every way they could and violence in the streets increased.

Savonarola's attempts to make of the city a new Jerusalem ultimately failed. He had fallen out with the religious authorities in Rome by 1495, though he continued to dominate in Florence until his excommunication in May 1497. The details of his rise, dominance and downfall can be followed in a very extensive literature, which is documented in the Notes and Bibliography; a summary version can be found in the Biographical Notes. Suffice it here to say that from 1492 onwards Ficino felt himself to be under attack by the friar, on grounds that must have especially pained him, as Savonarola sought to undermine everything he stood for: wisdom, moderation, tolerance, gentleness and patience.

All these developments formed the backdrop to this twelfth book of letters, and perhaps gave the signal that it was time to bring the collection to a close and get it into print.

The publication and dissemination of the letters

Earlier books of Ficino's letters had long circulated in manuscript, and several presentation copies had been made of various parts of the collection. Each book has its own dedicatee, but at some point a decision was made to settle on twelve books as a goodly number for the whole. As we have seen, the twelfth book has a slightly different character from earlier ones, having more short notes accompanying gifts and a smaller number of letters of philosophical substance. Perhaps this suggests that he felt some pressure to bring the collection to a conclusion, and such pressure would no doubt have originated in the political and social changes described above.

Ficino was well aware that the longevity of his legacy would depend on the still relatively new medium of print, which he had used so successfully before. Even though misprints and other errors could be frustrating, he was conscious of the advantages, giving access to a much wider readership, at much lower cost and much greater speed. In Letter 23 of this book he even appears to be jogging the memory of a German associate who had promised Ficino a new printing of his very popular *De vita*.

Ficino dedicated the twelfth book of letters to Girolamo Rossi (Preface) and added a further letter of dedication to him (Letter 20), which served as the preface to the whole collection. In the first, he indicates that the twelfth book notionally contains any other letters he might write thereafter. In the second (Letter 20), he speaks of his letters being born mortal, but now being born again as immortal through Rossi, who was involved in facilitating their printing. And indeed it was so.

When Ficino brought his collection to a conclusion in December 1494, he sent it to be printed in Venice. It had, as we have seen, been a momentous year, with many public disturbances, culminating in the arrival of the French troops in November, and it may have been on account of those disturbances, or of the hostile presence of Savonarola, that Ficino preferred his work to be printed outside Florence. The typographer and printer Matteo Capcasa of Parma had established a printing house in Venice and had been collaborating with Florentine publishers since 1485. It was he who produced a finely illustrated edition of Dante's *Divine Comedy* with Cristoforo Landino's commentary in 1491, reprinting it on his own account in 1493. Authority for the printing of Ficino's letters in Venice was duly obtained by Girolamo Blondi. The resulting *Privilegium* (Appendix J) is displayed at the front of the handsome folio volume, as one of three ornamented opening pages. The volume has decorative capitals at the start of each Letter throughout, and sometimes also at the start of new sections of longer letters.

Ficino did not stop writing letters in 1494: some, written in the following few years before he died, are included in the Appendix we have added to this twelfth book. But he clearly felt the collection was now in a form that could be circulated in print, just like his earlier translations of Hermes (1471–2), Plato (1484) and Plotinus (1492), and his own works *On the Christian Religion* (1474/6), his Plague treatise (1481) his magnum opus, the *Platonic Theology* (1482), and his *Three Books on Life* (1489).

By 1496, Ficino was again publishing works in Florence: his Platonic commentaries (1496) and his translation of and commentary on Dionysius (1496 or 1497). But he continued to be courted by publishers elsewhere, including Aldo Manuzio, who published the volume of translations not yet issued elsewhere, i.e. Iamblichus's *De Mysteriis* and other late Platonic works.

A second edition of Ficino's *Letters* followed only two years after the first, in 1497. This time it was brought out by the publishing house of Anton Koberger in Nuremberg, probably again with Blondi as the intermediary. Slightly less generous in format than the Venice edition, it nevertheless extended the influence of the Letters, especially in northern and eastern Europe. The Letters are also included in the two Basel editions of Ficino's *Opera omnia* (1561 and 1576, both by Henricus Petri), reprinted in 1959, 1962, 1979, 1983 (Turin) and 2000 (Paris), and in the Paris edition of Guillaume Pelé in 1641. Sebastiano Gentile has started a critical edition of the authoritative Latin text (see Bibliography). The most recent, and attractive, addition to this list is the facsimile of the 1495 first edition of Venice, with an introduction by Stéphane Toussaint, published in 2011 by the Société Marsile Ficin, Paris.

It is fitting to conclude by recognising the care Ficino took to bring his message of consolation and encouragement to as wide a circle as he could. His letters, like his longer writings, encompass many themes, ideas and interests, but the most insistent refrain in them all is perhaps his exhortation to the contemplation of higher things. At the very least, such contemplation provides a way of being able to live at peace with the vicissitudes of the world. Thus in the opening letter of this book, he urges two young scholars to dispel their doubts: they need not believe that they can taste the sweet savours of philosophy without some bitterness, but they should 'not lose hope, that the bitterness can one day, with the help of God, be changed to sweetness.' However, it is constancy in the practice of such contemplation that is the key to gaining so much more. As he reminds Martin Prenninger, through this kind of life the being will eventually be filled with light.

Valery Rees
1st October, 2020.

Translators' Note

This volume contains Ficino's twelfth book of letters, comprising letters written from September 1492 to December 1494, with a dedicatory preface to Girolamo Rossi. A substantial Appendix contains letters written after Ficino sent the book to press, as well as other pertinent material.

For the Latin text of the published letters, see the facsimile pages on pp. 175 to 197, with notes expanding unusual abbreviations and showing significant variant readings.

Textual Sources

The 1495 printed edition of Ficino's Letters was published in Venice by Matteo Capcasa of Parma. The copy in the library of the University of Durham, used here, shows some corrections in the hand of Ficino Ficini, Ficino's nephew. These may be regarded as corrections authorised by Ficino himself.

Besides the printed edition, there is one manuscript for Letters 1 to 5 and Appendices A and B: siglum Mo2, Munich, Bayerische Staatsbibliothek, MS lat. 10781. Letters 1–5 are on folios 94 to 101. Appendix A is on fols. 99–100 and B is on fols. 86 to 93. This manuscript was compiled for Filippo Carducci in November, 1492, and contains the letters of Books IX and X in addition to the above, together with some other correspondence unconnected with Ficino.

The sources for the Latin texts of the remaining Appendix items are given in the notes.

The Letters

Preface

Prohœmium Marsilii Ficini in duodecimum epistolarum librum ad Hieronymum Rossium dilectissimum suum

The preface of Marsilio Ficino to the twelfth book of his letters, dedicated to his beloved Girolamo Rossi

Marsilio Ficino to his beloved Girolamo Rossi: especial greetings.

WHEN I had brought the twelfth book of my letters to an end and was considering to whom in particular I should address it, I judged that it would accord with reason to dedicate the end of this long labour especially to you, for, in a word, you are the end for which I had long intended the entire work. Moreover, so that the whole endeavour of my letters may finally come to rest in you as its end, I have resolved that however many more I may write, even after this, will belong to this twelfth book, however long it may become and, in short, they will be kept together under the name of Rossi, or rather, Roscius.[1]

Be happy to read it, and live most happily, you who are, without any doubt, happily loved by us.[2]

I

Nullus mala penitus et curas extirpare potest

No one is able to eradicate evils and cares completely

Marsilio Ficino of Florence to his fellow philosophers, Giovanni Vittorio Soderini and Francesco Diacceto: especial greetings.[1]

YOU ask what that saying from the Gospel really means: 'It must needs be that offences come.'[2] In fact, this is just what Plato says: 'Evils cannot be completely eradicated,' but of necessity revolve around this mortal realm.[3] I pass over for now the many evils brought upon us by fate, nature, fortune, the elements, human beings, and animals. Those we inadvertently bring upon ourselves are surely far more serious. It should come as no surprise, then, that men given over to a busy life or enslaved by desires are overwhelmed by innumerable evils, since they subject themselves heedlessly to fate and fortune and frequently encounter agitation as if of their own free will. What is really surprising is that even men who have renounced the life of pleasure and the active life and have devoted themselves wholly to contemplation are still troubled by agitation. They appear to have avoided the causes of all disquiet, and yet they are often disquieted by heavier cares than are the pleasure-seekers or the men of action. For men of contemplation, spurning human affairs, betake themselves either to religion and holiness or to philosophy. In either instance they fall victim to Scylla in their desire to avoid Charybdis.[4]

Holy men, fleeing the delusions and frivolities of mortals, fall prey to tempting demons. For they 'wrestle not against flesh and blood', as Paul the Apostle says, but against wicked spirits, rulers of the dark air.[5] And so even while God is testing the pious, demons are afflicting them.[6] But what shall I say of the philosophers? Is it not true that, rejecting the duties of Jove or the delights of Venus, they often fall into the weariness and sorrows of Saturn and melancholy? Indeed, Democritus, Plato, and Aristotle think that all the cleverest men are vulnerable to this great evil,[7] with the result that they seem in some way to suffer the punishment that Prometheus the thinker suffered on Mount Caucasus for his theft from heaven.[8] Both kinds of thinker generally encounter heavier cares than do the followers of the active life or of pleasure, and to the same degree they encounter more powerful tormentors. Therefore, if the philosophers, who are thought to be the most likely to avoid evils, do indeed quite often fall into even more serious evils, then assuredly one can be confident that evils can never be avoided by mortals.

Perhaps, however, the difference is this: the evils of those we have just mentioned are gradually turned into the worst, but if these men were to follow their calling wisely and steadfastly, then finally, with the help of God and according to His promise, 'They that sow in tears shall reap in joy. He that goeth forth and weepeth, bearing precious seed, shall doubtless come again with rejoicing, bringing his sheaves with him.'[9]

I thought it good to remind you of these things, my beloved fellow philosophers, so that you do not believe that you can taste the sweet savours of philosophy without some bitterness, but also so that you do not lose hope that the bitterness can one day, with the help of God, be changed to sweetness, which is what nature commonly does in the case of apples.[10]

Be well and happy, and persevere in your contemplation with the wisdom and steadfastness you have already adopted.

27th September, 1492.[11]

2

Solem non esse adorandum tanquam rerum omnium auctorem

The Sun should not be worshipped as the maker of all things

Marsilio Ficino to Eberhard, illustrious Count of Württemberg and Elder of Mount Peligard: greetings.[1]

SOCRATES on military campaigns often stood still in his tracks under the heavens, looking up in astonishment at the rising sun, with unmoving limbs and unblinking eyes, like a statue, until he could greet the sun as it rose again the next day.[2] Led by these and similar signs, the followers of Plato will perhaps say that Socrates, regularly guided from childhood by a Phoebean daemon,[3] used to worship Phoebus above all. And for the same reason he was judged by the oracle of Apollo to be the wisest of all the Greeks.[4]

For the moment, I shall pass over what really seems to need saying about this daemon of Socrates, be it spirit or angel, but I certainly would venture to say that, in his heightened state of mind, Socrates was enraptured not by this sun but by another. For since wonder is usually aroused only by unfamiliarity, why would Socrates be so full of wonder and be so greatly amazed at this sun, which he saw daily and all of whose movements and powers he had for a long time understood by both mathematical and scientific reasoning? According to Plato, he called the sun not the first God but the son of God; not the first son of God, I would add, but the second, the one that is visible.[5] For he says that the first son of God is not this sun which is clearly visible to the eyes, but the other, namely the First Intellect, which is superior to this sun by far and can be contemplated only by the intellect. Socrates therefore, being reminded on occasion by the celestial sun, and surmising from this the supercelestial Sun, contemplated its majesty all the more keenly, and wondered in astonishment at the incomprehensible goodness of its Father.

James the Apostle calls Him 'the Father of lights,' meaning celestial lights and those beyond the celestial, 'with whom is no variableness neither shadow of turning;'[6] for he thinks that even the supercelestial lights have been made naturally changeable, and he has no doubt that the celestial lights are obscured by the regular turning of night and day. For these reasons he believes that 'every good gift', that is, those implanted naturally in the mind, and 'every perfect gift', that is, those bestowed after the natural gifts, comes down not from this sun and the stars in the sky, but 'from above', from the 'Father of lights' Himself. For relying on the powers of intelligence, as if on certain steps which have been received, not from the heavens, but from an even higher source, we ascend above the heavens and there experience, love, and worship many things more excellent than the heavens, and above all we revere the Maker of the heavens. However, it would be impossible for us to understand, or love through intelligence, anything incorporeal and better than the heavens if our understanding were exclusively from the heavens. But now, in case anyone, marvelling too much at the sun, moon, and stars, should pray to them and revere them as the authors of intellectual gifts and as fathers, Socrates has wisely reminded us that this sun is not the origin of the universe.

For the present, I shall omit the grounds on which we assert in our *Theology* that the origin of the universe is not body, soul, or intellect, but something far more sublime from which the sun in the heavens is so far removed that it is to be understood as just a shadow of that Sun, and not even an image.[7] However, the grounds which James touches on briefly here, I shall now briefly run through:

Since stillness, as the origin, ruler, and end of movement, is more perfect than all movement, surely God, who is Himself the origin, end, and ruler of all, cannot be in movement, whereas the sun is in constant movement.[8] Moreover, the power of the origin, being unlimited, reaches everything without loss and cannot be anywhere confined. The power of the sun, on the other hand, acting through its rays, is impeded wherever its rays are blocked.[9] The sun loses its power when eclipsed by the moon; its power is constrained by clouds, repelled by earthly density, and weakened by being so distant. Indeed, the sun itself is but a very small part of the cosmos. It is held within narrow confines. It is pulled round and round by its sphere but is also moved by the sphere that is ever above it, acting in opposition to the force of its own sphere.[10] It is impeded by unfavourable signs and is sometimes weakened by the stars and by the aspect of malefic planets.[11] Finally, the primary cause of the universe acts upon all things everywhere, always, and in everything. The sun, however, does not itself create the heavenly spheres, and it cannot through its own quality make anything cold or moist or dense or the like. Qualities like these in the heavens do not arise in any way from the sun. But although the sun is very far removed from the Creator of the cosmos, yet all the celestial bodies by divine influence seem to relate to the one sun as the regulator and measure in the heavens.[12]

Therefore, considering that all things in the heavens, below the heavens, and above the heavens are likewise related to the one primary cause of all, let us be fully persuaded at last to worship this one primary cause with at least as much reverence as is given by the heavenly bodies to the sun.

3

Copula philosophiae cum legibus, quod felix et nobilis sit philosophus

The bond between philosophy and the law; the happiness and nobility of the philosopher[1]

Marsilio Ficino to his especial friend Martin Uranius Prenninger: greetings.[2]

I HAVE always been a practising philosopher, never a lawyer. Yet two of my best friends are lawyers: in Italy there is Giovanni Vittorio Soderini;[3] in Germany, dear Martin, you excel in the profession.[4] Both of you have combined an extraordinary enthusiasm for wisdom with exemplary legal skill. So somebody is sure to ask: How is the law related to philosophy?[5] Well, how is Jupiter, author of the laws, connected to Saturn, who guides philosophy? As son to father.[6]

For the moment, I pass over the astronomers, who assert that Jupiter introduces new laws when in conjunction with Saturn, particularly on those occasions when their conjunction takes place at the cardinal points of the heavens and at the head of a group of three signs.[7] Do not the ancient poets and the theologians of old depict Saturn meditating in his sanctuary, and devising laws and obligations after long contemplation?[8] Saturn then hands them to his son Jupiter, who governs lawsuits, and Jupiter will instruct the citizens to follow them. Homer, too, says that King Minos, founder of the laws, used to withdraw every nine years to Jupiter's cave, where he received laws from Jupiter.[9] But no one versed in the ancient mysteries would dedicate a cave specifically to Jupiter, who always appears openly. This cave, therefore, can only be the permanent sanctuary, dwelling place or shrine of Saturn himself, in which Jupiter acting in fellowship with Saturn instructs King Minos in the laws that will then shape the people.[10]

But let us now turn from the functioning of the laws and pursue the study of wisdom. Through my letters I have encouraged many to engage in this with all their might and main. Since you are already well advanced in this, I see no need to give you encouragement, but rather strength and support. Now, we can observe ourselves, we can raise our eyes to God, or we can look around at our fellow men.

Suppose we observe ourselves: does not wisdom alone give us self-knowledge and enable us to live with ourselves, content with our own riches? Suppose we look up to God: is it not wisdom alone that makes us both godlike and dear to God as we continually contemplate what God Himself has created through contemplation and venerate Him as the acknowledged author of all our blessings? Suppose we observe our fellow men: is it not wisdom alone that establishes a wise ruler among rulers and the people, one who is ultimately worthy of veneration as a divine power?[11]

Granted, then, that the study of wisdom makes a man completely happy, does it also make him noble or show him to be so? If we may trust Plato, philosophers are undoubtedly the noblest of people, for he says they are a race of gold,[12] sprung from Jove himself, architect of the universe. If you place your faith in the Stoics,[13] you will recognise the nobility of philosophers from the future, for the Stoics assert that philosophers alone are immortal. Finally, it would be a sacrilege not to believe the prophet Daniel, who says, 'they that be wise shall shine as the brightness of the firmament; and they that turn many to righteousness as the stars for ever and ever.'[14] The 'firmament' seems to signify not only the eighth heaven[15] but the whole structure of the spheres, the firmament of all the stars and planets. This vault of heaven, quite apart from the stars and planets in it, somehow shines of its own nature, but with a finer, diffuse white light, which is for that reason less visible to the eye.

It is with a light of this kind that men of true learning and sanctity shall shine, both here and in their homeland, even if they have never taught anyone.[16] Those who have not just contemplated the divine for themselves but have also freely taught others and have given laws for the observance of justice shall shine with clearer brilliance than all the rest, sparkling most brightly like the stars. They shall shine, not for a limited time but for all time, not only for the entire duration of the universe but throughout the span of eternity that is more divine, a span which is never interrupted but is wholly perpetual and continuous. It seems just that instigators of public and divine good, who have always benefitted mankind and have not hidden their God-given light but have used it for the good of all, will be rewarded by God with eternal brilliance and goodness.[17]

4

Cur semper eadem & antiqua tractem

Why I keep coming back to the same ancient themes

Marsilio Ficino to Filippo Valori, Florentine ambassador to the Pope:[1] greetings.

YESTERDAY evening, when bidding farewell to our Franco,[2] I said, 'You will be my letter to our Valori.' But not long afterwards, I was somehow compelled to add some morning thoughts to last night's letter, as lovers are often wont to do, not being content with one letter at a time. So the 'Franco letter', if I may call it so, will tell you my state of health, while this present note will give you an account of our studies which Franco was too busy to hear. I see you ask what I am working on now. Actually, it is what I have been working on for a long time, dear Valori. Some fate or other keeps bringing me back to the same point.[3] From the outset, as you know, Saturn rising in Aquarius was the giver of my sign (I won't say guide). This is why I constantly return to ancient Saturnian themes. The first time Saturn returned to Aquarius, I translated Plato's ancient works, under the direction of the great Cosimo.[4] Now that Saturn has returned to the same place, I am returning to the same work. After translating Plotinus for Lorenzo, I am working on Plato again.[5] I am elucidating that great work with longer commentaries, as is only right. The brief commentary on *Timaeus*, composed at your country house in Maiano, is now expanding for me and I am about to start on *Parmenides* in the same way. Our great patron Piero de' Medici[6] has given me strong hope that he will breathe favourably upon a reappearance of Plato. And his inspiration is such that our hitherto wandering Plato will now found his Academy on this rock.[7] Therefore, when there is an opportunity while he is there with you visiting the Pope, please express my immense gratitude to him for this. In the company of Piero, who is like Jupiter to you, you will recognise the Bibbieni[8] as your Dioscuri, the heavenly twins, Castor and Pollux. After commending me to Piero, please commend me also to them.

Let me end this little note, which I must say has already become a letter, once I have let you know that the Martiana affair, which we should perhaps rather call Saturnian on account of its slowness, has now, through the authority of the Medici and with your care, been brought to completion.[9]

7th November, 1492.[10]

5

Similitudo Mercurii cum Saturno

Mercury's similarity to Saturn

Marsilio Ficino to his beloved Filippo Carducci: greetings.[1]

WHEN the letters I wrote had all been copied out for you and were almost ready to be brought to you by the messenger, I decided that a Mercurial work should not travel to a Mercurial friend without Mercurial auspices.[2] If the heavenly bodies have any power in such matters, it would then reach you more swiftly and be read more speedily. Moreover, so that it may receive much longer consideration[3] when you have re-read it, I have added Saturn to Mercury, either as his companion or as his leader.[4]

I have today read again, in the tenth book of the *Republic*, that among all the heavenly bodies Mercury and Saturn are most like each other in colour, that is, in their light.[5] It is therefore no wonder that their intelligences,[6] too, are of such similar light that the one encourages to wisdom, while the other, with God's favour, leads even higher.[7]

Mercury and Saturn signify that the Sun is the image of God: God Himself is the first author of wisdom, while they are the signposts to wisdom and companions of the image of God. For of all the heavenly bodies these two depart least from the Sun, in that Mercury almost always travels right under the Sun's splendour, while Saturn appears to wander least from the Sun's ecliptic path.[8] The astronomers think that the two planets are somewhat similar in nature, and that Mercury rejoices in the house and territory of

Saturn and in his aspect.[9] Hence, I surmise, it comes about that nearly all those who commence their journey or undertaking from Mercury, end it only in Saturn. May you, my Carducci, setting out from Mercury, eventually reach Jupiter.[10]

Farewell.
14th November, 1492.[11]

6

Apologia in librum suum de sole & lumine

Defence of his book on the Sun and Light[1]

Marsilio Ficino of Florence to Filippo Valori, Florentine ambassador to the Pope: especial greetings.

FOR a considerable time I was holding back the book on the Sun intended for the illustrious Piero de' Medici and, contrary to the Gospel precept, was improperly almost hiding my light, or the Sun, under a bushel.[2] But Piero del Nero, whom in our letters we have repeatedly called a man of pure light,[3] judged it proper that this light should shine for as many as possible, as God teaches. So I have yielded most willingly to that man of pure light to whom especially the care of light and radiance belongs, and besides entrusting the mystery to the magnanimous Piero de' Medici,[4] I have, with the support of Piero del Nero, permitted the book to be published by the printers for all to see.

Behold then, my Valori, dearer to me than light, this Sun of mine, however small, is at last arising in full view. But perhaps it may soon run into rising mists, or even prove troublesome to certain night-owls and bats.[5] In fact, winds will straightaway dispel the mists, or the sun itself, as it rises higher, will thin them out and dissolve them. As for the bats, dazzled and blinded by the light, advise them, if they are capable of taking advice, not to find fault with a light that is beneficial to others. But let them rather flee from this brilliance, as is their wont, and as is only right, being unworthy of the light, let them constantly hide from it.

In any case I have high hopes in summoning my Valori to this struggle, for he will fight most valiantly, like Hercules, not only against owls but also against insubstantial monsters. You often quote that saying of Boethius on Hercules, 'the vanquished earth bestows the heavens'.[6] The ancients present Hercules as a man fostered by the Sun, undergoing his twelve labours as if they were the twelve signs of the Zodiac, for true glory and for the splendour of truth, which are the special gifts bestowed by the Sun. Move briskly into battle now, my Valori, for I know that you will have at least three invincible champions: Hercules appearing as Poliziano, Phoebus as Pico, and Amphion as Landino.[7] These three have fought vigorously for my *Life* over the last three years and they will be just as successful in fighting hereafter for this *Light* of mine, however small it may be.

2nd January, 1493.[8]

7

Saepe in coelestibus gemini sunt. Item soles duo

There are often twins among the heavenly beings; there are also two Suns

Marsilio Ficino to Martin Uranius, his true brother[1] and unique friend: greetings.

IT is delightful to have discussions on the heavenly beings with you, my Uranius, as often happens, for you belong to the heavens. Not only are there the twins in the firmament, the Dioscuri, but there are also true brothers among the planets. For Mercury is as a younger brother to Saturn. As Plato says, they shine with a very similar light[2] and both preside over men of intellect. Kindly Venus[3] is the true sister of Jove, and Phoebe of Phoebus.[4] Mars, however, lacks a partner, as if too proud: he is the Sun's rival rather than his companion.[5]

For besides his own heat which competes with the Sun, Mars, as his rival, imparts to the Moon a kind of light, though this is observed by very few.[6] Besides these, the upper air,[7] like another Jupiter, is the brother and husband of the lower air, which is like Juno.[8]

But let us return to the Sun. Seeing that there are twin Suns in the heavens,[9] is it any surprise that twin Suns, as it were, have also been born in my house: first the greater *Sun* and then the lesser? You yourself saw the lesser *Sun* when you were in Florence at my home last summer, on your way as ambassador to the Pope, and it followed in your very footsteps when you left here for Germany to greet your illustrious prince, Eberhard. Piero de' Medici justly lays claim to the other *Sun*, which has come to maturity and taken its place among the *Platonic Commentaries*, and Piero justly lays claim to all the Platonic writings.[10]

In like manner twin lights, O my Uranius, have shone forth in the heart of my home, a lesser and a greater one. The lesser one has long been shining brightly for Febo Capella; the greater one now shines for the illustrious Piero de' Medici.[11] Therefore, heavenly man, happily contemplate them both. But you will contemplate successfully if, in an analogy of this light, you commit to memory the following Platonic mystery about divinity. Those things which give the least light we do not generally perceive except by trying in one way or another to get closer to them. When we are going to look at the Sun, we do not have to seek it, for it presents itself to us of its own accord, the most openly visible thing of all; rather we must cleanse our eyes, open and turn them and, as far as we are able, adjust them to it. Likewise, we are obliged to scrutinise the scanty truths of all other things through close reasoning, as if they were just sparks; however, we do not have the strength to approach the immeasurable light of God in this way, but it is through a loving conversion of the will and serenity of mind that we prepare ourselves for it, and when we are prepared it will show us its brilliance of its own accord. Hence that Platonic saying, 'Divine matters cannot be taught with words and reasoning like other things that are learned, but, through continual association with the divine and communion with it in one's life, suddenly a light blazes in the soul, like a spark from a fire, and thereafter it nourishes itself.'[12]

8

In librum de sole dono missum

My book 'On the Sun', sent as a gift

Marsilio Ficino to his fellow philosopher Lorenzo, high priest of the Laurentian temple.[1]

WHILE I was recently putting together my book *On the Sun and Light*,[2] which is small but was a great pleasure to write, you, though unaware I had been burning the midnight oil, with perfect timing discovered through your astronomical calculations that our entire study of wisdom is directed primarily to the Sun. This is because in my birth chart that part which the Egyptians call the portion of wisdom[3] had reached the heart of Leo, while the Sun, the lord of Leo, had occupied the ninth region of the heavens, which is assigned to wisdom.[4]

With excellent timing again, yesterday, just as the book *On the Sun and Light* was finished, you brought us your astronomical calculation. So today, with equally good timing, I in turn am sending you this very book. May this *Light* of ours seem fitting to reveal the Sun rather than the Moon.[5]

18th February, 1493.[6]

9

Amor ipse Deus amantem redamari iubet

Love, which is itself God, decrees that the lover is loved in return

Marsilio Ficino of Florence to Giuliano,[1] eminent Professor of Theology of the Order of Friars Minor, but himself by no means minor: especial greetings.

My dearest Giuliano, there is no need for you to excuse your silence towards us. For although you have seldom spoken to us, you have frequently spoken about us. And if anything happens to be missing in words, you make up for it all with your great love for us. I for my part have the strongest proof of your ardent love for me: in your absence, I have long been embracing you with a love that grows more ardent day by day.

In my book *On Love* and in some of my letters, I have explained with many lines of reasoning that well-known proverb 'If you wish to be loved, love'.[2] Yet it seems that the most compelling reason of all is the one that occurs to me even as I write, unless hasty judgement is deceiving me. But to reduce the risk of deception a little, let us discuss for a moment the following:

The ancients used to portray Apollo and Cupid as archers, the latter shooting flames, the former rays of light.[3] Apollo thus shoots light onto two people together, so that I see you by the same light by which you in turn see me. Cupid likewise shoots flames, so that when one of us is on fire, the other soon burns with the same flame.

Love, however, is in all respects a god, as Plato shows, and all antiquity bears witness. Our own theologians place the Holy Spirit, primal Love, above the seraphim, that is, the angels of love, and they always place the seraphim above the cherubim.[4]

Thus when the divine power of love, which supports reciprocal affection and union, sets someone on fire with love, by some wonderful hidden force, he immediately reflects upon the beloved the burning rays from this love as if from a mirror, so that the beloved, even if he is absent or unaware, is miraculously set alight and in turn will love the lover. For the divine power, being just, does not suffer the lover who has been aroused by an impulse from on high not to be loved in return.[5]

But that is enough on love for now.

You were also complaining in your letter that the books of Plotinus had failed to reach you, and you were almost going to blame me for being so slow. The books themselves were in fact completed by the printers last May, but the people who were entrusted by the Medici with the task of distributing the books, in Italy at any rate, have so far been rather slow to act and, despite my chasing them, are still slow.

I have not yet published the new version of Plato, more than half of which has already been completed.[6] You more than anyone urged me on with this, perhaps with the added encouragement of the angels in whose church you persuaded me, over dinner, to undertake this. In those times, after my lectures there, you too preached to large gatherings.[7]

I am sending you a little book, *On the Sun and Light*,[8] which I have recently published, for you to read, so that where great warmth has long been evident between us there may also be abundant light.

21st February, 1493.[9]

10

In Librum de Sole

My book 'On the Sun'

Marsilio Ficino to his fellow philosopher, the distinguished physician[1] Mazzingo: greetings.

ALL the astronomers, as you know, think that the Moon is exalted in the third region of the heavens from the ascendant, and that it is the leader of a short journey from there and of a small religion.[2] The Sun, however, is in the ninth, and is the ruler of a longer journey and a great religion – or, to be on the safe side, it is at least an indicator.[3]

Since you are very soon about to undertake a long religious journey to the Holy House of Loreto,[4] it is only right that I should now give you a *Sun* which has recently risen for me. I hope that it will be a good auspice for a clear sky and an easy journey.

11

In Librum de Sole

My book 'On the Sun'

Marsilio Ficino to George of Cyprus, eminent physician:[1] greetings.

SINCE all agree that Phoebus is the originator of medicine and father of physicians, it is right for me to send you my recently published book to read, a Phoebean book on the Sun and Light; for you have long been physician to our family.[2] Phoebus will then bear you truthful witness of my perpetual love for you. As Virgil says, 'The Sun will give you signs. Who would dare to say that the Sun is false?'[3]

14th June, 1493.

12

In librum de Sole missum

My book 'On the Sun' that has been sent to you

Marsilio Ficino to Baccio Ugolini: greetings.

SINCE Apollo and Bacchus are brothers, it is right that they greet each other.[1] But which one makes the first move? It is not Liber[2] who approaches Apollo, for he fears he might come back with words, but it is Phoebus who approaches Bacchus in the hope of coming back with wine.

15th June, 1493.

13

Foelicia ad philosophiam auspicia, a Mercurio et Saturno et Sole

Favourable auspices for philosophy, from Mercury, Saturn, and the Sun[1]

Marsilio Ficino to his beloved Niccolò Valori: greetings.

NONE of our friends has embarked on the study of philosophy under more favourable auspices than you.[2] For the moment I shall do no more than remind you how much the conjunction of Mercury and Saturn under Aquarius is thought to contribute to the pursuit of philosophy.[3] This conjunction occurred while I was preparing my book *On the Sun and Light* and you were taking your first steps in philosophy[4] and you were beginning with the Sun, clearly like a second Orpheus, beginning with Apollo rather than with the Muses.[5] So you at once looked up at this Sun with unblinking eyes[6] as was fitting under such great auspices. But then from this Sun, which rules among the heavenly bodies, you set out with remarkable speed towards the higher Sun, which is the source of the heavenly bodies, and you have very successfully made your way to the theology of the Platonists.[7]

Indeed in this theology you are daily examining all the most profound mysteries with as much insight as a person clearly would have who contemplates everything, not under the Moon but under the Sun.[8]

I beg you, my Valori, continue as keenly as you have begun and, with me as your constant companion and Apollo as your guide, you will soon attain the brilliant heights of truth and glory.[9]

14

Signa legitimi Platonici, atque de ideis

Distinguishing marks of a genuine Platonist; and also on Ideas

Marsilio Ficino to Francesco Diacceto, his fellow Platonist: greetings.[1]

THEY are entirely in error who hold that the Aristotelian teaching is in opposition to the Platonic, since a path cannot be in opposition to where it leads. Indeed, whoever considers it aright will find that the Aristotelian teaching is the path to Platonic wisdom, and that the natural world leads us to the divine. Hence it comes about that no one has ever been admitted to the deeper mysteries of Plato unless[2] he has first been initiated into Aristotelian teachings.[3]

Now there are three characteristics[4] of a fully developed Platonist, by which a priest of this kind may be distinguished from other philosophers and wise men.[5] The first is a noble intellect, which always turns itself from the lower to the higher; the second is religion; the third is a power of expression that verges on the poetic. The first pertains to Saturn, the second to Jupiter, the third to Apollo. So he alone is a genuine Platonist who is proceeding along the path I have mentioned, endowed with these characteristics and entrusted, so to speak, to these heavenly powers. That is why, Francesco, my fellow philosopher, I congratulate you as a genuine Platonist and I rejoice for the Academy.

Now so that I may respond to that question of yours on Ideas, please accept the short answer that a letter can provide.

You think that in the First Mind individual Ideas of particular entities are not completely separate from one another, but are in some way related. I have always thought so too. Nor do I think that this is inconsistent with Plotinus, whom you now have. Indeed, I explain this briefly in my commentaries on him.[6] And Proclus in his commentary on *Parmenides* says it is clear that individual Ideas of particular things are not completely separate.[7] This is undoubtedly in complete harmony with Plato when he says in the *Timaeus* that the archetype or Idea is eternal,[8] or when he shows that what is modelled on it and produced through it will be everlasting.[9] From this we may gather that the species of the natural world are formed entirely from the Idea, because they are everlasting, but it is not the same for individual instances, which are ultimately distinguished from one another by a series of subsequent causes. Such distinction, however, is by no means hidden from the First Intellect, the creator of the universal order. This is why, in the *Timaeus*, it is the younger gods[10] and the daemons who carry out the fashioning of the individual creatures under the Moon, while it is the Architect who gives order and instruction.[11] This is to ensure that in this realm there is not a vast multiplicity in what is absolutely united; that the many are not concealed from the One, who makes and perfects everything through His intelligence; and that the Ideas of individual things that are altogether changeable are not separated from one another in reality or by nature, but are distinguished only through the principle of the same intelligence applying itself now in one form, now in another.

Therefore you have thought this through well, my Francesco.

Farewell.
11th July, 1493.

15

Purgatio silentii diuturni

An apology for a long silence

Marsilio Ficino to Filippo Valori, Florentine ambassador to the Supreme Pontiff:[1] especial greetings.

YOU may be wondering why I have been silent for so long.[2] In brief, it is simply that there has been no obvious reason to write. For what in particular shall I write about? Shall I write about my health, I who am never sure whether I am ill or well? Should I give you some indication of what I am doing? Good heavens, I am not even sure about this! I certainly know what I want to do, what I am trying to do; but I still don't know what I am actually accomplishing. In fact, I am not even sure whether I am to believe you are here with us or not, for the company of your brother Niccolò, who is applying himself to philosophy with me every day, makes your presence so real that I do not notice any need for letters.

It is usual for people to express appreciation by at least sending quite long letters after lengthy periods of silence. Shall I, then, be now so unappreciative as to hope that a very short note will perhaps compensate for a very long silence? By no means; it is rather that my great love proves my loyalty and fulfils my obligation.[3]

Farewell.
15th June, 1493.[4]

16

In Librum de Sole

My book 'On the Sun'

Marsilio Ficino to Antonio Calderini: greetings.

THE Sun, lord among the heavenly bodies, surpasses other causes of natural phenomena principally because it creates all things by its heat and reveals them by its light. Even if I have no need to use the heat of the sun to warm Calderini,[1] whom I have found to be most warmly attentive in every aspect of the management and care of my affairs, yet I thought I should now use the light of the Sun to reveal openly to everyone, with Apollo as witness, our ardent love that has long been confirmed by so many proofs.

15th July, 1493.

17

Lumen est admirabile, quoniam est imago sapientiae: item quam mirabilis sit copula sapientiae cum potentia

Light is astonishing, because it is the image of wisdom; how wonderful, too, is the uniting of wisdom with power

Marsilio Ficino to Ramberto Malatesta, distinguished Prince of Sogliano:[1] greetings.

It is a universal, firmly-held opinion, the very voice of nature, as it were, that nothing is more beautiful to behold, nothing more lovable, nothing more astonishing, than light. Although all acknowledge this beyond question, yet when you enquire about the cause of so great and so evident a phenomenon, not everyone will readily find it. Only someone who has become aware of this light, which is so evident to the eyes, is likely to reply that it is nothing other than an image of the hidden light, that is, of wisdom herself. For, in truth, wisdom is nothing other than the very bright light of understanding.

Indeed, in the *Phaedrus* our Plato foretold that if ever this light can be perceived with the inner eyes, it will arouse a love for itself that is far more intense than the love that is daily inspired in lovers by the light seen in beautiful bodies.[2] The reason for this is that this light which is so apparent to the sight has acquired among us such great favour and admiration solely from that more hidden light of which it is an image: the light of divine wisdom. Thus divine wisdom has given universal pre-eminence to light, as though to her own deputy.[3]

Indeed, the eyes alone are the guides of our body; for among the bodily organs they alone are possessed of light, which serves as a kind of wisdom.[4] Among all the faculties of the soul, too, mind alone rules, for it shines with the attribute of wisdom. When it comes to the elements and similar bodies, fire alone is lord among them, like a wise man endowed with light.[5] In the heavens, likewise, the Sun itself, the sole source of light, rules over all.[6] In the view of astrologers, the Sun signifies power and wisdom; it rejoices in the ninth region of the heavens as in the temple of Minerva.[7] It is by being close to the Sun that Mercury seems to have obtained a reputation for wisdom.[8]

What more can I say? To put it briefly, supremacy over the whole world is not claimed by any extreme of heat or cold, by any violent burst of movement, or by any turmoil of surging bodies or their overwhelming mass; but it is that primary wisdom which, perceiving all, has power over all and, providing for everything everywhere, is thus also the mistress of everything. So she seems rightly to have enjoined us in our turn to unite wisdom and power, as far as we are able, just as she has plainly united them both in herself and in the universe. For this reason I consider that it was divinely brought about that the same light of the Sun which actually makes all things by its power likewise revealed all things through its wisdom and ultimately benefitted and delighted all things through its goodness.[9] This is why we are always urged to unite not only wisdom with power but also goodness.

The poets proclaim that a blessed union of this kind existed and was held in great reverence in former times when Saturn reigned.[10] This is what our Plato longed to see above all else, and what we, his followers, chiefly desire.[11] We shall love above all others that man who unites the pursuit of outstanding wisdom and probity of conduct with noble lineage and leadership of the state. Now at this point the whiff of flattery and insincerity, which is utterly inappropriate to philosophers, prevents me from stating at greater length what I feel. But let me at least speak my mind briefly. In Ramberto Malatesta, Prince of Sogliano, I have now found what I was wholeheartedly seeking.[12] This man I love with all my heart and, as the law of friendship bids me, I share all I have with him.[13]

18

Quomodo Venus per cupidinem commiscet amantes. Iuppiter amicabilis per Mercurium conflat amicos

As Venus brings lovers together through Cupid, so Jupiter, god of friendship, makes people friends through Mercury

Marsilio Ficino sends greetings to Ramberto Malatesta, the famous Prince of Sogliano.[1]

AMONG the nations of the ancient world, the theologians set such a high value on friendship that they worshipped Jupiter as god of friendship within the hosts of the heavenly powers, or rather, in many instances, above all the other gods. They considered him responsible for bringing about all occurrences of goodwill and true friendship.[2] It was therefore their view that, just as the gracious Venus kindled love and, if I may say so, joined lovers through Cupid, so Jupiter, god of friendship, engendered even stronger bonds of goodwill and created friendships through Mercury. If we were allowed to speak of Jupiter and Mercury nowadays, we would certainly say that this friendship of ours has been brought about not by any human agency but through the good offices of Jupiter, god of friendship, since Minerva, the instigator of our goodwill, is said to have been born from the top of Jupiter's head.[3] But can we say that it is through Mercury that she has done this for us?[4] It is certainly through Mercury, and not just through that rather mysterious celestial Mercury but also through a human Mercury better known to us. For Pietro Martelli, a very dear friend to us both, has brought us together.[5] He not only has a Mercurial spirit but also seems to carry before him the very appearance and nature of Mercury. These qualities are the ones I foretold before I had seen his birth chart (if I may mention my own prophecy, if I may call it that) and now that I have seen it, my prediction has been confirmed. Therefore, just as Pietro has hitherto played the part of Mercury serving Jupiter in forging a friendship between us, so will he henceforth really be Mercury, going back and forth between us, conveying and interpreting our thoughts to one another.

4th August, 1493.

19

Sol imago vicariusque Dei

The Sun is the image of God and His representative

Marsilio Ficino to his Lord and Reverend Father in Christ, Francesco Soderini, Bishop of Volterra: especial greetings.

I AM sending you my book *On the Sun*, which I recently dedicated to your kinsman, the magnanimous Piero de' Medici, for you to read also.[1] But it is to you, who are also my patron, that I am dedicating this summary of the whole book, so that the book itself may be seen to be dedicated to you too.[2]

There are three particular qualities that theologians attribute to God: power, wisdom and goodness.[3] As the image of God, the Sun through its power accomplishes everything in our world; through its wisdom it distinguishes individual things every day and reveals them to our eyes; through its goodness it brings us benefit and delight. It is said that God alone can perform miracles. This is why the Sun, God's representative, seems to bring about three wonders in particular: beneath the heavens, in spring and summer, it quickens so many things that seemed dead throughout the winter; in the heavens it illumines, measures and controls all the heavenly bodies; and above the heavens, all that is invisible not just to our eyes but to our minds also, the Sun renders visible, so to speak, by reminding us, through marvellous displays of the heavenly bodies, to contemplate all that is above the heavens.[4]

Reverend father, may you profit from considering this *Sun* of ours and *Light*, you who are worthier than all others of the true Sun and of its gracious light.

8th September, 1493.
Florence.

20

Prohœmium in epistolas

A preface to the Letters[1]

Marsilio Ficino of Florence to all his letters at the same time: greetings.

My letters, each time you greet my friends at my behest, offer immortal greetings to your dearest friend, Girolamo Rossi.[2] For I had fathered you mortal, soon to die by some misfortune or other. But Girolamo, a man well known for his loving care, has recently caused you to be born again, this time to immortal life, I hope. For you lay hidden a long while, yearning for the light, nor until now was there anyone to pluck you from the shadows, perhaps because this was not yet the will of destiny or deity. But our Rossi – or rather now your Roscius[3] – with that devotion he has always shown your father Marsilio, has now with the same inherited love[4] happily pursued you too, working diligently so that your long-hidden faces may be wholly revealed. Therefore greet this learned and caring man who has restored you, you who hitherto were full of sorrow but are now of good cheer, and for the prodigious gift of immortality give immortal thanks.

15th December, 1494.[5]
Florence.

21

Pro libro de sole, item de stella magorum, in solennitate Epiphaniae

My book on the Sun; also the star of the Magi at this solemn feast of the Epiphany

Marsilio Ficino to Angelo Niccolini, brilliant citizen and expert on law: greetings.

On this day the Magi, observers of the stars, with a wonderful star as their guide, greeted Christ, Maker of the stars, with three particular gifts: gold, myrrh, and frankincense.[1] On this day Christ is said to have been baptised by John in the waters of the Jordan, in the presence of the Holy Spirit shining down from heaven.[2] On this day Christ, Creator of water and wine, miraculously changed water into wine at the wedding feast.[3]

And so it is that you too, Angelo, a man of outstanding devotion, every year solemnly celebrate this day, which is renowned for three great miracles, with your threefold tribute of a banquet, music, and readings. I for my part am dedicating to these sacred readings at your home the book *On the Sun and Light*, which I recently composed with the purpose of raising the minds of readers through a comparison with the visible light of the Sun to a wholehearted contemplation of the invisible light of the Godhead.

Just as the wondrous Star led the Magi on this day to see Christ, who is both God and man, so may my *Sun* lead us to reflect on the presence of God this very day, 6th January, 1494.

22

Pro Bacchi dono. Item Evangelicum illud: ex aqua vinum factum

In return for a gift of Bacchus, and the Gospel account of wine made from water

Marsilio Ficino to Mazzingo, distinguished physician: greetings.

BEING constantly reminded by the morning readings for the eight days of Epiphany,[1] I was reflecting today on those words from the Gospel which relate how wine was made from water.[2] Do they also have a physical meaning in addition to their mystical and moral allegory? For nature transforms water into wine over a long period, just as Christ transformed water into wine in an instant.

Indeed, a physical interpretation, of particular interest to a physician, raises the question of why Christ chose this to be the first of his miracles.[3] Perhaps to show that wine would be the first and best support for our life. But why was 'the good wine' –a strong wine, like undiluted wine from Crete or eastern lands – 'kept until now'?[4] Why did Christ, the Master of Life, choose not to offer this wine at the beginning of the meal, but to hold it back for so long? Perhaps he wished to warn us that strong wine well-known for its potency should not be allowed to hot-blooded youth but should rather be kept to reinvigorate the colder disposition of old age. Finally, why did he change not just some of the water but all of it into wine? Clearly so that the good wine might be drunk undiluted, especially in old age.[5]

So while I was musing on these questions around midday, I began to long for, and even to seek out, such a wine to comfort me in my old age and my mother in her infirmity, for last autumn she completed her eightieth year, and I my sixtieth. But at that very hour you, as if divinely inspired, sent me a divine wine.

Both foresight and a gift from Bacchus are entirely fitting for an Apollonian physician such as my Mazzingo is, for that same Phoebus is called both the first physician and the author of prophecy and he is the brother of Bacchus, joined with him in sacred rites.[6]

This is in keeping with both the prophecy and service of Bacchus, inasmuch as Phoebus himself is called both the first doctor and the author of prophecy, and is the brother of Bacchus, joined (to him) by holy rites.

What I value most highly is that, together with your most excellent gift from Father Liber, you have sent a Galenic letter[7] giving useful advice for my life, in order to join remedy and advice in a friendly spirit.

Therefore, just as prognosis is linked with medicine, and Bacchus with Phoebus, so am I linked with you by love, and always shall be.

13th January, 1494.[8]

23

Pro libro de vita iterum imprimendo. Item auspicium de amicitia immortale

In support of the reprinting of my book 'On Life'; also a sign of immortal friendship[1]

Marsilio Ficino of Florence to the priest Johannes Menchen of Cologne, distinguished professor of canon law and secretary to the Archbishop of Cologne: especial greetings.

On 18th January, towards sunrise,[2] I seemed in my dreams to greet a man, previously unknown to me, who was endowed with a noble appearance and graced with fine clothes and a splendid retinue. After a discussion on natural science he held out his foot to me, as if to be healed.

That very day you yourself arrived in Florence on your way to Rome to represent Archbishop Hermann.[3] You expressed a wish to see me but were unable to come to me because of a severe bruise on your foot, so I came to you, as was both necessary and appropriate. As soon as I set eyes on you, I recognised immediately the heroic person I had seen in my sleep. After an initial greeting we soon fell to talking about my book *On Life* and discussed with each other many matters relating mainly to medicine. In fulfilment of what I had foreseen while asleep, you held out your bruised foot while we were speaking. And so it appears that I did not really see a dream but received a prophecy from on high, a sure sign, I think, that ours would be a divine friendship. But since divine things are also immortal, I foresaw, as I have just said, the immortal divinity of our friendship. You, meanwhile, have contrived its future immortality. For you have decided to take care of the reprinting of my books *On Life*, so that this *Life* of mine may be more widely disseminated; and from this kindness of yours towards me future generations may understand your great love for me, and mine for you; and so this divine friendship of ours may turn out in the eyes of posterity to be immortal.[4]

Live happily, my Johannes, disseminator of my *Life* and most worthy of life. Farewell and be happy.

17th January, 1494.
Florence.

24

Commendatio brevis in causa iusta

A brief commendation in a just cause

Marsilio Ficino to his Most Reverend Father in Christ, his lord Francesco Soderini, Bishop of Volterra: especial greetings.

I SHOULD like to commend to you the monastery of Settimo and to speak briefly in support of its Modena lawsuit.[1] Indeed I know how much you love those monks, those men of deep devotion. I, too, love them; in fact, I revere them. I think that as just men they demand just decisions; and you are the keenest defender of what is just. In short, I shall consider that any help that you give these men has also been given to me, who watch over them. The monk who is the advocate for this suit, Justus in both name and deed, will carefully report everything to you.[2] I also commend myself to you wholeheartedly.

Fare well and prosper.
25th January, 1494.
Florence.

25

Plato multa Christianis consentanea dixit. Platonici multi Christiana sunt imitati

Plato said many things that are consistent with Christian teachings; many followers of Plato seem to have adopted Christian teachings

Marsilio Ficino of Florence to his Reverend Father in Christ, his lord Jacopo Rondoni, Bishop of Rimini: especial greetings.

A HOLY friar, a distinguished Professor of Theology in the Order of St Dominic, greeted me in your name and declared most earnestly, with many instances of proof, that I am ardently loved by you.[1] Even though this had long been very clear to me, I had been hoping for news of your good health and I have now received the kind of news I have so long been wanting.

Philosophy, mother of all human blessings, long ago gave birth to our friendship which, as Plato says, is to be set above all other bonds and will not perish with time.[2] But all this is too well known to require verbal proof.

The friar also told us that another friar, though I do not know who it was, had arrogantly claimed in a public oration that the mystery of the Trinity, so holy to Christians, already existed in Plato, and that the first Christians received it from his writings. He said that you are awaiting my verdict on this question as Platonic teachings are known to me. So let me affirm beyond dispute that the mystery of the Christian Trinity was never in the books actually written by Plato, but there are some things that resemble it in words though not at all in meaning.[3] There are, however, greater similarities in the writings of those of his followers who flourished after Christ: in Numenius, Ammonius, Plotinus, Amelius, Iamblichus and Proclus.[4]

Since these men had all engaged with the Gospel of St John and some also with the books of Dionysius the Areopagite, they were happy to adopt some things similar to the Trinity and they took up the orders and names of the angels as being fully consistent with their Plato, a follower of Moses. That is why when St Augustine, formerly a Platonist but now considering whether to profess the Christian faith, came across these books of the Platonists and recognised that they were confirming Christian doctrines by their imitation of them, he gave thanks to God and became more eager to accept Christian teachings.[5]

How closely the Platonic resemble the Christian teachings you will be able to understand in a few words from the letter which I wrote a long time ago to Braccio Martelli on this subject, for I am now sending you a copy of it.[6] Fare well and be happy. Continue to love me who dearly love you.

2nd February, 1494.

26

Semper aliquid agendum, et quoad fieri potest, in eodem perseverandum

There is always something to be done and it should be persevered with as far as is possible

Marsilio Ficino of Florence to Callimachus,[1] a most learned man and excellent friend: especial greetings.

SINCE this universe of which we are part is always moving, certainly we neither can nor should ever abstain from action and movement, especially because, as the followers of Plato say, the first movement, which is everlasting, is natural to the soul itself and life is simply the movement and action of the soul.[2] So moving and acting are as necessary and desirable as living.

But have I made a wrong start here? It would perhaps have been more appropriate after a long silence to begin my letter to you with accounts of what I am doing and news of my health, than to start so abruptly with philosophy. Of course it would have been more appropriate, my dear Callimachus. But my rather longstanding practice and my own inner nature are responsible for the fact that I am making an inappropriate start with philosophy. You also are often accustomed to play the part of philosopher in your letters to me, but always at the right time and nicely. Let me then continue for a while as I began, in the hope that it is not so inappropriate.

There are three main kinds of movement through space in the universe.[3] Some things revolve around the same point in the same constant way; others continually change their place and position; yet others follow a combination of the circular motion and the straight.[4] Human beings, too, have different kinds of movement.[5]

But to speak now of my own movement, and not anyone else's, it is certainly my lot to revolve always in the same place. For what is Marsilio doing today? What he did yesterday. What will he do tomorrow? Again, what he is doing today. As you see, within the walls of the academy I always revolve around the same point again and again. But what I have been doing while circling thus for so long, and have done over and over again and am now putting together anew,[6] you will understand from the titles of my books, a list of which I am sending you to read, together with my book on the Sun, so that through the brilliant testimony of this Phoebean gift our friendship may shine out for present and future generations. In fact, I am sending you three copies of the book *On the Sun and Light*, so that I may please you and you may also be able to please your two friends.

So from all this you will see for yourself what I have written. Meanwhile I have heard from your Ottaviano[7] and the Tedaldi family[8] that you have now completed what you were working on, which struck me as extremely pleasing.

Farewell and be happy.
2nd April, 1494.

27

Sapientes filii sunt Minervae: haec Philosophiam parit: Philosophia philosophos

The wise are the children of Minerva: she gives birth to Philosophy and Philosophy gives birth to philosophers

Marsilio Ficino to his dearest brother, Germain de Ganay: greetings.[1]

THE poets are forever praising Minerva as a virgin. Yet no one else among the gods or mankind brings forth full-grown children, all the while preserving her perpetual virginity, since, being born herself from the head of highest Jove,[2] she likewise gives birth from the head alone.[3] Replacing the race of giants that was destroyed, she gives birth to the wise as heroes greater than the giants.[4] Philosophy, also a perpetual virgin and daughter of Sophia, that is, of Minerva, brings forth, from the crown of her head, philosophers in place of the wise.

Greetings again, therefore, my dearest Germain, whom Philosophy, the mother we have in common, bore as a true brother to me. Since our devoted mother[5] did not wish her children ever to be separated, she drew you into love for me (as you write) by sending her light to you, and in turn, by conveying the heat of that light to me, she seized me with love for you. But since all things should be shared among friends, and especially among brothers, I have decided that all I have shall be shared with you as you desire. So I shall first send you the books of Dionysius and many of the Platonists, which you have long been asking for. Then I shall send the commentaries on *Parmenides*, which are being copied out for you day by day. Perhaps the commentaries on the *Timaeus* will follow, and on the *Sophist*. Those on the *Sophist* which are now hurrying to their completion are being copied out, and at the same time even my letters are being reviewed. I had understood that you had the Plotinus already, together with other works, but recently you have written that you do not. If you wish it to be sent, please let me know.[6]

Farewell.

28

Pro libro de sole

My book 'On the Sun'

Marsilio Ficino to his lord Bernardo Bembo of Venice:[1] greetings.

ORDINARY love often grows cold or even perishes through long absence and lengthy silence. However, let Phoebus himself be the token, by his heat, and the witness, by his light, that our love is far from ordinary and can never cool down or fall into oblivion through absence or silence.[2]

19th [August, 1494].[3]

29

Pro libro de Sole

My book 'On the Sun'

Marsilio Ficino to his lord Antonio Cronico of Venice:[1] greetings.

ONE aspect of Jupiter that the ancients worshipped was 'the amicable', the intermediary between friends and the protector of friendship.[2] But tell me, what regions of the world does this Jupiter especially inhabit?

Perhaps he has placed his dwelling in the Sun, for friendship takes its name from love and is guided by love, and love is a kind of heat.[3] But the heat of love arises from knowledge.[4] It is engendered by beauty. But Apollo is, above all others, the author of heat, of knowledge, and of beauty.

So in this Apollonian gift may Jupiter the Amicable be the guarantor of our friendship.

19th August, 1494.

30

Quid sentiat de astrologia

My view of astrology[1]

Marsilio Ficino to Angelo Poliziano: greetings.

AGAINST a host of astrologers who strive vainly and impiously like the Giants to wrest heaven from Jupiter, Athena's child, Pico, and you, a Herculean warrior, are right to engage in frequent and successful combat.[2] Does not Orpheus famously sing of Athena as expeller of the Giants[3] and many poets tell how the Giant Antaeus was lifted from earth and life by Hercules.[4]

But what do I think? Truly, just as in all aspects of life I am of one mind with you, so also in this endeavour I agree with you, and although I may not be so quick to fight, I am entirely on your side.

In fact, nearly all the Platonists mention when appropriate the heavenly figures which the astronomers describe: they neither reject them nor are they eager to approve them. Plotinus, however, laughs such things out of court.[5] I too, interpreting him in my commentaries, as his translator, make light of them in the same way, partly relying on his authority and partly because I have no reliable means of determining things of this kind. Moreover, on the same principle, in those commentaries I call into question many of the astrologers' rulings.[6] But in the book *On Life*, in which I profess the art of medicine and conscientiously seek out from every quarter life-giving remedies of all kinds whenever I may, I neither utterly despise their representations nor spurn all their rules.[7] Even if I find in them no sound rational basis, yet as a zealous guardian of medicine for humanity, I hunt out remedies which are sure from the wise, as well as popular remedies which may well be effective, to gather from everywhere resources that will in some way be beneficial. In short, in order to leave nothing untried which may seem to anyone to be in some way conducive to health, I mix it with more reliable remedies; I also gather here and there many remedies which I pray may be of use even though I place less hope in them.

What I appear to be saying at the beginning of the third book – that the images in the heavens were mapped out by the earlier Platonists – is not what I mean. For it is not my purpose to assert there that the Platonists were advocates of celestial images, about which they say little or nothing, but that it was the view of some Platonists that the World Soul brought forth for itself the celestial bodies. It gave birth to the stars and the vault of heaven, and beyond the individual stars to the images,[8] if in fact there are any such images there. In that book I describe the arrangement of the signs and the images as I have noted them, not in the works of the Platonists, but in those of the astrologers.[9] But the development of the book already makes clear how far I believe in the celestial images and how far I trust those fashioned by art. Moreover, in my book *On the Sun* I am not teaching astronomy so much as pursuing moral allegories through astronomy and searching for means of rising up to the divine.[10]

In sum, while I have sometimes roamed rather freely and perhaps with too much licence in my books *On Life* as well as *On the Sun and Light*, blending the poetic with the philosophic, with Plotinus I conduct myself with more restraint and discipline, so that the fact that the imaginings of the astrologers have been refuted one by one by our Pico della Mirandola will be far from unwelcome to me. For nowhere do I support them: rather do I join Plotinus in laughing at them, and I am delighted that they are being driven off the stage by Mirandola. I rejoice with you, Poliziano, that, just as the Python's venom was nullified by Phoebus, superstitious nonsense is being nullified by Pico.[11] For in this matter, as in all others, you have always shown yourself to be a Hercules.[12] You have long been pursuing these portents of the astrologers, just as you have keenly pursued other monstrosities everywhere, so that you, as a most valiant Hercules, have overcome these monsters not only on earth but also in the heavens. In conclusion, may 'the vanquished Earth grant the heavens' to you as it did to Hercules.[13] Until then, live long on earth. Farewell and good fortune.

20th August, 1494.

31

Pro libro de sole

My book 'On the Sun'

Marsilio Ficino to Bernardo Rucellai, son of Mariotto: greetings.[1]

WANTING light for my friends and also desiring to enlighten them with its radiance, I have been taking care for a long time now that my books *On the Sun* and *Light* might be in the hands of all my friends.[2] So it is no surprise that you too, my dearest Bernardo, are now a recipient of this gift, now that you are beloved of us, that is, since we have recently got to know you – although it is not only now that you should be loved but for ever. Yet the fact that I love you so strongly is caused not just by your refined character and your uprightness but also because you are very dear to Girolamo Rossi, who is dearest of all to me and before all others most worthy of light.[3]

But let me clarify something with you about light in case you have doubts while reading this book: when I say that the Sun or the light was created first, please don't take this to mean that either the Sun or its light was made at the first moment or stage of creation, since Moses himself says, 'In the beginning, God created the heaven and the earth. And the earth . . .'[4] Understand, however, that angelic light was created at the first stage of the process, the light of the Sun will be present on the first day, and the orb and form of the Sun will eventually appear on the fourth day, but both the light of the Sun and its orb in all respects hold first rank among the heavenly bodies.[5]

Farewell now, and read happily, free from uncertainty.

32

Commendatio clientis apud Magistratum

Commending a client before the magistrate

Marsilio Ficino to Niccolò del Benino, a man of learning and fine character: greetings.[1]

FROM the very outset of your magistracy it was undoubtedly my privilege to rejoice with you in no small measure for the goodwill that we share, which is also of no small measure. For not only were you being honoured by this office but, even more, you were also going to conduct your magistracy in a fitting manner. It was also cause for my friends and clients to rejoice because, if they were innocent, they would receive protection from you, or if guilty, at least some measure of leniency and mercy. For I know your nature. I certainly know that you will combine justice with mercy in the proper manner, which God Himself teaches through His works.

Moreover, if I may say something about Jupiter in this context, the Jews call him Sedech,[2] which is Justice; and the Astronomers ascribe judgements and laws to their Jupiter. Poets sing of the same Jupiter as full of leniency,[3] though I would not include that line of poetry which leads towards licence rather than leniency: 'Jupiter established that whatever gave pleasure was right.'[4] Let it suffice that, in the view of astrologers, Jupiter applies, or indicates, mercy along with the laws.[5] In this way God clearly seems to have reminded men from the heavens that in a magistracy they should combine these two equally, but on account of your character I am sure you already know this well enough.[6]

Farewell and good fortune.
Florence.
31st August, 1494.

33

Gratiarum actio pro indulgentia in clientem impetrata

Giving thanks for the leniency granted in the case of a dependant

Marsilio Ficino to Niccolò del Benino, a man of learning and fine character: greetings.

SINCE good and evil are opposites and are therefore subject to opposite conditions, it certainly seems likely that, if good is fertile,[1] evil conversely will be sterile. But just as an offence is evil, to the same extent mercy is good, and thus it necessarily follows that a merciful favour is far more fertile than an offence and a wrong. And so, if a wrong committed by my dependant gave birth to our previous letter to you,[2] how much the more should your generous and merciful leniency give birth in its turn to a much better and more important letter. The first letter was Jovian, if I may call it so, relying on a comparison with Jupiter; the second letter will therefore not surpass the first, or even equal it, unless it is Apollonian, for only the Sun can surpass Jupiter.[3]

For this reason, so that this letter may be able to repay your kindness towards me under the auspices of Apollo, I am sending it to you as a companion of Phoebus and attendant on the Sun. Be kind enough to read our book *On the Sun*, which I am sending you as a gift, and live happily.

3rd September, 1494.

34

De Ioue amicabili & Apolline pro libro de sole

On Jupiter, the god of friendship, and Apollo, with relevance to my book 'On the Sun'

A message from Marsilio Ficino of Florence to Jean Matheron,[1] illustrious ambassador of the great king of France.

THE theologians of old were the first, and the poets the next, to worship Jupiter the Amicable amongst all the other deities, as the father of chaste love and steadfast friendship.[2] He won this title 'amicable' on account of both love and friendship equally. Since our Plato sometimes refers to this deity, in my commentaries I have often tried to find a clearer way of naming this god. Finally, after long contemplation, it came to mind that I should name him as the brightest of the gods, that is Apollo, source of light, heat, harmony, and knowledge.

Certainly, we never love what we do not know, we do not come to know anything without light, nor are we ever roused to love without some heat. Moreover, a harmonious accord is also needed for both love and friendship. Then again, for love physical beauty is often sought after, while for friendship beauty of mind is always desired. But both physical beauty and beauty of mind seem to be nothing other than forms of radiance. Now the giver of radiance is Apollo. So all these reasons compel us to name Apollo as the principal source of love and friendship. If, for the sake of discussion, we perhaps accept a number of gods, as the pagans do, we shall say that Phoebus Apollo is a god or divine power appointed as ruler of the Sun among the heavenly bodies. But if we take matters more seriously,[3] we shall declare that Phoebus is the supreme God, of whom the Sun in the heavens is a reflection. Thus Phoebus is the giver of virtuous love and constant friendship, while the Sun is their symbol.[4]

Since I love you ardently, being afire with the Phoebean radiance of your wisdom and your virtues, and since I endeavour to kindle friendship from love, it will be no surprise that I am coming to you under Apollonian auspices to offer you greetings.

35

Multifaciendum est laudari a laudato viro

Being praised by a man who is praised should be greatly valued

Marsilio Ficino to Germain de Ganay, a man of outstanding virtue: greetings.

WHAT I had long been hearing from many people of your outstanding virtue and high office has recently been confirmed for me with numerous testimonies by the noble gentlemen Cosimo Sassetti and Lorenzo Spinelli,[1] who are certainly most reliable witnesses in this matter. Furthermore, they have described how highly you think of me and how dearly you love me. I for my part greatly value your approval and love, since you above all are most worthy of praise and love. So I would wish that the pleasure you take in seeing our works may be as great as our desire to please you.

I hope you will soon see some followers of Plato coming from here to meet you.[2] You would have seen the Areopagite at the same time, the most eminent of the Platonists, if he were now able to join them in a condition befitting both him and you, but neglect by the copyist and the bookbinder has hampered his arrival.[3] I hope he will arrive in a few days, together with some letters. The commentary on *Parmenides* has already been copied out for you. The one on *Timaeus* is being rewritten day by day.

Farewell and good fortune, my dearest Germain. Continue, I beg you, to love your brother in Plato, Marsilio, who loves you most dearly.

16th October, 1494.

36

Pro libro de religione. Purgatio de tarda salutatione

My book on Religion and an apology for a belated greeting

Marsilio Ficino to Giovanni di Stefano,[1] most illustrious knight and ambassador from Milan: greetings.

ALTHOUGH your virtues and high position, as well as my immense love for you, have long been requiring me to greet you time and again and on my own initiative, yet the turbulence of your official duties has prevented me from interrupting you except on some vital matter. I am therefore greeting you now, since I think that you will perhaps be less occupied and also our common interest requires it (as has been the case for a long time). Greetings to you, of all men the most worthy of salvation; greetings always in God, the very author of everlasting salvation.[2]

Now I would not like to come empty-handed before a man of such virtue and high position, to approach the celebrated ambassador of the most illustrious Duke without a leader. So Christ is now my leader, full of grace and truth, as I bring to you a book treating of the Christian religion.[3] Let not the poor and humble appearance of the book offend you, I pray, since the Christian religion has taught humility from the beginning and gladly endures poverty. In fact, a book written on Christian piety[4] is wholly fitting for you, a man distinguished for piety. Moreover, love, to be complete, seems to long for two things in particular: fervour and constancy. How fervent is my love for you can be witnessed by that *Sun* of ours[5] which you already have, the source of heat as well as light; this book *On Religion* now in your possession will be the proof and pledge of how constant my love for you will be. For nothing is more constant than religious piety, and 'love never fails'.[6] Farewell and prosper, and love me, I pray, who have loved you long and fervently.

4th November, 1494.

37

Oratio Marsilii Ficini Florentini ad Carolum magnum Gallorum Regem

An address by Marsilio Ficino of Florence to Charles the Great, King of the French.[1]

KING Charles, ever unconquered, your exalted Majesty is sometimes accustomed to say, as many report, that he is being sent on this military campaign by the will of God. This indeed is what we and the whole of this your people of Florence firmly believe, strongly hope and passionately rejoice in. For it appears to be true that the most Christian king of the French is being sent by Christ and also that Charles, the king famed above all others for his sense of duty, is being guided by his duty as a Christian, especially since you have undertaken such a great journey and such a great task with the intention of redeeming for the Supreme Redeemer of the human race the holy city of Jerusalem, which is in the hands of ferocious barbarians.

We certainly hope that you will redeem the holy kingdom with ease, after retaking your hereditary kingdom[2] on the way, since throughout this journey you are following in the footsteps of Christ with all your might. For Christ, the King of Peace, frequently promises peace to those who wish for peace; you, too, as a most Christian king, endowed with a unique sense of devotion,[3] promise the same, we hear, and we hope you will assuredly deliver it. You will actually accomplish what the dutiful Aeneas and his descendants were commanded to do long ago by his father: 'Spare the conquered and subdue the proud.'[4] For this reason, since you will be the author of peace for all who desire peace, you will present yourself as the peacemaker especially for your own people, that is for us. You will look upon your city of Florence with an outstanding sense of duty and protection. Florence is named after a flower, the lily, and is everywhere full of lilies.[5] You will come unto your own and your own will receive you wholeheartedly.[6] Moreover, you, following Christ, your leader, will proclaim to the people, 'Come unto me all ye that labour and are heavy laden and I will give you rest.'[7] And so the people present and those who will come after through the ages will forever sing the praises of the Gracious King Charles, known for his graciousness and favour.[8] 'Blessed be he that cometh in the name of the Lord.'[9] Charles is dear to us and exalted as the peacemaker king. 'This is the day which the Lord hath made; we will rejoice and be glad in it.'[10] The people of Florence, present and future, will proclaim these very things about your glory. Moreover, the entire world and the history we all share[11] will recount, I think, what I am about to say: Charles, invincible King of the Gauls, has so far surpassed that saying of Caesar's, 'I came, I saw, I conquered'[12] – great when said and far greater when performed – that it can now be rightly said: 'I have not yet come, I have not yet seen, but I have already conquered.' He has even surpassed Hercules, universally acclaimed as the most renowned hero. For Hercules is said in his labours to have fought with his hands, with fire, with sword, and with club;[13] Charles the Great, however, has shaken the whole world, not by the machinery of war but with a single nod, so to speak, like Jove, so that he will be seen and will one day be called the lord not only of France but also of the world.[14] Just as Almighty God has freed the human race from hidden enemies, so the exalted Charles seems to have been sent from heaven to subjugate the Turks and thus reclaim the sacred city of Jerusalem from those who are clearly her enemies.

38

Cur providentia permittat adversa. Item de vaticiniis remediisque malorum

Why providence permits adversities. Also on prophecies and on the remedies for evils

Marsilio Ficino of Florence to Giovanni Cavalcanti, his unique friend: greetings.[1]

It is often asked by the Platonists why it is that divine Providence always permits men, the just and the unjust alike, to be troubled by countless evils.[2] To put it briefly, they usually answer in the following ways. Firstly, mortals do not know whether such things are evil or good, for the affairs of human beings are just like shadows, and their thoughts like dreams.[3] This is what is meant by the sayings of the Prophets: 'All is vanity'[4] and 'All men are liars'.[5] They further reply that, even if it is agreed that those things which seem evil really are to some extent evil, at worst, evil is allowed by the highest Good only for the sake of good. For difficulties and adversities remove a defect which is curable, but punish one which is incurable, and thus the good shines forth in both the cleansing of the one and the justice of the other. Again, in times of adversity good men distinguish themselves from evil men, are exercised and put to the test. But the testing, the training and the steadfastness are the good.

Besides this, it is worth considering carefully what Plato says in the *Phaedrus* concerning the cunning sorcery of an evil spirit. Right from the beginning a certain spirit mingled pleasure with as many vices as possible.[6] There Socrates says, by way of warning, that the chief endeavour of evil spirits is to detain for longer souls that are forgetful of their supreme Father, in this place of exile, cut off from their heavenly home, and to contrive long delays for them through enticements and worldly delights. Captivated by these, as if by the potions of the sorceress Circe and the sleep-inducing songs of the Sirens, the souls never return to their heavenly home, or at best do so more slowly.[7] To counteract these demonic snares, however, the kindly providence of God has ordained that bitter tastes be sometimes mingled with these sweet and joy-giving tastes, lest we be caught like fish on a hook by this kind of pleasure which Timaeus calls the bait of evils. The Platonists in general, and Plotinus and Synesius in particular, think that this is largely the reason why divine providence wished souls on earth to be afflicted by so many great disturbances. This is the meaning of that well-known statement of Plato in his book *On Knowledge*, a statement which I sent you a long time ago, my dear Giovanni, with a brief explanation, and which accords with the Gospel: 'It is impossible, O Theodorus,' he says, 'for evils to be rooted out completely, for there must always be something which is opposed to the good. Evils cannot exist among the gods, but of necessity they hover around our mortal nature and this lower region. This is why we must try to flee from here to there as swiftly as we can, and fleeing there means using all our strength to make ourselves like unto God; but it is justice, holiness and wisdom that make us like God.'[8] This is what Plato says.

With these words Plato makes it clear that this is the main reason why we should consider fleeing from here to God before it is too late, so that we may escape from the evils which necessarily afflict us here, that is, from this transient evil, to be able to gain everlasting good. No one, however, goes to find a doctor unless troubled by sickness, nor do sailors appreciate the skill of the helmsman unless they are being buffeted by the waves. Human beings are actually so dull that they completely fail to recognise the good except by comparison with evils, and so ungrateful that they do not readily honour God, the bestower of all good, unless they are oppressed by evils. For this reason, tormented by a host of illnesses and troubles, they are forced to fly for refuge to God Himself, as their doctor and helper. They are also obliged to acknowledge that their homeland is not this earthly region, where they are in constant distress and never find rest; their homeland is heaven. No better reason can be given why God permits evils and adversities than the Gospel account which teaches that people are sometimes born blind or crippled to reveal to mankind the wonderful power and goodness of God,[9] which means that ills that cannot be cured by human means will be cured by miracles. It is not ordinary illnesses or storms, but very severe ones, that bear witness to the best doctor or helmsman. Often, then, both in public and in private, men are hemmed in on all sides by such extreme difficulties that no escape is apparent anywhere; human deliverance is no longer hoped for, but only divine remedies are sought. At such a time, stretching out a gracious hand from on high to God's children who are humbly entreating Him with devotion, divine goodness and power proclaim that God alone is the saviour in extreme calamities. This is shown even more clearly when great perils are predicted through one of the prophets long before they arrive. It is the duty of the human doctor at least to give a prognosis even if he cannot preserve health; but it is the duty of the divine physician to care equally for both. And if we may bring forward examples of these things from scripture, how very many there are which are plain for all to see.

However, my purpose is, and always has been, to bring to light things which are not so well-known, and, as far as I can, to confirm Christian mysteries with Platonic ones. So, my Giovanni, being both a worshipper of divine mysteries and a devotee of Platonic ones, hear the words with which Socrates, in Plato's writings, confirms divine guidance on the remedies for human ills and substantiates the words of the prophets. For in the *Symposium* he says that the priestess Diotima, a woman of prophecy and well versed in divine matters, foretold a plague threatening the Athenians. Accordingly, by the performance of sacred rites during the ten years before the plague, she delayed the onset of the disease.[10] Thus also in the *Phaedrus,* 'If we mention the Sibyl and anyone else who has had recourse to prophecy, predicting so many things which would be of benefit in the future, we shall over-extend our already long discourse and be offering something that is obvious to all.'[11] And a little later he says, 'The ancients attest that prophecy accomplished by divine frenzy far surpasses both augury and human wisdom. So against those very grave diseases and hardships which sometimes threaten mortals through divine displeasure at ancient transgressions, divine frenzy comes from somewhere to particular people, predicts future events and miraculously finds remedies for those in need, resorting to prayers and acts of divine worship. So it comes about that, having attained expiations and propitiations, the divine frenzy makes safe the person possessing it, obtaining for him who is frenzied and possessed in the right way absolution from present evils both now and in the future.'[12]

Moreover in the first book of *Laws,* Plato says, 'Epimenides of Crete, a divine man, warned by a divine oracle ten years before the Persian War, came to Athens and made certain sacrifices ordained by the divine oracle and foretold to the Athenians, who were in dread of the Persian fleet, that the Persians would not come for ten years, and that when they came, they would go away again without accomplishing their object.'[13]

Plato certainly judges such a man to be wisest of all, even though he is often held by the people to be most foolish. Thus in the *Phaedrus* he describes this extraordinary fact in the following way: 'He who makes proper use of divine meditations and is always filled with the perfect mysteries, he alone becomes truly perfect, set apart from human pursuits and cleaving to the divine. Reviled by the multitude, as if beside himself, he is in fact unknown to the multitude, being filled with God.'[14]

After this, when he has placed the prophet and the divinely inspired priest far above human wisdom, Plato describes a mind which is altogether fired with divine love, experiencing the ecstasy of love, and he puts this kind of frenzy and alienation not only above human wisdom, but also above all divine gifts.[15] With this the words of the Apostle clearly agree: 'The greatest of these is love.'[16] Avicenna, too, agrees with Plato that prophets are sent from God and why they are sent, giving many reasons in his book on divine matters.[17]

But now, leaving these rather lengthy digressions, let us return briefly to our purpose. It is surely worthy of more than ordinary consideration that Plato says in the passage quoted earlier that God, displeased by ancient transgressions, in some way intended calamities for mankind. Hence we have the saying that adversities happen because of iniquities[18] and the Mosaic account that all adversities have befallen us because of the transgression of our first parents.[19] Plato further adds that God, moved as it were by compassion, often inspires prophets to foretell scourges that will come upon us, so that, being thus admonished, we may take refuge in prayers and holy purifications. Having performed these rightly, we frequently escape unharmed, and this surely seems to confirm all the mysteries of our Church. Therefore perhaps we should seek no further for examples of so great a matter. Was it not on account of many transgressions that dire destruction was threatening our city this autumn[20] – a destruction that could in no way be averted by human power? Was it not God's most tender mercy to the Florentines that foretold this very thing to us a full four years before this autumn through Girolamo, a man distinguished in holiness and wisdom, who was divinely chosen for this purpose from the order of preachers? Did we not miraculously avoid the most certain destruction already hanging over our head, through the forewarnings and divine admonitions provided through this man, certainly not by any power of our own, and beyond our hope and expectation? 'This is the Lord's doing; it is marvellous in our eyes.'[21]

It remains, my best Giovanni, that not only myself and you, but also all Florentines, complying with the health-giving counsels of so great a man, should henceforth give thanks to God, who is most merciful to us, and should publicly proclaim, 'Strengthen, O God, that which thou hast wrought for us.'[22]

12th December, 1494.

39

Gratulatio pro litteris diu expectatis

Joy on receiving a long-awaited letter

Marsilio Ficino to his most beloved Germain de Ganay: greetings.[1]

THE continuing difficulty of these troubled times has often prevented the arrival of your letters to me and of mine to you. Yesterday, 'your devotion overcame the hardships of the journey'[2] and yielded up to me your long-awaited letter. Arise now, my letter, already to hand. 'Go thou to our valiant one: enjoy a happier fate!'[3]

But what am I to write first? Surely I should begin with what has been especially pleasing to me: that I have been commended through your letter to your brother Jean,[4] that royal Achates, President of Paris. That has been and will be something well worthwhile for us. For almost all of Italy, certainly all of Tuscany and especially Florence, is shaken daily by disturbances from outside and from within.[5]

I recently met our Jean myself, in the presence of your noble king.[6] He is a man who deserves our good wishes on all occasions. It was a joy to see him on account of his own splendour, but I also took great delight in the fact that in your most eminent brother I seemed to see my own dearest brother-german, consoling me all the while in these present difficulties.

So, even though our calling requires a clear mind, I am nevertheless continuing as far as I can amidst these alarms to work unremittingly on the Platonic commentaries, and, God willing, shall complete them very soon.[7]

40

Pia Platonis sententia, de amicis et inimicis dei

The piety of Plato's view concerning the friends and enemies of God

Marsilio Ficino to his unique friend Giovanni Cavalcanti: greetings.

I DISCUSSED yesterday with you and that honourable man, your son-in-law, Gherardo Gianfigliazzi,[1] Plato's opinion in the *Philebus* concerning the friends and enemies of God. You then wanted me to set down for you the actual words of Plato and our own commentary on them. So here they are. Enjoy reading them.

This is what Plato says:[2]

'Is not a man who is just, godly and honourable a friend to God? On the other hand, is not the unjust and dishonourable man an enemy?

He certainly is.

Now every man is led by powerful hope. For there are inner conversations in each of us which we usually call expectations and hopes, but they are in fact highly-coloured imaginings. For instance, everyone can imagine himself taking possession of a large heap of gold, being awash with various pleasures, and bathing in every delight. Can it not be said that such expectations and imaginings often turn out to be true for good men because they are friends of God? On the other hand, for bad men are they not repeatedly false?

Of course!

Depraved men do have certain pleasures, but they are often contrived and are ultimately false. Therefore depraved men often exult in false pleasures. On the other hand, good men are always nourished by real joys.'

This is what Plato says. What follows is our commentary:

A good man, Plato thinks, is temperate in himself, reverent towards God and just towards men. Such a soul is more of a friend to God because of its likeness to God, but a bad soul, because of its unlikeness, is an enemy. And so, since God moves us inwardly and provides for us everywhere, it is not surprising that the expectations, imaginings and hopes of good men frequently turn out to be true, but those of bad men turn out to be false. Both kinds of men devise, choose and hope for so-called pleasures. For good men, being divine and truthful, these pleasures often happen to be true, but for bad men they turn out to be false. Bad men, being untruthful to themselves, are frequently deceived by expectation, and consequently often devise false delights. In short, if hopes ought not to turn out well for depraved men, who are in conflict with divine truth and yet who seem to meet with outward success, it follows, at the very least, that inwardly they do not turn out well. Therefore they are always tormented within; they are enfeebled and their pleasures are like the false pleasures of the sick, of dreamers and the insane.[3]

20th December, 1494.

41

Pro libro de Sole

My book 'On the Sun'

Marsilio Ficino to Jean de Ganay,[1] highly distinguished President of the Parliament of Paris: especial greetings.

BEING unable to practise philosophy peacefully in the city because of the great number of guests in the house and the public disturbances,[2] yet unwilling to interrupt my continual philosophical duties,[3] I withdrew to the solitude of the countryside. But before leaving, I often sought out your splendour, which I had desired for a long time.[4]

Since I have not yet been able to greet your splendour in person, I now greet it from afar with a Phoebean gift. Just as Phoebus himself reaches with his rays what he fails to touch with his orb, so does your splendour, by its rays, reach me even here.

Through the very heat of Phoebean light I beseech you, my resplendent Jean, to love Marsilio, who is full of ardent love.[5]

Farewell.

42

Pro libro de Sole

My book 'On the Sun'

Marsilio Ficino to Paolo of Verona,[1] a man outstanding for his learning: greetings.

I WAS at least able to see you in Florence, for which I was most grateful. It would also have been very gratifying to see the President of Paris,[2] a man of most distinguished appearance. Yet in fact, if you are both, as I think, reciprocally bound by that kind of love where the one is in the other, as soon as I caught sight of Paolo, I beheld Jean within Paolo. This, of course, is what Phoebus does: while he looks outwards with his splendour he is, as it were, simultaneously looking inwards with his heat.

In conclusion, by means of this Phoebean gift, which I am also sending to you, I earnestly beseech you to commend me often to the Apollonian John.[3] Farewell.

The end of the twelfth and last book of letters
of Marsilio Ficino of Florence to his friends.
Thanks be to God.
Amen.[4]

Appendix

This Appendix contains a number of letters from or to Ficino that were not included in the edition of his Letters that he prepared for publication in print in 1495. Letter A, present in the manuscript, had already been published in the form of a chapter in *De vita*. Likewise, item B, the original text of *De sole*, was removed and published separately. Letters D to I and K to P postdate the printing of the *Letters*. Some documents are included for their particular interest, such as the *Privilegium* (J), permitting publication of the *Letters*, Ficino's defence before the College of Cardinals after the execution of Savonarola (Q) and Ficino's will (R).

Items A to R are ordered chronologically apart from instances which should obviously be grouped together because of their recipient or theme. Three items, S to U, are from earlier years; two of these (S and U) came to light only recently. The final item V is the epitaph inscribed below Ficino's memorial bust in the Cathedral of Santa Maria del Fiore in Florence.

Appendix Letters

A

Exhortatio ad moralem et contemplativam religiosamque vitam

An exhortation to lead a moral, contemplative and religious life[1]

Marsilio Ficino to his friends: greetings.

THOSE who desire truth need to look after their bodily spirit with the full care of physicians, for if it is completely neglected, it may hinder or ill serve those seeking truth. If this is so, how much more carefully should one cultivate the incorporeal spirit, that is, the intellect, through the precepts of moral discipline, since truth itself, being incorporeal, is acquired by the intellect alone. For it is an offence against divine law to cultivate the body, the mere servant of the soul, but neglect the soul, the lord and sovereign of the body, especially as the opinion of the Magi and Plato[2] is that the whole body so depends on the soul that, unless the soul is in good health, the body cannot be. That is why Apollo, the father of medicine, judged Socrates, not Hippocrates, to be the wisest of men, even though Hippocrates was of Apollo's own lineage.[3] For Socrates devoted himself to the healing of the soul just as much as Hippocrates did to the healing of the body; but what they attempted, Christ alone achieved. Accordingly, if we are bidden by Socrates to cultivate our mind by the best practices, so that with a clear mind we may more easily follow the light and truth we naturally seek, is it not all the more proper to venerate divine truth first and foremost through holy religion?

The mind has been created to seek and attain this truth in just the same way that the eye has been created to discern the light of the sun.

And as our Plato says,[4] just as sight sees no visible thing anywhere except in the splendour of the supremely visible, that is, the sun itself, so the human intellect does not apprehend any intelligible thing except in the light of the supremely intelligible, that is, the light of God, which is always and everywhere present to us: I mean, the light 'which lighteth every man that cometh into the world',[5] the light about which David sings, 'In thy light shall we see light.'[6]

Indeed, when the eyes have been cleansed and are looking upon the light itself, suddenly its brilliance streams into them and is fully resplendent with the colours and forms of things. Likewise, as soon as the mind has been cleansed of all bodily agitations through moral discipline, and turns with a devout and burning love to divine truth, that is, to God Himself, divine truth suddenly pours into the mind, as the divine Plato says, and happily unfolds the true principles of things which are contained within it, and by which all things are established.[7] It floods the mind with light and at the same time, in equal measure, imbues the will with abundant joy.

B

De Sole

On the Sun

[*Translators' Note:* The Sun held an important place in Ficino's thinking, not only because of its astronomical importance but also because of Plato's use of the Sun as an analogy for the One, calling it the child of the Good, and the visible representative of the Good or the One in the Creation. This Appendix presents the first version of his work on the Sun in the form that was written for, and sent to, Count Eberhard of Württemberg in 1492.

An earlier essay on the Sun, entitled 'Orphic Comparison of the Sun to God' was sent as a letter to Lotterio Neroni on 19th December, 1479, under the joint authorship of Ficino and Giovanni Cavalcanti (*Letters*, **5**, 27). The theme of the Sun's significance on several levels recurs frequently throughout Ficino's writings. Plato was undoubtedly one of his principal sources for *De sole* (On the Sun), as is evident from the text itself, but we know that he also studied the Greek *Hymn to the Sun* of the Emperor Julian (331-363), also known as *Hymn to King Helios*, and he made copious notes on his copy of it (MS Riccardiana 76). He had already made use of those notes in an extended passage of his commentary on Plato's *Republic*, VII (see Farndell, *When Philosophers Rule*, pp. 33-35). Giovanni Pico della Mirandola also studied this manuscript of Julian's work. For the text of Ficino's notes and Pico's unpublished commentary, see Eugenio Garin, *Studi sul Platonismo Medievale*, Florence, 1958, pp. 190-215.

In addition to Plato and Julian, Ficino drew on Iamblichus and on Proclus's commentary on the *Timaeus*. By 1492 he was familiar with Proclus's commentary on Plato's *Republic*, including its eleventh treatise dealing with the allegory of the Sun. He was also familiar with numerous works on astronomy, including the widely known *Almagest* and *Tetrabiblos* (known in Latin as the *Quadripartitum*) of Ptolemy of Alexandria (second century AD) and several Hebrew and Arabic works that circulated in medieval Latin translations. These included writings of Māshā'allāh and Abū Ma'šar (9th century), Alcabitius (10th century), Abraham ibn Ezra (12th century) and more. Several of these works were being published or republished in print around the time Ficino was writing *De sole*, indicating that there was a considerable interest in such matters among the reading public. Printed editions of particular note are Abū Ma'šar's *Introductorium in astronomiam* and *Great Conjunctions* printed by Erhard Ratdolt (Augsburg, 1489). Ratdolt had already printed Ptolemy's *Quadripartitum* in Venice in 1484 before he moved back to Germany; it was printed again in 1493 in Venice (which served the book trade in Italy, Germany and beyond) in a major new compendium by Bonetus Locatellus, who combined it with works by Haly Abenragel, Almansor, Zahel, Māshā'allāh and others. Ratdolt had also published Haly Abenragel's *Book on the Judgment of the Stars* (Venice, 1485), and there were five editions of Alcabitius between 1485 and 1491.

The influence of all these works can be seen reflected in Ficino's *On the Sun*, but it is often not possible to distinguish which was a principal source in any particular passage, especially as these works often draw on one another. In addition, Ficino uses arguments that he had developed elsewhere in his own work, for example in the *Platonic Theology* and the third book of *De vita*. He was thoroughly grounded, as were all trained physicians, in matters related to astronomy and astrology. References in our notes are therefore confined to points of particular importance or interest.

Ficino first wrote this '*Comparison of the Sun to God*' in 1492. It had been begun by April of that year and was still in progress in June 1492, but was completed and sent to Eberhard, Count of Württemberg, some time before 13th September 1493, by the hand of Johannes Streler. This copy is now in the Landesbibliothek of Stuttgart, codex H.B. XV 65, having passed afterwards into the possession of the Monastery of Weingarten, where a letter from Caspar Vollandius to Nicholas Buchner, Abbot of Zweifalten, was added in 1547. An edition of the work under the title *De comparatione solis ad deum* was printed at Tübingen that same year by Ulrich Morhard. A copy of this very rare edition is held at the Library of Fribourg (see Kristeller, *Sup. Fic.*, I, p. LXXI).

The dedication letter written to accompany this first version of *On the Sun* remained in Ficino's letters as published, in the eleventh book. (Due to the numbering of our volumes this is *Letters*, **10**, 33 in our series.) Most of the text was also originally part of the eleventh book but was later removed since the work on the Sun had already been published – except that it remained in MS Mo2, which was written before the twelfth book of letters was finished. The final chapter (ch. 13) of the work as published was based on a further letter to Count Eberhard in the twelfth book (Letter 2 in this volume), which was also in MS Mo2 but was not removed from the printed editions of the *Letters*.

The letter dedicating the work to Count Eberhard (*Letters*, **10**, 33) is undated, but refers to Streler's return to Germany after his mission in Rome. Further reference occurs in Letter 7 of this volume, to Martin Prenninger, dated 18th January, 1493. In fact, Letters 6 and 7 were included in the printed edition of *De sole* when it was published by Antonio Miscomini in Florence, on 31st January, 1493, Letter 6 serving as an *Apologia*. The letter from Bindaccio Ricasoli to Gregorio Alexandrino (included here as Appendix C) was also included. The 1493 edition was a twin volume, with the title *De sole et lumine*, and included a new dedicatory Preface, to Piero de' Medici, a new first chapter, additional passages through the book, and an extra two and a half chapters at the end before the final chapter, ch. 13, mentioned above. *De sole* is accompanied by a greatly expanded version of a treatise *On Light* that Ficino had written in 1476 (ed. Gentile, *Lettere*, II, 9, *Quid sit lumen*). This carries its own dedication letter to Piero de' Medici.

De sole et lumine was published again in Leipzig by Conrad Tockler in 1502 and purportedly with *De christiana religione* and *De vita* in Venice by Bernardino de Vitalibus in 1503, though all four copies we have been able to consult contained only *De sole et lumine*, with the letters as added in the 1493 version. *De sole et lumine* was also included in a popular anthology called *Margarita Facetiarum* (Pearl of Wit), published by Johannes Adelphus in Strasbourg in 1508 and 1509. The letter from Bindaccio Ricasoli (Appendix C) is appended there but not its list of books.

Both *De sole* and *De lumine* (as separate works) were added by Aldus Manutius to the second edition of Ficino's translation of Iamblichus and other late Platonists, published in 1516. *De sole* and *De lumine* are also in the Basel edition of the *Opera omnia* on pages 965-975 and 976-986 respectively. In all the printed editions, both works are dedicated to Piero de' Medici, who was still at the head of government in Florence in 1493.]

De sole

Comparatio solis deo

On the Sun

Comparison of the Sun to God

How the Sun is the image of God and lord of the heavenly bodies

NOTHING reflects the nature of the Good more than light. Firstly, light appears as the purest and most conspicuous thing in the sensory realm. Secondly, of all things it spreads out most easily and abundantly, and in a moment. Thirdly, being harmless, it presents itself to all and penetrates most mildly and most pleasantly. Fourthly, it brings with it life-giving heat, warming, generating and stirring all into motion. Fifthly, though it is present to all and within all, it is tainted by none, it mingles with none.

In the same way the Good itself stands above the whole order of creation. It spreads out most abundantly. It soothes and attracts all. It forces nothing. Everywhere it has as its companion love, like warmth, by which individual beings in all places are allured, and gladly welcome the Good. Though absolutely present everywhere in the innermost heart of things, it has dealings with none. In short, just as the Good itself is beyond estimation and expression, so to a great extent is light; for as yet no philosopher has explained the fact that nothing anywhere is clearer than light and that nothing seems more obscure, just as the Good is the best-known of all and equally the least-known.

As a result Iamblichus finally resorted to calling light a kind of impulse, and a visible image of divine intelligence, just as a ray flashing forth from the eye in the act of seeing is an image of sight itself.[1] We, in our way, usually speak of light by way of analogy, as a trace of the life of the cosmos presenting itself in this way to the eyes, or as the life-giving spirit between the soul of the cosmos and its body. But we have said enough about this in our *Theology*.[2]

The Sun, illuminator of the heavenly bodies, and their lord and governor

As the manifest lord of heaven, the Sun directly rules over and governs all the heavenly bodies. For the moment I shall overlook its vast magnitude, which is reckoned to exceed that of the earth one hundred and sixty-six times.[3] First of all, it brings light to all the stars. In themselves these have either a faint light of their own, as some believe, or none at all, as most people think.[4] Next, as Haly and Abraham[5] say, that light coming chiefly from the twelve signs is spoken of as living, and actually appears so, because the Sun is at the same time imparting its energy. More precisely, the Sun fills the two signs on either side with so much energy that both spaces are termed by the Arabs the *dustūrīya* of the Sun, that is, the royal throne.[6] While planets are there, they avoid the burning heat of the Sun but are empowered with a wonderful energy, especially if in this particular space the higher planets rise before the Sun, the lower planets after the Sun.

Again, Aries, the sign in which the Sun rules, thus becomes the head of the signs and signifies the head in any living being. Also, Leo, the sign which is the domicile of the Sun, is the heart of the signs and has command of the heart in any living being. Moreover, the yearly prosperity of the whole globe always hangs upon the entry of the Sun into Aries, and from this rightly comes the nature of a spring. The quality of a summer, however, can be judged from the entry of the Sun into Cancer, the nature of an autumn from its entry into Libra, and the quality of a winter can be found in its entry into Capricorn, discovered in each case, that is, through the prevailing configuration of the heavenly bodies.[7]

Undeniably, since the season depends upon the movement of the Sun, it is the Sun that marks out the four seasons of the year through the four movable signs.[8] Again, from the Sun's return to its original degree at each person's nativity, that person's fortune that varies through the year goes back to its starting point.[9]

In addition to this, as Aristotle says, the movement of the Sun, as the first and foremost of the planets, is very simple: it neither departs from the middle of the Zodiac, as the others do, nor does it move backwards.[10]

The characteristics of the planets in relation to the Sun

Again, everywhere in the heavens certain fixed courses appear to be marked out from the Sun itself. As soon as the planets have traversed these, they change their motion and disposition. For when Saturn, Jupiter and Mars come through the third part of the heavens from the Sun, into trine aspect with the Sun,[11] they immediately change their motion and move either forwards or backwards.[12] Venus and Mercury, however, range through certain shorter fixed courses towards and away from the Sun: Venus is prevented from departing by more than forty-nine degrees, Mercury by twenty-eight.[13] In whatever aspect the Moon is to the Sun, it changes its form and nature, producing four phases, and, as if it were another Sun, represents the four seasons of the year; and whenever it is in conjunction with the Sun, it shows the nature of the month to come from the actual degree of the conjunction and from the configuration of the heavens.

Similarly, each of the planets, as soon as it reaches the heart of the Sun, has dominion over the others at that time, however brief it may be. On the other hand, drawing near to the Sun, they are meanwhile free of their usual function. Coming into conjunction with the Sun, Saturn is thought to lay aside his ancient severity, Mars his usual ferocity.[14]

The higher planets rise as the Sun approaches them but sink as it departs. When in conjunction with the Sun they are at the height of their epicycle, but when they are opposite the sun they are at the lowest point.[15] The Moon is at its height on reaching both positions, but is lower when square to the Sun.[16] If Venus and Mercury in their forward motion are conjunct with the Sun, they are exalted; if they are retrograde, they are at their lowest. From what we have said, when the higher planets change their course in trine aspect with the Sun, they undoubtedly seem to venerate the royal gaze of the Sun, and when they are in conjunction with the Sun, they seem to be at their highest and in forward motion, inasmuch as they are at such time in concord with the king. When the opposite is the case, they are at variance with the king, that is, in opposition to the Sun, retrograde and at their lowest. When Venus and Mercury reach the Sun, if at that time they are in forward motion, that is, in obedience to their Lord, they proceed with intense brightness, but if slanting at an angle, like rebels, they are for the time being powerless.

Now if the Moon is also in opposition to the Sun, it is very bright, and this should cause us no surprise. For what is the light of the Moon, but the self-same light of the Sun reflected back from either side by the mirror of the Moon? And at full Moon the light is reflected back to the Sun from its whole surface. The Moon, however, appears to grow fainter when it is square, since at that time it is looking askance at its Lord.

Again, just as the Sun does not go backwards, so neither does the Moon regress, the swiftness of its epicycle preventing backward motion. In short, when the Moon, with energy from the Sun, travels north along the Sun's path, to where the stars form the mighty head of the Dragon, there it shows its waxing phase; but when it travels south, where the tail of the Dragon is thrust forward, it shows its waning phase.[17]

All the planets, when they are east or west of the Sun, change their characteristics and their title accordingly. Indeed, they are all in awe of the Sun's path, which is called the ecliptic. The lower planets therefore digress to the side of the ecliptic more and more in succession, ending with the female planets, that is, the Moon and Venus, digressing the most. In short, all are either positioned on this path or digress from it. Again, proceeding at other times to the north or south, they are thought to change their characteristics accordingly. The Moon, mistress of generation, has no light except from the Sun, and as Proclus says,[18] it receives the strength of all the heavenly bodies from a perfect aspect of the Sun, as though they were all in the Sun, and it sends down a similar strength to our world.

The power of the Sun in procreation and in the seasons

Put simply, at the birth of each human being, it is the position of the Moon that declares the lord of the natal chart and the import of the conception. In addition, the conjunction or opposition of the Moon with the Sun that takes place before the rise of a human being reveals the truth of the birth and its fortune; and in the prevailing configuration of the heavens, that portion of heaven in which the *pars fortunae* falls is said by the ancients to be the *daimon* of the birth:[19] it foretells or ushers in, as the Egyptians have it, the tenor of the whole life. This *pars fortunae* is marked out firstly by the distance observed between the Sun and the Moon, and then projected from the position of the Ascendant.

For the moment I pass over the fact that astronomers discover and measure, through the well-known movement of the Sun, the movements of the planets; that by its own movement the Sun marks out the nights and days, the hours, months and years; that from its light and heat together it generates, invigorates, sets in motion, and regenerates everything; that it gladdens and nourishes, and with its first arrival makes manifest what had been hidden; that by means of its approach and withdrawal it brings about the four parts of the year in turn; and that regions which are too remote from the Sun are equally remote from life. Spring is the best of the seasons, since it begins from Aries, the realm of the Sun, whereas autumn is the worst,[20] since it takes its beginnings from the Sun's weakest point in Libra.[21] Finally, a birth by day is generally reckoned to be better than a birth by night, the first being considered chiefly from the Sun, the second from the Moon, as the Sun's mirror.

In a birth chart, the configuration of the heavens is divided into twelve parts,[22] where, since the ninth house is appointed to the Sun,[23] and the third to the Moon, the former is called God, the latter Goddess, and they are thought to signify all that is best: wisdom, trust, religion, everlasting glory. Furthermore, as the Sun ascends to the mid-heaven,[24] on either side[25] it nourishes the vital spirit and the animal spirit in us in a wonderful way.[26] But as it descends, both spirits are weakened. The Moon, also, consort of the Sun, likewise refreshes our spirit and natural humour in waxing, but withdraws its support in waning. In addition, the fuller it is with the light of the Sun the more it promotes life and health for all.

For now I pass over how the Moon as it approaches the Sun should be heeded so long as it has some light, according to its aspect with the Sun, signifying this limb or that as it moves from one sign[27] to another; and thus the power of all the heavenly bodies needs to be transferred from the Sun via the Moon to nourish limbs through medicines duly prepared at that time. For we have already said enough about these matters in the book *On Life*.[28]

Praises of the ancients for the Sun

It is for these reasons that Orpheus called Apollo the life-giving eye of the heavens, and I am going to give brief quotations gathered from the Orphic Hymns: 'the Sun, the eternal eye which sees all', 'which is above the light of the heavens', 'regulating heavenly things and earthly', 'guiding — or drawing — the harmonious course of the world', 'lord of the world'; 'immortal Jupiter', 'encircling eye of the world'; 'holding a seal shaping all the beings in the world'; the Moon is 'pregnant with stars', 'the Moon, queen of the stars.' These are from Orpheus.[29]

Iamblichus adds the view of the Egyptians: 'What good we have, we have from the Sun, that is, either from the Sun alone, or from other things also; what is more, that good is unconditional, whether from the Sun or from the Sun through others.' Again, 'the Sun is the master of all elemental powers. By the power of the Sun, the Moon is the mistress of generation.'[30] For this reason, Abumasar says that life is poured into all through the Sun and the Moon.[31] Moses deems the Sun to be the lord of the heavens by day, the Moon by night, like a nocturnal Sun.[32] The natural philosophers of old called the Sun the 'heart of heaven'.[33] Heraclitus called it the fount of heavenly light.[34] Most of the Platonists located the world soul in the Sun. This soul, filling the whole sphere of the Sun, pours out rays through that 'fiery' globe, as through its heart, as spirit pouring out thence through all. By these rays it allots life, sensation and movement to the universe.

Perhaps for these reasons most astrologers believe that, just as God alone allots to us an intellectual soul, so He alone sends it under the influence of the Sun, that is, no later than the fourth month after conception.[35] But this is their viewpoint. Certainly Mercury, which signifies the movement of our mind, departs least of all from the Sun; finally, Saturn, which signifies the state of the mind withdrawn, departs least from the ecliptic path.[36]

The dispositions of the signs and planets around the Sun and Moon

Accordingly, the actual disposition of the signs in the Zodiac clearly shows that the Sun is king of the heavenly bodies, and the Moon, both sister and consort of the Sun, is queen. For Leo, seat of the Sun, and Cancer, seat of the Moon, are next to each other, as are Aries, kingdom of the Sun, and Taurus, kingdom of the Moon. However, the rest of the planets place their respective seats all around the king and queen, as if they were in the middle. On the one side Mercury holds Virgo, next to Leo, but on the other side, Gemini, next to Cancer. Moreover, on one side Venus holds Libra, on the other Taurus; Mars, Scorpio on one side, Aries on the other;

Jupiter, Sagittarius on one side, Pisces on the other; Saturn, Capricorn on one side, Aquarius on the other.[37]

But once, when I was setting out the seats of the planets like this in relation to the Sun and the Moon, my close friend Bindaccio Ricasoli, a man of profound judgement, interposed thus: 'Do you see, Marsilio, that the same seats are disposed in the same sequence, although in reverse order, on both sides of the houses of Saturn?'[38]

I said, 'I realise that this scheme fits particularly with the Sun itself. But at the same time it also relates to lofty Saturn. What does this mean? If Saturn is worthy of this honour, it is because it seems to deviate least of all from the royal path of the Sun.'[39] But let us return to the matter in hand.

So these five planets each occupy two seats: one following the Sun as though at its back, the other in full sight of the Moon. The former seats are called westward of the Sun, the latter eastward of the Moon. But the Sun and the Moon claim the whole Zodiac for themselves. For the province of the Sun contains Leo, Virgo, Libra, Scorpio, Sagittarius and Capricorn; the province of the Moon contains Aquarius, Pisces, Aries, Taurus, Gemini and Cancer. But perhaps they called Cancer the gateway of human beings because it is there that the Sun already seems about to descend, and they called Capricorn the gateway of the gods because there the Sun seems immediately to ascend. But we have also made this clear in a different way elsewhere.[40]

To be sure, these two signs, together with Aries and Libra, have claimed dignity for themselves, so as to be called the pivots of heaven,[41] because it is there that the Sun determines the four changes of the seasons, and because, as it advances through Aries and Libra, it keeps a middle course, whether ascending or descending, and holds day and night in balance. Thus the arc produced from Aries to Libra is named by the Egyptians 'the arc of Minerva', that is, of wisdom and justice.[42] Ptolemy reckons that the Sun and Moon are the authors of life: the Moon demonstrates this because it pertains to growth and invigoration, the Sun because it is concerned with the senses.[43] Moreover, he reckons that Jupiter and Venus are beneficial to life, because they are in concord with the Sun and the Moon in a particular harmonic relationship: Jupiter mostly with the Sun, and to some extent with the Moon, but Venus with each in turn.[44]

On the other hand, Saturn and Mars are hostile to life, because they are discordant with the Sun and the Moon: Saturn is more at variance with the Sun, Mars with the Moon. Jupiter, however, is more life-giving than all the others because, if the light of the Sun and the Moon be brought completely together, Jupiter gains strength from both. Nor indeed should it be overlooked that when planets regard the face of the Sun or the Moon as if with a kind of greeting, they suddenly acquire a new power, which the Arabs have called *almugea* ('proper face')[45] because when following the Sun they are separated from it by as great a distance as that of their house from the house of the Sun; or, when preceding the Moon they come as close to the Moon as their domicile is to the domicile of the Moon. In this way therefore, whenever it has risen in the west, that is, behind the Sun, Saturn will greet the Sun in the sixth sign from the sign of the Sun. Jupiter will regard the Sun when in the fifth, Mars in the fourth, Venus in the third, Mercury in the second. Similarly, when they have risen eastward of the Moon, that is, in front of it, they will greet the Moon and will behold it at the same intervals.

Hereupon appears the concord of Jupiter and Venus with the Sun and the Moon, but the discord of Saturn and Mars with them both.[46] It is clear that Jupiter has placed his own seat Sagittarius in perfect trine aspect with Leo, the seat of the Sun. Again, Venus has placed Libra in a sextile aspect with Leo, which is also propitious. Mars makes Scorpio square [to Leo], which is a dissonant interval. Saturn is both in the sixth, which is not harmonious, and in the seventh, directly in opposition. For it makes Aquarius opposite to Leo, and likewise Capricorn opposite to Cancer. Similarly, in relation to Cancer, Venus makes Taurus sextile and Jupiter makes Pisces trine, Mars makes Aries square, and Saturn, as we have said, is in both the sixth and the seventh. So Jupiter and Venus are said to be fortunate, being in harmony with the king and queen of the heavens, but Saturn and Mars, being out of harmony, are said to be unfortunate.[47]

The Sun is an image of God.[48] *A comparison of the Sun to God*[49]

Having contemplated these matters with the utmost care, our Plato called the Sun the visible child of the Good itself.[50] He also thought that the Sun is the clearly visible image of God in this temple of the cosmos, placed by God Himself to be marvelled at everywhere before all other things by those who reflect upon it.[51] As Plotinus says, and Plato likewise, the people of old used to worship it as a god.[52] The ancient theologians of the nations placed all the godly powers of the gentiles within the Sun. Indeed, Iamblichus, Julian and Macrobius bear witness to this.[53] In short, anyone who does not see that the Sun is the image[54] of God in the cosmos and His representative, has certainly never observed the night-sky, never looked up at the rising Sun, never contemplated how far it surpasses our senses or how quickly it brings back to life things which when far away from it were thought to be dead. Nor has he observed the munificence of the Sun, by which it alone does what all the stars together cannot do. Therefore, together with the Platonists and Dionysius, I conclude that the Sun, or Phoebus, leader of the Muses, that is, of intelligence, is the visible image of God.[55] In addition, Phoebe, the Moon, is an image of Phoebus, just as Phoebus is an image of God, and, as Hipparchus says, the Moon is a mirror of the Sun, in that she deflects to our world the light which is falling on her from the Sun[56] – but now is not the time to examine this.

We should not, however, omit that Platonic comparison which I have described more fully elsewhere: just as the Sun generates both eyes and colours, and bestows upon the eyes the power by which they see, and on the colours the power by which they are seen, and unites them both, with light joining them, so is God thought to relate to all intellects and intelligible things, and He surpasses all these, just as the Sun surpasses both eyes and colours.[57]

But one may ascend from the image to the original, partly by removing what is worse, partly by adding what is better. So, if there is no objection, take away fixed quantity from the Sun, just as Averroes removed matter from it.[58] But at the same time leave its power, together with its light, so that the light itself remains, filled with wondrous power, not bounded by fixed quantity or by any shape, and therefore touching the limitless space in your imagination by its presence all around, surpassing your intelligence at this point, just as it already exceeds the keenness of your eyes.[59] By this very course of reasoning, from the Sun, you will seem, according to your ability, to have found God, 'who has placed His tabernacle in the Sun.'[60]

In fact, just as there is nothing more alien to divine light than completely unformed matter, so nothing differs more from the light of the Sun than does the earth. Thus bodies in which an earthy condition predominates receive no light within, being, as it were, utterly unfit for light. It is not because light is incapable of penetrating them; for although it does not light wool or a leaf from within, yet it instantly penetrates a crystal which in other respects is much more difficult to penetrate. Thus the divine light shines even in the darkness of the soul, but the darkness comprehends it not.[61]

Amid all this the question is asked: What was the very first thing that God created? Moses answers, 'Light.'[62] For as a natural consequence, there immediately emanates from the divine light itself, which is above the intelligible, a light which is more similar than anything else to God. Intelligible light, that is, the angelic intellect, is in the incorporeal world above us. Sensible light, that is, the actual light of the Sun, is in the corporeal world. But at its first stage, as on the first day of creation, this light has the unreserved power to shine within and illuminate without; at the second stage, it has the power through its ability to generate heat both to be strong itself and to quicken everything else; at the third stage, through its own efficacy and at the command of God, it has the power to grow to a vast size; lastly, at the fourth stage of nature and of order, as on the fourth day of creation,[63] it has the power to share its vast size with the world, just as the light of divine intelligence is reflected back upon itself from which it has emanated.

C

Nonnulla de lumine. Item Catalogus librorum Marsilii[1]

Some words on light. Also a list of Marsilio's works

Bindaccio Ricasoli to the distinguished physician Gregorio Alessandrino: greetings.[2]

I AM sending you the book *On the Sun and Light* recently published by our Marsilio, in the hope that it will please you in no small measure because it treats of light which is most pleasing to all, because it comes from Marsilio the Platonist who is dearest of all to you, and especially because it is through this light that you will also see what is invisible, which is more to be desired than anything else. For our Marsilio, with whom I am on familiar terms, frequently says that light was created by divine providence not only that we might discern physical things by it but also, and much more importantly, that through it we might discern the incorporeal. For he says that other proofs that affirm this are either less clear to us or are deduced from elsewhere, but while the light itself strikes the eyes openly, it shows that it is not corporeal by many indications. This is so that we may recognise that anything incorporeal coming to us through the corporeal is something incorporeal above the corporeal. And while we find innumerable rays joined together yet distinct within the single light of the Sun, from this we may observe how the ideas of all things, in their different kinds, exist in the divine mind. Furthermore, when we see that the rays falling upon various clouds and vapours produce different colours there, we can understand how the ideas frequently produce different effects in vastly different kinds of matter. Lastly, when we see by the Sun's splendour the different colours, which are also in its power, bursting forth on earth, we clearly recognise how the seminal principles of all things exist in nature, and come forth from it. This is what he says in conversation, but you will be able to see these things far better expressed in the book *On the Sun and Light* which we are sending. And so that you can see all Marsilio's books in this light, as I know you wish to, here is a list of them.

A List of the works of Marsilio Ficino of Florence

Original Works

The views of the philosophers on God and the soul

Platonic statements in four books written in his youth

On Pleasure

On Love. Giovanni Cavalcanti, his beloved friend, a man of deep faith and gravitas, encouraged him to write this book, with the purpose of recalling the lost lovers of empty beauty to the love of immortal beauty

On the Christian Religion

Platonic Theology, divided into 18 books, on the immortality of souls

Partial Commentary on the *Philebus*

Eleven books of *Letters*, mostly Platonic and moral[3]

Three books *On Life*, that is on a healthy life, on a long life, on the life to be obtained from the heavens

Summaries of all the books of Plato

Summaries of all the books of Plotinus

A book *Against the Plague*

Some summaries on Theophrastus or Priscianus *On the Soul*

In the second book of letters are contained these eight short treatises:[4]

Five Keys to 'The Platonic theology' and a digest of the same
On the Rapture of Paul to the Third Heaven
On Light

A short work on *The Star of the Magi*

Summaries on Dionysius, *On Mystical Theology* and *The Divine Names*

A commentary on the *Timaeus*

On the Sun and Light

Translations

A number of extracts from Hermias, *On the Phaedrus* and from Iamblichus, *On the Pythagorean sect* and from Theon of Smyrna, *On Mathematics*

Hermes Trismegistus *On Divine Wisdom and The Creation of the World*

Alcinous's *Digest on Plato* together with *The Definitions* of Speusippus and *The Sayings* of Pythagoras and Xenocrates, *On Consolation*

All 56 books of Plato
All 54 books of Plotinus
Iamblichus, *On the Mysteries of the Egyptians and Assyrians*
Synesius, *On Dreams*
Psellus, *On Daemons*
Porphyry, *Gateways to the Realm of Mind*[5]

The commentary of Priscian of Lydia on Theophrastus, *On the Soul*

A number of extracts from Proclus on *Alcibiades,* on *The Republic* and on the Priesthood

Some extracts from Porphyry, *On Abstinence*

The book of Dionysius the Areopagite, *On Mystical Theology*

Dionysius the Areopagite, *On The Divine Names*

Some extracts from Athenagoras, *On the Resurrection*

He is daily revising the books of Plato wherever they happen to have been corrupted by other hands, dividing them into chapters, and throwing light on them with longer summaries and commentaries.[6]

D

Marsilio Ficino to Jacopo of Volterra:[1]

I HAVE so greatly loved you, my Jacopo, and have always thought so highly of you that I have boldly promised myself whatever can be rightly asked of a friend, and I know for a certainty I will receive it from you: I cannot be wrong. For what may a friend not presume to hope for or to expect from a good and generous man, since it is in the nature of goodness to pity those who are in need and of a generous man to practise liberality? Therefore, seeing that in both these respects we are presently in need of a favour, I am, for that reason, not afraid to ask for or to expect from you what my soul promises itself, from your goodness and from the bond of friendship. And to come at last to the matter in hand: Michele the priest, my close friend and tutor in the Valori household, pays me such respect and so attends upon me that not only do I wish him well, but I also think that the favours he receives from anyone are all conferred upon me, too.[2] Well then, Michele thinks that the matter is in your hands because you are seeking, through your agent, Francesco Strozzi, that under the authority of certain edicts, an annual payment be made of eight gold pieces, from Santo Stefano of Butiano, of which he is currently the rector.[3] However, he finds this very hard to bear because although for the last six years, before there was a notion of any levy, he always held that priesthood in undisturbed possession, now, after all this time, he is being oppressed by an unexpected and unfair burden. Unfair, I say, for since he only gets from that benefice just ninety-six measures of wheat from the annual produce of the parish, I do not hesitate to affirm that such a trifling amount from so great a yield will be thought hardly fair, at least with you as assessor.

That is why I am making this extraordinary request: that you consider the case of this man in accordance with my goodwill and your highest humanity. For he is a poor man, a keen scholar, and, as I have said, a close friend of mine. But if you will treat him with kindness, as I hope and desire, then indeed you will be thought worthy of the name of a loyal and learned friend, and you will bind to yourself a man who will constantly pour out prayers for you every day, faithfully and religiously, in accordance with his own goodness, as long as he lives. For me, however, nothing can be more touching or more pleasing than to know that I have found such favour in your eyes that my Michele may be relieved of the whole burden if possible, or at least of the greater part, so that he may manage to meet the remainder of that payment.[4]

Farewell.
Florence.
4th September, 1496.

E

Letter of Jacopo of Volterra to Ficino[1]

To Marsilio Ficino:

If I am briefer than I should wish, it is because of illness. My head has been so beset by a humour that I am hardly able to stand, let alone write. I had not risen from my bed when your letter and your little book on the sun and light were delivered to me. It was indeed timely, since up till then I was in darkness. For when I had handed the letter to my servant to be unsealed, and when he was telling me who the writer was, at the name 'Marsilio' I said: 'It is something great.' I got up right away, took the letter, read right down to the end. I undid the book, read its title, and said to myself, 'Was I not a true prophet, when I had an inkling that something great would come from Ficino?' For what can be greater than the sun, if, as the Arabs say, and you confirm, it is the royal throne?[2] What again is greater than light, which illumines every man?[3]

Thus, half-dressed, boots hanging down, I glanced over almost the whole book, through the chapter headings, and, so help me God, I was reading without hindrance and without the help of a glass, like a young man, as if that light had not only lit up my bedroom, but had put light into my now dim eyes. So thanks are due, first to you for such a great gift, and then to Michele, who provided the reason for the gift and the light.[4] In a moment my heart was opened by this light of yours, because you make haste to help, being good by nature, perceptive, persuasive, and also innocent, I hope, of any wrong. Although you love Michele, you do not bear Jacopo ill-will; on the contrary, you love him, too, most wonderfully. Thus both your letter and the things you say about me, which are always respectful, display [the evidence] of your supreme love towards me . . .

F

Marsilio Ficino of Florence to Germain de Ganay, presiding judge in Paris: greetings.[1]

YOU would like to know more about the death of Pico della Mirandola, as it seems you are still unclear about it.[2] Surely what you want, Germain, is to grieve more deeply. For although you are grieving deeply while still in doubt about this loss, I think you will soon grieve very bitterly indeed once you have definite news. Perhaps it was better to grieve over a loss that is uncertain than to be tormented by one that is beyond doubt. Alas, what are you asking, my dearest Germain? Personally, I would rather remain in doubt, and even now I am not able to tell you about this without weeping.

Last November, on the very day that Charles, great King of France, entered our city of Florence, our Mirandola deserted us; and the grief he brought to the learned was almost as great as the joy the king brought to the city at that time.[3] Thus the caring spirit that looks after Florence balanced the grief of the learned with the joy of the populace and at the same time lit the royal flame to replace the extinguished philosophic light, so that the city might not appear bedimmed on that day. The Mirandolan light that has been extinguished on earth has been restored to heaven. For with that carefree nature of his, the playful Pico has departed from this shadow of life, to make it clear beyond doubt that he is going to return from a kind of exile to his celestial home.[4]

You also want to know what Pico has written and what he was writing most recently. He has written the *Hexameron*, an *Apology,* and a treatise on *The One and Being,* as well as many letters.[5] The writings he had once composed on the subject of love while adolescence was still raging, he subsequently condemned with more mature judgement; he wanted them suppressed completely and they cannot now be published without doing him wrong. I am certain this is the good man's final wish. For in age Pico was a son to me, in friendship a brother, and in affection none other than my second self.

He would toil at three things every day: the harmonisation of Aristotle with Plato, expositions of the sacred scriptures, refutations of the astrologers. All these were argued with as much fluency as precision, but however brilliant in style, they were obscured by such strange and illegible handwriting that they could scarcely be read, even by him. And so they have not yet been completed or revised by him, nor can others copy them out, unless they happen to be seers! For if they could do this, we would not miss our Pico so very much as one gone from our midst, nor would we ever suppose him to have died. But his good nephew, Giovanni Francesco, strong in learning and ability, is every day endeavouring to draw those works out of darkness into the light, and is writing about his uncle's life and deeds.

And so receive this epitaph we have written for him.

The High Priests all too rarely grant a glimpse of the more secret mysteries, and straightway hide them again.

In the same way God granted to mortals the divine philosopher Giovanni Pico della Mirandola and hid him from our eyes at the early age of thirty.[6]

So that you should know the other loss to the world of letters which occurred in Florence last autumn, our Angelo Poliziano, a learned master of Latin and Greek, departed this life at the age of forty in September just before Pico's death. He had long since published his *Miscellanies* and *Silvae*, some speeches, and many letters, all of them composed with penetration and elegance.[7] He was also daily making many corrections needed for the sake of style, but, like Pico, in obscure handwriting, so that with both of them the loss to the world of letters has been very grave.

23rd March, 1495.[8]

G

Dedication Letter for the translation of Athenagoras[1]

Marsilio Ficino of Florence to his Lord Germain de Ganay, Royal Counsellor of Paris, a most learned man: especial greetings.

I HAVE loved you greatly for a long time and for many reasons, no less than a brother, my dear Germain. As you can see, I frequently enjoy playing with your name, Germain, and perhaps you enjoy hearing that.[2] Although, as I say, I have loved you in no small measure for your many virtues, yet it is most of all for your outstanding esteem for the dead, especially the most distinguished among them. For this is a kind of devotion to duty that is divine; it is very rare and most noble. Indeed, only those seem to love freely who love the dead from whom, for the most part, they can expect nothing, although Plato and Plotinus argue that many benefits can be drawn from them. I therefore decided to send you the excerpts I made long ago from the book on the Resurrection by the Christian philosopher Athenagoras of Athens[3] and translated from the Greek, in order to console you as best I can while you are mourning the bitter deaths of those outstanding men, Poliziano and Pico. If you consider these matters and others on resurrection which we deal with in the *Platonic Theology*,[4] you will perhaps grieve less heavily. So read and live happily, a man and friend most worthy of a long and happy life.

H 1[1]

Marsilio Ficino to his beloved brother:[2] greetings.

My brother, you wish to read in Latin the Orphic Hymn on Nature.[3] Since the will of brothers should be the same, just as their nature is almost the same, receive now this little gift you desired. Your wish is equally my wish. But before you read the words of Orpheus, hear the ancient mystery about Nature to help you define and analyse Nature in the way they do.

Universal Nature is a fertile power, giving birth to good things that pertain to essence, movement and life. Now, Nature has four levels.[4] The lowest level is in the universal body of the world. The one above this is in the very soul of the world. The next higher level is in pure mind. The highest is in the Good itself. Her scope and character are much the same throughout, but her potency varies at each level. All the many and various good things in the creation arise from four principles: they derive from the Good itself, and from pure intellect; they are also dependent on the world soul and on the power of the world machine. But none of these principles is called Nature on account of bestowing gifts which relate to intelligence, sense, or the order and distinction of forms and the like; it is on account of their power to give substance, movement, and life that each one of these principles is called Nature. For their other powers and remaining effects other names are allotted. That is why in one name there are various other names. But Nature is everywhere seen as the most ancient of the divine powers, since she is always the first to bestow the gifts which are the foundations of all else that is good. Whilst discussing the nature of the cosmos, Timaeus declares that Nature is to be described as being within the machinery of the cosmos and within the cosmic soul;[5] Cratylus says the same when he shows that the soul was so called among the Greeks because it contains nature herself;[6] and so says Philebus, when he calls this cosmic being Jove, and adds that a royal intellect and royal soul lie within the nature of Jove.[7] In the fourth book of the *Laws*, Plato also names Nature within the pure Intellect, when he says God moves in a circuit in accordance with Nature.[8] Then, in his first letter to Dionysius, he names Nature within the very first principle of the universe, when he says: you have asked me about first Nature.[9] Similarly, in his letter to the Syracusans, where he effectively says 'I would gladly bring Nature into the light for the human race.'[10] Following the earlier naming, Plotinus places Nature in the world soul as the quickening power of this soul.[11] Proclus, however, places Nature below the soul, that is, within the world machine itself, calling it a shadow, a trace, a power and instrument of the world soul for moving and regulating the very body of the world.[12] I think it was certainly in this sense that Aristotle called Nature the principle of movement, for the soul and its power within the body exist as the principle of movement.[13] But when Pan is called the god of Nature, he is to be understood not as the creator of nature but as her servant, for Pan is everywhere the lordly power ministering to universal Nature.[14]

Thus Orpheus in this hymn praises as one this universal Nature which is arranged on four levels, since each subsequent level, depending on the previous one, is in harmony with the whole. Therefore, while you are reading these various and often disparate names, you must assign each of them to its own level. For example, when Orpheus proclaims Nature 'as end without end, in whom all partake equally,' or as the 'father of her own self' and so forth, you will understand that he means the Good itself. When he proclaims Nature as 'craftsman', 'fashioner', 'far-sighted wisdom', you will understand her as pure intellect, the child of the Good. When he proclaims her as 'mother', the 'nourisher' who 'transforms' and 'sets in motion', then you will consider her as the soul of the world, created by pure intellect. When he proclaims her as 'daemon of the heaven', 'of the upper air', 'of the sea', 'of the earth', you will think of her as the strength of the soul, and as the spirit that governs the world.

In short, the Orphic hymn on Nature is of this kind.[15]

H 2[16]

Marsilio Ficino commends himself to Cosimo de' Medici, Father of his Country

RECENTLY, when I took up my lyre to relax the mind with the strains of music, I was recalling the Hymn of the divine Orpheus which he himself also sang to Cosimo, that is, to the Cosmos.[17] The meaning of that hymn, if I may express the Greek literally in Latin, was as follows:

O Heaven, begetting all things,
Thou ever indomitable part of the Cosmos,
Of ancient and venerable origin,
Beginning of all and end of all,
O Cosmos, our father, who encirclest the orb of the earth
with thy spherical motion,
Thou home of the blessed,[18]
whirling round on thy course,
O celestial and terrestrial Cosmos,[19]
protector and guardian of all,
Embracing everything,
holding the invincible necessity of Nature in thy heart,
O thou of sky-blue eyes, indomitable [one],
of varying form, varying all things,
O thou omnipotent Father of time,
O thou blessed and most exalted spirit,[20]
Hear our prayers, O Cosmos, and grant a peaceful life to a dutiful youth.

I[1]

Marsilio Ficino of Florence to Giovanni Francesco della Mirandola, Count of Concordia: greetings.

AFTER your departure, I sent a short letter to France concerning the death of Pico and in praise of him. My lengthy and exceptional praises of Pico may be found throughout my many writings over the years: from my books of letters, especially the later ones (for twelve books of letters have now been printed), the preface to *Plotinus*, the book *On the Sun*, and the commentaries on *Timaeus* and *Parmenides*.

Read his epitaph:

The High Priests all too rarely grant a glimpse of the more secret mysteries, and straightway hide them again.

In the same way God granted to mortals the divine philosopher Giovanni Pico della Mirandola and hid him from our eyes at the early age of thirty.

Let this be his epitaph.[2]

God seems to have bestowed on Giovanni Pico all the abundant gifts of fortune, both of mind and of body. If only He had granted him a longer span of life! But it is not right to blame providence for this. For if God had already brought him in such a short time to his peak, beyond the powers of nature, perhaps Pico was not able to proceed to anything higher. The inconstancy of nature does not suffer anything to remain the same, whereas consummate goodness does not allow a relapse into something worse. But you yourself have written better and in more detail about these and other such matters in your *Life of Pico*,[3] not so much to give him glory (for who could add light to the sun?) as to shed light on his hidden works, so deserving of the light, once the clouds have been dispelled. Men will therefore admire and praise your devotion to your extraordinary uncle, and God will judge it worthy of no small reward.

1st November, 1495.

J

Privilegium Hieronymi Blondi

Writ of privilege[1] in favour of Girolamo Biondo

APPEARING before the Most Serene Council, the Eminent Ambassador of the Most Illustrious Lord of Rimini stated that Girolamo Biondo, a man of foresight from Florence, had in his keeping, as a result of his great zeal, expenditure, and diligence, the letters of the remarkable, most excellent and worthy Marsilio Ficino of Florence, a man of great learning, and the book *On the Heavenly Life* by Master Giovanni of Ferrara of the Order of Friars Minor.[2] These remarkable and most useful works the said Girolamo, with the same great zeal, expenditure, and diligence, intends to have printed, asking in his own name that the aforesaid Most Serene Council should deign to proclaim that no one except for the said Girolamo alone be permitted to cause the aforesaid works to be printed either in this city of Venice, or in any other place or state which is under the authority of the aforesaid Council; and that they cannot be sold through anyone if they have been printed elsewhere, that is, among foreign jurisdictions and authorities.

Wherefore the aforesaid Most Serene Council, namely the undersigned Noble Councillors, deeming it proper that in this matter the said Girolamo should receive a profit and recompense befitting his books and determining in favour of the view of the said Eminent Ambassador who is urgently seeking this, have decreed and established and they decree, establish and command that no one in the whole jurisdiction and authority of Venice, except for the said Girolamo, shall from this day forward be permitted to cause the above-named works to be printed, or to sell within the said authority those which might be printed elsewhere, with an irrevocable penalty of the confiscation of the books and a fine of 10 ducats for each volume thus discovered, the total to be divided into three equal parts, the first to go to the informer, the second to our Council, and the last to the said Girolamo Biondo.

Councillors: Jacopo Leone, Niccolò of Treviso, Andrea Venerio, Leonardo Mocenigo.[3]

K[1]

Piero of Bibbiena to Marsilio Ficino:

YOU will be surprised, Marsilio, and rightly so, that I, Dovizi, an exile, am now sending you a letter in which there is nothing to make you angry with me, fearing, as you may be, for your own safety.[2] Not long ago you knew me to have been uneasy in my official position, which was as demanding as it was important and as coveted as it was prestigious. For after that sad and bitter misfortune which befell our city, we are in no hurry to write or hear about any serious matters. Having no occupations to distract me, however, I have settled down in Venice and am returning, half educated, I might say, or rather as a late learner, to my literary studies and indeed, to the study of both Latin and Greek. I have long lamented and wept over these studies; in part I am distressed when I remember the time I have wasted, because this type of loss is most grievous, and in part I rejoice, because no joy other than the literary can dispel this wretched example of broken fortune.

You are at a loss, now, Marsilio, and you are asking, 'Where is all this leading?' Hear my answer in a few words:

If any Italian city excels in literary pursuits, then this one excels above all and it would take too long to list individual examples. For whether you are looking for those studies pertaining to philosophy or to music, poetry, and rhetoric, or again to civil law, you will find the most learned men, and very many of them, well versed in Latin and Greek literature. For my part, I marvel that there are many men like Ermolao,[3] or rather, I think that there will be. But you will marvel even more when you learn of the incredible enthusiasm and close attention given to the education of children. For when children reach the age of four, they are handed over to teachers from whom they learn, first of all, good conduct and, soon afterwards, the noble arts. However, the person from whom, in particular, they learn to speak well in this first stage of life is of the utmost importance. It is not servants, slaves, or wet nurses, who instruct the very young, but only the poems of our divinely inspired poets, Dante and Petrarch. And so it is that they have so much time to devote themselves to oratory that they soon become well grounded in liberal studies. Incidentally, we ought to rejoice that our poets are so well known and are of such good repute beyond our border in another state.

Now what I say regarding the children I also say about their elders. For there is no one who does not admire, does not honour with reverence, these poets, no one who does not have figures and likenesses of them in their houses or a great part of their poetry committed to memory.

This situation prompted me to ask among the most eminent men of the state about you: whether your reputation is spreading by word of mouth, and whether you have gained a reputation worthy of your exalted Platonic achievement and worthy of your own virtues.

O true and sincere praise, O vast reputation and truth-speaking acclaim, how fitting you are and how well you promote the glory appropriate to my Ficino! How wonderfully events have unfolded according to our desire. For 'your fame is known in the heavens above'[4] and in all the world, you are praised, loved and embraced by people you have never seen just as much as you are known within our city. For indeed the works of Plato, rendered by you for Latin speakers, abide and shine forth. Having been translated with consummate wisdom, believe me they travel widely, full of approval on the lips of Venetians.

Just recently the book of your letters was published, and I am filled with delight and even astonishment to hear people speak of it. I would express my views if I were wise enough to understand a wise man.[5] When I actually read the book, however, as carefully as I could, I was delighted to see that I was counted among your dearest friends. I hope that I really live up to your expectations, since you have linked my name with many outstanding minds.

Therefore I congratulate you, splendour of our country, or rather of our age, who have built so many monuments to your eternal memory. And I do not know whether or not I should add 'I envy you', since the life of nearly all of us is death if we compare ourselves to you. For your immortality is already set out before men's eyes, something which seldom happens to the living. But the hope for the future is even greater. So, although you may consider this to be beyond what you intended, I would urge you to publish other works worthy of your remaining years and as beneficial to the living as to posterity.

Venice.
31st March.[6]

L

Marsilio Ficino of Florence to his fellow philosopher Paolo Orlandini, a monk in the Church of the Angels: greetings.[1]

YESTERDAY, after debating many divine matters with me with your usual precision, you finally asked why in my letter on Happiness I place will above intellect, although in the *Philebus*, following Plato's view, I had put intellect above will.[2]

I could reply that in the *Philebus* I was presenting the Platonic view but in the letter my own; yet I would not want Marsilio's view to disagree with Plato's. So my reply in brief is that our mind has two ways of operating; one is natural, the other supernatural, which we rightly call ecstasy.[3] In the first way, the intellect leads the will as a companion, using its naturally infused light, and having led it rightly, it eventually fills it, and for that reason it is put first. In the second way, in ecstasy, a new light and power, divinely infused, fills the intellect with divine splendour but not until it has fired the will with a wondrous love.

The will thus fired, through the transformative efficacy of heat and love, leads the mind to God, where love itself, whose role in the universe is that of generation, regenerates the soul and makes it divine.

Indeed, in the *Philebus* we dealt with the natural operation of the mind, in full agreement with Plato,[4] but in the letter we are touching upon ecstasy, which is higher than natural movement, and we touched on it, agreeing with Plato, in the *Phaedrus* and *Symposium*; and in the commentaries on Dionysius we have shown how the divine love which is kindled in the will carries the intellect into the highest unity, and this is principally how we enjoy God.[5] But this is enough for a letter. You could happily take it further in your theological commentaries.[6] Commend us frequently to your[7] Venerable Father, or rather our Venerable Father, Guido di Lorenzo, restorer of the Church of the Angels.[8]

Florence.
13th November, 1496.

M[1]

Robert Gaguin to Marsilio Ficino: greetings.

YOUR goodness and wisdom, my Ficino, are so widely known, particularly here at our Academy in Paris,[2] that in the colleges of our most learned men, and also even in the classrooms of boys, your name is loved and praised. For them your magnificent efforts in undertaking the translation of Plato into Latin bear witness to your fine qualities. And Plotinus, the follower of Plato, whom you have rendered into Latin, enhances your renown. Furthermore, the other volumes of your works and the letters to your friends are read and held in high regard. Consequently, large numbers of our scholars are on fire to know you in person and to gaze on the man from whom such brilliant monuments to learning have come forth.

Among them is this friend of mine, Gaucerus Barterius,[3] who is setting out for Italy and has resolved to see you. He has no less enthusiasm for acquiring learning than Plato had when he went to the Egyptians or those men of Cadiz when they travelled to Rome to seek out Livy.[4] This youth is zealous in his studies and is already running of his own accord. But it would be in keeping with your wisdom and renown, finest of men as you are, if you welcomed him and spurred him on in his pursuit of learning.

Farewell from Paris.
1st September, 1496.

N[1]

Marsilio Ficino of Florence to Aldus of Rome: especial greetings.[2]

THANK you for your kindness and careful work. It saddens me that in these difficult times I am less able to apply such care myself.

I can well believe that there are many errors in these books through the fault of the copyists. For on receiving your letter I immediately spotted two mistakes near the beginning of the Iamblichus.[3] That was no surprise, as I did not personally check the pages you have, being at the time busy with my commentaries on *Parmenides*[4] and Dionysius,[5] but some of my helpers did, though they were quite careless, but I did not notice their carelessness until after the books had been sent to you.

I received the Greek texts just in time from the Medici.[6] They are not easily to be had now, or found by chance. I think the Synesius[7] is particularly faulty, for which my copyists, or rather friends, are not entirely to blame, for the copy I had was full of errors. In sum, all these works were produced in some way or other at a time when my hands were full with other matters.

Nor am I able to attend to them in these troubled times. Quite apart from my physical infirmity, I cannot live safely either in Florence or the suburbs, nor can I gather together my books, which are scattered about the city. For a long time three Furies have persistently afflicted wretched Florence: plague, famine and sedition,[8] and what is still more grievous, a hidden pestilence, among all the other things that people conceal.[9]

I have read your corrections to the Synesius and approve them. Accordingly I entrust all the rest to your conscientiousness and commit it to your judgement.

To conclude: if you will send me further quinternions, in the same way as you have sent one now, I too shall correct them as best I can, and once the whole work has gone to press I shall send a list of corrections for you to print at the end of the text before the books themselves are put on sale.[10]

Fare well. Please greet in my name Girolamo Biondo, who has done his utmost to support my reputation, and thank him.[11]

1st July, 1497.

(*On the back:* To Aldus of Rome, a most learned man, in Venice.)

O[1]

Egidio to Marsilio Ficino: greetings.[2]

I WAS about to set out for the city of the learned,[3] chief city of most of the world, on my way to teach the philosophy of the godlike Plato. Though utterly divine, it had been all but consigned to oblivion and the dullness of our ignorant age had made it unfamiliar. Fearing I would not be strong enough to withstand the venomous attacks of the sacrilegious Peripatetics,[4] I left Padua and came to you as the one person who has restored lustre to the Academy. I considered the points you touched on in your summary of the *Parmenides* would be insufficient unless I also heard you in person discoursing on the lofty theme of Ideas.[5]

When I had done this, I left you with joy in my heart. I felt so much admiration for what you taught and for your eloquence, fluency and vigour that I thought I had not met Marsilio Ficino, teacher of the highest arts and high priest of the Muses, but had consulted the oracles of Jupiter Ammon, Dodona and Delphi,[6] or some even more trustworthy oracle. Your presence while speaking was so powerful that I believed I was Alcibiades at Socrates' side while he was debating, to the point where I felt myself filled with his divine spirit.[7]

So, afire with such eagerness for the sacred contest, I completed my journey with all speed. Full of confidence, I entered Rome. I propose the Platonic arguments that are to be defended against the Peripatetics. I announce the day of battle. The fiercest troops assemble, swollen with spite and envy; they pitch camp; they put their strongest men in command of the left and right wings; the light-armed soldiers enter a battle that at first sight seems just a skirmish. But once they had set up the whole of their battle line it was fiercer than Thermopylae or Cannae.[8] You could see[9] the Thracian spear of Priam's son making a lightning strike at Plato's breast,[10] Memnon hacking at his flanks with a blood-stained blade,[11] the Amazons charging in with two-edged axes,[12] and Paris lying in ambush.[13]

What a furious onslaught, what anger on their faces, what a shouting from the whole army! You would have said the sky was falling in and all the buildings collapsing. I heard the din of clashing arms and falling trees and the enemy pressed with such might and main that they seemed about to destroy Plato's reputation utterly. Indeed, had not the support of the high priests, called cardinals, come to its assistance, I believe it must have perished. Nonetheless, the divine doctrine could not be overthrown by the frenzy of those accursed men and with the help of God and his guardian angels we escaped, and escaped in such a way that the enemy were shamed by the grandeur of Plato.

I was going to come to you straightaway, Marsilio, so that you who urged the racehorse on when it was about to leave the starting gate might also see it prancing with wondrous joy at its victory. But when I reached Siena I was advised to stop, being informed of a suspected plague. However, I thought I ought to write to you, for otherwise you would not know. I am awaiting your letter most eagerly by the same messenger. Indeed, there is nothing I desire more.

I want to know whether your new translations of Porphyry and others have been printed.[14] I am confident that with this work you will do more for the Republic of Letters than those who are commonly supposed to have benefitted it most.[15] This recognition was the one thing missing from the high praise your works have received. For by your translation of Plato you have made all good men keen followers of the Academy; by your works on Plotinus you have made them learned; with your *Platonic Theology*[16] you have raised them to heaven; with your three books *On Life* you have given them sound health; with your book *On the Christian Religion* you have filled them with holiness; you have made them shine brilliantly in the rays of your *Sun*; you have made them natural scientists with your commentaries on the *Timaeus*; with your elucidation of the *Symposium* you have filled them with love; you have meticulously prepared them with your summaries of the entire Platonic corpus; you have so filled everyone with your many admirable late-night studies,[17] your great exertions and your many writings that they call you the Father of Learning, though we are uncertain whether it is as soldiers of the Athenian or the Florentine Academy that we should salute you.[18]

Good heavens, how much the Latins owe you, because you rejected the study of vain and commonplace doctrines and steeped them in the disciplines of true and holy philosophy, raising their eyes to the light of divine contemplation. No less will the Greeks stand in your debt, whom you redeemed from deepest darkness to their unimaginable glory when they lay worn out with decay and disuse in the night of oblivion and the deepest waters of Lethe. As a result we hold that Marsilio Ficino has been sent by divine providence to make clear that the mystical theology of Plato is in perfect accord with our sacred doctrines and was their forerunner. This, my dear Marsilio, is the reign of Saturn; this is the Golden Age so often prophesied by the Sibyl and the bards;[19] these are those times when Plato foretold that his works would become best known.

Farewell.

P

[*Translators' Note:* These three letters are of considerable importance to early Renaissance ideas in England. John Colet read Ficino, may have met him in Florence, and corresponded with him on his return to England. The letters below were found in his heavily annotated copy of the 1495 edition of the *Epistolae* belonging to All Souls College, Oxford. They were discovered by J.H. Lupton, biographer of Colet, in 1869, and were shown by the distinguished palaeographer Neil Ker to Ficino's biographer Abbé Raymond Marcel in 1952.[1] They were then translated and published by Sears R. Jayne in 1963.[2] The first letter from Colet to Ficino has not been found, but Jayne thought it was probably written in December 1498. He tentatively dated Colet's second letter (P2) to April 1499 and Ficino's replies (P1 and P3) to April and July 1499. John B. Gleason in a more recent biography of Colet proposes a different dating, placing P3 first, in 1495, while Colet was still in Italy, with the proposal that Colet gave it pride of place in his copy, before the other fragments, on account of its more substantial nature; he suggests that P2 was a response to P3, written in the hope of being invited to meet Ficino.[3]]

P 1

Marsilio Ficino of Florence to John Colet, who cherishes and is to be cherished in equal measure.[4]

LOVERS are accustomed to create within themselves an image of the beloved's face that is more beautiful than its actual form.[5] For the power of love is not only to transform the lover miraculously into the beloved, but also to enhance the form of the beloved in the eyes of the lover, because natural love is the source of generation and increase. Therefore, my most loving John, as soon as you saw the light of our spirit shining in our writings like the moon in water,[6] you loved it passionately as being in harmony with your own spirit and, seized by love, you suddenly saw it as the sun instead of the moon. And so you often call me the sun.[7] I am the sun to you and to those who love me, but to all others, the moon. Clearly, this view of yours, my dear Colet, favours me, by reflecting to you a more beautiful Marsilio than the one it observed. It would be more favourable still if it rendered Marsilio equally beautiful to others. May your ardent and elegant letter be as pleasing to others as to me, so that I may be as pleasing to others as to you.

Farewell, my most loving and most beloved Colet.

P 2

John Colet to Marsilio Ficino[8]

WHEN I read your books, I seem to come alive; how much more alive would I be were I to see you, Marsilio, who should be seen and cherished. Thanks to your letter, I seem not merely to live but to live well. If I can now see you and set eyes on you in person, I shall be blest. In the hope of seeing you I live,[9] but waiting too long to behold you, I die in that hope. Or so it seems to me. But in the meantime sustain me in that life which is part of you. You have kept me alive this year with your letter. Add to it another, and I shall live another year. If you add one more, then I shall live for a third year.[10]

P 3

Marsilio Ficino to John Colet

THE difference between understanding and love, I think, is this: understanding comes first and love comes after.[11] Understanding gives birth to love, love expands in understanding. Understanding is more inward, love more outward. In short, understanding is simpler, clearer and more truthful; love is somehow more complex, more clouded and more condensed.

Hence, although love depends on understanding, yet, because love comes after and is more outward-going than understanding, whatever is presented to the mind, in any way and at any time, is loved before it is understood. For with external objects it must surely be the case that love, which comes after and is closer to the object, grasps it sooner than understanding, which comes first, is more inward and further away. This, indeed, accounts for the fact that fire gives heat before it gives light and, by heating things placed near it, it refines them so that it wholly and inwardly makes them shine. This is also why every desire is more fervid than the actual sense to which it belongs, and why the will is more blind and heedless than the intellect. For when will sets forth from intellect and declines into something more clouded, it becomes less heedful and more apt to rush into everything.

My dear John, my will is for you to understand this mystery, namely that will is clouded intellect, whereas intellect is will that is clear and unclouded. So will knows and intellect wills. Or rather, in these matters, whatever is is intellect. But understanding is itself intellect and is self-sufficient or at any rate less needy than will, whereas will is an intellect which is needy and therefore greedy and in want. Being closer to things than intellect is, and sensing them sooner and very keenly, will allows and regards as good what would meet with disapproval were it to come before clear intellect. If the intellect eventually considers the thing and rejects it, the will does not allow this rejection, for it is closer to the thing known and clings to it. Even if it has been considered and spurned by the intellect, nonetheless will does not allow it to be rejected. Will, being nearer to the thing known, clings to it more closely and more tenaciously.[12]

Q[1]

Apologia Marsilii Ficini pro multis Florentinis ab Antichristo Hieronymo Ferrariense hypocritarum summo deceptis ad Collegium Cardinalium

The defence by Marsilio Ficino before the College of Cardinals on behalf of the many Florentines deceived by the Antichrist, Girolamo of Ferrara, greatest of hypocrites[2]

FOR my part, venerable Fathers, I know that very many members of the Sacred Council wonder that one single hypocrite from Ferrara deceived so many otherwise intelligent and learned Florentines for a period of almost four whole years.[3] And they are right to be greatly astonished when they reckon how many eminent men have been taken in by one man. In truth, no mortal, but a most cunning demon, and not one, but a horde of demons ensnared unhappy mortals by the most treacherous means and captivated them with astonishing devices.

Surely no one now wonders, but all accept without argument, that the first parents of the human race, armed with divine wisdom and virtue as children of God, established in Paradise, and instructed by angels, were nevertheless deceived by one diabolical spirit.[4] Why, then, should it seem strange that a vast crowd of demons in the guise of an angel besieged and led astray the Florentines, who, especially at that time, were greatly afflicted?[5]

Surely we must believe him to be the very Antichrist who will use extraordinary means to corrupt so many men of outstanding prudence and probity. There is much evidence that Girolamo, prince of hypocrites, was inspired not by a human but by a diabolical spirit to lead us astray, and that he not only practised trickery but even used force against us.[6] In this Antichrist there was a matchless cunning that steadfastly put on the face of virtue to mask vice. He had a monstrous spirit marked by fierce recklessness, empty boasting, and Satanic pride. His brazen lies were invariably backed by imprecations and oaths. When he declaimed, his face, voice, and language were often thunderous, so that his listeners were battered into submission rather than willingly persuaded.[7]

In the midst of a debate he would flare up, shout, fulminate and be transported by passion, like those whom the poets describe as raving and possessed by demons. On occasion he even burst into prophecy. He mixed all his predictions with falsehoods more easily to deceive or convince the common people. Finally he was refuted by his own lies and wicked deeds.

This is not the place to discuss why the Astrologers, together with the Platonists, concluded that Savonarola had been subject to a wide variety of malign influences from the stars. But briefly, they may perhaps have guessed from diverse malefic stellar influences and convergences, or at any rate from certain signs, that Savonarola or, as I should more accurately name him, Saevonerola,[8] had been prey to various evil demons. It is not clear whether he fell victim to supernatural influences or rather laid himself open to evil spirits through his own pride and wickedness. What is certain is that these influences streamed into his diabolical soul as into their very own workplace, whence they at once exhaled the deadly poison that had gathered there. This poison infected and destroyed not only Saevonerola but all who came near him for any reason, even the common people who had been committed to his care and trusted him too much.

Apollonius of Tyana[9] is said to have detected and expelled a similar misfortune threatening the Ephesians from a filthy old man possessed by evil demons. For a long time I too had detected the same threat from Saevonerola. There had been a sudden change in our government and the French were tormenting Florence with every kind of terror. At first I was as thoroughly frightened as the fearful people by this demon and for a short while was taken in. However, I soon came to my senses and for more than three years, mostly in private but often in public and not without risk, I told many of my acquaintances to flee far from this venomous monster, created for the destruction of our people.

I say nothing of the insurrections, deadly enmities, neglect of public affairs, and the heavy expenses and losses that resulted. Without doubt Saevonerola's worst effect was this: he infected as many people as he could with his pride and heretical obstinacy, drove them mad and like a stingray[10] utterly stunned them. Such were the fruits of his diabolical seed. As a strong witness that this can and often does happen, we have the Apostle Paul castigating the Galatians: 'O foolish Galatians, who hath bewitched you, that ye should not believe the truth?'[11] I think a refusal to believe the truth can only come about through subjection to some great secret power. For those who have been beguiled by seducers and have rashly consented to falsehood are not only deprived once of the light of truth but when the deception is eventually detected they often harbour bad feelings towards everybody more learned and are more wary of receiving the truth.[12]

Preachers are often accursed or fanatical, and anyone who hearkens to them should be warned always to keep this verse of Saint Matthew before the eyes and ears of his mind: 'Beware of false prophets which come to you in sheep's clothing but inwardly they are ravening wolves. Ye shall know them by their fruits.'[13] Paul summed up the matter in his second Epistle to the Corinthians: 'For such are false apostles, deceitful workers, transforming themselves into the apostles of Christ. And no marvel; for Satan himself is transformed into an angel of light. Therefore it is no great thing if his ministers also be transformed as the ministers of righteousness; whose end shall be according to their works.'[14]

I shall conclude my brief defence likewise. No one ought to be surprised that so many Florentines – not all, for a large number had long ago realised the evil tyranny of Saevonarola[15] and his satellites –

were led astray by his diabolical trickery. Some were even led into the same wickedness by that devil's goading, since Florence had to struggle not only against one demon but against the fearsome legion of demons[16] crowding round Saevonerola.

From this pestilence God's mercy, the foresight of the Pope and your diligence, Cardinals, have of late happily delivered us. We were also helped by the heavenly favour of the seraphic Saint Francis,[17] by our Cathedral College of Canons, and by the care of several eminent citizens, notably Giovanni Canacci,[18] who took the lead in urging this endeavour. We did not take up arms against the heavenly powers, as Aeneas and his comrades are said unwittingly to have done when they fought vainly in defence of Troy, so that afterwards they cried: 'Alas, no one may place any trust in the gods against their will.'[19] By contrast, we fought against the infernal powers and Tartarean monsters, as did Orpheus to recover Eurydice, and Hercules to win glory.[20] Inspired by God, we fought to preserve the liberty of both Florence and the Church of Rome, so that after the battle we sang: 'God rose up and scattered his foes who fought for the Antichrist. All those who hated God fled from His face, and vanished like smoke. As wax melts before fire, so those hypocrites and arrogant sinners perished before the face of God, for the Almighty, who opposes the proud and favours the meek, by the strength of his arm hath scattered Lucifer and his followers in the imagination of their hearts.'[21]

The punishment of all other sins God often defers to future judgement, but against impious pride, a crime graver than any pestilence, He more often strikes with immediate judgement. For what is clearer than the following miracle? God bore with this sacrilegious man indulgently so long as, like a conjuror, he was only deluding the common people in the name of Christ and His Cross. But once Saevonerola sought publicly to contaminate and imperil the very body of Christ in the Eucharist with fire,[22] Almighty God, by shaking the heavens with violent rainstorms, thunder and lightning, exposed his savage and overweening impiety, and suddenly roused the people to burn him in that self-same fire.

Accordingly, after expressing the especial gratitude owed above all to God, we give profound thanks to the Pope and to your holy College, and humbly commend the people of Florence and the Cathedral College which is utterly devoted to the Church of Rome.[23]

R

The will of the outstanding and most worthy philosopher, the venerable Marsilio Ficino.[1]

IN the name of God Amen. In the one thousand four hundred and ninety-ninth year of our Lord of His saving incarnation, on the twenty-ninth day of September, in the third indiction,[2] enacted in the congregation of San Marco in Florence in the presence of venerable members of the Order: Brother Giorgio Antonio Vespucci of Ser Amerigo of Florence, Brother Vincenzo Nicolai of Ranga, Brother Pietro Antonio, formerly Ser Leonardo of Colle, Brother Honofrio of Pietro Dati of Florence, Brother Bonifazio of Giovanni Landino of Florence, Brother Donato of Bonaventura of Florence, Brother Francesco of Master Antonio Gondi of Florence, in the aforesaid church of San Marco of the Order of San Domenico, all sworn witnesses to each and every thing written below, called, retained, engaged and consulted at the particular request of the undersigned testator.[3]

Let it be openly manifest and known to all in what manner this venerable and prudent man, this exalted and famous professor of philosophy and canon of the Cathedral Church of Florence the venerable Marsilio, son of the late Master Ficino d'Agnolo,[4] an outstanding doctor of arts and medicine, whose memory should be honoured, wisely and discreetly considering in advance the causes of unexpected death, and desiring therefore to provide for the health of soul and body by disposing of his temporal goods and to depart testate rather than intestate, by the grace of our Lord sound in mind sense sight and intellect, albeit infirm in body, by this declared testament, spoken not written, has attended to the provision and distribution of his goods and substance in the following way, that is to say:

First, putting the eternal before the temporal and transitory he has humbly and devotedly commended his soul to our Redeemer the Lord Jesus Christ and his glorious mother the Virgin Mary and all the triumphant court of paradise, and in the matter of his funeral rites and the appointment of the place for his tomb he has instructed that the manner order and will of his undersigned executors be observed and put into effect.[5] For his tomb, which he has ordered to be of humble construction in every way, he has asked his friend the Magnificent Lorenzo di Pierfrancesco de' Medici to pay the cost, because the latter would wish to undertake this expense from his own purse out of his customary kindness towards the said testator, such expense not to exceed what will be stated by his worthy noble unique friend Giovanni di Niccolò Cavalcanti and by me Jacopo, undersigned notary, greatly loved and close friend of the same testator, both being in agreement.[6]

Item. He bequeaths for the maintenance of the main church in Florence the sum of three pounds of small florins.[7]

Item. He wills that immediately upon his death masses known as those of Saint Gregory be celebrated in the Church of San Marco in Florence at the expense to his said estate of one large gold florin in gold.[8]

Item. For the love of God he bequeaths to the church of San Cristoforo in Novoli in the district of Florence six gold florins in gold, and to the church of the community of Pomino of the same district he bequeaths four similar florins to be disbursed in the following way, that is: one florin from the said six florins bequeathed to be for the relief of the poor of the congregation of the same church in Novoli, and another similar florin from the said four florins bequeathed to be for the relief of the poor of the congregation of the same community of Pomino.[9] And the rest of the said bequeathed monies he wishes to be disbursed for the needs of the said churches by referring each case individually to the express decision of the undersigned executors.

Item. For the relief of his soul he bequeaths to the daughters of the lady Antonia his servant, for them all, four florins of large gold in gold, provided however that they be disbursed for the provision of dowries for one or more of these girls at the choice and judgement of the same lady Antonia their mother.[10]

Item. For the love of God he bequeaths to the venerable brother, professor of Holy Writ, Master Bastiano of Bartolomeo[11] and to Ser Luca Fabiano[12] the Florentine notary as follows: to each of them, a cloak, hood and cap of new cord cloth from San Martino, in black, for the use of each to wear on the death of the said testator.[13]

Item. He orders that the book of Plato in Greek with all the dialogues on good paper, which is in the house where he lived,[14] should be bequeathed to the Magnificent Lorenzo di Pierfrancesco de' Medici as one well deserving, and because of certain just reasons that are prompting his mind and conscience.[15]

Item. He similarly orders that the book with certain dialogues of Plato in Greek on best quality paper[16] which is currently with the prudent Francesco of Zanobi Diacceto[17] should be restored to the heirs of Amerigo da Benci, the said heirs to show by trustworthy records that the said book of the said Amerigo had been given or lent for a time to the said testator.[18] Otherwise he bequeaths that same book to the same Francesco his friend as he well deserves.

Item. For the relief of his conscience he wills and instructs that satisfaction should be made to all his creditors by the undersigned executors of his said estate and that this shall be done as quickly and conveniently as possible, and specifically to the lady Antonia his servant[19] in respect of total payment for her service rendered and to be rendered to the said testator, and to Ser Luca Fabiano[20] the Florentine notary in respect of sixty gold ducats and in large gold,[21] for which he asserts he is indebted to the said Ser Luca having settled accounts with him, partly for the monies held by him for their mutual benefit and partly for expenses incurred in the domestic requirements of the said testator.

Item. On account of the outstandingly faithful services rendered to him by the said Ser Luca and in recompense for services of this kind, he acquits and frees the said Ser Luca from all expenses and provisions whatsoever, acquired or to be acquired in the home of the said testator or elsewhere in consideration of the said testator, and from each and every other thing whatsoever which may be sought by him in any way whatever and for whatever reason, even things unknown and which he could have considered in general or in particular. And furthermore, he likewise obliges his beneficiaries named below, whoever they may be, under penalty of forfeiting what is stated below, that directly or indirectly or under any excuse sought they should not trouble the said Ser Luca for any reason put forward nor even under pretext of any other reason at all which they might state or wish or be able to propose to the said Ser Luca to put him under future obligation or in debt to any of them, since he altogether intends to free the said Ser Luca from the same beneficiaries, and to keep him free and quit of all obstacles and opposition which will directly cease and be removed.[22]

Item. For the purpose of curtailing disputes he likewise frees and acquits all those his beneficiaries mentioned below from and concerning all and everything which any of them hitherto owed or for which they had been under obligation to the said testator for whatever reason even one unknown, and from all and everything which he had spent or made available, more on or for one than on or for another, and he forbids them to make any claim on one another or to seek to equalise the distribution for any reason. They are expressly ordered under penalty of forfeiting what is stated below.

Item. As recompense for the services rendered to the same testator by Ficino his nephew by blood,[23] and for some monies that have come into the hands of the said testator from the monies of the said Ficino, he leaves to the same Ficino, son of the late Cherubino of Master Ficino, all the books and note-books of the said testator of whatever quality and subject matter, with the exception of the books of Plato specifically bequeathed above; and also all and each of the furnishings and movable goods which are found to be in the master's house[24] and that of the worker of the estate of Careggi, with the exception of the wine-casks and barrels; concerning which books and note-books and other bequests to the said Ficino the said Ficino may dispose of as he wishes.[25]

Item. He leaves to the same Ficino his nephew, for his lifetime, the estate at Careggi situated in the community of San Pietro di Careggi in the environs of Florence with the master's house and the labourer's cottage and with the wine-casks and barrels (the terms and conditions are made clear below).[26] And after the death of the said Ficino he bequeaths the said goods to the heirs male in the first degree legitimate and natural of the said Ficino, and after the death of all the said heirs male in the first degree legitimate and natural of the said Ficino he bequeaths the same goods to the grandsons of the said Ficino to be born from the same heirs male legitimate and natural: by grandsons of the said Ficino to be understood grandsons and not others i.e. great-grandsons or others in a further degree. And after the death of all the said grandsons of the said Ficino, and with the said third generation in direct descent from the said Ficino ended, he freely leaves the same said goods to the Chapter of Canons of the Cathedral Church of Florence. And meanwhile for as long as the said estate and goods shall remain in the possession of the said Ficino and his aforesaid descendants, he obliges those to whom these goods shall fall from one generation to the next each year on the 19th day of October by way of registration and recognition of the true and rightful ownership of the said goods to pay to the said Chapter of Canons four pounds of small florins for celebrating on the said day one office for the soul of the said testator insofar as it shall seem good to his undersigned executors. And in default of settlement of the said annual payment or registration for three years he wills that these goods freely fall back and revert to the said Chapter of Canons, to which Chapter in such case he freely leaves and bequeaths the said goods, with the duty however of performing the said office each year, which duty he enjoins on the same Chapter even at the end of the said third generation both in perpetuity and beyond a hundred years.[27]

Item. With the duties stated below he leaves to Arcangelo, the brother by blood of the same testator, and son of the said late Master Ficino, and to Zenobio, son of the late Cherubino of Master Ficino, and to Dietifeci, son of the late Daniele of Master Ficino, his nephews, for the lifetime of the said Arcangelo Zenobio and Dietifeci several plots of arable land situated in the commune and jurisdiction of Monte Varchi, from which each year ninety-two sesters of grain are collected as rent, their terms and conditions made clear below.[28] And after the death of the said Arcangelo Zenobio and Dietifeci he leaves the same said property to the sons and grandsons of the heirs male legitimate and natural of the said Arcangelo Zenobio and Dietifeci, save however with the prerogative of degree as stated above concerning the sons and descendants of the said Ficino, and after the death of the said Arcangelo Zenobio and Dietifeci and their aforesaid sons and grandsons in the first and second degree and not beyond, he leaves the same said property to the aforesaid Chapter of Canons of the Cathedral Church of Florence; with the duty also that the said Arcangelo Zenobio and Dietifeci and their aforesaid descendants from one generation to the next to whom the said property shall fall, each year for as long as the said property shall remain in their possession, by way of registration and recognition of the true and rightful ownership of the said property, should pay to the said Chapter four pounds of small florins to be disbursed for the said office as stated above concerning the duty imposed on the said Ficino and with the same penalty of forfeiture and reversion of the said property to the said Chapter of Canons, in the event of their ceasing settlement of the said payment or registration for three years; and with the duty also that the said Arcangelo Zenobio and Dietifeci and the other above mentioned legatees to whom the said property shall fall should be obliged each year to give and supply to Ser Luca Fabbiano the Florentine notary during his lifetime out of the grain contribution of the said properties twelve sesters of grain, out of which in any year the said Ser

Luca should be obliged to assign two sesters to the Church of Santa Maria or Santa Lucia of Monte Martiano, the pensionary of the said testator for the sake of his soul.[29] He declares that, even after the death of the said Ser Luca these two sesters of grain must be supplied each year to the said church by the said Arcangelo Zenobio and Dietifeci and their aforesaid descendants, for as long as the said property shall fall to them. And he wills that the said Arcangelo Zenobio and Dietifeci and their aforesaid descendants with the cessation of all opposition as to difficulty and impossibility should be obliged to ensure and effect that those holding the said property present and future shall promise by a public document, and they shall pledge themselves to the said Ser Luca, to assign to the same Ser Luca in any year the said twelve Florentine sesters of grain just as the said possessors are obliged to do concerning that part of the said payment and they should be obliged to ensure that the foregoing are carried out no later than a month from the day of the death of the said testator under penalty of forfeiture of what is stated below.

In the matter of all his other goods however both present and to come he appoints as his general beneficiaries the aforesaid Arcangelo Ficino Zenobio and Dietifeci in equal shares[30] and he places responsibility upon these his beneficiaries and he enjoins that they must acquiesce in and comply with all the dispositions in the present testament and should not contravene such dispositions even in the least degree or stand in opposition to them directly or indirectly nor should one disturb or provoke another and vice versa or one bring or advance litigation against another and vice versa nor do or attempt anything but to pursue all the aforesaid dispositions made by the said testator as well as those stated below and should assign them with fullest effect according to his exact will.

But he deprives from all share in and benefit of his estate those acting to the contrary and not complying with the straightforward legal declaration and summary of the undersigned executors; and for the purpose also of curtailing disputes the said testator declares that all bequests made in the present testament are intended to compensate his said appointed beneficiaries and as recompense for whatever amount or items each one of them might have been able to request or to acquire on whatever plea or pretext from the said testator for whatever reason wishing that they should in every way acquiesce in and remain content with what has been stated above.[31]

In addition he debars his said legatees whoever they may be from the alienation of immovable goods from his family and home and from the hiring out for any length of time of the said immovable goods and every kind of alienation and every means transaction or contract whereby any kind of alienation could be arrived at by intermediaries. Indeed he deprives those acting to the contrary of every advantage and bequest of the present testament and transfers such advantages and bequests in equal shares to those who remain compliant, or else to be transferred to the said Chapter of Canons.

In addition the said testator wills and declares that his undersigned executors including their agents and administrators immediately following the death of the said testator should without lapse of time acquire and take possession of all and each of the moving and movable goods the furnishings clothing and whatever else shall be found belonging to his said estate except items as specifically bequeathed above and equally with the exception of what he freely declares to belong to the said Ficino of what remains in the house where he lived.[32]

And likewise they should acquire and take possession of the monies to be found in the charge of the director of Santa Maria Nuova[33] of Florence or those elsewhere belonging to the said testator, and they should complete a careful inventory of all the aforementioned in the presence of at least two of his above-named beneficiaries; which beneficiaries whoever they may be he altogether debars except for their presence from any meddling or interfering with the foregoing but they should promise to his said undersigned executors that the foregoing be carried out and fulfilled under penalty of forfeiture of his said estate for those contravening and interfering with the aforesaid, the penalty to be applied as is stated and declared above.

Moreover he makes and appoints as his executors trustees and implementers of this his present last will the aforesaid Chapter of Canons of the main church of Florence with full and absolute power capability and authority as much as can be granted and accorded to such executors; as also of fulfilling and of commissioning the fulfilment and effectively procuring and bringing about the commission and fulfilment of each and every point expressly laid down and instructed above by the testator himself; of completing and of bringing about the completion of the said inventory of movables furnishings clothing and whatever else ought to be included in the

1. Detail from *Miracle of the Sacrament*, 1485-86, by Cosimo Rosselli, showing portraits of Marsilio Ficino, Pico della Mirandola and Agnolo Poliziano. Fresco. Church of Sant'Ambrogio, Chapel of the Miracle of the Sacrament, Florence. © 2020, Photo SCALA, Florence. Letter 30 refers to the shared interests of the three friends.

2. *Memorial plaque to Callimachus* (Filippo Buonaccorsi), 1496. Designed by Veit Stoss, cast by Peter Vischer the Elder. Cast bronze. Dominican Church of the Holy Trinity, Kraków. Photo by courtesy of Chris Rees and by kind permission of the Church (March 2009). Letter 26 is to Callimachus.

3. Portrait of Germain de Ganay, jurist, canon of Cathedral of Notre-Dame, Paris, and Bishop of Cahors from 1510. Artist unknown, Cathedral of Cahors. © VTR / Alamy Stock Photo. Letters 27, 35, 39 and Appendices F, G, and H1 are addressed to de Ganay.

4. *King Charles VIII of France (1470-1498)*, 16th century, French School (after Jean Perréal, 1450-1530). Oil on panel. Musée de Condé, Chantilly. Photo © RMN-Grand Palais (domaine de Chantilly) / René-Gabriel Ojéda. Letter 37 is an address to the King.

5. *Entry of Charles VIII into Florence*, c.1515–7, Francesco Granacci. Oil on wood. Inv. No. 3908/1890. Reproduced by kind permission of Gallerie degli Uffizi and the Ministero per i beni e le attività culturali e per il turismo. © Gabinetto Fotografico delle Gallerie degli Uffizi. Commemorating the arrival of French troops in 1494.

6. *John Colet, Dean of St Paul's*, c.1535, Hans Holbein the Younger. Black and coloured chalks, pen and ink, brush and ink, and metalpoint on pale pink prepared paper. Accessible at www.rct.uk/collection/912199. Royal Collection Trust, © Her Majesty Queen Elizabeth II, 2020. Appendix P presents the surviving correspondence between Ficino and Colet.

7. Portrait of Fra Girolamo Savonarola, c.1498, Fra Bartolomeo. Oil on wood. Reproduced by kind permission of the Museo di San Marco, Florence, and Ministero per i beni e le attività culturali e per il turismo. © Museo di San Marco. See Letter 38 and Appendix Q.

8. *Execution of Savonarola in the Piazza della Signoria*, 1498, sometimes attributed to Francesco di Lorenzo Rosselli. Tempera on wooden panel. Reproduced by kind permission of the Museo di San Marco, Florence, and Ministero per i beni e le attività culturali e per il turismo. © Museo di San Marco. See Appendix Q.

said completion of the inventory for removal and sale, as far as they see it to be more expedient for his said estate; furthermore also of exacting and enforcing payment from debtors to his said estate whoever they may be and of recouping whatever might be owed to his said estate; as also of recouping and raising from the said hospital director the whole sum of monies of the said testator which will be found in his possession or in that of the said hospital at the time of his death and of making quittance full and final settlements and acknowledgements of receipt if need be, as far as they see fit; further of satisfying the creditors of his said estate whoever they may be and of releasing to the legatees named above and of ensuring the release of the sums of money and movable items and the cost of his funeral and furthermore of estimating what is due and paying out the amount to those persons in both that manner and form according as the said executors wish and judge suitable for the quality circumstances and rank of the said testator.[34]

And in addition also in the event of disagreements which could arise he wills and declares that if among his said appointed beneficiaries there should arise in the future any dispute or controversy concerning the estate or the hereditary goods of the said testator his said beneficiaries must without delay and without legal quibble and according to the facts acquiesce in adhere to and comply with every judgement and declaration to be made concerning the aforesaid by his said executors, which executors the said testator chooses forthwith for the purposes already stated as arbitrators and friends proceeding in common and exercising judgement amongst his said beneficiaries, and he lays a burden on the consciences of the aforesaid executors in the foregoing in relation to all that has been committed and assigned to them concerning all the foregoing although the said testator is wholly assured of the goodness loyalty and law-abiding nature of those executors.

In addition when satisfaction has been made concerning all bequests and obligations of the present testament and for the cost of his funeral and other matters needing to be settled by the said executors the said testator imposes upon his said executors that they distribute and assign all residuary ready monies and all residual proceeds of goods and items which were to be disposed of as above or payments exacted or demanded from debtors in the following way, that is: to Ser Luca Fabiano notary of Florence one half, but the other half to his above-named appointed beneficiaries in equal portions.[35]

The said testator also forbids all discounts from the said bequests under the Falcidian Law[36] either Trebellian[37] or deductions, because he altogether wishes all the foregoing bequests to hold good unimpaired and without appropriation or any deduction in the manner and order as he deposes and instructs above.

The aforenamed testator asserts that this shall be and is intended to be his last will deposition and judgement, which he wills and declares to be valid and binding and to have force by the law of testament and if by the law of testament it is not valid, should not be valid or will not be valid, he wishes it to be valid and binding by the law of gift of codicils in the event of his death or of any other last will whatsoever even with all other better means form and title as well by which it may be might be or in any way shall be able to be more and better valid in law in the future; revoking cancelling and annulling all and any other testament whatsoever and any other last will of whatsoever kind at whatsoever time both whensoever and howsoever composed made or composed and made or drawn up hitherto by him even if in them or in any of them there had been appended or inserted any modifying words general penalising or precise and or modifying clauses general penalising or precise, concerning which special particular or precise mention ought to have been made in the present testament, which words all and singular and which clauses all and singular the said testator wills and declares sufficiently particularly and individually to be considered appended and inserted here in the present testament and the said testator asserts that he has regretted and does regret these modifying words all and singular and expressly has revoked does revoke has wished and does wish them all to be considered revoked asking me Jacopo undersigned public notary to complete from the foregoing one public document or more also as often as I shall be required to do so.

S[1]

Marsilio Ficino, ancient servant of the House of Medici, wishes happiness to Lorenzo, his one and only patron.[2]

I HAVE just sent you happiness, Lorenzo, from the bottom of my heart, believe me.[3] But if anyone thinks that you have happiness from one so wretched, he is wrong, for to such a one all things are so utterly wretched that even happiness will present itself as extreme unhappiness. If anyone imagines that you have received from him anything pleasing, he is likewise wrong. For he is so lacking in grace that while he tries his utmost to fulfil his duty of gratitude towards you he is considered the most ungrateful of all. He also errs who when he strives to give you great praise – O most unhappy man! – he is deemed to vilify the outstanding man who praises him. It has been so decreed by some fate for wretched mortals that those who anxiously devote themselves to their studies for a very long time eventually perish in those very studies. Thus the philosophers Diagoras, Protagoras, Anaxagoras, Pythagoras and Socrates perished while engaged in fine points of discussion;[4] and so did the orators Demosthenes and Cicero through the very exercise of their eloquence.[5] But those orators are said to have perished as a result of a wondrous skill in exposing people's faults.[6] Your Marsilio, on the other hand, is perishing through his lack of skill in giving praise.[7] In those men, therefore, it is not the art but the will that is to blame. But in my case it is not the will but ineptitude that is to blame. Far be it from me ever to have wished or to wish now to offend him on whom alone after God I recognise that my whole welfare depends, through whom alone I am whatever I am, whom alone out of all others I wish to be favourable to me, at whom alone I shudder when he is even a little annoyed. Happy, ah too happy, had I but died before the Ides of May.[8] For that is when, trusting in the grace of the Holy Spirit on those solemn feast days of the Holy Spirit, which were unfortunate and extremely hostile to me alone, I, wretched as I am, crossed your threshold with those two insignificant gifts. Would that I had dedicated them – not because they are yours, but because they are mine and most unsuitable – would that I had dedicated them to Vulcan or Pluto rather than to Castor and Pollux.[9]

But since I have dedicated them to my noble patrons, let it be by their own fate that they rise or fall. It is something to have wished to honour my kindly masters. But what I judge to be most unfortunate is that it is now the eighth month since my rejection, or rather my downfall. It laid me low in misfortune for seven months so that I could not think of any remedies until Mercury, recently retrograde, by chance revealed this downfall which had been brought upon me a long time ago by Saturn and Mars. Where then, philosopher, is your usual tranquillity of mind? Alas, our philosophy has melted away through grief, all our tranquillity has now turned to storms. Only Phoebus with his nod of assent can clear the sky and calm the tempests.[10] But see, even now while I am writing, some tiny shred of hope is rising up in the midst of my unspeakable sorrow. Caesar is said to have frequently spared his enemies even when they did wrong of their own volition.[11] Will not our Scipio pardon his servants when they make mistakes through want of skill and beg for forgiveness?[12] Surely the malignity of this fate of mine will modify the beneficence of your exalted mind and of your fate; or will that limitless love of the Holy Spirit, on whose help I relied at the outset, be less powerful for forgiveness and reconciliation, if appropriate, than the hatred of Saturn and Mars is for causing trouble and discord if perchance that hatred strikes?

I dare not foolishly further trouble the ears of that man whom I once unintentionally offended. The great Cosimo, who sometimes smiles upon me even in my dreams as I frequently bewail my lot,[13] is the patron I should call upon to win over the grandson who is so like him. Cosimo strongly commends his Marsilio to Lorenzo.

T 1[1]

Lorenzo de' Medici to Giovanni Lanfredini in Rome:[2]

. . . Concerning the bishopric of Cortona: if it should fall vacant for any reason, I would greatly desire our Lord[3] to grant it to our Messer Marsilio, whose teaching and worth are assuredly well known where you are and in many other parts of the world; and in addition to the pleasure that I myself would receive from this, our Lord would be well commended for his virtues and his good life. Be advised that this thought is mine alone and that I have not shared it with him. It is my will that this matter be executed in such a way that neither he nor anyone else come to know of it beforehand . . .[4]

Spedaletto.
6th October, 1487.

T 2

Lorenzo de' Medici to Giovanni Lanfredini:

YOU know in what esteem I hold Messer Marsilio Ficino. And because it might soon come about that I shall be able to bestow on him a small benefice with cure of souls, which is about to fall vacant,[5] it would be necessary, since he already has two such benefices, for him to have a dispensation to hold three such benefices, which would usually be inadmissible.[6] I should like you to do everything in such a way that this dispensation will quickly be to hand, even though such a permit is not entrusted to churchmen unless of some standing. You can assure our Lord that he may as readily give permission to Messer Marsilio as to any other such person.
29th October, 1489.

U[1]

Sebastiano Salvini humbly commends himself to Guido, Reverend Prior of Santa Maria degli Angeli.[2]

IN the very nature of things, most excellent and devout man, a harsh sequence of difficult times has now fallen upon us,[3] with the result that we attach the greatest importance to honours, riches, resources, abundance, nobility of birth and other numerous benefits of fortune, which we should value lightly, while our blessings of the soul, as if they were not ours, to our shame we hold in low regard. We want to know and understand more and more rather than put better things to the test. Alas! While we are plucking 'the golden bough that lies hidden in the shady tree, with its leaves and pliant stem,'[4] our duty is not to know more than we should but always to do more, in a good way. Wisdom is the perfect blessing of the human mind: not only the knowledge of matters divine and human, but their enactment, because 'the whole glory of virtue consists in action.'[5] As you well know, venerable Father, the mark of a wise man is not so much to know everything as to live honourably, justly, piously, wisely, and to fear God: for 'The fear of the Lord is the beginning of wisdom.'[6] 'And by the fear of the Lord men depart from evil.'[7] What is good for us is what makes us good, so let us love the supreme good with all our might. Is not the soul the place of the highest good?[8] Unless the soul be pure and holy, it can at no time take hold of supreme and immortal God. If I do not know how to share a thing with a brother or his child, it profits me little to divide it into parts. We want to measure the stars, but we do not measure how large or how small the soul is. We really want to know the straight line with precision, but we do not know what will succeed in leading to our welfare, honour and straightness of conduct. Why do wretched mortals strive so keenly for riches, which always turn out to be evil, indeed the worst of all, for bad people. Why are wretched men so enamoured of glittering caparisons for their horses rather than the true ornaments of the soul?[9]

> Golden chains hang down on their breasts from the neck;
> Covered with gold, they champ the yellow gold with their teeth.[10]

These things cannot make the master or the horse any better. That which is truly good, as we have said, makes us good. Why have many beds? We lie in one bed; where we are not is not really ours. If we, like many men of your religion, as I have been able to perceive, will 'drench our single cover with our tears',[11] we shall sculpt our own highest good within the mind. It will not be an ivory Minerva that is sculpted for us, such as Phidias made, but a living immortal Minerva, most beautiful of all.[12] We shall always make our soul more beautiful by the operations of the virtues, if we measure its greatness, if we seek its true beauty, that is wisdom, with Plato, who prayed to immortal God, prayed that He would make his soul ever more beautiful.[13] For divine wisdom is the true beauty of the soul, which cannot be bought with silver or gold, or with precious stones,[14] but with faith, hope and love:[15] with faith, as will not escape you, we come close to God, and by it we turn to religion, we fear God, we hope that we shall one day possess eternal goods in abundance.

If the Athenians showered Herodotus with the greatest honours at the 84th Olympiad when he had recited his histories,[16] then Melissus the natural scientist, Euripides the tragedian, Theaetetus the mathematician, Aristophanes, Sophocles the tragic poet, Democritus of Abdera, Empedocles, Hippocrates the physician,

Gorgias, Hippias, Prodicus, Parmenides, Aristotle and Zeno, how much more praise should philosophers have heaped with their words upon Socrates, Diogenes and Plato, who through their life and conduct instructed far more people than the others I have named? How much the more is it incumbent on us to praise Christ, the Master of Life, 'who began both to do and teach' more excellently than all?[17] And on everyone to praise His Apostles, Peter and Paul? And those eminent Church Doctors Augustine, Jerome, Gregory and Ambrose? And the almost countless others whom Christ 'loved equally'[18] should we not extol to the stars, or rather to God, to Christ, maker of the stars, for they, through love for Him, either underwent martyrdom or wrote countless most beautiful works on the Christian truth with the greatest integrity and care, and they confirmed all those things at their peril?

Wherefore, most pious and devout man, we are sending you the book *On the Christian Religion*, produced as attractively as the matter permits and in great detail, by our Marsilio, who, as I think, is no less a Christian than a Platonist, and he is no less zealous for you than for himself.[19] In this book you will find the true humanity on which the fine religion of the Christians is founded, its modesty, moderation, justice, sanctity, hope, love, faith, and at the end, the obstinacy, errors and false statements of the Jews, and the Mohammedans' arrogance, ineptitude, temerity, and delight in the physical.

Farewell.
Florence.
1st January, 1487.

V[1]

Stranger, behold!

Here is Marsilio, Father of Wisdom, who brought to light the Platonic teaching that lay buried beneath the dust of ages.

While preserving its Attic grace, he was the first to offer it to the Latin peoples, inspired as he was from on high to open the sacred portals of the divine mind.

In former times he lived happily through the munificence of Cosimo and Lorenzo de' Medici, and now he lives again for the benefit of all.

The Senate and People of Florence, in the year 1521.

Notes to the Letters

Preface

1 Sextus Roscius Amerinus (fl. 1st century BC) was famous as the subject of Cicero's first major lawsuit, when he defended him from a false accusation of murdering his father. Cicero presented him as a model of filial devotion (Cicero, *Pro Roscio Amerino)*. See also Letter 20.
Girolamo Rossi's role was to ensure a future for Ficino's letters, and to act as Ficino's representative in Venice, in matters relating to the publication of these and perhaps other works.
The name Roscius was also often applied to actors of excellence, after the famous Roman actor, Quintus Roscius Gallus (ca. 126 BC – 62 BC).

2 Ficino uses repetition, *feliciter*, *felicissime*, *feliciter*, to emphasise his wishes for happiness, success and good fortune.

I

1 This letter marks the beginning of Diacceto's association with Ficino. He was studying in Pisa with Giovanni de' Medici and Giovanni Vittorio Soderini. It is thought that Ficino was replying to a letter from both Diacceto and Soderini, but it has not survived.

2 St Matthew 18:7. See also St Luke 17:1.

3 Plato, *Theaetetus*, 176AB. Ficino had already addressed this theme in *Letters*, **1**, 50 to Giovanni Cavalcanti, in **4**, 33 to Francesco Sassetti, and, most extensively, in **5**, 48 to Lotterio Neroni. Ficino begins here by quoting the exact words of his *Theaetetus* translation, but lapses into paraphrase. Cf. Plotinus, *Enneads*, I, 2, 1. In the last years of Ficino's life, his pupil Diacceto went beyond Ficino, regarding physical matter as itself evil (*De pulchro*, II, 7, and his *Oratio* on the Soul).

4 The danger attendant on trying to sail between the rock of the sea-monster Scylla and the whirlpool of Charybdis in the Sicilian straits of Messina is described by Homer in *Odyssey*, XII, 73-110 and 235-239 and by Virgil in *Aeneid*, III, 420-432; it is also mentioned by many other authors including Ovid, Propertius, Cicero and St Jerome. The proverbial form, 'they fall victim to Scylla in their desire to avoid Charybdis' can be traced back to the *Alexandriad* of Walter of Chatillon (1135-1180), a medieval epic poem based on the history of Alexander the Great, rarely read now but popular in its time and still known for this line (*Incidit in Scyllam qui vult vitare Charybdim*).

5 See Ephesians 6:12. 'For we wrestle not against flesh and blood, but against principalities, against powers, against the rulers of the darkness of this world, against spiritual

wickedness in high places.' For Ficino the lower air is the realm of Juno but also of the daemons.

6 Cf. Job 1:6-12; St Matthew 4:1-11.

7 Plato discusses the effects of evil and melancholy on body, mind and soul in *Timaeus*, 86-90. Aristotle discusses melancholy as an affliction particular to philosophers in *Problemata*, 30, 1 (953a-955a); Democritus, who neglected his estates and blinded himself when his eyes distracted him in his contemplations, is mentioned by Cicero, *De finibus*, V, 29, 87 and Diogenes Laertius, *Lives of the Philosophers*, IX, 36. Ficino discusses the dangers of melancholy for philosophers in *Platonic Theology*, XIV, 10 (ed. Allen and Hankins, vol. 4, pp. 307-311) and then at length in his *De vita* (passim).

8 Prometheus was one of the sons of the Titan Iapetus; his name means 'forethought' and he is famous for attempting to outwit the gods (Hesiod, *Theogony*, 510-70; Boccacio, *Genealogy of the Gods*, IV, 44). Zeus punished him and his three brothers for their presumption. In Prometheus's case, it was for climbing up to heaven to steal fire from the gods for mankind. He was chained to a rock in the Caucasus for eternity, with an eagle (or vulture) daily devouring his liver, which each night was renewed. Hercules rescued him from this endless punishment by killing the bird. Prometheus was also the mythical founder of many arts. In his *Philebus* commentary, Ficino presents Prometheus as the archetype of human intelligence (see Marsilio Ficino, *The Philebus Commentary*, ed. by M. J. B. Allen, ch. 26).

9 Psalm 126:5-6. Ficino uses plural forms for verse 6, which is in line with the Greek Septuagint and with Jerome's various Latin versions. Singular forms are used in the Vulgate of modern times and the King James Version, following the original Hebrew.

10 There is a traditional Christian association of apples and evils through the story of Eve and the serpent in Genesis, and through the similarity of the Latin words *malus*, 'apple tree' and *malum* 'evil'.

11 MS Mo2 adds Florence as the place of writing.

2

1 This letter became chapter 13, the final chapter, in the published edition of Ficino's *De sole* (1493), a work first written for Count Eberhard and sent to him in 1492. The dedication letter that accompanied the first version was included in the previous book of our translation of Ficino's letters (see *Letters*, **10**, 33); other chapters followed in the manuscript Mo2 but Ficino did not include them in his published *Letters*, perhaps because *De sole* was already in print by the time the *Letters* were published (1495). He had added to it further material and published it together with a companion work on light, under the title *De sole et lumine*, dedicating it this time to Piero de' Medici. *De sole et lumine* was printed in Florence by Antonio Miscomini on 31st January, 1493. Further editions followed, in Leipzig in 1502, Venice in 1503 and Strasbourg in 1508. The chapters from Mo2 are now presented in Appendix B below. The last section of this letter is quoted at length and discussed by Michael J.B. Allen in 'Marsilio Ficino and the Language of the Past,' in *Forme del Neoplatonismo*, edited by L. Simonutti, Florence, 2007, pp. 35-50, esp. pp. 40-42; reprinted in Allen, *Studies in the Platonism of Marsilio Ficino and Giovanni Pico* (Abingdon: Routledge, 2017). Allen suggests that this letter is an adaptation made from the last chapter of *De sole*,

but more likely it is the other way around: that this letter became, with slight adaptations, the last chapter of that book See notes to Appendix B.

2 This differs a little from the description given by Alcibiades in Plato, *Symposium*, 220 CD which refers only to a single occasion, as does Diogenes Laertius (*Lives of the Philosophers,* II, 23). However, in Aulus Gellius, *Attic Nights*, II, 1, 1-3, or 2.1.2, drawing on the now lost writings of Favorinus of Arles (80-160ad), Socrates's long meditation on the Sun is described as a regular practice.

Ficino also discusses this episode in *Platonic Theology*, XIII, ii, 2 in relation to deep contemplation.

3 *A Phoebean daemon*: Phoebus, Apollo and the Sun are all the same: Apollo is the name given by the Greeks to the god *Helios*, the Sun. He wards off evil, and inspires prophecy, music and all the arts, from agriculture to government. He is the leader of the Muses. The name used by the Romans, Phoebus, derives from the Greek word *phoibos*, 'shining, pure, bright'. On the *daemon* of Socrates, see Plato, *Apology*, 31D; Plutarch, *De genio Socratis* (in *Moralia*, Loeb edition, VII, pp. 361-509); Apuleius, *On the God of Socrates*, esp. 19, and Proclus, *Commentary on the First Alcibiades*, 78-83. On the guardian spirit more generally, see Plotinus, *Enneads*, III, 4; Proclus, *Commentary on the First Alcibiades*, 68-78. For illuminating discussions, see Michael J.B. Allen, 'Socrates and the Daemonic Voice of Conscience' in *Synoptic Art*, ch.4, pp. 125-47; Anna Corrias, 'From Daemonic Reason to Daemonic Imagination: Plotinus and Marsilio Ficino on the Soul's Tutelary Spirit', *British Journal for the History of Philosophy*, 21, 3 (2013) pp. 443-62.

In his summary of Plato's *Apology*, Ficino discussed the nature of the daemon of Socrates, calling it by turns 'fiery', in that it raised him aloft in contemplation, and 'Saturnian' in that it drew the focus of his mind away from the body and restrained him from actions. See Farndell, *Gardens of Philosophy*, p. 124.

4 Plato, *Apology*, 21A-22E. Socrates was told by his friend Chaerophon, who had consulted the oracle of Apollo at Delphi, that no one was wiser than Socrates.

5 Plato calls the Sun the 'son of the Good' in *Laws*, X, 898D-899A. See also Plato, *Republic*, VI, 508-9. Ficino comments on the latter passage in several places: first in his *De amore*, II, 2, and in the *Philebus* commentary, ch. 31 (translated by Allen, *Marsilio Ficino: The Philebus commentary*, see pp. 302-4) as well as his commentary on the *Republic* itself (*Opera*, p. 1408, translated by Farndell, *When Philosophers Rule* London: Shepheard-Walwyn, 2006, p. 29). In his commentary on Plato's *Cratylus*, Ficino explains the name Apollo as signifying a threefold Sun: divine, angelic and celestial (*Opera*, p. 1313; Farndell, *When Philosophers Rule*, p. 104). Isidore of Seville likens the Sun to Christ (*On the Nature of Things*, 20).

6 James 1:17.

7 In *Platonic Theology*, I, ii-vi, Ficino unfolds the principles governing the creation of soul and the nature of the creative forces. See also *Platonic Theology*, XII, i, 11-13.

8 Ficino's discussions of creation in *Platonic Theology* are expressed in terms of motion and action, as this chapter of *De sole* reflects. He also summarises these principles in two letters written around the same time, the third and fourth letters of Book II (*Letters*, **12**, forthcoming; Latin text in Gentile, *Epistolae*, II, 3-4, pp. 34-43). Cf. *Platonic Theology*, I, v, 9.

9 Ficino's view of the Sun here as limited in influence stems from the prevailing Ptolemaic view of the cosmos in which the Sun is just one of seven planets circling the earth, although Pliny singles out the Sun as having special influence as 'the life or rather the mind of the universe, the chief regulator and the God of nature; he

also lends his light to all the other stars.' Pliny, *Natural History*, II, 4. Set against this is the Biblical tradition of the Sun ruling and setting measures (Genesis 1:14-18). Ficino draws on many ancient sources, both pagan and Christian, including Julian's *Hymn to King Helios* and Isidore of Seville, *On the Nature of Things*, 20-23 (for details of modern translations, see Bibliography).

The very fact that the Sun is in motion presents limitations discussed by Ficino in the paragraph that follows, since being in motion separates it from the creative powers of God that are held in stillness. Some medieval writers even represented the Sun as following a zigzag course along the ecliptic (see Bruce Eastwood, *Ordering the Heavens*, III, 5). However, in other parts of *De sole* Ficino distinguishes the visible sun which moves from an invisible higher Sun, which is representative of God. The views expressed in this section, therefore, do not conflict with Ficino's philosophical ideas (see, for example note 5 above) which place that higher Sun beyond the planetary system. In this he follows Julian's *Hymn to King Helios*, which also distinguishes between the invisible and visible Sun. See John Dillon, 'The Theology of Julian's *Hymn to King Helios*', *Itaca*, 14-15 (1999), pp. 103-115, reprinted in *The Platonic Heritage*, Routledge Variorum Series, 2016, (first published by Ashgate, 2012), essay XXIII.

10 In the view of most ancient astronomers, all the seven planets move in the same direction, from west to east, each in its own sphere, nested one within another, while the heavens themselves, in which they are held, and the fixed stars, rotate from east to west. See, for example, Ptolemy, *Almagest*, I, 8; Pliny, *Natural History*, II, 6 (II, 8 in Teubner edition). The theologians agreed: see, for example, St Basil, *Hexaemeron*, III, 3.

11 In *Letters*, **6**, 17 (p. 25) Ficino notes how the influences of all the stars can be blocked or countered. The entire system of influences may be hard to follow and interpret, as was readily acknowledged even by Ptolemy, e.g. *Tetrabiblos*, I, 2.

12 For the Sun as the 'regulator and measure' the prime source is Genesis 1:14-18. Egyptian cosmology also gave great importance to the Sun, as is reflected in Plato, Ptolemy and Pliny.

3

1 This letter is also discussed in Allen, 'Marsilio Ficino and the Language of the Past,' at pp. 47-8; see Letter 2, note 1.

2 *Amico unico* was a term Ficino reserved to indicate a special connection of friendship. Giovanni Cavalcanti is always called *amico unico*, a unique or especial friend. This may reflect the fact that Cavalcanti had been his friend from early times but was from an aristocratic family, which would have set a social distance between him and Ficino. Some friends are called *dilectissimo*, 'beloved', (e.g. Antonio Calderini, Amerigo Corsini, Filippo Carducci, Filippo Valori); Giorgio Antonio Vespucci and sometimes Filippo Valori are called 'his own'. *Familiarissimo* is used of Bindaccio Ricasoli as well as *dilectissimo suo*. Other dear friends may be called 'fellow philosopher' (e.g. Lotterio Neroni, Giovanni Pico della Mirandola, Pier Leone of Spoleto) or sometimes 'fellow Platonist' (Pico della Mirandola, Pier Leone) or 'fellow priest' (e.g. Girolamo Pasqualini). Senior members of the Church are usually addressed formally, with Ficino humbly commending himself, as are kings and princes. Bernardo Bembo, a good friend but of considerably higher social status, being an eminent Venetian aristocrat, usually receives a rather formal greeting, as a

distinguished nobleman and knight. Friends perhaps a little less close to Ficino are often noted as 'distinguished' in their field (e.g. Domenico Benivieni). Niccolò Michelozzi is always addressed as 'a true man', which is intended as a constant compliment. Some correspondents never receive an epithet, e.g. Francesco Bandini, but it would be hard to ascribe a reason for this. Martin Prenninger first receives the designation of 'unique friend' in the preface dedicating to him the ninth book of letters, and written after that book was completed, on 4th July 1490. From that time onwards, Prenninger, like Cavalcanti, is always addressed as *amico unico*. Before that, Prenninger was also called *Uranius*, alluding to the heavens, which may have been a name he had adopted, as was the fashion in humanist circles.

3 Giovanni Vittorio Soderini (1460-1528), youngest of the four sons of Lorenzo de' Medici's trusted adviser, Tommaso Soderini, all of whom had distinguished careers. Giovanni Vittorio started teaching Law at the Florentine *Studio* in 1485 and moved with the faculty, temporarily to Prato in 1486, and to Pisa from 1487. He would later serve as one of the senior lawyers in the city. But at the time of this letter he was in Pisa, alongside Diacceto, providing company for Giovanni de' Medici, who was studying at the university. See Letter 1 and Biographical Notes.

4 For Prenninger's legal career, which included a professorship at the University of Tübingen as well as the posts of Chancellor to the Bishopric of Constance and Counsellor to the Duke of Württemberg, see Biographical Notes. Prenninger's legal judgements (*Consilia sive responsae*) were collected and published in 1597.

5 Plato stressed the link between justice and wisdom, for example in *Laws*, 864, and in *Republic*, V, 473D where he uses the famous model of the philosopher-king.

6 In Greek mythology, Saturn devoured most of his children at birth because of a prophecy that one of them would usurp him. Jupiter was hidden at his birth and survived, and in due course he did usurp his father's power, confining him within a cave. Jupiter then introduced law and order, but poets pined for the golden age of Saturn when laws were not needed because everything in nature and society regulated itself, and they longed for its return. See Hesiod, *Works and Days*, 109-120; Virgil, *Georgics*, I, 125-8; II, 513-40; *Eclogue* 4; Ovid, *Metamorphoses*, I, 89-150. Plato refers to the age of Saturn in his *Laws*, IV, 713 and *Statesman*, 272.

7 The cardinal points of the heavens, as on earth, are North, South, East and West, with East holding special significance, defining the ascendant. 'At the head of a group of three signs' (*triplicitatum capitibus*): a group of three signs of the Zodiac, either linked by their connection to one of the four elements, or by a seasonal association, is called a triplicity, and the first in each group is called its head. Libra is the head of an autumnal triplicity in ancient astrology, containing Libra, Scorpio and Sagittarius.

Guido Bonatti (13th century) had discussed the connection between great conjunctions and the birth of religions, drawing on the authority of Albumasar (9th century) in *De magnis coniunctionibus*. See also Ficino, *Letters*, **6**, 17 and Appendix, 'On The Star of the Magi'.

In a well-known passage of his Commentary on the *Comedia* of Dante, Cristoforo Landino refers to a conjunction of Saturn and Jupiter that was due to take place on 25th November, 1484 at 1.41 p.m., in Scorpio in the ascendant of the fifth degree of Libra, signifying a change in religion. He interpreted this as a change in Christianity for the better, quoting Virgil's line on the return of the Virgin and the Golden Age (Virgil, *Eclogues*, IV, line 6). It is not surprising that Ficino chose to publish his Plato translations in that year: the task of printing it was begun on 25th January in that year and was completed by September or October. (Landino, *Comento sopra la Comedia*, on *Inferno* I, 100-111, Edizione Nazionale dei Commenti Danteschi, edited by P. Procaccioli, 4 vols. Rome, 2001, I, pp. 320-21.)

In his summary of Plato's *Statesman*, Ficino alludes to the characteristics of the two reigns, of Jupiter and Saturn, remarking that the reign of Saturn is more closely associated with happiness and prosperity because of its engagement in contemplation of the divine. Jupiter's reign is focused on human activity. (Farndell, *Gardens of Philosophy*, p. 63; Ficino, *Opera*, p. 1296.)

8 Saturn's contemplative role is described by Ficino in the Preface to his Commentaries on Plato, where he is represented in the innermost sanctuary of the Academy, contemplating the secrets of the heavens. See *Gardens of Philosophy*, p. 7; *When Philosophers Rule*, p. 31. On the role of Saturn in favouring human contemplation, see *Platonic Theology*, XIII, ii, 3 and *De vita*, III, xxii, 27-44. On Saturn in general, see Michael J.B. Allen, 'Marsilio Ficino on Saturn, the Plotinian Mind, and the Monster of Averroes,' *Bruniana & Campanelliana*, 16 (2010-11), pp. 11-29, reprinted in *Studies in the Platonism of Marsilio Ficino and Giovanni Pico*, Variorum Series, London, Routledge, 2017, pp. 253-71.

9 Minos, one of the sons of Jupiter and Europa, was the original king of Crete, ruling at Knossos. He is named at the opening of Plato's *Laws* as the lawgiver for Crete and, citing Homer, *Odyssey*, XIX, 178-9, he is described as consulting with his father Jupiter every ninth year (Plato, *Laws*, I, 624). This myth is developed further in the dialogue *Minos*, 319DE, a dialogue no longer regarded as authentic but still within the canon in Ficino's time and translated by him. On the significance of this myth, which invokes the transition from the Golden Age, and the linking of Saturn, man and the cosmos, see Michael J.B. Allen, 'Marsilio Ficino and the Language of the Past,' at pp. 47-8. On Plato's dialogue *Minos*, see Michael Davis, 'Plato's Minos: the Soul of the Law,' *The Review of Politics*, 78 (2016), pp. 343–63.

Minos was celebrated as the foundational lawgiver for Crete and after his death he was made a judge in the underworld by the gods. When he is described in this role in *Odyssey*, 11, 568-71, it is as 'glorious son of Zeus, with a golden sceptre in his hand'. In Proclus's *Platonic Theology,* VII, 46 (as translated by Thomas Taylor), Minos and his fellow judge Rhadamanthus are described as 'heroes illuminated by Jupiter, who raised themselves from generation to true being, and meddled with mortal concerns no further than absolute necessity required'.

Jupiter's cave is traditionally on Mount Dikte, or may be the cave on Mount Ida in Crete where Jupiter was born.

10 People had often mused on the fresh possibilities that might arise when Saturn and Jupiter were in conjunction in the heavens. In *Letters*, **6**, 41 Ficino expresses hope for a return to good government under the conjunction of 1484, which was predicted to occur on 25th November of that year. In fact, he timed the publication of his Plato translations to take advantage of such an auspicious time. For Cristoforo Landino's hope that the 1484 conjunction would bring a reform of society, see note 7 above.

11 Ficino presents these last three sentences as statements rather than rhetorical questions. But in the spirit of enquiry this letter engenders, and the court-room experience of its recipient, we feel justified in modifying the style. In *Laws* IV, 713, Plato discusses the nature of the earliest rulers of mankind as being of a superior race, i.e., demigods, a point elaborated further by Ficino in his commentary (Farndell, *When Philosophers Rule*, pp. 96-7). Behind Plato's description lies Hesiod's account of the successive Ages: Golden, Silver, Bronze and Iron (Hesiod, *Works and Days*, 109-20).

12 The real reference here again is to the poet Hesiod, *Works and Days*, 109-120. Plato is referring to him when he speaks of golden men in *Cratylus*, 398. See also *Republic*, III, 415A, though this relates to rulers rather than philosophers.

13 For the Stoics the soul (*psyche*) is that part of the all-pervading divine spirit present in each of us. We are thus parts of a greater whole and our soul is the divinity within us. The soul was perishable, because material, composed of a mixture of fire and air, but it survived death for a certain time. The Stoics differed, however, over how long. Some thought it would survive for only a short period. Cleanthes (300-232BC) who succeeded Zeno of Citium as the leader of the Stoic school held that all souls would survive to the great conflagration which closed the cosmic cycle, whereas his successor Chrysippus (280-204 BC) declared that only the souls of the wise would survive until then. It is to Chrysippus and his followers that Ficino probably refers in this passage.

14 Daniel 12:3, 'And they that be wise shall shine as the brightness of the firmament; and they that turn many to righteousness as the stars for ever and ever.'

15 The eighth heaven was the sphere of the Fixed Stars, and therefore would have a sense of fixity or '*firmamentum*'. According to medieval cosmology, heaven consisted of nine concentric spheres with the earth at the centre. The first seven spheres contained Moon, Mercury, Venus, Sun, Mars, Jupiter and Saturn respectively. The eighth contained the fixed stars, and the ninth was that of the prime mover. In Dante's *Paradiso* the eighth heaven is also the sphere of the Church triumphant, where Dante sees the Virgin Mary and is questioned by Saints Peter, James and John. Beyond the spheres is the Empyrean, the abode of God.

16 By 'homeland' Ficino is indicating the heavenly homeland he so often refers to.

17 Basel adds 'Farewell'.

4

1 Filippo Valori was appointed as Florentine ambassador to the newly-elected pope, Alexander VI (Roderigo Borgia). The pope was elected on 11th August, 1492 and the delegation set off from Florence on 7th November, 1492 (the date of this letter). Valori sent numerous dispatches from Rome between 1492 and 1494.

2 Matteo Franco was appointed a member of the delegation to Rome. The diary of the Florentine chronicler, Luca Landucci, records that it included Francesco Valori together with Piero di Lorenzo de' Medici, Pier Filippo Pandolfini, Tommaso Minerbetti and Gentile Becchi, Bishop of Arezzo. These would have been the senior delegates, with Matteo Franco in a supporting role. For further details on Francesco Valori, Tommaso Minerbetti and Matteo Franco, see Biographical Notes. Gentile Becchi and Pier Filippo Pandolfini were both distinguished representatives of Florentine interests, resident in Rome. (See Biographical Notes to volumes **5**, **8** and **9**.)

3 Around 1485, Ficino wrote to John of Hungary (*Letters*, **7**, 19, undated) that his constant interest in the restoration of ancient teachings was attributable to divine providence, not to Fate or the stars. He says there that Aquarius rising and the positions of the Sun and Mercury signify, but do not produce, a restorer of the ancient teaching. So Ficino's comments here may be read as a light-hearted engagement with astrological lore rather than a serious astrological explanation.

4 Ficino's first translations from Greek were in 1462. The ten dialogues comprised *Hipparchus*, *On Philosophy*, *Theages*, *Meno*, *Alcibiades* I and II, *Minos*, *Euthyphro*,

Parmenides and *Philebus*. Two copies of the list and argumenta survived, but only one copy of the first versions, which is in Bodleian MS Canonicanus lat. 163. See Kristeller, *Sup. Fic.*, II, pp. 103-105; Allen, *Marsilio Ficino: The Philebus Commentary*, pp. 3-7; Hankins, *Plato in the Italian Renaissance* (1990), 1, 308-9 and Valerio Sanzotta, 'Marsilio Ficino as a Commentator on Plato for Cosimo de' Medici'.

5 The translation of Plotinus with commentaries was complete by 1489 but published only in May 1492 (Florence: Miscomini). A single circuit of Saturn (one complete orbit around the Sun) is reckoned to be 29.46 years – the length of time that had elapsed since Ficino's earliest work on Plato. He published this new round of commentaries and summaries in December 1496 (Florence: Francesco da Veneto). It includes new material on *Parmenides*, the *Sophist*, *Timaeus*, *Phaedrus* and *Philebus*. Ficino discusses Saturn's role in establishing order for mankind in his commentary on Plato's *Laws*, IV (see tr. Farndell, pp. 96-7).

6 Lorenzo de' Medici (the Magnificent) died on 8th April, 1492. His son Piero succeeded him and Ficino's published works of this period, 1492-1493, carry dedications to Piero.

7 Matthew 16:18. 'Thou art Peter, and upon this rock I will build my Church.' In Greek and Latin Piero's name, *Petros* or *Petrus*, echoes the word for a rock (Latin *petra*, Tuscan *pietra*).

8 Bibbieni: the brothers Piero and Bernardo Dovizi (they were not twins) are here called the 'Bibbieni' after their birthplace Bibbiena, in the province of Arezzo, but it has been suggested, by Ornella Pompeo Faracovi (1999) that the name is also a play on the astronomical term for the bright fixed stars in any constellation, known in the works of the Arabic writer Abu-Bakr, as the *stellae Beibeniae*. Piero Dovizi become chancellor to Lorenzo and after the death of Lorenzo in 1492 he become very influential thanks to Lorenzo's successor Piero. His brother, Bernardo Dovizi, become a cardinal and close friend of one of Lorenzo's sons, Giovanni. There is a record of Piero Dovizi accompanying the Medici delegation on 7th November, 1492 and it seems, from this letter, that both brothers were in Rome at the same time.

9 The identification of this matter has remained obscure, but in *Letters*, **10**, 18 Ficino expressed thanks for a benefice, namely the Martiana church, to Giovanni de' Medici. In the will Ficino signed on 29th September, 1499, reference is made to the payment of two 'sextarium' measures (pints?) of grain to be paid to the churches of Santa Maria and Santa Lucia of Monte Marciano, 'as a pension' for Ficino's soul – presumably for masses to be said in his memory. Present-day place names referring to 'Marciano' include an isolated Monte Marciano in the province of Grosseto; a commune of Marciana on the Island of Elba (on the lower slopes of Monte Capanne); a Monte Marciano in the province of Ancona; a Monte Martano not far from Spoleto, in Umbria (province of Perugia). Most of these have churches to Santa Maria and Santa Lucia in or nearby. Otherwise, see notes to *Letters*, **10**, 18.

10 The Basel edition gives '1482', but this is obviously incorrect.

5

1 A close friend of Ficino's. See Biographical Notes.

2 The copy of earlier letters that Ficino says he has prepared for Carducci, identified as MS Mo2 (Bavarian State Library, Munich, Clm. 10781) has turned out to be a

highly important manuscript as it contains material not found elsewhere. The collection was sent, with this letter, to Carducci shortly after Luca Fabiani had finished writing it. At some point, letters sent by the Signoria between 1465 and 1469 (mostly composed by Bartolommeo Scala) on foreign affairs were added. The Ficino section of the manuscript consists of 100 folios; the Scala section adds a further 159 folios. From a private library in Italy it came to the library of the Electors of the Palatine in Mannheim and eventually to the royal library of Bavaria in Munich. It seems that Books I-VIII may also have been part of the same copying enterprise, since MS L28 is also in Fabiani's hand, and was completed a little earlier, on 19th October, 1490.

MS Mo2 contains the letters of Books IX-XII up to this point, where it stops. The additional items that are included in it but omitted from the printed edition of 1495 have been included in this translation series, generally as Appendix letters.

Since this letter is dated 14th November, 1492, an interested reader would be able to ascertain the exact position of the planets at the time. A basic assumption would be that Mercury and Saturn were conjunct and in the ascendant. Mercury is especially associated with speed and intelligence, communication and eloquence, Saturn with philosophy and wisdom. For a general account of Mercury in Ficino's thinking, see Susanne Beiweis and Lauri Ockenström, 'Memory, Mercury and Magic in Marsilio Ficino's *De Vita*', in *Rinascimento*, 2nd series, 59 (2019), pp. 271-96.

3 *Consideraretur*: in Latin, the word for 'consideration' allows Ficino to make a play on words between the usual meaning and the equally relevant *con* with *sidera* – suggesting the involvement of the stars.

4 Saturn, slow by nature, is nevertheless also concerned with intelligence, especially that inwardly directed intelligence that is called for in contemplation. See also note 7. As Ficino explains below, Saturn and Mercury follow the Sun in two different ways, one by remaining close, the other at a distance but in the same orbit.

5 Plato, *Republic*, X, 617A, where Saturn and Mercury are described as being like one another, with a yellower light than that of the Sun or the Moon.

6 The intelligence of the planet is distinct from its physical body. During the Middle Ages, and based on Aristotle's suggestions, there was a general belief that the movement of the celestial bodies was caused by intelligences or angels, with some variation on exactly how this process worked. See Edward Grant, *Planets, Stars and Orbs, the Medieval Cosmos, 1200-1687* (Cambridge: 1994, reprinted 1996), pp. 523-545.

7 In the *Platonic Theology*, Ficino says that both these planets through their nature 'gather our spirits round a centre' and 'they recall the mind's attention from alien matters to its own concerns, and bring it to rest in contemplation, and enable it to penetrate to the centres of things.' *Platonic Theology*, XIII, 2, 3.

8 Mercury is never more than 28° from the Sun. The ecliptic is the apparent path taken by the Sun through the sky, so called because eclipses happen only when the moon is on or near this line.

9 According to Ibn Ezra, some of the qualities attributed to these two planets overlap and are therefore strengthened when in favourable aspect to one another (Abraham ibn Ezra, *The Beginning of Wisdom*, ch. 4).

10 Often, for Ficino, Jupiter (Jove) represents the World Soul. But in the context of this letter it would seem to represent God, of whom the Sun is an image. Ficino's use of astronomical terms is not rigidly bound and allows for playful associations.

11 MS Mo2 adds 'Florence'.

6

1 This letter was appended to the published version of Ficino's *De sole et lumine*. For the publication of that work, see Letter 2, note 1.

2 St Matthew 5:15; St Mark 4:21; St Luke 8:16.

3 *Letters*, **6**, 36 and **7**, Appendix B. See also **2**, 55 where *candidissimo* was translated as 'of the greatest radiance'. There is a deliberate play in all these cases between *candidissimo*, literally 'whitest', and Piero's surname Nero, 'black'.

4 In the preface to *De sole et lumine*, dedicated to Piero de' Medici, and in the first chapter, again mentioning Piero, Ficino stresses the nature of the work as the exposition of a mystery.

5 Ficino is expecting some opposition to this work from conservative theologians.

6 Boethius, *Consolation of Philosophy*, IV, 7, 34–5. Previously quoted by Ficino in his letter to Pier Leone of Spoleto, *Letters*, **9**, 45.

7 As in the call to defend his *Three books on Life* (*Letters*, **7**, Appendix B), Ficino identifies his three friends with three great defenders from the classical world. Hercules was noted for his courage, strength and the performance of twelve immense labours; after his death he was admitted to the realm of the gods. Phoebus denotes Apollo the Sun god. Amphion and his twin brother Zethos constructed the walls of Thebes: while Zethos laboured arduously carrying the stones, Amphion played his lyre and the stones followed him, gently gliding into place, a story generally taken to signify not only the power of music but also the importance of eloquent speech.

8 The 1503 edition of *De sole* replaces this date with 11th January, but for no apparent reason, except perhaps a misreading of a Roman ii.

7

1 Ficino calls Martin *Germanus*, which, besides indicating a German, means a full brother, as opposed to a half-brother, or it may suggest someone genuine, real or true. A twin would be *geminus*, as in the title.

2 For the similarity of their light, see Plato, *Republic*, X, 617A. It is described as less white (more yellow) than that of the Sun, Moon, Jupiter or Venus.

3 In some versions of her myth, Venus is said to be born from the seed of Saturn (Kronos), the father of Jove; she would therefore be Jupiter's sister.

4 Phoebus and Phoebe, also called Apollo and Diana, were the twin children of Leda and Zeus (Jupiter).

5 Mars, the red planet and god of war, did have a partner in Roman mythology: Nerio, the Sabine personification of valour. However, she is rarely referred to and much better known is his dalliance with Venus, a popular subject in poetry and painting.

6 Nicholas Oresme (14th century, France) and Albert of Saxony (14th century, Paris and Germany) both supported the view of Macrobius (fl. 400 AD, Rome) and Avicenna (10th century, Persia) that the planets and stars were mildly self-luminous, quite apart from the light they received and reflected from the Sun. Followers of Aristotle and Averroes maintained that the Sun was the sole source of light. The debate between these two views was never fully settled.

7 The Durham copy of Venice, with alterations in the hand of Ficino Ficini, corrects the printed word *aeternus* to *aeterius* (often spelt *aetherius*), meaning 'of the upper air', and also a title of Jupiter.

8 Besides being brother and sister, children of Saturn and Ops, Jupiter and Juno were husband and wife. Jupiter ruled over the upper air (*aether*) and Juno governed the lower, denser air (*aer*), closer to earth.

9 Ficino previously mentioned a double sun in *Letters*, **5**, 49. The phenomenon of a double sun, parhelion, or sometimes even a triple sun (also known as the Sun with sundogs) is an optical illusion caused by sunlight passing through hexagonal ice crystals that may be contained within cirrus cloud. A contemporary illustration appears in the Nuremberg chronicle of 1493. Appearances in ancient times were discussed by Aristotle, Aratus, Cicero and Seneca. There was a recent sighting, recorded photographically, in 2011.

10 The volume of Ficino's Platonic Commentaries was eventually published in 1496, See Letter 4, note 5.

11 A reference to the twin volume, *De sole et lumine*. *De sole*, written originally for Count Eberhard of Württemberg, was dedicated afterwards to Piero. See Letters **6**, 7 and 19 and Appendix B. *De lumine* was an expansion of the letter addressed to Febo Capella in 1476-1477, *Quid sit lumen*, included in the second book of his letters which consists of short treatises and will be added to this translation series as a final volume. See also *Letters*, **3**, 10.

12 Plato, *Epistle* VII, 341D (and cf. *Symposium*, 210E for the suddenness of mystic vision). Ficino expands on the meaning of this passage in a most helpful way in his commentaries: on Plato's Seventh letter, see *Opera*, p. 1534-5, translated in A. D. Farndell, *Gardens of Philosophy*, pp. 169-70. See also *Platonic Theology* VIII, iii, 5; XII, i, 10; XIV, x, 12 and in Ficino's Dionysius commentaries, the longer letter of dedication to Giovanni de' Medici (*Marsilio Ficino On Dionysius the Areopagite*, tr. by Michael J.B. Allen, 2 vols., (The I Tatti Renaissance Library, Cambridge MA, 2015), I, pp. 440-3 as well as towards the very end, in ch. 349.4 of the *Divine Names*, ibid. II, p. 403.

8

1 Two possible candidates meet the requirements for consideration as 'Lorenzo, high priest of the Laurentian temple'. The more likely of the two is Lorenzo Guiducci, Prior of San Lorenzo from 1482 until his death in 1496. The Basilica of San Lorenzo was one of the principal churches of Florence, and was particularly associated with the Medici, whose town house lay within its parish boundaries. Its foundation dates back to the fourth century, and later served for some centuries as the city's earlier cathedral. Under the patronage of Cosimo de' Medici it was rebuilt and became the Medici family's church. Medici family members are buried there. In the 1520s, under Duke Cosimo I, further additions to the complex of buildings were designed by Michelangelo, including the famous Laurentian Library. Guiducci wrote a short work (*Opusculum*) in 1482, on God, Angels, the Soul and eternal happiness; he was also interested in astronomy and mathematics, transcribing at least one work of the 10th-century Arab astronomer Alcabitius in 1460.

The second 'Lorenzo' is Guido di Lorenzo, Prior of the Camaldolese Convent of Santa Maria degli Angeli, which supported philosophical study and was also under Lorenzo de' Medici's personal patronage. Guido himself had been appointed by Lorenzo (see Biographical Notes) and was his close friend and his personal confessor.
Lorenzo Guiducci, however, is the more likely, because of his specific interest in the heavenly bodies and because the church of San Lorenzo is more properly called 'Laurentian'.

2 This small work was composed of expanded versions of two earlier works: *De sole*, first written for Count Eberhard in 1492 and *Quid sit lumen*, written for Febo Capella in late 1476. It was published in 1493. See Letter 2, note 1 and Introductory Note to Appendix B.

3 In Ficino's birth chart, of which there are two versions, Jupiter occupies the central portion of Leo. See *Letters*, **8**, 18 and a diagram of his birth chart in *Letters*, **5**, p. 122. Wisdom, connected with the ninth house, is traditionally associated with Jupiter and his daughter, Athena, the goddess of wisdom who was born from his head, but Saturn also denotes a kind of wisdom: see Letter 5, notes 4 and 7. The *pars sapientiae* is an Arabic term for the fifth part of the ninth house. Such terms had been explained by Guido Bonatti, in his *De astronomia tractatus*, written in the thirteenth century. In chapter 12 of that work the *pars sapientiae* is described as having characteristics of Saturn (stability, philosophy, profundity), Jupiter (wisdom, patience, reason) and Mercury (writings, experiments, wisdom).

4 The ninth house as a whole is associated with wisdom, religion and travel to distant parts. When in the ninth house, the Sun is said to be 'exalted' (i.e. its effects are magnified). The planetary positions given here accord with Ficino's horoscope as described in *Letters*, **7**, 19 and **8**, 18 as printed in the Venice edition, and shown in **5**, p.122. In another version of his horoscope, given in *Letters*, **2**, 24 and the manuscript Mo2 for **8**, 18, Jupiter is said to be in Cancer, not Leo. However, the Sun is in all cases in the ninth house and in the zodiacal sign of Scorpio. It is not known how or why Ficino came to have two slightly different versions of his natal chart.

5 By this rather unusual remark, Ficino may be suggesting that the knowledge to be gained from this work was received directly from the source rather than being reflected knowledge.

6 All printed editions of this letter agree on 1493 (there is no manuscript). By this twelfth book of his Letters, Ficino appears to have abandoned Florentine dating, in which the new year started on Lady Day (March 25th), a system which gave all dates from January 1st up to Lady Day the number of the year which had already ended on the previous December 31st according to the system we use nowadays.

9

1 See Biographical Notes under Giuliano of Istria.

2 *De amore,* II, 8 has a full discussion of reciprocal love. See also *Letters*, **1**, 129; **4**, 25 and passim. The proverb comes from Seneca's *Epistle* 9, where he attributes the saying to Hecato of Rhodes. Hecato was a Stoic philosopher who is known today only from references in Cicero and Seneca.

3 Apollo was famed as an archer, as shown in the ancient sculpture known as the Apollo Belvedere, rediscovered in 1489. Amongst his epithets were *ekebolos* (far-

shooting) and *arcitenens* (holding the bow). At the beginning of Homer's *Iliad*, he unleashes a stream of arrows on the Greek troops before Troy (*Iliad,* I, 33-53); for his slaying of the Python at Delphi, see Ovid, *Metamorphoses*, I, 441-4. Cupid is always portrayed with a bow and arrows which inflame desire in those he shoots. Ovid describes the rivalry between Apollo and Cupid as archers in *Metamorphoses*, I, 453-73.

4 Ficino's actual words here are *veris amoribus*, 'the true loves'. Traditionally, from earliest times, the seraphim are associated with love and the cherubim with knowledge. See Dionysius, *Celestial Hierarchy*, VI, 2, echoed in Aquinas, *Summa contra gentiles*, III, 80; *Summa theologica*, Q108, art. 4, obj.2 and art.6; and in Dante, *Divine Comedy: Paradise*, 98-102. By the Renaissance, cherubim had also become identified with the winged figures representing love in the ancient world (of which Cupid is an example). For a full discussion, see Valery Rees, *From Gabriel to Lucifer: A Cultural History of Angels*, London, 2013, chapters 5 and 6.

5 On the fire of love, cf. *Letters*, **7**, 55 and 56. On reciprocal love, see *Letters*, **1**, 129 and *De amore*, II, 8.

6 Ficino had hoped, with Lorenzo's support, to publish a revised edition of his Plato translations together with all his commentaries, but the luxury edition intended was never produced. See *Letters*, **10**, 13; also Kristeller, *Sup. Fic.*, I, cxviii and clv; James Hankins, *Plato in the Italian Renaissance*, Leiden, 1990, p. 301. In the event, the translations were reprinted in 1491 together with the *Platonic Theology*, but the commentaries appeared only in December 1496, published in Florence by Lorenzo Veneto.

7 Giuliano had been invited to preach at Santa Maria degli Angeli, the church of the Camaldolese Order in Florence in February 1493. The exact date is unknown, but we can presume it was shortly before this letter was written. This letter confirms that philosophical discussions were still taking place in the church alongside its more regular activities, despite the unease of their inspector, Pietro Delfin (see *Letters*, **7**, 53).

8 Ficino's *De Sole et lumine* was published in Florence by Antonio Miscomini on 31st January, 1493. For the earliest version of *De sole*, see Appendix B. For the full text of both works, see *Opera*, pp. 965-986.

9 This letter has not followed the Florentine dating system, but must be 1493, as shown in the Venice edition, because of the precise reference to the Plotinus printing.

10

1 Mazzingo was Ficino's own physician. See Biographical Notes. The term *phisicus* may also imply a 'man of science'. In Letter 11, another physician who had cared for him, Giorgio Ciprio, is described as *medicus* rather than *phisicus*. The two terms are probably interchangeable, but in the present letter Ficino is using the astronomers as his authority; in Letter 11 his authority is Phoebus, god of the healing arts.

2 Ficino uses the term *plaga* here, to indicate a portion of the heavens, even though it is not the astronomical term one might expect. Exaltation of the Moon is always in Taurus, and so the ascendant at this time must be Pisces. The third house in an astrological chart is traditionally associated with short journeys.

3 Although Ficino is speaking of regions of the heavens (*plagae*) he seems to have in mind the ninth house (*domus*), which is associated with long journeys. When Pisces is the ascendant, the ninth house is Scorpio, which is ruled by Mars, friend of the

Sun. If the Sun is there, its influence is powerful, especially upon anything governed by the ninth house.

4 Loreto was a popular pilgrimage site in the Marche. In 1469, a large basilica was constructed over the Holy House, a structure which was said to have been the actual home of the holy family in Nazareth, miraculously transported first to Croatia in 1291, then moved, again by angels, to Recanati, and in 1294 finally transferred to Loreto, nearby.

11

1 George of Cyprus or Giorgio Ciprio is called *medicus*, whereas Mazzingo in the previous letter was called *phisicus*, though both were physicians. George was currently physician to Giovanni de' Medici, who had been quite ill in 1491, though George had cared for Ficino and his mother over a long period.

2 On *De sole et lumine*, see Letter 9.

3 Virgil, *Georgics*, I, 463-4.

12

1 Apollo and Bacchus are both sons of Jupiter, though by different mothers. In *De vita*, II, 20 Ficino quotes a verse from the poet Tibullus: 'Phoebus and Bacchus alone have youth eternal, For uncut hair befits both gods.' He says they are inseparable brothers and practically identical, with Phoebus as the celestial sphere of the Sun and Bacchus as the Sun itself. They each have three gifts for humankind to preserve youth: Bacchus gives sunny hills, sweet wine and freedom from care; Phoebus gives sunlight, aromatic herbs and songs for the lyre.

In this letter Bacchus also refers to Baccio. Phoebus or Apollo – often a nickname for Pico, in Ficino's circle – here refers to Ficino himself, with his book on the Sun.

2 *Liber* is another name for Bacchus, referring to the freedom from care brought by wine, or perhaps to an early myth that he liberated certain cities. *Liber* is also 'a book', adding another nuance to this playful covering letter.

13

1 Auspices indicate the influences favouring the beginning of an enterprise. The term comes from the ancient Roman priestly practice of observing the chirping or flight of birds (*avis* + *spicio*) for signs of the future. The term soon lost that specific meaning and stands for the favouring influences themselves.

2 Niccolò was studying with Ficino by the time Ficino wrote his letter to Prenninger listing his friends (*Letters*, **10**, 28), which he placed into the volume between letters dated 22nd July and 3rd August, 1492. It would appear from what follows that Niccolò began his study of philosophy early in 1492. See note 4.

3 When Mercury and Saturn are in conjunction, those aspects of their influence that are in concordance with each other are strengthened. Saturn was associated with discipline, contemplation and serious study; Mercury was linked with eloquence

and intelligence. In Aquarius, Saturn is the natural ruler and therefore especially powerful. Such a conjunction would not occur frequently, as Saturn's cycle is long, taking 29 years to complete one orbit.

4 In 1492, Mercury entered Aquarius on 20th January and was conjunct with Saturn on 27th January. So perhaps this allows us to date the beginning of Niccolò's studies. He would have been 27 years old. This was also the year in which Ficino began his book on the Sun in its first form for Duke Eberhard. The complete work on the Sun and Light (*De sole et lumine*) was published on 31st January, 1493.

5 Orpheus held the Sun to be greater than his brother Dionysus (Bacchus). In one version of the tale, Bacchus, enraged, sent the Bassaridae to pursue him and cut him to pieces. The Muses gathered up the fragments of his body and buried them on sacred ground. In the more familiar version of the story, Orpheus is attacked by the Bacchantes (followers of Bacchus) after entering the underworld to try to save Eurydice.
For Niccolò, beginning with Apollo would mean beginning his studies with Ficino's *De sole* rather than with the arts, which are associated with the Muses (even though they are led by Apollo).

6 *Aquilinis oculis*, 'with the eyes of an eagle'. The eagle was noted as the only creature able to look steadily at the sun without blinking. Pliny, *Natural History*, X, iii, 9 relates that the great sea-eagle raised only those chicks who were able to do so, throwing any others out of the nest.

7 Ficino discusses the supercelestial Sun beyond the sun we see in the sky. See Letter 2 above, which became ch. 13 of *De sole*.

8 The Moon shines only with the reflected light of the Sun. Knowledge obtained through its light is therefore less than the full and direct knowledge obtainable through the light of the Sun. See Plato's Cave allegory, *Republic*, VII, 514-7, expounded in Ficino's commentary and also in *Letters*, **3**, 26; **5**, 48 and *Platonic theology*, VI, ii, 14-15. He also refers to it in *Letters*, **1**, 51.

9 Niccolò was still studying daily with Ficino in June 1493 (see Letter 15) and remained close to him for the rest of Ficino's life. See Biographical Notes.

14

1 Diacceto is named during the discussion of beauty in Ficino's commentary on Plato's *Parmenides*, ch. 84 (tr. Farndell, p. 165), a topic on which Diacceto later wrote. His *De pulchro* was written between 1496 and 1499, although not published until 1514. For a modern edition, see Sylvain Matton, *Francisci Catanei Diacetii: De pulchro libri III* (Pisa: Scuola Normale, 1986).

2 Reading '*nisi*' with Durham correction and Basel edition of 1576. Venice 1495 has *visi*.

3 For a short account of the steps in Platonic training, see *Letters*, I, 123. In his Commentary to Plato, *Republic*, VII, *Opera*, p. 1412 (*When Philosophers Rule*, pp. 39-40), Ficino lists the programme of study that should be followed by anyone hoping to achieve insight into the deeper matters discussed by Plato, especially those concerning the divine. These start with the traditional studies of the Aristotelian path, such as arithmetic, geometry, astronomy, music, natural sciences, and progress to dialectic when discussing metaphysics or theology. See also his *Epinomis* (*Opera*, 1526-7; *When Philosophers Rule*, pp. 162-3).

4 Ficino uses the word *symbola* here, which has Pythagorean overtones.

5 Reading *philosophis sapientibusque* with Basel edition of 1576. Venice 1495 has *septisque*, presumably for *sectisque*.

6 Ficino, *In Plotinum*, commentary on *Enneads*, V, 3, x-xii and V, 9 (*Opera*, pp. 1760-61 and 1771).

7 Proclus, *In Parmenidem*, II, 730-732 and III, 814-836. See also Ficino's commentary on *Parmenides*, ch. 5 (ed. Van Haelen, pp. 50-55; tr. Farndell, *Evermore Shall Be So*, pp. 12-13) and Plato, *Parmenides*, 128-130.

8 Plato, *Timaeus*, 29A.

9 Plato, *Timaeus*, 29AB.

10 Plato, *Timaeus*, 42D. The Venice edition of 1495 has *iuniores;* The Basel edition of 1576 has *seniores*. For consistency with Plato, *iuniores* is clearly to be preferred.

11 Plato, *Timaeus*, 42E-43A. See also 41B-D.

15

1 Filippo Valori was ambassador to Rome in 1492-3, and Ficino asked him to defend his *De sole* there against accusations of heterodoxy. See Letter 6 above. For the long-standing relationship between Ficino and Valori, see Biographical Notes.

2 It is just over six months since Ficino last wrote to Filippo (Letter 6).

3 We follow the reading of the contraction *offô* by Nuremberg (1497) and Basel (1576) as *officio*. An alternative reading *offenso* would yield 'make amends for my offence.'

4 The Venice edition has '1493'; the Basel edition has '1494' but Valori's embassy to Rome was completed in 1493. Valori died on 25th November, 1494, while on an embassy to Naples.

16

1 Ficino's choice of words here, *calore . . . calderinum . . . calefaciendum*, plays on the fact that all three words are related to heat. Ficino is sending his old friend, still in Rome, a copy of the new book.

17

1 Sogliano was a fortress town within the territory of Rimini, ruled by the Malatesta family from 1295 to 1500. Sogliano is on the river Rubicon some miles inland from the coast. The Malatesta family provided several *condottieri* (mercenary captains) during the 14th and 15th centuries. On Ramberto, see Biographical Notes.

2 Plato, *Phaedrus*, 250D, also picked up in Ficino's *Phaedrus* commentary, I, 17 and II, 29.

3 On the light of wisdom, see Ficino, *Phaedrus* commentary, II, 9, 2-3. Ficino also discusses light extensively in his Commentary on Book VII of Plato's *Republic* (the Cave Allegory, *Republic*, 514A–520A), and in his Orphic Comparison of the Sun to God (*Letters*, **5**, 27).

4 For the view that the eyes possess light which they emit in order for vision to take place, see discussions in *De amore*, VII, 4 and Commentary on the *Timaeus*, 30.

5 On fire as the superior element, associated with wisdom, cf. St Matthew 3:11-12.

6 'The heavens' is used here in the limited sense of the heavenly bodies, i.e. what we would call the solar system.

7 The Sun is exalted in the ninth house, the house of wisdom. See Letter 8 above.

8 In *De vita*, III, 24 Ficino speaks of men of learning being primarily Mercurial and Solar – combining the qualities of both. On the qualities of Mercury that derive from his staying close to the Sun, see *Letters*, **9**, 42.

9 See also Letter 19.

10 This refers to the mythical golden age: see Hesiod, *Works and Days*, 106-120, Virgil, *Eclogues*, IV, 4-63, Ovid, *Metamorphoses*, I, 88-112.

11 Plato, *Republic*, V, 473DE, VI, 501E and VII, 540A-C. This is not the first time Ficino has looked for a 'philosopher-king' in the political world around him: see, for example, letters addressed to Matthias Corvinus, King of Hungary (*Letters*, **2**, Preface) and to Federico da Montefeltro, the Duke of Urbino, *Epistolae*, II, Preface and *Letters*, **6**, 22.

12 Cf. Virgil, *Aeneid*, IV, 100.

13 According to Diogenes Laertius, the saying that 'friends have all things in common' is ascribed to Pythagoras by Timaeus of Locri (*Lives of Eminent Philosophers*, VIII, 10). Timaeus is presented as a member of a Pythagorean school in Calabria in Plato's dialogues *Timaeus* and *Critias*. Some have doubted his real existence as he is not mentioned elsewhere, beyond Plato's writings, but other characters in Plato's dialogue have been shown to be historic personages, so it is reasonable to suppose that Timaeus was too, and would have lived around the 5th century BC. The saying is also commonly quoted from the much later writings of Seneca, in the 1st century AD: *Epistles*, 6.

18

1 See note 1 to Letter 17.

2 Jupiter was especially associated with friendship and hospitality in the ancient world. In *Letters*, **1**, 51, Ficino ascribes that role to God, but equates Jupiter with God in this context. For *Jupiter amicalis* (Jupiter the friendly), see Letter 29 below. Ficino's views on friendship are expressed in many places, but see especially *Letters*, **3**, 32 and **5**, Appendix.

3 For this myth, see *Homeric Hymns*, 28; *Orphic Hymns*, 32; Hesiod, *Theogony*, lines 886-929. Ficino also referred to the myth of Minerva's birth in *Letters*, **6**, 12.

4 Amongst Mercury's many attributes was his role as messenger of the gods, expressed visually in his winged helmet and sandals. Mercury was also seen as fastest moving of the planets. See also Beiweis and Ockenström, 'Memory, Mercury and Magic', cited in Letter 5, note 2.

5 On Pietro Martelli, see Biographical Notes.

19

1 On Ficino's *De sole et lumine*, see note 1 to Letter 2 and Appendix B. More than half the letters in this volume are related in some way to *De sole et lumine*.
Francesco Soderini was a close kinsman of Piero. Francesco's mother, Dianora Tornabuoni (1422-1462) was the elder sister of Piero de Medici's grandmother, Lucrezia Tornabuoni (1427-1482).

2 Ficino speaks frequently of the Medici and Valori families as his patrons, less often of Soderini. However, patronage within the Church was equally important to him. Previous letters to Francesco Soderini, Bishop of Volterra, include expressions of thanks for help and support given. See *Letters*, **9**, 20, 31; **10**, 16, 19. Their friendship, however, can be traced in letters in much earlier volumes (*Letters*, **1**, 127; **4**, 29; **5**, 36, 40).

3 From early in his career, Ficino had been interested in how these three qualities were manifested in the creation. In his *Di Dio et Anima* of 1457 or 1458, he noted that Hermes, Plato and Homer all thought that 'the divine mind, as substance and presence, is above the first heaven, but as goodness, consciousness and power, it is throughout the universe' (Kristeller, *Sup. Fic.*, II, p. 132). He also observed, as Lactantius (3rd-4th century AD) had done before him (*Epitome* of the *Divine Institutes*, 42), that Hermes, in *Asclepius*, 8, describes the making of a second God, before the creation of the world, who is the word of God and wisdom and full of goodness. Others linked power with the Father, wisdom with the Son and goodness with the Holy Spirit. The triad of qualities, power-wisdom-goodness, was a topic of heated debate among Christian theologians from Abelard and Hugh of St Victor to Aquinas, especially in respect of how it might be applied to the Trinity. As a formula, it was of course much older, and relates to statements in St Augustine and the Church Fathers, but Ficino here seems not to be engaging in that debate, but referring mainly to the Platonic and Proclan view as a basis for the discussion that follows. Aquinas treats power, wisdom and goodness as names of God in *Summa contra gentiles*, I, 30; see also Augustine, *City of God,* XI, 24; Marcia Colish, *Peter Lombard* (Leiden: Brill, 1994), ch. 3.

More recently, Ficino's translation of extracts from Proclus's commentary on Plato's *Republic* offered new emphasis on these three qualities. See *Letters*, **10**, 29, especially the opening paragraph. The source text in Plato is *Republic*, II 379-82, where the primary qualities of a god appear to be goodness, immutability and truth. In *Laws*, X, 900-902, the primary qualities are knowledge, power and goodness. Proclus manages to unite the two statements, and Ficino also adds a reference to Proclus's *Elements of Theology* where the three main attributes of a god are given as goodness, power and knowledge (Proclus, *Elements,* propositions 119 and 121; Ficino, *Letters*, **10**, 29, p. 36).

4 These points are discussed in more detail in chapter 9 of *De sole*. See Appendix B.

20

1 This preface was written at the end of 1494 to serve as a preface for the first printed edition of Ficino's collection of letters (*Epistolae,* Venice, 1495) where it occupies a highly decorative frontispiece page; it also appears in its proper chronological place here in the twelfth volume. No manuscript copy is extant.

2 *Amicissimo vestro*: your dearest friend. A variant here is *amicissimo nostro Hieronymo*, 'our dearest friend Girolamo', but this appears in the Basel *Opera omnia* (not in a manuscript as indicated in the first edition of our volume 1). It was nevertheless translated as 'our' in our revised volume 1, because by implication he is Ficino's dearest friend too. Even in the Basel edition, the version '*nostro*' appears only at Book XII, 20, not in the Preface, which follows the more common *vestro*. Sebastiano

Gentile's critical edition of Book I showing this letter as a Preface (Gentile, *Lettere* I, p. 3) makes no mention of a variant. No manuscript copy of this letter is known.

3 The classical form of the name invokes Roscius Amerinus. See note 1 to the Preface letter in this volume.

4 '*charitate haereditaria*': this suggests that Rossi was a descendant of Roscius Amerinus, inheriting the qualities of filial devotion Cicero famously ascribed to him; it also suggests that the letters, as children, inherit the love already shown to their father, Ficino. The role envisaged for Rossi was to ensure a future for Ficino's letters, and to act as Ficino's representative in Venice in matters relating to the publication of these and perhaps other works.

5 In the Venice edition, although the date given for this letter in the twelfth book is 15th December, 1493, it is shown as 15th December, 1494 when used as a preface. The latter date is thought to be correct. There is no manuscript version available for this letter.

21

1 St Matthew 2:11. See Ficino's sermon, *On the Star of the Magi*, translated as an Appendix to *Letters,* **6**, pp. 60-65 (*Opera*, pp. 489-91. See the critical edition of Daniele Conti, *Marsilii Ficini Florentini Praedicationes*, Turin, 2014, pp. 61-68 and his introductory material on pp. cvii-cxxx). Epiphany, on 6th January, is the feast celebrating this occasion.

2 St Matthew 4:13-16. In the Anglican and Lutheran Churches the baptism of Christ is celebrated on the Sunday after Epiphany, but in the Catholic Church it is celebrated at Epiphany.

3 St John 2:1-11. The marriage at Cana was also celebrated at Epiphany. These three events were all held in the Catholic Church to mark moments of the revelation of glory (which is the meaning of *epiphania*).

22

1 Until 1955, the Latin Church celebrated Epiphany as an eight-day feast, known as the Octave of Epiphany, beginning on 6th January and ending on 13th January.

2 St John 2:1-11.

3 St John 2:11.

4 St John 2:10.

5 See Ficino, *De vita*, II, 7, lines 62-66, quoting Galen.

6 See Letter 12, note 1 for Bacchus and Apollo as brothers. Both Bacchus (Dionysus) and Phoebus Apollo were honoured in rituals at sacred sites such as Delphi.

7 Galen of Pergamon (130-216 AD): one of the leading Greek physicians of the ancient world. Mazzingo's letter appears not to have survived.

8 Although Venice and Basel both show 1493, from its place in the sequence of letters this letter would seem to belong to January 1494. Two methods of counting the months between Christmas and Lady Day were still in use in Florence at the time, which may account for the apparent discrepancy. The later date is confirmed by the mention of Ficino's age, and was also adopted by Figliucci's translation of 1548.

23

1 We have taken *immortale* as an ablative, on the authority of Ciceronian usage (the more usual ablative form would be *immortali*).

2 Ficino gives the date as the 15th day before the Kalends of February, which by traditional inclusive counting is 18th January. However, the letter is dated 17th January, so the dream described and the subsequent meeting may have have happened a year before the writing of this letter, the only letter we have from Ficino to Johannes.

3 See Biographical Notes. Johannes served the Archbishop as chancellor for many years.

4 It is not clear to which printing of the *De vita* this letter may be referring, or indeed whether the edition envisaged was ever printed. It may be that Johannes was instrumental in arranging one of the early editions listed below, without his name appearing on it, or it may be that he never fulfilled his promise. Kristeller inclined to the latter view: see *Sup. Fic.*, I, p. LXXXV and *Marsilio Ficino and his Work after 500 years*, p. 116.

If he had not yet fulfilled his promise, then the dating of the letter one (or more) year(s) to the day later than the dream and the events in the letter would act as a reminder to Menchen to fulfil his promise. That would explain the *Pro* in the title – Ficino is pleading on behalf of the reprinting of *De vita*, which would not be necessary if it had already taken place, and reminding Menchen of the 'immortal sign of friendship', rather than the 'sign of immortal friendship' to which he refers in the body of the letter. It would also explain the closing phrase that their immortal friendship would be published to the world and posterity through the second printing.

Editions of *De vita* that did follow after the first printing of 1489 (by Antonio Miscomini in Florence) include:

i. Paris, printed by Georg Wolf and Johannes Philippi, undated but either 1494 (according to GW 9884) or 1492-6 (according to J R Clark); thought to have been instigated by the French theologian and humanist Jacques Lefèvre d'Étaples.
ii. Venice, 1498. No names are shown on copies of this edition, but associated with it have been the names of Bartholomaeus Pelusius, Gabriel Bracius, Johannes Bissolus and Benedictus Mangius.
iii. Basel, printed by Johannes Amerbach, undated, but ascribed to 1489-95 (according to GW 9883) or 1497 (according to GW 9885). There is no information to suggest Menchen's involvement with this edition.
iv. Bologna, 1501, printed by Benedictus Hectoris.
v. Venice, 1503, printed by Bernardino dei Vitali. According to its title page, this is a composite work containing *De sole*, *De christiana religione*, *De vita*, and an *Apologia* on Magic, but extant copies we have seen contain only *De sole*.

Many more editions followed, in France, Italy and Germany, and translations too, from 1505.

24

1 The Abbey of San Salvatore at Settimo was originally a Benedictine monastery founded in the 10th century by Lothar of Cadolo. Its location at the seventh staging post or milestone outside of Florence (in what is now Scandicci, south west of the

city) gave it the name Settimo. The Cluniac order obtained control in the 11th century and attracted such rich endowments that in 1048 the title of count was conferred on the abbot. During this period the monastery was deeply influenced by the Vallombrosan reforms of St John Gualberto. On 12th February, 1068, the Vallombrosan monk Peter Aldobrandini here sustained a famous ordeal by fire to defend the abbot from charges of simony. He passed unharmed through the flames. By 1236, the Abbey had become a Cistercian house. Its position, at the junction of major road and river routes, gave it strategic importance and it grew in size and significance. Its impressive buildings, in ruins since the late eighteenth century, are currently undergoing restoration. During the fifteenth century, the monks of the abbey played a leading part in the financial administration of the city and the city also contributed to its upkeep, especially after the floods of 1487 and 1488. It is not clear what problems were the cause for Ficino's intervention at this time, but Soderini, as Apostolic Secretary and *referendarius* in Rome, had become a central figure in the network of Florentine contacts and was well placed to pass on requests to the papal courts.

2 It has not been possible so far to identify the monk named here.

25

1 Dominican Professor of Theology: among the Dominicans in Florence at this time were several outstanding theologians and preachers, amongst whom were Giovanni Caroli and Vincenzo Bandello (see Biographical Notes). However, it is not possible to be sure who this 'holy friar' might be. It must, however, be someone who has come from Rondoni, who was probably in Rome.

2 Plato, *Laws*, VIII, 837A-C; *Gorgias*, 508A.

3 In his commentary on Plato's sixth Letter, Ficino discusses how close Plato's formulations appear to come to the idea of a Father, a Son and a Holy Spirit. He does, however, point out there that it would be a heretical, Arian view. (Translated in Farndell, *Gardens of Philosophy*, pp. 163-4).

4 Numenius, Plotinus and Amelius are mentioned by Eusebius in his *Praeparatio evangelica* as being close to Trinitarian doctrines (XI, 16-19). Numenius of Apamea was a Pythagorean/Platonic philosopher of the second century AD, who sought out the harmonies between religion and philosophy, calling Plato a 'Moses speaking in the Attic tongue'; most of his writings are lost. Ammonius Saccas (175-242) is best known as the teacher of Plotinus and Longinus in Alexandria; Plotinus (205-270) studied with Ammonius, then taught in Rome. He is considered the founder of Neoplatonism; his interpretation of Plato was more easily reconciled with Christian thought than was Plato himself. Amelius (3rd century) was born in Tuscany, studied with Numenius in Rome, and then became Plotinus's first pupil. He praised the opening of St John's gospel, noting its likeness to Plato's teachings on the *logos*. Iamblichus (d. c.325) and Proclus (412–485 AD) also figure in the list of non-Christian philosophers Ficino gives in *De christiana religione*, XI, of philosophers who studied Christian teachings to emulate them rather than to criticise (*Opera*, p. 17). Cf. *Platonic Theology*, II, iii, 5. While these philosophers might indeed have come upon the Gospel of St John, as St Basil and St Augustine had maintained (St Basil, *Homily*, XVI, on St John 1:1; St Augustine, *City of God*, X, 29) and Eusebius confirmed (*Preparation for the Gospel*, XI, 18-19), they could not have read Dionysius, who lived much later than he indicates in

his works. Ficino and his contemporaries were unaware that he was, in all likelihood, a Syrian monophysite monk of the 6th century, a follower, not a precursor of Proclus. See also *Letters*, **10**, 3. Ficino discusses the likely transmission of ideas from St John, St Paul, Hierotheus and Dionysius in *De christiana religione*, XXII (*Opera*, p. 25). For a full discussion of this letter, see M.J.B. Allen, 'Marsilio Ficino on Plato, the Neoplatonists and the Christian doctrine of the Trinity,' *Renaissance Quarterly*, 37 (1984) pp. 555-84, reprinted in *Plato's Third Eye*, 1995, item IX.

5 St Augustine, *Confessions*, VII, 9.

6 Ficino, *Letters*, **7**, 7.

26

1 See Biographical Note on Filippo Buonaccorsi, still living in Poland at this time. Ficino's earlier correspondence with Callimachus is in *Letters*, **7**.

2 To follow the ideas of Plato's followers on the soul as conveying life, a good place to start is Plotinus, *Enneads*, V, i, 2, which was quoted in part by Eusebius in *Praeparatio Evangelica*, XI, 17. See also Proclus, *Elements of Theology*, propositions 188 and 189. Proclus is mentioned in the commentary on *Timaeus*, 41D (Division 25), *All Things Natural*, pp. 121-4.

3 See Proclus, *Commentary on Parmenides*, VII, 1155-1169 (pp. 510-520 in tr. Morrow and Dillon).

4 Ficino discusses the motion of the heavenly bodies in his *Platonic Theology*, IV, i, 17-24 and *Timaeus* commentary, *Distinctiones et summae*, 22, (tr. Farndell, *All Things Natural*, p. 116-7); in section 101 he discusses other kinds of movement. He discusses straight and circular motion more generally in his *Platonic Theology*, e.g. III, ii, 8; IV, ii, 9-11, VI, xii, 9-16.

5 *Platonic Theology*, XVI, vii, 7.

6 Ficino uses the word *retexam*, a term which suggests either unravelling a piece of work or reweaving it. In *De sole et lumine*, he is putting to new use much material that he has already used elsewhere. See Introductory Note on the composition of *De sole* (Appendix B).

7 Ottaviano di Guccio de' Calvani or Galvani was resident mainly in Poland. He was related to Arnolfo Tedaldi and worked with him. When Callimachus died, it was he who reported the death and funeral in full detail to the Tedaldi family.

8 Arnolfo Tedaldi, a relative of Callimachus on his mother's side, had been settled in Poland for a long time, holding an influential position in the salt trade. He had been responsible for Callimachus finding refuge in Poland, back in 1470, and they remained closely associated. Arnolfo died in Cracow in 1495, a year before Callimachus. Other members of the Tedaldi family were within Ficino's circle (*Letters*, **1**, 2nd edition, p. 259). See also Biographical Note on Buonaccorsi and Plate 2.

27

1 In calling Germain de Ganay his dearest brother Ficino is taking advantage of the fact that *germanus* means a full brother (as opposed to a half-brother or step-brother)

in Latin. This enables him to enlarge upon their common interests and callings. See Biographical Notes for Germain's high position at the French court.

2 Hesiod, *Theogony*, 924; *Homeric Hymns*, 28; *Orphic Hymns*, 32; Fulgentius, *Mythologia*, XI, 1; Apollodorus, *Library*, 1.3.6. Christian authors generally accepted that Minerva represented prudence and some report her miraculous birth, without in any way endorsing her (as for example, Augustine, *City of God*, IV, 10; *Contra Faustum*, XX, 9). Ficino holds a much more sympathetic view, integrating Minerva within a theological framework, as in *Platonic Theology*, XI, 4, 13.

3 For the birth of Minerva's daughter, Philosophy, see *Letters*, **7**, 12.

4 For the defeat of the giants, in which Athena/Minerva played a major part, see the Greek sources in note 2 as well as Ovid, *Metamorphoses*, I, 151-62; Apollodorus, *Library,* I, 6, and cf. Letter 30 below.

5 In Latin, *pia mater.* Curiously enough, this became an anatomical term for one of the three membranes surrounding the brain and spinal cord, in use in late medieval medical texts as a translation of the equivalent Arabic term, and in English from 1400 to the nineteenth century and beyond. Some versions of Minerva's birth specify that she was born from Zeus's brain.

6 Ficino was preparing manuscript copies of these commentaries for Germain. The printed version did not appear until 1496. The Letters were, however, printed in 1495. For a progress report some months after this letter, see Letter 39.

28

1 Bernardo Bembo, a Venetian nobleman (see Biographical Notes), had become a close friend of Ficino during his first visit as ambassador to Florence in 1475. Since that time he had been in the city only rarely, living either in Rome or in Venetian territory.

2 In the literature of antiquity, calling one of the gods to be a token or witness indicates the solemn nature of the undertaking. Here the appeal is to Phoebus, who is also (as Phoebus Apollo, the Sun) the subject of the book Ficino is sending Bembo.

3 Only Figliucci gives the month and the year for this letter.

29

1 Antonio Vinciguerra Cronico (c.1440-1502): Venetian humanist and diplomat, Cronico accompanied Bernardo Bembo on some of his embassies, including one to Florence during which he participated in discussions on the soul (reported by Ficino in *Platonic Theology*, VI, 1, probably dating to the spring of 1474). He also served as secretary to the Venetian senate from 1470 to 1500. He was a friend and correspondent of Pico and Poliziano. Ficino wrote three letters to him (*Letters*, **4**, 42, **5**, 2 and this present letter).

2 Jupiter was especially associated with friendship and hospitality. *Jupiter amicalis* (Jupiter the friendly) is reported as a cult title for Jupiter, especially in Pergamon. *Amicabilis*, used by Ficino here, is less common, but is explained in his *Philebus* commentary, ch. 26 (ed. M.J.B. Allen, p. 242).

3 In *De sole*, ch. 9, where Ficino takes the Sun as an analogy for God and adapts the familiar words of Psalm 19:4, 'In them [the heavens] hath he set a tabernacle for the sun', to refer to His dwelling place. In Latin and Italian, friendship (*amicitia*) and love (*amor*) are presumed to share the same root (*am-*).

4 Knowledge: Ficino uses the less usual word *notitia* here, rather than the broader term for knowledge and understanding, *scientia*. He sometimes uses *notitia* to indicate a mere concept or common notion, but it can also carry a deeper sense, as here, of awareness, cognisance or familiarity.

30

1 *Quid sentiat*: lit. 'what he thinks'. This letter presents Ficino's view of astrology, and we have therefore used the title 'My view'. It is addressed to Poliziano but also concerns Pico della Mirandola. Both Pico and Poliziano were engaged in polemics against certain aspects of the practice of astrology, an area in which they had some disagreement with Ficino. Pico was compiling a major work, called *Disputations against divinatory astrology*, published only posthumously in 1496. Poliziano wrote a reply to this letter, of which we published a translation in *Letters*, **8**, Appendix L. He also wrote to Pico (Poliziano, *Epistolae*, XII, 7) with some information gleaned from ancient calendrical texts, but also complaining about Pico's prolonged absences from the city, caused by the time he had wasted in conversation with astrologers. He included with that letter a Greek epigram against these time-wasters (Poliziano, *Greek and Latin Poetry,* Greek Epigram XLIX, ed. O. E. Knox, p. 230).
For interpretations of this important letter, see Carol Kaske, Introduction in *Marsilio Ficino: Three Books on Life,* ed. by C.V. Kaske and J. Clark (Binghamton, NY, 1989), pp. 3-70; John North, 'Types of Inconsistency in the Astrology of Ficino and others', in *Christian Humanism. Essays in honour of Arjo Vanderjagt*, ed. by A.A. MacDonald, J.R. Veenstra, Z. von Martels, (Leiden: Brill, 2009) pp. 281-302; Valery Rees, 'Celestial Bodies in the writings of Marsilio Ficino' in *Heavenly Discourses*. Proceedings of conference held at the University of Bristol, September 2011, ed. Nicholas Campion, (Ceredigion: Sophia Centre Press, 2016), pp. 111-17; Remo Catani, 'Astrological Polemics in the Crisis of the 1490s', in *Italy in Crisis*, 1494, ed. by Jane Everson and Diego Zancani (Oxford, 2000), pp. 41–62.
On Pico, see especially H. Darrel Rutkin, 'The Use and Abuse of Ptolemy's *Tetrabiblos* in Renaissance and Early Modern Europe: Two Case Studies (Giovanni Pico della Mirandola and Filippo Fantoni)' in *Ptolemy in Perspective*, ed. by Alexander Jones, New York: Springer, 2010, pp. 135–50. Ovanes Akopyan, '*Princeps aliorum* and his Followers: Giovanni Pico della Mirandola on the "Astrological Tradition" in the *Disputationes adversus astrologiam divinatricem*' in *Renaissance Studies,* 32/4 (2017), pp. 547-64. Ptolemy's writings formed the basis of university studies of astrology, but other works were popular too. For printed sources of ancient and medieval astronomical texts newly available at this time, see notes to Appendix B. There were some sources, too, of impeccable theological credentials, such as the *Speculum Astronomiae* of Albert the Great.

2 Ficino is comparing the astrologers in question to the Giants of old, who tried to oust Zeus (Jupiter) and the Olympian gods. Athena played an important part in the battle, but the gods were able to defeat them with the help of a human, Hercules. The fullest account of this battle is in Apollodorus, *Library*, I, 6, 1-2.

The battle (called the Gigantomachy) was understood as a primordial battle between order and chaos. It was also associated with volcanic disturbances. It became a favourite motif in Greek art. Athena's leading role was signalled by its representation on the inside of her shield in Phidias' colossal gold and ivory statue in the Parthenon.

3 *Orphic Hymns*, 32, 12.

4 Antaeus was the son of Poseidon, god of the sea, and Gaia, earth. As a result of his parentage he was extremely strong, so long as he kept in contact with the earth (his mother), but when lifted in the air he became as weak as water. Exploiting his strength, he used to challenge strangers to wrestle with him, easily killing them. Hercules, who was set to defeat him as one of his twelve Labours, discovered the secret of his power, and was able to lift Antaeus above the ground and could then crush him. See Apollodorus, *Library*, II, 5, 11. This was another favourite theme in art, especially in bronzes, such as those by Antonio del Pollaiuolo, in the 1470s, and by Bertoldo di Giovanni and Giambologna in the sixteenth century.

5 Plotinus lampoons astrologers, especially at *Enneads*, II, 3, 2-6. In particular, he accuses them of giving powers to the planets that properly belong to the ruler of the universe. Hence Ficino's opening remark in this letter, comparing such people to the Giants who tried to seize heaven from Jupiter.

6 For Ficino's commentaries on Plotinus, see *Opera*, pp. 1537-1800. An English translation is in progress, of which two volumes are so far in print, covering *Enneads* III and IV, *Marsilio Ficino*: *Commentary on Plotinus*, edited and translated by Stephen Gersh, Cambridge MA: Harvard University Press (I Tatti Renaissance Library), vols. 4 and 5, 2017 and 2018.

7 See *De vita*, esp. III, Preface, chapters 1 and 26, and the *Apologia* that accompanied it (reprinted in *Letters*, **8**, Appendix B).

8 By 'images' Ficino refers to the constellations, for which there was an established traditional imagery.

9 Like most other philosophers of his time, and certainly all medical men, Ficino was well acquainted with all the standard works on astrology. See note 1 above and introductory note to Appendix B.

10 See Appendix B.

11 Python was a serpent said to have sprung from the mud after the deluge. He was slain by the arrows of Apollo. Ovid, *Metamorphoses*, I, 416-47. In a famous quotation, Fulgentius (5th century AD), says that the meaning of this myth is that 'false belief is crushed like serpents when the true light appears', *Mythologia*, I, 17.

12 Poliziano repeatedly protested against being compared to Hercules. See *Letters*, **8**, Appendix B, note 43.

13 Boethius, *Consolation of Philosophy*, IV, 7 (poem), 34-5. See also Michael J.B. Allen, 'Homo ad zodiacum: Marsilio Ficino and the Boethian Hercules,' in *Forma e parola: Studi in memoria di Fredi Chiappelli*, ed. by Dutschke *et al.*, Rome, 1992, pp. 205-21, reprinted in *Plato's Third Eye*, Aldershot, 1995.

31

1 This Bernardo Rucellai (see Biographical Notes) should not be confused with Bernardo di Giovanni Rucellai (1448-1514), the husband of Lorenzo de' Medici's older sister Lucrezia (Nannina).

2 See Introductory Note on *De sole*, Appendix B.

3 Bernardo's friendship with Girolamo Rossi may have led to his apparently recent introduction to Ficino, although Ficino was also close to the other branch of the Rucellai family.

4 Genesis 1:1.

5 Genesis 1: 3-5 and 14-18. Cf. Basil, *Hexaemeron*, Homily II, 7 and III, 3; also VI, 3. In Pico's *Heptaplus*, written in 1489, the light of the sun is equated with the true light accessible only after death, but nothing is made of the difference between days 1 and 4.

32

1 On Niccolò del Benino, or Benin, see Biographical Notes.

2 Ficino uses this transliteration for the Hebrew form צדק (*tzedek*). This is usually transliterated as *tzedek*, meaning righteousness or justice. The term is used by Abraham ibn Ezra, who connects Jupiter with justice, judges, 'worshippers of the Lord', and men of wealth (e.g. in *Sefer Ha-olam, The Book of the World*). Ibn Ezra's works gained wide circulation through the Latin translations of Petrus Abanus (1257–1316). He attempted to correct some of Abū Ma'šar's observations, especially on the conjunctions of Saturn and Jupiter.

3 Jupiter's reputation for indulgence rests partly on the example given below and partly on his being the grandfather of fatherless Cupid, whom he treated with indulgence. In the story of Cupid and Psyche, Cupid appeals to Jupiter, who shows mercy despite Cupid's misdemeanours (Apuleius, *Golden Ass*, VI, 22).

4 Ovid, *Heroides*, IV, 133.

5 The qualities of Jupiter, as well as the other planets, are listed in Abraham ibn Ezra, *The Beginning of Wisdom*, ch. 4.

6 The combination of divine justice and mercy is alluded to in Psalms 89:14 and 85:10. From the letter that follows this one, it becomes clear that Ficino was asking for a favourable judgement on someone's behalf. He does so here with such great discretion that it is scarcely apparent. He also takes care to separate the sending of a gift (Letter 33) from the asking of the favour.

33

1 In the Durham copy of the *Epistolae*, corrected by Ficino Ficini, there is an illegible marginal alteration, indicating a replacement for the word *nam*. It may, however, have been intentionally deleted.
For the productive nature of good and the sterility of evil, cf. the fable in *Letters*, **9**, 48 (p.52).

2 Letter 32.

3 In classical mythology, Zeus/Jupiter might be considered to hold superior rank, being king of the Olympian gods as well as being represented by the largest of the planets. However, in a Christian context, the Sun, representing Phoebus Apollo, clearly has superior power.

34

1 Jean Matheron de Salignac: see Biographical Notes. This letter is placed between letters written on 3rd September and 16th October, 1494. The main body of French troops arrived in Italy in September, reaching Pavia unopposed by 21st October, 1494, but not entering Pisa until 8th November. It is, however, likely that Matheron, as Ambassador, travelled ahead of the troops and may well have been in or near Florence by the time he received this.

2 On *Jupiter amicabilis*, see notes to Letters 18 and 29. It is a post-classical term, being projected back to earliest times on the strength of the Greek *Zeus philios* spoken of by Plato. English fails to preserve the connections that are obvious in Latin between *amicabilis* and love (*amor*) and friendship (*amicitia*). Apuleius refers also to Jupiter as *hospitalis*, the hospitable god, or god of hospitality.

3 *Sin ratione potius seria nitimur* ('but if we take matters more seriously'): Ficino uses *nitimur* 'rely on', from the verb *nitor*, perhaps carrying the hint of a pun with *niteo*, to shine or be brilliant. It is certainly audacious to identify Apollo and Jupiter as he does here.

4 Symbols became important in later Neoplatonic philosophy, from Porphyry onwards. In general, they indicate a meeting point between material reality and the spiritual world. They may have more material presence, like the Sun, or have less materiality, as in forms of speech or ritual.

35

1 Lorenzo Spinelli and Cosimo Sassetti, both members of the banking community in Florence with connections in France, appear to have provided the means for the initial introduction to Germain de Ganay, who became an important contact for Ficino. This is not the first letter, however. See Letter 27 above, and also 39 below. For a brief note on the two bankers, whose careers do not otherwise intersect with Ficino, see Biographical Notes.

2 By 'some followers of Plato' Ficino may mean a copy of his Plotinus translation and commentary accompanied by some of his translations of Proclus, Iamblichus and Porphyry which were ready at this time. The two commentaries of his own that are mentioned were not printed until 1496, so he evidently is having manuscript copies made. He later sent Germain a beautiful presentation manuscript of his St Paul Commentary (1496-7), which is held as a 'Special' item in the British Library Collection (BL MS Harley 4695).

3 Ficino had written a dedication letter to accompany an unfinished version of Dionysius's *Divine Names* by the end of 1492. It was addressed to Giovanni de' Medici. The manuscript sent to Germain de Ganay was completed in 1494. The first printed edition bears no date, but reference is made to it in the printer's colophon to Ficino's Plato Commentaries 'being published separately here' (in Florence), i.e. around December 1496, or early 1497. Part of the intervening time between the dedication letter and publication in print was probably spent on further revisions, but little is known of the contract with Lorenzo de Alopa or any delays that may have arisen: the political situation in the city may have made life difficult for

many businesses, including printers. This letter was not included in the collection of Ficino's letters published by Felice Figliucci in the sixteenth century (Venice, 1546-8).

36

1 See Biographical Notes under Gian Stefano Castiglioni.

2 Salvation: the terms of greeting Ficino uses (*saluto*, *salve*, *salus*) all cover a wide range of meanings including health, wholeness, safety, salvation and simple greeting.

3 Having already given Castiglioni a copy of his recent *De sole*, presumably in person, Ficino now adds a copy of his *De christiana religione,* which had been in print since 1476.

4 Ficino's book covers many topics, including the piety of the Apostles and early followers of Christ. But *pietas* covers a wide range of meanings and Ficino's book encouraged a wide range of responses to the Christian tradition, especially those based on love.

5 On Ficino's *De sole*, see Letter 2, note 1 and Appendix B.

6 1 Corinthians 13:8.

37

1 King Charles VIII of France arrived outside Florence on 8th November, 1494. The current *Oratio* is written as an address to be presented to the King in person as part of the ambassadorial mission to his encampment, in which Ficino took part. There is no record of what actually took place at that meeting, but the text was included in its proper chronological place in the collection of Letters.

The main purpose of Charles VIII's expedition was to reclaim the Kingdom of Naples after the death of King Ferrante. Before Aragonese rule in Naples, established by Ferrante's father, the kingdom had belonged to the House of Anjou, of which Charles was now the heir. Pope Alexander VI had encouraged his expedition, hoping for various gains, including the recapture of Jerusalem from the Turks. This latter cause was uppermost in Ficino's mind as well as Savonarola's. See Introduction.

Calling Charles *Carolum magnum* invokes the memory of Charlemagne, King of the Franks (747-814), recognised as the first Holy Roman Emperor, crowned on Christmas Day 800 by Pope Leo III.

We have been greatly helped in our translation of this oration by Robert W. Scheller's article 'Imperial themes in art and literature of the early French Renaissance: the period of Charles VIII', in *Simiolus: Netherlands Quarterly for the History of Art.* Vol. 12, No 1 (1981-1982), pp 5-69, translated from the Dutch by Michael Hoyle. Scheller in turn records his indebtedness to Dr. C.I. Heesakkers for assistance with the Latin.

2 i.e. Naples.

3 Ficino uses the term *pietas*, which we have translated here as 'devotion' but it also has strong associations with duty.

4 Virgil, *Aeneid*, VI, 853. In the underworld Aeneas' father, Anchises, instructs Aeneas on his future role in words that resound through Latin literature.
5 The lily or *fleur de lys* was the symbol of the royal house of France and prevalent on French royal coats of arms as well as being featured on the coat of arms of the city of Florence from medieval times in the form of the *iris fiorentina*, which grew there in abundance. From 1465, the Medici family also used the lily on their coats of arms, but this was a right granted by the French king, not by the city.
6 A reversal of the rejection of Christ in St John 1:11 and 5:43.
7 St Matthew 11:28.
8 Ficino is linking *gratiosus* (gracious) correctly with *gratiis* (graciousness) and *Carolus* (Charles), more imaginatively, with *charitas*, 'love, or charity', here rendered as 'favour'.
9 Psalm 118:26.
10 Psalm 118:24.
11 See Scheller, 'Imperial Themes,' cited in note 1 above, p. 7, footnote 6.
12 The famous words '*veni, vidi, vici*' were attributed to Julius Caesar, reporting his swift victory in the Pontic war to the Roman Senate in 47BC. Suetonius in his *Life of Julius Caesar*, 37, reports that they were displayed during his Triumph procession.
13 The exploits of Hercules are recounted by many classical authors. He used each of these weapons on famous occasions, but the club is one of the defining attributes by which he can be recognised in art.
14 Throughout classical literature, Jupiter (Jove), king of the Olympian gods, indicates his will and decisions with a simple nod. See, for example, Homer, *Iliad*, I, 530. Any desire on Charles's part to be considered 'lord of the world' would imply a challenge to the German Emperor Maximilian. The rivalry of these two monarchs was well known. The 'machinery of war' is brushed lightly aside here, but Charles's army was known for its heavy-duty machines: 'French artillery . . . consisted of thirty-six bronze cannon, eight feet long. They fired lead balls as large as a man's head; each was drawn on a wagon by a team of thirty-six horses. In addition, there were a number of smaller-caliber guns. Charles's army was the first in history to take a wagon train of cannon on a long march. More powerful than anything the Italians had ever seen and far more easily transported, his cannon could batter breaches in massive stone walls in a few hours. Fortified castles were no longer capable of withstanding sieges. The Italians were horrified by such monstrous weapons.' (Orville Prescott, *Princes of the Renaissance*, New York, 1969, pp. 10-11.)

38

1 Ficino had not written to Giovanni Cavalcanti since 1482 (see *Letters*, **7**). This letter is the first of two in this final volume. They had been close friends from Giovanni's childhood – he was about twenty years younger than Ficino - and over the years Ficino addressed more letters to Giovanni than to any other correspondent, 47 in all. He always addressed him as his 'unique friend' (though he was not the only person to receive this epithet), and they wrote some letters together. Ficino composed much of his *Platonic Theology* while staying with the Cavalcanti family in their country house at Rignano in the Val d'Arno, not far from Ficino's birthplace of Figline. For more on Cavalcanti, see Biographical Notes.

2 Plato raises this question in *Laws*, X, 906, *Theaetetus*, 175C–77A and a few other places (see below) but gives it no systematic enquiry. Other discussions of the subject among the Platonists include Plotinus, *Enneads*, I, 8; II, 4; II, 9; III, 1; a treatise of Proclus, *On the Existence of Evils* and two on *Providence*. See also Augustine, *Confessions*, VII; Aquinas, *De Malo,* Q.1-5 and *Summa Theologica*, Ia, Q.48-9. In the Bible, the classic texts on this subject are the Book of Job and St Matthew 5:45. Michael J.B. Allen has discussed this letter in '*In principio*: Marsilio Ficino on the Life of Text' in *Res et verba in der Renaissance*, ed. by Eckhard Kessler and Ian Maclean (Wiesbaden, 2002), pp. 11-28; reprinted in Allen, *Studies in the Platonism of Marsilio Ficino and Giovanni Pico* (London: Routledge, 2017), pp. 67-84. He notes how Ficino looks for good purpose in the existence of suffering.

3 This is most forcibly expressed in Plato's Cave allegory, *Republic*, VII, 514-7.

4 A constant refrain through the book of Ecclesiastes.

5 Psalm 116:11.

6 Plato, *Phaedrus*, 240AB. This passage is also discussed in Ficino's commentary on *Phaedrus*, III, 9 and in the *Platonic Theology*, XVI, vii, 14, where Hermias's commentary is cited. The form of Ficino's Latin translation of the Greek is slightly different there but in each place Ficino uses the term *daemon*, translated here as 'spirit'.

7 The delays caused to Odysseus on his return home by the enchantments of Circe and the song of the Sirens are described by Homer in *Odyssey*, X and XII.

8 Plato, *Theaetetus*, 176. Ficino quoted this at length in a letter to Lotterio Neroni on 3rd December, 1480 (of which he presumably sent a copy also to Cavalcanti), *Letters*, **5**, 48.

9 The healing of the man born blind is related in St John, 9:1-41; verse 3 specifically says he was blind 'that the works of God should be made manifest in him.' For the healing of the cripple, see Acts 3:1–10.

10 Plato, *Symposium*, 201D.

11 Plato, *Phaedrus*, 244B, as translated in Ficino's own version.

12 Plato, *Phaedrus*, 244DE, though slightly paraphrased.

13 Plato, *Laws*, 1, 642DE.

14 Plato, *Phaedrus*, 249CD.

15 Plato, *Phaedrus*, 250–252.

16 I Corinthians 13:13.

17 Ficino frequently draws on Avicenna. He is probably here referring to Avicenna's *Metaphysics* commentary or his treatise on the soul, *De anima* (part of *Al-Shifā*). For discussion of ideas on prophecy shared with Avicenna, see Masoumeh Soleymani Chaharfarsakhi, 'Avicenna and Ficino on Divine Prophets,' *Accademia*, XIV (2012), pp. 23-43.

18 Anonymous proverb, also taken up by St Augustine. Cf. St Matthew 18:7 'Woe unto the world because of offences! It must needs be that offences come . . .'

19 This is the doctrine of original sin, which is based on the account of Adam and Eve's disobedience (Genesis 3). St Paul gave the doctrine great importance and St Augustine elaborated it further.

20 The French invasion in November 1494 gave rise to great fear, which was exacerbated by the preachings of Savonarola.

21 Psalm 118:23.

22 Psalm 68:28.

39

1 Ficino calls his addressee *Germanus*, a natural Latin transcription for 'Germain', de Ganay's name. *Germanus* is also an archaic term for a full brother, sharing both parents, as opposed to a half-brother. Germain was unrelated to Ficino except in the allegorical sense described in the text of the letter. For his keen interest in Ficino's work and its reception in France, see Biographical Notes.

Like Letter 35, also to Germain de Ganay, this letter was not included in the 16th century collection published by Felice Figliucci (Venice, 1546-8), although the letter to Germain's brother Jean (Letter 41) is there.

2 The words of Anchises to his son, Aeneas, when the latter eventually reaches the Elysian Fields on his journey through the underworld: Virgil, *Aeneid*, VI, 687-8.

3 Virgil, *Aeneid*, VI, 546. Ficino cleverly adapts Virgil's memorable line: '*I decus, i nostrum: melioribus utere fatis*' to place the idea of honour or glory wholly on de Ganay: '*I nunc ad decus nostrum: melioribus utere fatis*.'. The Basel edition barbarously omits the crucial verb, 'i' (go). '*Decus*' includes meanings of honour, glory, splendour, a man of valiant deeds or honourable achievements.

4 Jean (or Jehan) de Ganay was a leading statesman of the French court and President of the *Parlement* of Paris, who accompanied his king to Italy. When they reached Naples in February 1495, his position was given formal recognition with the title of Chancellor of France.

5 Florence was riven with inner strife as Piero de' Medici became increasingly unpopular. On 8th November, 1494, King Charles VIII of France reached the territory of Florence, on his way south to claim the throne of the Kingdom of Naples. On 9th November, Piero was driven out of the city, never to return. See Introduction, pp. xx–xxiii.

6 Ficino took part in the embassy deputed to meet the French king encamped outside the city in early November 1494.

7 The volume of commentaries was duly completed for publication in print in Florence, by Lorenzo Francesco da Veneto, on 2nd December, 1496.

40

1 Member of a leading noble family in Florence.

2 See *Philebus*, 39E-40C, a dialogue between Socrates and Protarchus. Ficino returned to the *Philebus* several times, regarding it as a key introduction to Plato. An early translation was read to Cosimo de' Medici before he died in 1464; lectures on the text followed and a first written version of the commentary by 1469. The revised commentary appeared in 1496. Meanwhile the discussion of questions arising in the *Philebus* had informed many of his other works, such as the *Platonic Theology*.

3 This section was written for the third version of his *Philebus* commentary, prepared for the 1496 publication of his *Commentaria in Platonem*. It can be found in Appendix V to Allen's edition of Marsilio Ficino, *The Philebus Commentary*, pp. 502-3, as the summary of chapter 34.

41

1 See Biographical Notes and references to him in Letters 39 and 42.
2 For dissensions in the city and a sense of panic at the approach of the French army, see Introduction.
3 Ficino was determined to continue his translations and commentaries, convinced of their value to his contemporaries in these difficult times.
4 This would suggest that Ficino may have gone more than once to the French camp. The sentence which follows, declaring that they have not yet met, is in contradiction to the previous letter in which he tells Germain he has now met his brother. One explanation might be that this group of letters is not in strict chronological order and that Letter 41 preceded Letter 39. Publication of the *Letters* took place in Venice early in 1495 and these letters were written quite close to the time of publication, at the end of 1494. Another possible explanation might be that Ficino saw Jean but only from far off, without personal contact. A third possibility is suggested by Letter 42. For another possible explanation of the discrepancy, see Letter 42.
5 The overlapping qualities of heat/love and light/intelligence constitute a main topic in *De sole* as well as other late works of Ficino's such as the commentaries on Dionysius and on St Paul.

42

1 See Biographical Notes under Paolo Emili of Verona.
2 Jean de Ganay.
3 This letter suggests he did not meet Jean in person, at least on this occasion, but only a virtual form of Jean, in Paolo, albeit a radiant form. Whether the previous letters play on this, or are simply out of date order, must remain a matter of conjecture.
4 In the Venice edition this is followed by a colophon (see p.197), which includes an astrological birthchart for it in which each element is of good omen: 'The Letters of that most eloquent man, Marsilio Ficino of Florence, are brought to a successful conclusion, paid for by the provident donor, Girolamo Blondi of Florence sojourning in Venice, printed in Venice with the care and diligence of Matteo Capcasa of Parma, at the entrance of Phoebus to the spring equinox, with Leo in the ascendant, on the day and hour of Mercury, on the feast of St Gregory, in the 1495th year of our salvation.' The feast of St Gregory the Great was formerly held on March 12th.

Notes to Appendix Letters

A

1 The Latin text for this letter can be found in Kristeller, *Sup. Fic.*, I, pp. 64-5. It comes from MS Mo2, which contains Books IX to XI of the letters and the first five letters of Book XII. It appears on fol. 99v°, between the fourth and fifth letters of Book XII. This might suggest a date between 7th and 14th November, 1492. However, it was later noticed by Kristeller that apart from the title it is identical with Chapter 26, the final chapter, of Book I of the *Three Books on Life*, which was published in 1489 (having been started in the early 1480s, as shown in *Letters*, **6**, Preface and Note to the Reader). A decision had been made (whether by Ficino or someone else) to add to the collection of letters being transcribed at this time a copy of an item already perhaps well known. This could be because it fits well with the general theme of the Sun, but it could also be linked to the growing controversy over the status of philosophy in the Christian life. Savonarola had already attacked philosophers during his Lent sermons of 1492. By the end of that year, he was speaking of the 'Sword of the Lord held by a hand in the sky' that he had seen in a vision, and a trinity of faces coming from a single light, that proclaimed in unison a warning of the punishments to come. According to this voice, the worst miscreants of all were the 'wicked prelates and preachers of philosophy'. See Donald Weinstein, *Savonarola: The Rise and Fall of a Renaissance Prophet* (New Haven & London: Yale University Press, 2011) pp. 82-96. Ficino is here defending the pursuit of philosophy as being fully in accordance with the highest ideals of Christian life. Savonarola had himself read Plato (see L. Tromboni, 'Girolamo Savonarola lettore di Platone: Edizione e Commento del *De doctrina Platonicorum*,' in *Rinascimento* 46/2 (2006), pp. 133–213) but ultimately rejected him.

2 For the Magi, see *Chaldaean Oracles*, 11 and 12 in the series passed on by George Gemisthos Pletho (ed. Brigitte Tambrun Krasker); the same oracles are numbered 97 and 96 in the edition of Ruth Majercik; for Plato, *Charmides*, 156-7.

3 Socrates was declared the wisest man by the oracle of Apollo at Delphi. See Plato, *Apology*, 21AB. Hippocrates, regarded as the father of Greek medicine, was naturally aligned with Apollo, the god of medicine.

4 Plato, *Republic*, VI, 507D-509A. See also Ficino, *Platonic Theology*, I, vi, 4-6.

5 St John 1:9.

6 Psalm 36:9.

7 Plato, *Epistle* VII, 341D.

B

1 Iamblichus, *De mysteriis,* I, ix, 32. Ficino's Latin for 'impulse' is *actum*, a term laden with implications for the effective action of light, translating here the Greek *energeia*. Iamblichus himself appears to be drawing on earlier discussions in Plotinus, e.g. *Enneads*, IV, v, 6-7.

2 Ficino has a long disquisition on the nature of the soul in *Platonic Theology*, VI, ii (based on Plato's cave allegory) which dwells on the affinity of light and life. See also XV, v, 4-5 and XVI, viii, 6.

3 Ptolemy's estimate was just a little higher, putting the sun's volume at 'about 170 times' that of the earth (*Almagest*, V, 16). According to modern data from NASA, the diameter of the sun is 109 times that of the earth.

4 Plato, Aristotle and Averroes all seem to have believed that the Sun was the sole source of light for all planets and stars (see, for example, Plato, *Timaeus*, 39B); Macrobius, however, agreed that the Moon reflected the light of the Sun but regarded the other planets as self-luminous (*Commentary on the Dream of Scipio*, I, 20; Albert of Saxony, and Nicholas Oresme, two fourteenth-century astrologers, credited some others with this belief too, including Heraclitus, Cicero and Avicenna. They also maintained that the fixed stars, i.e., what we call stars as opposed to planets, had light of their own. In the *Argumentum* to the *Platonic Theology*, Ficino took this discussion a little further (section 8).

5 There are two Arabic astrologers whose names were Latinised as Haly. The first is Ali ibn Ridwan (988-1061), who wrote on both medicine and astrology. His Arabic commentary on Ptolemy's *Tetrabiblos* was translated into Latin in 1136-8, and was regularly included with Ptolemy's work, including the first printed edition of Venice, 1484. The second is Abu l-Hasan 'Ali ibn Abi l-Rijal, sometimes called Haly Abenragel (c. 1015-1063), a court astrologer in Kairouan (Tunisia), who wrote one of the largest astrological compilations of the Middle Ages. His *Distinguished Book on Horoscopes from the Constellations*, (*Al-Bari fi akham al-nujum*) was translated from Arabic into Old Castilian and thence into Latin in 1254 as *Libri de iudiciis astrorum*, or *Praeclarissimus liber completus in Judiciis astrorum*. It survives in several manuscripts, and was also published in print by Erhard Ratdolt in Venice in 1485.

Abraham is Abraham Ibn Ezra (d. 1167), who wrote several works on astronomy, many of which were translated into Latin by Petrus Abanus (c.1257-1316). Ratdolt printed ibn Ezra's *Liber de nativitatibus* in 1484. All of the works mentioned were thus available in Florence, in printed form as well as manuscript. In fact, on 13th January 1493 (or possibly 1494) Bonetus Locatellus published in Venice an edition that contained all of these works, as well as some other popular items such as the *Introductorium* of Zahel.

6 The Persian term *dustūrīya* (or *dastūrīya*), used by the great authority Abū Ma'šar and others, indicates a position of power for any planet, and an extension of its influence over the two signs on either side.

7 Aries, Cancer, Libra and Capricorn were known as the cardinal signs because the entry of the sun into each marked the beginning of a new season. Charts for the moment of entry into each of the cardinal signs could be drawn up to predict the quality of the season to follow.

8 The movable signs are the same four cardinal signs.

9 It was considered a valid practice, amongst others, to cast 'genethliacal' charts on an annual basis, refining the indications of the original birth chart to determine a person's fortune for the coming year.

10 Although attributed to Aristotle, the source of this comment is in Julian's *Hymn to King Helios*, 138b, where he says 'The Sun makes the simplest movement of all the heavenly bodies' and that Aristotle took this to show its superiority. It cannot be traced directly in the works of Aristotle, but he envisaged the Sun as having perfect

spherical motion. Primary (i.e. spherical) motion and motion along an inclined path that causes coming-to-be and passing-away are discussed in *On Generation and Corruption, 10*. The apparent path of the Sun through the Zodiac became known (after Aristotle's time) as the ecliptic. Other planets diverge from the ecliptic, moving round the Sun, and, as viewed from the earth, they appear to slow down, to stop, to move backwards and then to move forwards again. That process is called retrogression. See note 12.

11 i.e. at an angle of 120° from one another.

12 For the idea of retrograde motion, Ficino draws on ancient tradition based on epicycles e.g. Ptolemy, *Almagest*, XII, ii, 3-6. It had become a commonplace notion and would remain so until Copernicus's theories of a heliocentric universe were established (see note 16 below). Ficino frequently refers to the retrograde movements of planets in his letters, e.g. *Letters*, **7**, 65.

13 Modern measurements would correct the figure for Venus to 47°, but have not altered the 28° of Mercury.

14 When a planet is 'combust' (i.e. in conjunction with the Sun), its negative energies are markedly curtailed.

15 In the later version, Ficino adds that when they are square to the Sun (i.e. at 90°) they are in the middle, between high and low.

16 This would appear to mean that the moon reaches a high point of its elliptical epicycle at both full moon and new moon, but in the two intermediate phases, when it is square to the Sun, i.e. at first quarter and last quarter, it is low. Ficino may be speaking of apogee and perigee within epicycles. Apogee marks the moon's farthest point from the earth, and perigee its closest – but here he seems to be considering their relation to the Sun and not the earth. The whole system of epicycles, that is, of smaller circles on the circumference of larger ones, appeared to account for irregularities in planetary speed and movement in the geocentric system that prevailed prior to the discovery of heliocentrism by Nicholas Copernicus (1473-1543) and the confirmation of elliptical orbits by Johannes Kepler (1571-1630).

17 The head and tail of the dragon mark the lunar nodes, that is, the points where the orbit of the moon crosses the ecliptic, the 'head' when it is ascending, the 'tail' when it is descending.

18 It is difficult to find exactly where Proclus says this, despite notes provided in a statement of something similar in Kaske & Clark's edition of Ficino, *De vita*, III, vi, 48. Both there and in III, iv, 25, Ficino stresses the fact that the Sun contains the powers attributed to all the heavenly bodies, but the references given (p.436 n.5) are not helpful. Ficino did not know the later treatises of Proclus's commentary on Plato's *Republic*, and the references to his *Timaeus* commentary are obscure. Perhaps Ficino had in mind a general picture of the place of the Sun in Proclan thinking, or even the Proclan hymn to the Sun (lines 8ff).

19 The *pars fortunae* was calculated from the positions of Sun and Moon in relation to the Ascendant. The *daimon* presiding there would serve as guardian spirit, and would be constant through the life, determining the kind of beneficial gifts that might be available to an individual.

20 '*Autumn*' in the printed editions, 'Saturn' in manuscript.

21 *Casu solis*: the Sun is in exaltation in Aries; its decline (*casus*) or debilitation (i.e. the weakest point of its cycle) is in Libra.

22 These are known as houses.
23 i.e. is ruled by the Sun.
24 i.e. the tenth house.
25 i.e. while it is in the 9th house and the 11th house.
26 Ficino distinguishes three kinds of spirit in the human framework, as well as a *spiritus mundi* that links the world body to the world soul. Of the three, the natural spirit (not mentioned here) is responsible for nutrition, growth and reproduction; the vital spirit is responsible for life, the passions, and song; the animal spirit serves the functions of the soul. See Ficino, *De vita*, I, 2 ed. Kaske & Clark, and their Introduction. p. 43.
27 *Signo* is the correct reading, present in this manuscript and some early editions. The widely used edition of Basel erroneously has *igno* (fire).
28 Ficino, *De vita*, III, 6. See also *Apology* attached to *De vita,* esp lines 42-53.
29 *Orphic Hymns*, VIII, to Helios, and IX, to Selene (ed. Athanassakis and Wolkow). Further instances are added in later editions, including a quotation found in Proclus's Commentary on Plato's *Timaeus* (at III, 95, 18-19) that suggests the Sun is the offspring of Athena (divine intelligence).
30 Cf. Iamblichus, *De mysteriis*, VII, 3.
31 Ficino quoted this more fully in *De vita*, III, vi, 79-80. probably using Abū Ma'šar's *Introductorium*, VI.
32 Cf. Genesis, 1:16.
33 Reported in Macrobius, *Commentary on the Dream of Scipio*, I, xx, 6.
34 Ibid., I, xx, 3.
35 Months of gestation were traditionally related to the planets: the first month to Saturn, the second to Jupiter, the third to Mars, the fourth to the Sun and so on.
36 The association of the moving mind, thought, and eloquence with Mercury and the deeply still contemplative mind with Saturn runs right through the writings of Ficino and many other writers. See especially, *Platonic Theology*, XIII, ii, 2-3 and *De vita*, I, vi, 22-28. See also Letter 5 in this volume.
37 In this section, Ficino expounds the theory of the planetary domiciles according to Ptolemy, *Tetrabiblos*, I. 17. A glossary and diagrams can be found in *Letters*, **7**, pp. 148-9.
38 Ficino and Ricasoli discussed several topics of astronomy (for example, *Letters*, **9**, 42). See Biographical Notes.
39 The 'royal path of the Sun' is the ecliptic.
40 E.g. Ficino, *Platonic Theology*, XVIII, 5, 2. The principal source here is Macrobius, *Commentary on the Dream of Scipio*, I, xii, 1-2. Porphyry also elaborates on the two entrances to the afterworld in his *Cave of the Nymphs*, xi, a commentary on Homer, *Odyssey*, XIII, 109-112. Cancer and Capricorn also give their name to the tropics, where the Sun is directly overhead, because of the earth's tilt, at noon on the June and December solstices respectively.
41 Cardinal points: the Latin term *cardo* denotes a hinge, around which things pivot. See also notes 7 and 8 above.
42 In the 1493 printed edition, Ficino adds a summing up of the Sun's importance in the universal order, then starts a new chapter with the sentence that follows.
43 Ptolemy, *Tetrabiblos*, III, 11.
44 Ptolemy, *Tetrabiblos*, I, 4-5; cf. Ficino, *De vita*, III, 4-5, where the three Graces are included in the beneficial relationship.

45 *Almugea* is the transliteration of an Arabic term meaning 'face to face', and is applied to a normal or usual aspect. See Ptolemy, *Tetrabiblos*, I, 23. It was used by some translators of the Arabic, such as Plato of Tivoli (12th century), but others, including William of Moerbeke (13th century), translating the same text from Greek, did not use the term, translating it as *facies* and *propria facies*.

46 'Concord' denotes a positive relationship, 'discord' a negative one.

47 This description of favourable and unfavourable aspects, or auspicious and inauspicious placements, is based on the fact that each of the planets named rules the sign mentioned. Trine and sextile aspects are considered favourable. The planets are in signs and in houses. The first house is the one occupying the eastern horizon at a given time, such as the moment of birth. Houses indicate particular areas in the life, e.g. matters affecting the body, the family, the spouse, activities in the public domain, whereas the signs indicate the quality of the event. In both cases it is the planets that are considered active, the house or sign playing a passive role. See the detailed explanation in Ficino, *De vita*, III, 10.

48 Ficino uses *statua* not *imago* (used elsewhere), a term picked up enthusiastically later by Francesco Giorgi in his book *On the Harmony of the World* (Venice, 1525), IV, 1.

49 Comparisons of the Sun and God run through Platonic philosophy, biblical imagery and, in particular, texts where those two streams come together, e.g. Dionysius, *Divine Names*. See introductory note above for Ficino's earlier *Orphic Comparison of the Sun to God.*

50 Plato, *Republic*, VI, 508B. Cf. Julian, *Hymn to King Helios*, 133A.

51 Plato, *Republic*, VI, 508B-509C.

52 Plotinus, *Enneads*, IV, 4, 30. Plato, *Laws*, XII, 966-7 and see section above on Praises.

53 Iamblichus, *De mysteriis*, I, ix, 30; Julian, *Hymn to King Helios*, 133-5; Macrobius, *Saturnalia*, I, xvii, 1-2. Ficino made copious notes on all these pagan authors (see Eugenio Garin, in *Studi sul platonismo medievale*, Florence 1958.)

54 Image: on this occasion, Ficino uses *imaginem* (not *statuam*).

55 Plotinus, *Enneads*, I, 7; Dionysius, *Divine Names*, 700B-C.

56 Hipparchus of Rhodes, Greek astronomer, 2nd century BC, whose works are now all lost, but who enjoyed a great reputation, especially for his observations on the Sun and the Moon, his development of trigonometry, the theory of epicycles. and his discovery of the Precession of the Equinoxes. He is cited frequently by Ptolemy in the *Almagest*. The nature of the moon's light is confirmed by Ptolemy in *Almagest*, IV, 1.

57 This passage is enlarged in the printed edition, but had its origins in Ficino's *Orphic Comparison of the Sun to God*, written jointly with Giovanni Cavalcanti and sent to Lotterio Neroni (*Letters*, **5**, 27).

58 Averroes, *De substantia orbis*, 2. This argument is developed in Ficino, *Platonic Theology*, I, iii, 19 and is summarised in the *Argumentum* (Introduction) 4-5, where it provides the basis for the first step of contemplation in the ascent of the soul (*Platonic Theology*, ed. Allen and Hankins, vol. 6, pp.222-25).

59 This could be described as a thought experiment of the kind favoured by Plotinus and used by Ficino, e.g. in *Letters*, **5**, 13. Cf. also Dionysius, *Divine Names*, I, 4, 592D-503D.

60 Psalm 19:4. The King James Version differs slightly from the version familiar to Ficino. We have preserved Ficino's version, which is still reflected in the Douai-Rheims Bible and older editions of the Vulgate (as Psalm 18:6).

61 St John 1:5. Following this is material that appears as the beginning of chapter 10 in the published version but which concluded Ficino's first version for Count Eberhard. The final chapter (ch. 13) of the later versions was formed from the letter sent to the Count (Letter 2 above) on 27th September, 1492.

62 Genesis 1:3.

63 Although light was created on the first day of Creation (Genesis 1:3) the luminaries, sun and moon, were not created until the fourth day (Genesis 1:14-18).

C

1 Text printed in Kristeller, *Sup. Fic.*, I, pp. 73-4 and 2-4. This letter was added to printed editions of *De sole et lumine*.

2 From the time he was a student, Ricasoli was close to Ficino and continued to promote his teachings after Ficino's death. The physician, Gregorio Scuto of Alessandria, a small city in Piedmont, had been in correspondence with Ficino earlier while he was living in Siena (*Letters*, **9**, 29) and retained a keen interest in his work. See Biographical Notes on both.

3 Ricasoli counts eleven books, which correspond to our volumes 1-11. He separates Book 2 (as we have done), see note 4 below.

4 The manuscripts of this second book of letters contain eight items. By the time Ficino added the second book to his collection for printing, in 1495, a ninth was added (though eighth in position), namely a letter to Alamanno Donati. The same letter, however, appeared in some manuscripts in Book VI, and was therefore also included as an appendix in our *Letters*, **5**.

5 This work has various names. Ficino calls it *De occasionibus, sive de causis ad intelligibilia nos ducentibus*.

6 A collection of Ficino's commentaries on Plato was published in Florence in 1496, but the third complete edition of the translations, incorporating numerous corrections and revisions, never appeared.

D

1 The Latin text is in Kristeller, *Sup. Fic.*, II, p. 94. Jacopo was an Apostolic Secretary in Rome. For his career, see Biographical Notes under Jacopo Gherardi.

2 This is thought to be Michele Mercati, who had entered a monastery but may have later left it and been serving as a priest and tutor. He outlived Ficino.

3 Butiano is unknown. There is a village of Buriano (in case Butiano is a mistranscription), in the region of Grosseto, in the Maremma, some 90 miles south of Florence, but it has no trace nowadays of any church of Santo Stefano. There are several churches of Santo Stefano in the region of Tuscany, but we have no means of determining whether one of these might be relevant here.

4 Appendix E is Jacopo's reply to this letter, and informs us that Ficino sent a copy of *De sole et lumine* with it.

E

1 Latin text in Kristeller, *Sup. Fic.*, II, p. 317, but only part of the original letter survived.

2 For the royal throne, see *De sole*, Appendix B, where Ficino confirms the use in Arabic astronomy of the term *dustūrīya* as applied to the sun, meaning royal throne, but it is '*regium solium*', not '*solum*', as Jacopo uses here.

3 Cf. St John 1:9.

4 See Appendix D.

F

1 The Latin text is found in Kristeller, *Sup. Fic.*, II, pp. 91-3. Germain de Ganay held the position of Counsel to the Parlement of Paris, a high court of appeal. In 1485 he was appointed Ecclesiastical Counsel and later became President of the Chamber of Requests. The 'Parlement' was a judicial body not a legislative one. For his subsequent importance, see Biographical Notes.

2 Giovanni Pico della Mirandola died on 17th November, 1494, the day that King Charles made a formal entry into the city from the Florentine countryside.

3 Most Florentine citizens would have taken a far more negative view of the King's entry, but Ficino is here writing to a member of the King's entourage.

4 With epithets such as 'playful' and talk of Pico's 'carefree nature' we glimpse Ficino's forgiving attitude towards Pico's misdemeanours and personal slights. Cf. their earlier correspondence in *Letters*, **6**, 31; **7**, 10, 31, 35, 51, 58, 62, 63, 65, 66, 67, Appendices A, B, C; **8**, 15, 17; **10**, 15, 21.

5 The work described here as *Hexameron* is more commonly known as *Heptaplus* (1489); the *Apology* (1487), followed Pico's *900 Theses* for debate (1486). The introductory essay to the 900 theses, later known as *An Oration on the Dignity of Man*, was also intended as a defence but was considered ill-judged and was condemned by the Church. The third work, named *De ente et uno* (1491), was the first part of an unfinished attempt to establish complete concord between Plato and Aristotle. See Historical Note on Pico della Mirandola in *Letters*, **7**, pp. 142-47.

6 Pico was 31 at the date of his death.

7 Poliziano's published Latin works include a set of essays on classical philology and literary criticism, known as the *Miscellanea*, or *Miscellaneorum centuria prima* (1489), an unfinished second set of miscellanies, four course-introductions known collectively as the *Silvae* (1482-6), and *Lamia* (1492). These were republished, together with a collection of further speeches and twelve books of correspondence, in a posthumous edition by Aldus Manutius in 1498. Poliziano also wrote Italian verse and a lyrical drama, *Orfeo*. He died just before Pico, on 24th September, 1494.

8 The Latin reads 23rd March 1494, but this is Florentine style (in which the New Year began on 25th March).

G

1 The Latin text of this letter can be found in *Opera*, p. 1871. It appears to have been written shortly after the deaths of Poliziano and Pico, which occurred on 24th September and 17th November, 1494. The translation of Athenagoras' *De resurrectione* was first published on 18th August, 1498, by Guido Mercator in Paris, together with Ficino's early translation of *Axiochus*, on death, which he believed to have been written by Xenocrates (a Platonist of the 4th century BC) but which is now considered to be a 1st century composition. This volume has been attributed to the supervision of Jacques Lefèvre d'Étaples in Paris. It also contains the late Stoic *Tablet of Cebes* translated by the Paduan scholar Ludovicus Odaxius, first published in 1497. Ficino's letter of dedication would have accompanied a manuscript version of *De resurrectione* sent directly to Germain de Ganay, probably closer to 1494 than to 1498.

2 Germain's name is taken as cognate with *germanus*, a brother, and Ficino repeats here the play on *germanus* that he used earlier in correspondence with Martin Prenninger in Germany. See also Letter 39 and Appendix H. On De Ganay and the significance of his title as Royal Counsellor, see Biographical Notes.

3 Athenagoras (2nd century AD) was a Church Father living in Athens who defended Christian beliefs and practices in a work addressed to the Emperor Marcus Aurelius and his son Commodus. A second work on the Resurrection is cautiously attributed to him. Before his conversion he had been a Platonist, but in this work he moves away from Plato's suggestion that the body is a prison for the soul and accepts a complementary role for body and spirit in manifesting God's image, as well as upholding the idea of bodily resurrection after death.

4 See especially *Platonic Theology*, XVIII, ix, 4–15.

H

1 The text of this letter to Germain de Ganay is found in Kristeller, *Studies in Renaissance Thought and Letters*, I, pp. 96–7. For its date, see note 2.

2 Ficino calls him *Germano*, which denotes a true brother. It can equally mean 'a German' and Ficino uses the same epithet in both senses to his German friend, Martin Prenninger, as in Letter 7 of this volume. In Letter 39 he uses the term to denote brotherhood with Germain de Ganay.

3 Ficino was reluctant to share his translations of the Orphic Hymns and some other ancient religious material. See *Letters*, **9**, 25 to Martin Prenninger, which did include two other Orphic Hymns, ones that had an acceptability based on their use earlier by Eusebius. Although Prenninger had seen Ficino's own translations, Ficino declined to publish them and the versions he sent Prenninger were translations already published by George of Trebizond. The present letter, to de Ganay, appears to have included his own version of the *Hymn to Nature*, but de Ganay in turn decided not to add it with this letter to the volume of Ficino's Athenagoras translation, dedicated to him and published in Paris in 1498 (see Appendix G). This letter therefore belongs to the period between 1494 and 1498. The text of the hymn has not been found, but a short extract from another hymn in the same series that Ficino sent to Cosimo de' Medici as early as 1462 is given below (Appendix H2). For

English translations of the whole hymn, from the Greek, see *The Orphic Hymns*, 10 (ed. Athanassakis and Wolkow, with notes), or in a verse version, 9 (ed. Thomas Taylor, with Greek).

4 These four levels seem to follow Plotinus in envisaging three active hypostases and a fourth lower passive layer, but Nature is here presented as a power that is present in all four.

5 Plato, *Timaeus*, 30–34.

6 The names for soul (*psyche*) and nature (*physis*) are discussed in *Cratylus*, 399D–400A.

7 Plato, *Philebus*, 30D. Soul here is *animus*: so far in this letter Ficino has used *anima* for 'soul' but either can translate the Greek *psyche*, which is the word found in Plato's *Philebus*.

8 *Deus secundum naturam se revolvit*: Plato, in *Laws*, IV, 716A, states that God 'travels according to his nature in a straight line'. This raises questions about straight and circular movement that Ficino's language here (*se revolvit*) does not address. However, Ficino resolves the apparent conflict between moving in a circuit (as here) and moving in a straight line (as in the *Laws*) in his commentary on *Laws*, IV, by saying 'Plato shows that God is the founder of all laws when he says "He defines and acts with a straight line," that is, He determines all things by the straight rule of law', and that straight motion also governs 'the outflow of creation from God and the inflow of God throughout the whole creation' but this straight motion depends on God's circular motion, a circular act that Timaeus says is natural to the divine intelligence, which from itself looks back to itself, and, by looking back, gazes unceasingly upon all things.' (*Opera*, II, p. 1499; Farndell, *When Philosophers Rule*, p. 98). A mature summary of these views can be found in his translation of and commentary on Dionysius, *Divine Names* (ed. Allen), chapters 107–8 (including spiral motion for the soul) and chapter 303 where God's motion is of all three kinds. For a striking description of other heavenly motion, see the Orphic Hymn to the Cosmos, given below as Appendix H 2.

9 Plato, *Letters*, II, 312D. Ficino attributed the first Letter to Dionysius to Dion, hence in his understanding Letter II is the first letter of Plato to Dionysius. The passage in which he expounds 'first Nature' is 313A, a famously riddling description, which leaves the soul searching for knowledge about the three levels of creation that are beyond its own level.

10 Plato, *Letters*, VII, 341D.

11 Plotinus, *Enneads*, III, 8 deals with Nature, especially in the context of creation and contemplation. See also note 12 below.

12 This remark corresponds to a note Ficino made for himself while reading Proclus in MS Riccardiana 70. See H. D. Saffrey, 'Notes Platoniciennes de Marsile Ficin dans un Manuscrit de Proclus', *Bibliothèque d'Humanisme et Renaissance*, 21 (1959), pp. 161–84 at p. 177. Ficino's note summarises Proclus's view of nature in just these words, followed by a summary of the view of Plotinus. Kristeller suggested a parallel with Proclus, *Elements of Theology*, 21, but the parallels with Proclus's *Platonic Theology* are more obvious, e.g. the arguments contained in its first book, chapters 14, 15 and 18.

13 Aristotle, *Physics*, II, i, 192b21.

14 Proclus uses the expression '*to pan*' to refer to the whole universe, but, as Thomas Taylor points out, he also relates to the god Pan all the gods and daimons of the sublunary world (Taylor, *Proclus: The Theology of Plato*, VII, xxxvi).

15 Ficino is careful to say the hymn is 'on Nature', whereas in the original Greek it is clearly 'to' Nature.

16 This extract is taken from a letter written by Ficino in 1462 to Cosimo de' Medici found in only one manuscript, the *Collectiones Cosmianae*, assembled by Bartolomeo Scala on Cosimo's death, MS Biblioteca Laurenziana LIV, 10. The letter was published by Della Torre in his *Storia dell'Accademia Platonica di Firenze*, (Florence, 1902, repr. Turin 1968, pp. 537-8) and was re-edited by Kristeller (*Sup. Fic.*, II, pp. 87-88). For an English translation of the entire letter and a discussion of its relevance to Ficino's situation in 1462, see James Hankins, 'Cosimo de' Medici and the "Platonic Academy",' *Journal of the Warburg and Courtauld Institutes*, 53 (1990), pp. 144-62, esp. p. 149. In it, Ficino expresses gratitude for Cosimo's early patronage and identifies himself with the 'dutiful youth' in the last line of the hymn. English translations of the original Greek of the hymn are found in *The Orphic Hymns*, 4 (ed. Athanassakis and Wolkow or ed. Thomas Taylor).

17 This hymn is to Ouranos, who is the father of Zeus. His name may be variously translated as heaven, cosmos or sky.

18 Ficino has consciously adapted the Greek here: 'home of the blessed gods' becomes 'home of the blessed'.

19 The heaven or sky is seen as belonging to both worlds, celestial and earthly.

20 The Greek here, for spirit, is *daimon*.

I

1 The Latin text of this letter can be found in Kristeller, *Sup. Fic.*, II, p. 93. Giovanni Francesco was the nephew of Giovanni Pico della Mirandola and inherited the title Count of Concordia on his uncle's death. He also took upon himself the editing and publication of his uncle's works, making some alterations to protect his uncle's orthodoxy. See Biographical Notes.

2 Ficino had composed this as an epitaph and sent it to Germain de Ganay earlier in the year. See Appendix F.

3 *Ioannis Pici Mirandulae Vita* (1496). This was written as an introduction to the first edition of Giovanni Pico's *Opera*, first published in Bologna in 1496 and included in subsequent editions. A reduced version of it was translated into English by Sir Thomas More in 1504.

J

1 The Latin text of this *Privilegium* is found as a frontispiece to the 1495 edition of Ficino's *Epistolae*; see also Kristeller, *Sup. Fic.*, I, p. 67. A writ of privilege authorised publication of a work and provided protection similar to that of modern copyright.

2 Venice was known as 'La Serenissima', hence 'the most serene Council'. The ambassador of the principality of Rimini was Antonio de Cauchorio, who lent his support to this application, enabling it to succeed. The author of *De coelesti vita*, mentioned here too, was the Franciscan Johannes Ferrariensis, possibly to be identified as Johannes de Curribus or de Canalis, who had died in 1462. That work was printed by Matteo Capcasa di Codeca for Girolamo Blondi on 19th December, 1494, and Cauchorio's name is also associated with it. Although the *privilegium* is not

dated, it probably predates the publication of that work, as well as Ficino's *Epistolae* printed on 12th March, 1495.

3 All four signatories are Venetian officials. In 1499 Jacopo Leone was serving a second term as governor of Verona, which was under the dominion of Venice. Niccolò Franco was Bishop of Treviso from 1485 to 1499, but had also served as a governor of Verona in 1490. Leonardo or Lunardo Mocenigo belonged to a distinguished patrician family from which came several doges. He served as rector of the *Gymnasium* of Padua in 1500. Andrea Venerio held the same post in 1503.

K

1 The text of this letter from Piero Dovizi is given in Kristeller, *Sup. Fic.*, II, pp. 218-220.

2 On the expulsion of the Medici from Florence in 1494, Dovizi, principal secretary in the Medici household, had gone into exile too. See Biographical Notes.

3 Ermolao Barbaro, a diplomat and outstanding scholar from Venice, had been a good friend of Ficino's, visiting him in 1490 on his way to Rome. By the time of this letter, however, he was no longer alive, but left his mark with his contributions to the revival of Aristotelian science and philosophy, his translation of Dioscorides, a commentary on the *Natural History* of Pliny, and another on the first-century geographer, Pomponius Mela. See Biographical Notes in *Letters*, **8** and **9**.

4 Virgil, *Aeneid*, I, 379.

5 Adapting a saying from Pliny (*Letters*, I, 10) derived ultimately from the great orator Quintilian.

6 Dovizi seems to be writing just after the publication of the *Letters*, which were issued at the spring equinox of 1495. According to the Julian calendar, this fell on 11th March that year. The feast of St Gregory, also mentioned in the colophon of the *Letters*, used to be celebrated on 12th March but may have been counted as commencing the evening before. So Dovizi's letter may be dated to 31st March, 1495.

L

1 For the Latin text of this letter, see *Opera*, pp. 1425-6, where it comes between the end of the commentary on Book VIII of the *Republic* (following Ficino's exposition on nuptial arithmetic) and the beginning of that on Book IX. It was also included in the Appendix to M.J.B. Allen, *Marsilio Ficino. The Philebus Commentary*, on pp. 487-9. We have adopted Allen's emendations.

Paolo Orlandini (see Biographical Notes) was a monk at Santa Maria degli Angeli. In the late 1480s and 1490s Ficino 'delivered numerous Platonic commentaries' at Santa Maria degli Angeli. Ficino is recorded in the Cathedral Chapter archives as having permission to preach in the church of Santa Maria degli Angeli every single day of December 1488. After Ficino's death Orlandini served as prior. See D.F. Lackner, 'The Camaldolese Academy: Ambrogio Traversari, Marsilio Ficino and the Christian Platonic Tradition,' in *Marsilio Ficino: his Theology, his Philosophy, his Legacy*, eds. M.J.B. Allen and V. Rees (Leiden: 2002), pp. 15-44, at pp. 32 and 42.

2 For Ficino's letter on Happiness (c.1473), see *Letters*, **1**, 115; his *Philebus* commentary underwent several revisions: the first version was written in 1469, a second in 1490-91 and the third, final version in 1496.

3 Reading, with Allen, *excessum* not *excelsum*. Ficino's views on *excessum*, a kind of ecstasy, were developed most fully in *Platonic Theology*, XIII.

4 See *Philebus* commentary, especially ch. 15 on intelligence, ch. 23 on dialectic, and ch.33 on the distinction between human and divine intelligence.

5 For discussion of ecstasy in Plato's *Phaedrus,* see especially Ficino's commentary ch. 26, on *Phaedrus* 1249C-250C; in the *Symposium*, see *De amore*, IV, 4 on divine light in the soul and IV, 5 on the proper use of that light. In his commentary on *The Divine Names* of Dionysius, which was released in the same year as this letter, analysis of love as a path to the divine pervades the entire work, but see especially chapters 16.2; 97.3; 98; 99.3-4.

6 Reading, with Allen, *commentationibus* not *commemorationibus*. Orlandini wrote seven works on a variety of topics, philosophical and theological. They remained in manuscript, unpublished, but under the collective title *Eptathicum*.

7 Reading, with Allen, *vestro* not *nostro.*

8 Guido di Lorenzo was Prior of the monastery at the Church of the Angeli from 1487 until 1498, being summoned to that post by Lorenzo de' Medici from the Cistercian abbey at Settimo (hence he is sometimes called Guido da Settimo). The aim was to introduce reform and clear the Angeli church's debts. See Biographical Notes and Appendix U.

M

1 The Latin text of this letter can be found in Kristeller, *Sup. Fic.*, II, p. 242.

2 Gaguin was teaching at the University in Paris. See Biographical Notes.

3 Although this letter is often quoted by scholars of Gaguin, no one has identified the young man concerned. Suggestions have included a Gualterus mentioned by Erasmus in a letter to Servatius in 1493, and William Walter (Guielmus Gaulterius) mentioned by Fausto Andrelini (1462-1518, another friend of Erasmus and Professor of Humanity at Paris from 1489) in the dedication of his *Elegies*.

4 According to Hermodorus (4th century BC), a fellow pupil, Plato travelled after the death of Socrates, and spent some time in Egypt studying under the priests (Diogenes Laertius, *Lives of the Philosophers, III*, 6). St Jerome confirms the travels in his Letter 53 to Paulinus. Ficino mentions Plato's travels in Egypt in his *Life of Plato*, (*Letters*, **3**, 19, pp. 34 and 44). For the 'men of Cadiz', Pliny the Younger refers in his letters to a man who went from Cadiz all the way to Rome just to set eyes on Livy, so stirred was he by his reputation (Pliny, *Epistles*, II, iii, 8).

N

1 The Latin text of this letter is found in P.O. Kristeller, *Sup. Fic.*, II, p. 95.

2 Aldus Manutius, or Aldo Manuzio, (1444-1515) is considered the finest printer of the Italian Renaissance. See Biographical Notes. He was preparing a folio volume of translations and short works by Ficino, to which this letter refers, which was published in September 1497, a few months after this letter. The volume was dedic-

ated to Cardinal Giovanni de' Medici. A second Aldine edition came out in 1516, and several other editions followed from printing houses in Lyon.

3 The volume begins with a Latin paraphrase of *De mysteriis Aegyptiorum Chaldaeorum Assyriorum* by the 4th-century Syrian Neoplatonist Iamblichus, which lent its title to the whole volume. It also contains Ficino's translations of works by Proclus, Porphyry, Synesius, Psellus, and other Neo-Platonists, as well as his own early *De voluptate*.

4 Ficino's major commentary on Plato's *Parmenides* was published in 1496. For translations of this commentary, see A. Farndell, *Evermore Shall Be So: Ficino on Plato's Parmenides* (London: Shepheard-Walwyn 2008) and M. Vanhaelen, *Marsilio Ficino Commentaries on Plato*, vol 2, *Parmenides*, 2 vols. I Tatti Renaissance Library (Cambridge, MA: Harvard University Press, 2012).

5 Dionysius is not the Athenian who was converted to Christianity by the preaching of St Paul on the Areopagus (Hill of Mars) during his visit to the city, as related in the Acts of the Apostles 17:19-34. During the sixth century a series of mystical writings, full of late Platonic idealism, was attributed to him. Their author is now known as Pseudo-Dionysius the Areopagite. Ficino translated two of his works, *Mystical Theology* and *The Divine Names*, adding commentaries of his own. These are now translated by M.J.B. Allen, *Marsilio Ficino on Dionysius the Areopagite*, 2 vols, I Tatti Renaissance Library (Cambridge, MA: Harvard University Press, 2015).

6 Ficino may have been able to borrow some works before the Medici hastily left Florence but he is probably referring to later events: On 9th November, 1494, when Piero de' Medici fled, seventeen chests of books were taken from the Medici palace to the monastery of San Marco where they remained until at least the following year. On 31st August, 1495, a committee was selected to choose items to be kept by the Signoria, and Ficino was a member of that committee.

7 Synesius of Cyrene (c.373–c.414) was a Greek Christian Platonist living in Libya. In 410 he became Bishop of Ptolemais. In 1484 Ficino had translated into Latin his *De insomniis* (*On Dreams*), a treatise on divination by means of dreams. It was published in the volume being prepared by Manutius.

8 Florence was repeatedly affected by epidemics: that of 1478-9 had been a particularly bad one, prompting Ficino to write his *Consilio contro la Pestilentia* (printed in 1481, but circulated in manuscript straight away), and the spring of 1497 was another. Then, as now, famine and shortages were associated with economic downturns caused by epidemics or war, and civil unrest is described in many sources.

In 1494, the year of the expulsion of the Medici, there had been frequent violent incidents in the streets. By January 1496, the city was divided, with some wanting to appease the French and others favouring a new alignment with the Pope and Milan. Public life was strikingly volatile, with several factions contending for dominance (see Introduction). Ficino remained in the city, though troubled with failing health and the death of his mother in November 1496.

9 Some have interpreted the 'hidden pestilence' referred to here as a reference to Savonarola. In Appendix Q Ficino applies that term to him.

10 From this, it is unclear whether Manutius was able to incorporate the first round of corrections into the text and Ficino was anticipating a second round – or whether it was too late for changes to be made to the typesetting, but errata would be recorded. However, no errata seemed to have appeared.

11 According to the colophon of the book, Girolamo Blondi or Biondo paid for the printing of the first edition of Ficino's letters, in Venice, 1495, for which he obtained

the necessary *privilegium* (Appendix J). The volume bears his imprint of a red phoenix. He was also thought to have been involved in the printing of the second edition in Nuremberg, in 1497, although the better-known name of Hartmann Schedel has also sometimes been associated with it. It appears that he also obtained the *privilegium* for the printing of the volume discussed in this letter, in April 1496. See Biographical Notes under both Blondi and Rossi.

O

1 The Latin text of this letter can be found in Kristeller, *Sup. Fic.*, II, pp. 314-6.

2 Egidio is often known as Giles of Viterbo. See Biographical Notes.

3 To a member of the Augustinian Order, like Giles, the chief city and centre of learning would have been Rome, the seat of the Church and the home of the largest library, in the Vatican.

4 Peripatetics: Aristotelians. Aristotle taught at the Lyceum in Athens, where he reputedly lectured in the *peripatoi,* the colonnades or covered walkways, walking up and down, and followed by his students as he did so. Hence his followers became known as the Peripatetics. At the time of this letter, Aristotelian philosophers dominated the University of Padua.

5 Plato believed in the existence of perfect, eternal, unchanging entities he called Forms (*eidē*) or Ideas (*ideai*). They were the only truly real things, and formed a hierarchy, with the Form of the Good at the summit. The Forms could not be perceived by the senses but only by the intelligence (*nous*) or understanding (*epistēmē*). The many sensible particulars in the phenomenal world derived what reality they had according to the degree to which they imitated or participated in the Forms. The word 'idea' is misleading: the Forms were not merely mental concepts. Plato held that they had an independent existence apart from the mind. Aristotle sharply criticised the theory on a number of grounds.

6 Egidio refers to three famous oracles: those of Jupiter Ammon in Libya; of Jupiter at Dodona in northwest Greece, where the god was supposed to speak through the rustling leaves of an oak; and of Apollo at Delphi in central Greece, where the god spoke through a priestess, the most celebrated oracle in the ancient world.

7 The effect Socrates has on the young Alcibiades is described in Plato's *Symposium*, 215D-216C. Alcibiades comes to appreciate the true qualities and inner nature of the philosopher. Being 'filled with the divine spirit of Socrates' may also refer to Socrates's *daimon* (see, for example, Plato, *Apology*, 31CD; Apuleius, *On the God of Socrates*, XIX) and this calls to mind the effect of the godly *daimon* of Plotinus in the temple of Isis, narrated by Porphyry in his *Life of Plotinus*, X, 14-25 and translated by Ficino, *Opera*, pp. 1541-2. For more on the *daimon* of Socrates, see Apuleius, *On the God of Socrates*.

8 Egidio's text is here seriously corrupt. The Latin reads '*et Thermopylis et canis acrioris*', literally 'and Thermopylae and of the fiercer (or keener) dog', which is meaningless in the context. We have conjectured '*Thermopylis et Cannis*', although it is possible that several words are missing. The version printed in Giles's own letters suffers from the same defect. Giles of Viterbo, *Lettere Familiari*, ed. by Anna Maria Voci-Roth (Rome: Institutum Historicum Augustinianum, 1990), I, 101–102. Thermopylae and Cannae were the sites of two decisive historic battles against deadly enemies. The Greeks lost

to the Persians at Thermopylae in 480 BC and the Romans to the Carthaginians at Cannae in 216 BC. What follows is an imaginary battle scene, set in the days of the Trojan War, but the presence of Plato is anachronistic.

9 'You could see': following a Greek usage for '*cernere erat*', cf. Virgil, *Aeneid*, VIII, 767.

10 Priam had, by various concubines and wives, fifty sons, amongst whom were both Hector and Paris. Egidio probably refers here to Hector as he was the leading warrior on the Trojan side. The most famous of the deaths at his hand was that of Patroclus, in revenge for which Hector in turn was slain by Achilles. However, Egidio has written 'Plato' here – even though the philosopher lived some 800 years later than the Trojan War. Plato did see active military service, but from 409 to 404 BC.

11 Memnon was an Ethiopian king who brought an army to Troy to help the beleaguered city. He was killed by Achilles. A statue of Memnon in Egyptian Thebes was said to make a sound like a broken lyre string when touched by the first rays of the rising sun.

12 The Amazons were a race of fierce warrior women said to have lived in Pontus, in Asia Minor, by the Black Sea. It is now thought they may have been nomadic Scythian women, obliged to defend themselves and their flocks during the long absences of their menfolk. Their queen, Penthesilea, led them to fight on the Trojan side in the war, in which she was slain by Achilles. The name Amazon is traditionally said to have been derived from *a-mastos,* without a breast, because they were said to have their right breast seared during childhood to enable them to use a bow and arrows more easily, but their favourite weapon was a two-sided axe.

13 Paris was a son of Priam. Before his birth his mother, Hecuba, had a dream that she would give birth to a flaming brand, interpreted to mean that her son would be the destruction of Troy. So it proved. Paris was chosen to judge the beauty contest between Hera (Juno), Athena (Minerva) and Aphrodite (Venus), which led to the outbreak of the Trojan War. Paris awarded the golden apple to Aphrodite, who had promised him the love of the most beautiful woman in the world, that is, Helen, who was already the wife of the Spartan king Menelaus. Paris duly abducted Helen, which led the Greeks, under Menelaus's brother Agamemnon, to launch a great expedition against Troy to recover her. Homer depicts Paris as cowardly. It was he who (with Apollo's help) lay in ambush for Achilles and killed him by firing an arrow into his heel, the only part of him that was mortal.

14 Egidio refers to Ficino's translations into Latin of various texts by Iamblichus, Synesius, Porphyry, Proclus, Xenocrates, Psellus and other Neo-Platonists, published in one volume by Aldus Manutius of Venice in September 1497.

15 Egidio refers to the 'Republic of Letters', a phrase that became much more popular with the rise of the Academies in the 16th century, but can be found as early as 1417 in a Florentine context (in a letter from Francesco Barbaro to Poggio Bracciolini dated 6th July, 1417).

16 The *Platonic Theology* (*Theologia platonica*) was Ficino's *magnum opus*. In eighteen books, it was written between 1469 and 1474, and published in 1482.

17 i.e. burning the midnight oil.

18 The editor, Kristeller, marks this passage 'seriously corrupt' (*locus graviter corruptus*). The switch from third person plural (*appellent*) to first (*fateamur*) is awkward in the extreme. We further suspect that *utros* should read *utrum*.

19 Egidio here alludes to the famous 'Messianic' Fourth Eclogue of Virgil, written in 40 BC. In it the poet foresees the coming of a new Golden Age inaugurated by the birth of a child (*puer*).
In late antiquity and the Middle Ages the poem was thought to be a prophecy of the birth of Christ, and Virgil was regarded as a prophet like Isaiah. Hence Dante calls Virgil the master, and chooses him as his guide to the very gates of Paradise.
The Golden Age was supposed to have taken place under the reign of Saturn (*Saturnia regna*), Jupiter's father and predecessor as king of the gods, when peace and harmony reigned, and man did not have to work by the sweat of his brow to cultivate the earth, which of its own accord produced food in abundance.
A Sibyl was a prophetess with oracular powers. There were several, the most famous being the Sibyl of Cumae near Naples, who foretells the birth of the child saviour in the Fourth Eclogue, and whom Aeneas consults before his descent into the underworld in Book VI of the *Aeneid*.

P

1 R. Marcel, *Marsile Ficin* (Paris: Les Belles Lettres, 1958), pp. 575-6.
2 S.R. Jayne, *John Colet and Marsilio Ficino* (Oxford: Oxford University Press, 1963).
3 J.B. Gleason, *John Colet* (Berkeley: University of California Press, 1989).
4 The word play here between *colet* (John's name), *colenti* ('to one who cherishes') and *colendo* ('one who is to be cherished') cannot be fully rendered in English. The verb *colo* itself covers many meanings, including to cultivate land, to worship a deity, and to dwell in a place, and to cultivate the friendship of someone through constant attention.
5 For the image in the lover's own soul, see *De amore*, II, 8; on the formation of a superior image, more beautiful than the first, *De amore*, VII, 1.
6 A reference to one of the stages of gradual clarification in vision and understanding, from Plato's Cave allegory, *Republic*, VII, 514A–520A.
7 Jayne suggests that Colet had reflected back to Ficino his own musings on Phoebean characters, which is expressed in many of his letters.
8 We have not replicated here the initial draft and later changes Colet made to what survives of this letter. They can be found in Jayne, *John Colet and Marsilio Ficino*, p. 82.
9 Cf. Romans 8:24-25.
10 Colet's apparent end of life concerns were probably not specific but an expression of a common trope. He did not have serious health issues until 1514, and died from his third bout of 'sweating sickness', during the epidemic of 1519, at the respectable age of 52.
11 The Latin terms used here are *intelligentia* and *amor.* Ficino discusses the different roles of love and understanding, or will and intellect, in several places, notably *Letters*, **1**, 115 and **6**, 42 and 44. Colet made notes against the first of these (Jayne, p. 102). The description here, though, is expressed in rather different terms, not unlike those in St Augustine, *De Trinitate*, IX, 12, 18. For the controversial nature of such discussions, see the notes to *Letters*, **1**, 115 in the revised edition (2018). See also *A Companion to the Study of St. Augustine*, ed. by R.W. Battenhouse (New York: Oxford University Press, 1955), pp. 300-4.

12 This is an abrupt end, and may therefore indicate it is only part of a letter Ficino sent, but no other version is extant. We should also remember that Colet's transcription is sometimes faulty.

Q

1 The Latin text of this *Apology* was preserved in two manuscripts, the 16th century Magl. VIII, 1443, on folios 144-5, published by Luigi Passerini (*Giornale Storico degli Archivi Toscani*, III, 1859), then by Kristeller, *Sup. Fic.*, II, pp. 76-9. The second manuscript was discovered more recently and was bought by the Bridwell library of Perkins School of Theology, Southern Methodist University. It was published by Volkhard Wels, *The Antichrist Girolamo of Ferrara, Greatest of all Hypocrites* (Dallas, 2006). Neither manuscript is in Ficino's hand.

The *Apology* has been discussed by many scholars, including Lorenzo Polizzotto in *The Elect Nation: The Savonarolan Movement in Florence 1494-1545* (Oxford: Clarendon Press, 1994), pp. 94-104. Doubt has been cast on whether it was in fact ever sent to the College of Cardinals, since another statement was submitted on behalf of the cathedral canons and the Florentine people, that of Giovanni Francesco di Poggio Bracciolini (a canon lawyer, cathedral canon and son of the famous scholar of the same name (1380-1459). Bracciolini's well-reasoned apology was also addressed to the College of Cardinals and covers comparable ground, though in a different tone. It was judged expedient to send it, even though the canons had already been exonerated by the Pope once Savonarola had been imprisoned. Bracciolini's version was published in Rome by Eucharius Silber (c.1500) and also in Nuremberg. This *Apology*, if it really was penned by Ficino, may have been intended for circulation among his friends and patrons in Florence or Rome, to make his position publicly clear, or perhaps it was only a draft for use by the cathedral chapter, one that was not ultimately used. At all events it serves as a good demonstration of imaginative thinking on a difficult issue at a time of great local distress.

2 Girolamo of Ferrara is Girolamo Savonarola (1452-1498), the Dominican friar and preacher who returned to Florence in 1490 and held sway between 1494 and 1498. He denounced clerical corruption, despotic rule, and the exploitation of the poor. He prophesied the coming of a divine scourge and a conqueror from the north who would reform the Church. In 1494, when Charles VIII of France invaded Italy and threatened Florence, his prophecies seemed about to be fulfilled. Savonarola took part in the embassy to the French king, while the Florentine citizens expelled Piero de' Medici, who had surrendered fortresses to the invading army. At Savonarola's urging, they established a popular republic. Savonarola's influence was at its height and he instituted a campaign of extreme austerity with denunciations, bonfires of the vanities, processions, and pious theatricals. In May 1497, following Florence's failure to join the Holy League, which was attributed to Savonarola's influence, he was excommunicated by Pope Alexander VI. Public opinion began to turn against him, though there were strong factions for and against. In May 1498, he was imprisoned, tried, and eventually hanged and burned with two of his supporters, Fra Domenico Buonvicini da Pescia and Fra Silvestro Maruffi, in the main square of Florence. Ficino had initially supported Savonarola when he first arrived in

Florence but later rejected his views and was criticised by Savonarola in his sermons.

3 The Latin term, *lustrum*, usually means 'a period of five years'. However, the word was sometimes used of a four-year period, and so we have taken it, given that Savonarola's 'reign', or period in power, can be considered as lasting from November 1494 to 23rd May 1498.

4 This invokes the example of Adam and Eve in a way that minimises their responsibility, just as he will seek to minimise the responsibility of the ordinary citizens of Florence for what happened in the city. The nature of Adam's error had been the topic of a famous theological dispute in Florence in 1489 between the Dominicans, represented by Niccolò de Mirabilibus, and the Franciscans, represented by Giorgio Benigno Salviati. Ficino had been among the large audience present at the debate (See *Letters*, **8**, pp. 128 and 131-2).

5 The arrival of the French troops posed a real threat to the city and its wider territory. It also introduced a period of increasing factional division within the city. It is interesting that Savonarola is now characterised as not just demonically inspired, but as having a whole host of demons crowded into him – though his reputation was nevertheless that of a holy man.

6 The 'force' included the bands of youth, *fanciulli*, orchestrated from San Marco, who went round the city shaming people by collecting 'instruments of vanity', often accompanied by intimidation. Street violence was nothing new in the city, but demarcations between factions were more drawn at this time than any other. See Introduction.

7 The contrast in preaching styles between Savonarola and Ficino could hardly have been greater. Contemporary hearers would have been used to strong language from preachers, especially Dominicans. One contemporary reported '. . . visions of ruin, voices, candelabras, trumpets . . . his sermons inflamed everyone's mind. It seemed as if it was not he who was talking, nor was it organized in the usual way. It was as if the spirit was talking through his mouth.' (Fra Giovanni Caroli, a fellow Dominican, quoted in Weinstein, *Savonarola: The Rise and Fall of a Renaissance Prophet*, p. 78), but there were also many preachers who favoured gentler persuasion and expressions of love. Many of Savonarola's sermons are available in translation, although the written versions do not convey the drama with which he infused them in the pulpit. See, for example, *A Guide to Righteous Living and other Works*, tr. by Konrad Eisenbichler, Toronto, 2003, pp. 81-176.

By contrast, some of Ficino's sermons may be read within his letter collection, for example *Letters*, **7**, 41. Eleven earlier sermons were also translated into the vernacular for wider circulation, in a volume of *Sermoni morali della Stultitia et Miseria degli Uomini*, addressed to Jacopo Guicciardini in 1478 (*Letters*, **1**, 57, 58, 59, 68, 69, 95, 110; **2**, 62 joined with **3**, 27; **3**, 1; **4**, 1 and 5). Further sermons of Ficino await an English translation (in preparation) but are in the *Opera omnia*, pp. 473-93 and a new critical edition by Daniele Conti, *Marsilii Ficini Florentini Predicationes*, Turin: Aragno, 2014.

8 The author points up Savonarola's cruel character by distorting his name as 'Saevonerola'. *Saevus* means 'fierce', 'cruel' or 'savage'. The term *Saevus Nero*, identifying the Antichrist with the Roman emperor of evil repute, was also used in early patristic literature.

9 Apollonius (first century AD) was a Greek Neo-Pythagorean holy man from Tyana, in Cappadocia. He was a contemporary of Jesus, to whom he was compared by

several Christian and other writers. The main source on his life, including his miracles and his travels to India, is not entirely reliable but became very popular during the Renaissance: *Life of Apollonius of Tyana*, by the Athenian writer, Philostratus (170-247AD). Ficino had already cited from it in his *Platonic Theology*. Alamanno Rinuccini (1419-1499) produced a Latin translation of it, but it was not published until after his death, in 1501 (revised by Filippo Beroaldo and published by Aldus Manutius).

10 In Plato's *Meno* (79E-80B), the numbing effect of Socrates's questioning is compared to that of the 'torpedo fish' or electric ray (*narke* means numbness as well as the name of the fish).

11 Galatians 3:1. The King James Version of the Bible, which we generally follow, translates *credere* as 'obey' rather than its other meaning to 'believe', but the latter is more obviously relevant here.

12 Following the Bridwell manuscript, which supplies text missing because unreadable in Kristeller's source.

13 St Matthew 7:15-16.

14 2 Corinthians 11:13-15. This underlines the difficulty people had in avoiding falling for deception.

15 An alternative spelling is used here.

16 Cf. the demon who became 'legion' in the story of the Gadarene swine, St Mark 5:1-13.

17 This may be a reference to the Franciscan order in the person of Francesco da Puglia, a friar at Santa Croce who challenged Savonarola to an ordeal by fire in a sermon on 25th March, 1498. Responding on behalf of the Dominicans, since Savonarola was himself under interdict, Domenico Buonvicini da Pescia accepted the challenge. After much public consternation, in Florence and Rome, and the substitution of another Franciscan friar for the original challenger, an elaborate bonfire was duly prepared for the two friars to go through, to see whose innocence would be upheld by divine protection. The date was set for 6th April, then changed to 7th. On the day, everything was ready and crowds had assembled but, by the time they had argued about removing specific items of clothing and whether or not the Host could be carried, a heavy thunderstorm broke out, soaking the logs and brushwood, and the trial was abandoned.

18 Ficino's good friend, Giovanni Canacci, held office as a prior during the ascendancy of Savonarola, and played an important part in bringing him to account. See Biographical Notes.

19 Virgil, *Aeneid* II, 402.

20 Both Orpheus and Hercules had to enter the underworld in pursuit of their quests, Orpheus to regain his bride Eurydice and Hercules to fulfil his twelfth labour. The most familiar versions of these stories were recounted by Virgil, *Georgics*, IV, 457-503 and Ovid, *Metamorphoses*, X, 3-63 (Orpheus) and by Seneca, *Hercules Furens*, 46-62; 662ff. (Hercules).

21 This is based on Psalm 68:1-2 'Let God arise, let his enemies be scattered: let them also that hate him flee before him. As smoke is driven away, so drive them away: as wax melteth before the fire, so let the wicked perish at the presence of God,' followed by the injunction to rejoice and 'sing unto God' in verses 3-4, then the words of the Magnificat (Luke 1:51): 'He hath shewed strength with his arm; he hath scattered the proud in the imagination of their hearts.'

22 See note 16 above for the revival of the ancient ritual of trial by fire. The determination of the Dominicans not to send their champion into the flames without the Host caused great controversy and accusations of sacrilege. After the fiasco of the thunderstorm, an enraged populace clamoured for Savonarola's downfall. On 8th May, 1498, he was arrested by the Signoria and tried for heresy, together with Fra Domenico Buonvicini and Fra Silvestro. On 23rd May all three were hanged and their bodies were burned. See Plate 8.

23 The first 'College' here refers to the College of Cardinals in Rome, the second 'College' is the Cathedral Chapter of Florence Cathedral.

R

1 From the State Archives of Florence, Archivio Notarile, vol. M 239, f.68 and published in *Sup. Fic.*, II, pp. 193-201. Ficino's title is given in Latin as *Dominus*, while the witnesses are all *Fratres* ('friars' or 'brothers'). As there is no justification for applying the honorific 'Lord', or making him a 'Father' of the monastery, we have rendered *Dominus* here as 'the venerable'.

2 An 'indiction' indicates a particular year within a 15-year cycle, commonly used for dating legal documents.

3 Some of the monks of San Marco listed here have been noted in other volumes of the letters: Giorgio Antonio Vespucci (1435-1514) was a confidant of Ficino, a fellow canon of the cathedral, and a highly respected educator. He had joined the monastery of San Marco in 1497 after a distinguished career (*Letters*, **2**, 21; **3**, 5; **4**, 47; **6**, 3 and Biographical Note *Letters*, **6**, p.111); Amerigo is mentioned here as his father but the more famous Amerigo is his nephew, who gave his name to America. Friar Vincenzo Nicolai of Ranga is thought to be the Vincenzo who was taken prisoner while on a mission to Hungary in 1483 (*Letters*, **7**, 33, 37, 52 and 61). He is described as a *necessarius* of Ficino, suggesting he was in some way dependent on him. Kristeller suggests an identification with Vincentius of San Gimignano (Vincenzo Mainardi, 1481-1527), who would have been just 18 years old, and who later became procurator of the Dominican Order at the Roman Curia and wrote a life of San Antonino of Florence. But the name as given clearly rules this out. Pietro Antonio appears to be the name taken on entry to the monastery by Leonardo of Colle, a well-known notary who held several magistracies (*Letters*, **5**, 24 and, according to some, **9**, 8); Onofrio of Pietro Dati (or Onofrio Dazzi) is recorded as being 86 in 1560, so would have been a young monk of 25 at the time of this document; Bonifazio Landini (d. 1527) is known for at least one song setting written for the monastery; a Donato di Bonaventura of Florence is known only as a Dominican, in Florence and in Lucca; Francesco Gondi was a member of a leading family of bankers.

4 The full name of Ficino's father was Dietifeci (or Diotifieci) d'Agnolo di Giusto of Figline. The title *Magister*, Master, refers to his status as a graduate of the higher degree of Medicine.

5 Ficino died two days after this will was written, on 1st October, 1499. He was buried in the Cathedral of Santa Maria del Fiore, with due honours. An oration was delivered by the Chancellor, Marcello Virgilio Adriani, in the presence of a large number of people of all ranks. In 1521, the famous bust by Andrea Ferrucci

(reproduced as the frontispiece to *Letters*, **1** was added, with an inscription to honour Ficino's memory. This is offered in translation as Appendix V.

6 Lorenzo di Pierfrancesco de' Medici and Giovanni Cavalcanti, both noblemen, had been Ficino's friends for many years. For letters to Lorenzo (sometimes called the Younger, to distinguish him from his cousin, Lorenzo the Magnificent), see *Letters*, **4**, 46; **9**, 2 and 12 and perhaps **6**, 10. The letters to Cavalcanti or written jointly with Cavalcanti are too numerous to list, but see *Letters*, **1-6**, and 38 and 40 in this volume. The notary is Jacopo di Martino Martini (cf. *Letters*, **9**, 1, and Biographical Notes).

7 The Florentine gold coin, or florin, was a currency of international trade as well as domestic exchange. Of fixed weight and purity since first minted in 1252, and therefore of assured value, it had been issued in more than one form: most versions were small, a little smaller, thinner and lighter than our current 10p coin (cf. 5 euro, US nickel), and thus convenient to handle, but a larger coin first minted in 1422 was meant to challenge the Venetian ducat. This was known as the 'large florin'. Although of larger diameter, it was also thinner, therefore nominally similar in value, though values fluctuated somewhat. There was also a notional currency, the so-called 'florins of account', used for accounting purposes. Their value was calibrated against the gold florin and varied with time. These monies of account included the *fiorino largo d'oro* and its later replacement, the *fiorino largo d'oro in oro*. Both are mentioned in the course of this will. 'Three pounds of small florins': Given the small weight and size of gold florins, three pounds in weight would be a sizeable sum. This is therefore more likely to be an expression of monetary value in terms of the pound or *lira*. Originally the gold florin had been worth one lira in the old Roman system of lire, soldi and denarii (terms which, unlike their English equivalent of pounds, shillings and pence, were all used as units of weight and linear measure as well as value) but that parity had long since vanished with the economic expansion of the thirteenth and fourteenth centuries and the gradual debasement of silver.

The 'main church' is presumed to be the cathedral, Santa Maria del Fiore, of which Ficino was a canon and where he was buried. It was by far the largest church in the city, although Santa Maria Novella was regarded as the main Dominican church, and the cathedral is named again for a bequest later in the will. Curiously the masses in Ficino's honour were to be said at San Marco rather than either of the two larger churches. This was perhaps in recognition of its special place in the spiritual life of the city ever since its restoration by Cosimo de' Medici in 1438.

8 Gregorian masses, first instituted as a cycle of 30 masses by Pope Gregory the Great in 590, were believed to release from purgatory the soul for whom they were said. The sum of money mentioned here as 'large florins of gold in gold', a money of account, could in practice be settled in silver or gold (see note 7).

9 Ficino had been rector of the Church of San Cristofano in Novoli (which still stands in what is now a suburb of Florence) since January 1474, and of San Bartolomeo in Pomino since January 1473. He was ordained a priest in December 1473.

10 In *Letters*, **7**, 24, Ficino spoke of his domestic obligations, in terms of needing to support his orphaned nephews and provide dowries for his nieces, but his housekeeper and her daughters are named here for the first time. A dowry of 850 florins for his niece, Alessandra (d.1510), is attested in the diary of her husband Biagio Buonaccorsi on 15th April, 1495.

11 Sebastiano Salvini was Ficino's cousin, who served also as scribe for some years and as collaborator on theological matters. Theirs was a close relationship over many decades. See Biographical Notes.

12 Luca Fabiano (d.1520) served Ficino as a scribe and amanuensis from 1476 or 1477. In the early period of his employment Ficino wrote him a curious letter on appropriate behaviour and speech (*Letters*, **3**, 46); he also added a personal note at the foot of Ficino's letter to the musician Sebastiano Foresi (*Letters*, **4**, 11). By 1491, Luca was also a notary, and by 1492 was also an assistant in the chancery, although continuing to live with Ficino. His work for the chancery continued for 26 years. The closeness of his relationship with Ficino is shown by his treatment in the will, and by the fact that when Fabiano married and had a son, he named him Marsilius de Ficinis.

13 San Martino cloth was a generic name for cloth made in Florence from the finest English wool. It is not clear whether the cloaks, hoods and caps were to be new items specially purchased, or simply the best among Ficino's existing wardrobe. Even if not brand new, these would have been plain garments of distinction, suitable for an official occasion.

14 The 'house where he lived' could refer to the house in the Via Larga which he acquired on 15th September, 1497 (having lived previously, with his mother, in a house provided by Cosimo de' Medici near Santa Maria Nuova), or to the villa at Careggi. It is thought that he lived mainly in the city during his final year, on account of ill health.

15 Ficino owned two copies of the works of Plato in Greek and also at some time had access to Cardinal Bessarion's copy. One copy was given to him by Cosimo de' Medici in 1462: Laurenziana, MS LXXXV, 9. This is thought to have been a copy of the codex presented to Cosimo by the Byzantine Emperor John Paleologus at the Council of Ferrara/Florence in 1439. Although Ficino refers to it as being on good paper, it was in fact a parchment manuscript. He designated it to be left to Lorenzo di Pierfrancesco, partly on account of his interest in Plato, but also as a member of the Medici family still in Florence, and perhaps even also in recognition of the ways in which the elder branches of the Medici house (i.e. Lorenzo, Piero, Giovanni) had not always fulfilled their financial obligations to the younger.

16 *Carta bombacina* was the heaviest, best quality grade of paper available. Whether it was made from silk and cotton is a question still debated.

17 Although the will calls him Francesco of Zanobi Ghiacceto, this is unquestionably Ficino's pupil and successor, Francesco Cattani da Diacceto. Spelling of names was often fluid at that time.

18 The second Plato codex in Greek had belonged to Amerigo Benci, a senior member of the Medici bank and a wealthy collector, who gave or lent it to Ficino in 1462, or possibly 1464 (*Letters*, **1**, 3). Ficino lent it on to Francesco Cattani da Diacceto, and is here arranging for its return if required. It contained some but not all of the dialogues.

19 Antonia's daughters were provided for above. This is a separate provision for her, in return for services rendered.

20 Spelt 'Fabbiano' on this occasion, another example of fluid spellings.

21 The Venetian term 'ducat' was also in use in Florence. For the large gold florin, see note 7 above.

22 Ficino has obviously gone to some lengths to provide security for Luca Fabiani. He was not family, but their relationship was a close one. His work for Ficino was

extensive, even though he took on other tasks for the city even before Ficino died. See note 12 above.

23 This is Ficino Ficini, who lived with Ficino and served as his amanuensis in his later years. He was the son of Marsilio's brother Cherubino. After Ficino's death he remained a pupil of Francesco Diacceto.

24 From the paragraph that follows, this would appear to mean the house on the estate at Careggi.

25 The ultimate destinations of the books varied, and they ended up in different collections over time, many finding their way to the great libraries of Florence after one or two generations.

26 This was the estate given to Ficino by Cosimo de' Medici in April 1463.

27 This legal formula provides an interesting reflection on how long was expected of 'perpetuity'!

28 This land was inherited from Ficino's mother, who died in 1496, and was intended for the joint benefit of her sons. An arbitration of 1498 had adjusted the claims of the various parties. The 'sester' is a measure derived from the Roman *sextarius*. The size of a sester varied according to time and place and it has not been possible to verify what quantity is intended here.

29 A benefice in Monte Martiano had been given to Ficino by Giovanni de' Medici in 1492 (*Letters*, **10**, 18). From the income provided to Luca Fabiano by Ficino's family, he is to be responsible as *pensionarius* (in the mediaeval usage of that term) for the payment of a 'pension' to one or other of those churches that would presumably be honouring Ficno's name and praying for his soul.

30 Now that provision has been made for Luca and others, the remainder of his estate, as is to be expected, is shared among his family members and their heirs – but only for three generations, after which it reverts to the Cathedral. Ficino was survived by one brother, Arcangelo, two sisters, and the three nephews mentioned.
Dietifeci, his brother Daniele's son, died in 1507 as a result of a physical assault.
Dietifeci's sister Alessandra (who received a simple dowry, not a share of the estate inheritable by her heirs) died in 1510.

31 It would be interesting to know whether such a provision is frequent in wills of the period, or whether it is an unusual expression of wisdom from beyond the grave!

32 Here it is unclear whether this refers to the city house or Careggi, but would no doubt have been clear at the time. Ficino lived in the city as well as on the estate in Careggi. There were other houses where Ficino did not live: the *catasto* (tax register) of 1498 records a house shared with his brother Arcangelo in Figline as well as four *poderi* in Montevarchi and a house in Montevarchi.

33 It was not unusual for monies to be deposited with hospitals for safe keeping, cf. the Ospedale in Siena, which met all the needs of travelling pilgrims including care of valuables.

34 The canons who fulfilled these executor functions were Simone Rucellai and Giovanni Vespucci.

35 It is worth noting that Luca's share is a full half of the residual estate, but family had also been provided for. Given all the provisions in this will, it is interesting to remember that Ficino reminds his correspondents on several occasions that he lived a simple life on very restricted means, and he always claimed to be content with what he had. From the will it is clear that he had sufficient, especially after the inheritance from his mother in 1496.

36 The *Lex falcidia*: an ancient law, from Roman times, prevented a testator from depriving his natural heir, who must receive at least one quarter of the estate.

37 Another form of protection of bequests, especially the inheritance of the natural heir. During the reign of Nero, in the consulship of Trebellius Maximus and the philosopher Seneca, a Senate resolution of this name protected a beneficiary from deductions or charges against the estate that would diminish his inheritance. Both this and the Falcidian protection could be abrogated by the testator if he made specific mention of the intention to do so.

S

1 This letter was found recently in the Darmstaedter Collection of the State Library of Berlin by Eef Overgaauw and Valerio Sanzotta, and was published in *Interpres*, XXIX (2010), pp. 171–182.

2 The circumstances in which the letter was written are not entirely clear. Ficino calls himself 'ancient servant' of the Medici, whose orbit he entered in the 1450s. It is addressed to Lorenzo as 'sole patron', and must therefore have been written after the death of Piero de' Medici in 1469. It speaks of 'Castor and Pollux', certainly referring to Lorenzo and Giuliano de' Medici (see also letter to Jacopo Ammannati, *Letters*, **2**, 54), and therefore can be presumed to predate the death of Giuliano, murdered on 26th April, 1478. Although Ficino had dedicated the first book of his letters to Giuliano around 1473, and still referred to the two brothers as 'my patrons' both here and in February 1476 in the letter to Ammannati, Lorenzo may nevertheless have been considered his primary patron by 1475. Certainly that was the year in which Ficino and Lorenzo appear to have drawn apart from one another. Between 1474 and 1476 there were also strong rivalries in Lorenzo's court, with bitter feelings vented in the harsh satires of Lorenzo's companion, Luigi Pulci. Lorenzo's chaplain, Matteo Franco, came under attack, as did Ficino himself (see *Letters*, **1**, 113 and 114; **2**, 5 and 6). On Pulci, see *Luigi Pulci in Renaissance Florence and Beyond: New Perspectives on his Poetry and Influence*, ed. by James Coleman and Andrea Moudarres (Turnhout: Brepols, 2017).
Based on the date of Pentecost, which is given here as 15th May, the most likely year for the inauspicious visit to Lorenzo's house is 1475: Easter Sunday fell on 27th March (Julian calendar) that year, with Pentecost on 14/15th May. The letter itself tells us that the date of writing was more than seven months after that, and reference to the movements of Saturn, Mars, and Mercury were confirmed in the contemporary astronomical tables of Regiomontanus by Overgaauw and Sanzotta. This suggests a likely date for the letter of January 1476, but the nature of the untoward event and the identity of the two works that Ficino delivered at the time of Pentecost are not obvious. Few of Ficino's letters can be dated to this period, and those that are were not addressed to Lorenzo.

3 The 'happiness' referred to here is that in the greeting above, though Ficino may also have been wishing to recall the interest they both had in happiness, reflected in the treatise on happiness he had written for Lorenzo earlier (*Letters*, **1**, 115, dated tentatively to 1473) and in Lorenzo's own poem *L'Altercazione*.

4 Diagoras of Melos (5th century BC) died in Corinth, where he had fled to escape accusations of impiety in Athens. According to Diogenes Laertius, *Lives of Eminent*

Philosophers, Protagoras of Abdera (5th century BC), a great teacher of Sophistic argument, fled Athens after being charged with impiety. Anaxagoras committed suicide after his trial for impiety, on account of the indignity of it. Many legends surround the death of Pythagoras, but all agree on his having been murdered by opponents. The death of Socrates after his trial, including accusations of impiety, is narrated by Plato in *Phaedo*. The trial itself is described in the *Apology*.

5 Demosthenes, great orator of the 4th century BC in Athens, fled to a sanctuary on the island of Poros, during the disturbances that followed the death of Alexander of Macedon. Captured there, he preferred suicide by poison. Cicero, who was greatly influenced by Greek philosophers and also became the most powerful orator in the Roman courts, was murdered while fleeing from Rome in 43 BC during the turbulence that followed the assassination of Julius Caesar.

6 Both Demosthenes and Cicero were responsible for the successful prosecution of notable politicians, by fearlessly exposing their wrongdoings, even though this might bring enmity and revenge.

7 For Ficino's unpopularity at this time with some of Lorenzo's courtiers, see note 2 above and descriptions of Lorenzo's court such as André Rochon, *La jeunesse de Laurent de Médicis: 1449-1478*, Paris: Les Belles Lettres, 1963.

8 'Happy, ah too happy,' is deliberately reminiscent of Dido's lament in Virgil, *Aeneid*, IV, 657, as she is about to throw herself on the funeral pyre. The Ides of May fall on 15th May. See note 2 above.

9 Vulcan refers to the flames, Pluto to burying the gifts in question; Castor and Pollux, the famous twins rewarded with life as stars after they died, refer to Lorenzo and his brother Giuliano. This dates the letter to before 1477, as there is reference to Whitsun, the feast of the Holy Spirit, and Giuliano died in April 1478. But which of the years between 1469 (when Piero died, making Lorenzo sole patron) and 1477 is uncertain.

10 Either the celestial Phoebus or, more likely, Lorenzo. Lorenzo's adoption of the laurel as his emblem indicates his identification with Phoebus.

11 Julius Caesar (100-44 BC), who in general did not spare enemies in war, spared those in Spain (Caesar, *Civil War*, 74,1). On his return to Rome at the end of the war, he famously pardoned those who had opposed him, so as to make a permanent break with the previous culture of murder and proscriptions used by his predecessors. He was thereafter known for his clemency, even though some, like Cato, took such pardon as an affront to their honour and rejected it.

12 Publius Cornelius Scipio (236-183 BC) was famed for his victories in the Carthaginian wars. He earned a reputation for magnanimity and compassion, humility and forbearance. Livy, *History of* Rome, XXXIII-XXXVII; Seneca, *Epistles*, 86. He was also the subject of Cicero's *Dream of Scipio* and the hero of Petrarch's Latin epic *Africa*, becoming a symbol of clemency and restraint.

13 Cf. *Letters*, **6**, 7.

T

1 These letters, both in the vernacular, are printed in Kristeller, *Marsilio Ficino and his Work after Five Hundred Years*, p. 34.

2 Lanfredini was Florentine ambassador to Rome.

3 Abbreviated as N.S., for *Nostro Signore*, indicating the pope, Innocent VIII.

4 The bishopric did not in fact fall vacant in Ficino's lifetime.

5 Ficino already held two benefices in small communities outside Florence: he was parish priest in San Bartolomeo, Pomino, from January 1473, and of San Cristofano, Novoli, from January 1474. He held a canonry in the Cathedral from 1487, though that may not have been counted in the same way. On 25th April, 1492, he thanked Giovanni de' Medici for the gift of the benefice of 'the Martiana church', whose precise location is not certain (*Letters*, **10**, 18 and note on pp. 69-70). Ficino's will also mentions the grain revenues from this benefice (Appendix R). However, there may have been some other benefice in view in October, 1489, the date of this letter, since the Martiana church is described in 1492 as being a benefice that had been bestowed on Giovanni, rather than a vacant one.

6 Princes of the Church, like Giovanni de' Medici, held numerous benefices, but rules did apply to lesser persons, though they could be waived by dispensation.

U

1 The Latin text of this recently rediscovered letter appears as Appendix I in Guido Bartolucci's edition of Ficino's *De christiana religione* (Pisa: 2019), pp. 311-2.

2 See Biographical Notes under Guido di Lorenzo. For Ficino's letter to Paolo Orlandini, a monk in the same monastery, see Appendix L.

3 Besides the three scourges of disease, famine and civic unrest in Florence that Ficino referred to in his letter to Manutius at the same period (Appendix N), the monastery of the Angeli experienced in 1486 a number of disturbances, including riots with physical violence, leading to imprisonment of some of the monks. A subsequent visit from Pietro Delfin, the Vicar General of the Camaldolese order, led to a strongly worded letter (6th December, 1487), criticising the Prior for allowing use of the monastery's church for secular study. Ficino had close relations with the monastery throughout this period, and had permission to preach there in the evenings from his own cathedral chapter, confirmed just three days after Delfin's letter. (Though famous by now as a philosopher, Ficino was also a priest and had become a canon of the cathedral in April 1487.) Whether he was considered by Delfin to be among the outsiders teaching secular subjects later that year is still debated (see Stéphane Toussaint, 'Plotin chez les Moines. En marge des Ennéades: Marsile Ficin dans une lettre de Pietro Defino Camaldule?', *Accademia*, VI (2004), pp. 47-57.) But Salvini, the author of this letter, was himself a priest and a theologian, working in the papal Curia.

4 Virgil, *Aeneid*, VI, 136-7.

5 Cicero, *De officiis,* I, 6.

6 Psalm 111:10.

7 Proverbs 16:6.

8 Quoting Seneca, *Letter to Lucilius*, 87.

9 Cf. Aulus Gellius, *Attic Nights*, V, 5, 3.

10 Virgil, *Aeneid*, VII, 274-5. In the first line, Salvini has added *collo,* 'from the neck', often used in such contexts, though not in the original Virgilian lines.

11 Cf. Psalm 6:6.

12 The sculptor Phidias (5th century BC) was the artistic director for the building of the Parthenon in Athens, and made for it a gold and ivory statue of Athena, a standing figure holding a spear and a Nike (symbol of victory), completed in 438 BC. His gold and ivory statue of Zeus at Olympia, completed a few years later, was one of the seven wonders of the ancient world. The Roman goddess, Minerva, was accorded all the attributes of Athena.

13 Plato, *Phaedrus*, 279B-C.

14 Cf. Job 28:15-16.

15 I Corinthians 13:13.

16 Eusebius, in the second part of his *Chronicon*, records Herodotus being honoured for reading his books in the assembly at Athens just prior to the 84th Olympiad. All the following names are recorded as being 'well known', 'important' or 'notable', mostly in the 84th to 86th Olympiads (444-433 BC), with Socrates being 'celebrated for his superlative eloquence' in the 86th. Plato is mentioned several times, recording his birth, his death and periods of distinction in the 98th and 101st Olympiads, (389-373 BC); Aristotle is named as a young hearer of Plato in the 103rd.

17 Acts 1:1.

18 Virgil, *Aeneid*, VI, 129.

19 Salvini had contributed in significant ways to Ficino's *De christiana religione*, which was written in 1474, printed in Latin in 1476 and again in Tuscan with some additions in 1484. He provided some material on earlier religious controversies less familiar to Ficino, and discussed points of theology with him. See Bartolucci's edition, mentioned in note 1 above.

V

1 This epitaph is inscribed in Latin beneath the bust of Ficino commemorating him in the Cathedral (Duomo) of Florence. See Appendix R, note 5. The text of the inscription was printed by Raymond Marcel, with punctuation added, in his biography, *Marsile Ficin* (Paris, 1958), p. 734. The version found in Kristeller, *Sup. Fic.* II, p. 202 varies slightly from the stone version followed here.

Note on the Latin Text

The Latin text displayed on the following pages is from the first edition, printed in Venice in 1495, by Matteo Capcasa of Parma. As with all early printed books, it follows a system of abbreviations, the most important of which are given below. Likewise, its punctuation and orthography differ from more modern texts in ways also summarised below.

The copy used is by kind permission of Durham University Library (shelf mark SR.2.C.22). It shows corrections made to the printed text by Ficino's nephew, Ficino Ficini, under Ficino's own supervision. The corrections are referred to in the annotations as Dur, to distinguish them from the simple printed version of Venice, V. They are not, however, always legible.

The annotations below the text on the following pages indicate these corrections if they are not clearly visible, and show alternative readings from the one surviving manuscript of this book, MS Mo2 (Munich, Staatsbibliothek, MS lat. 10781). Significant variant readings from the Basel printed edition of 1576 are also indicated. These two latter sources are referred to in the annotations as MS, and B respectively. MS Mo2, written before the conclusion of the book, lacks the Preface and stops after Letter 5. The writing on the last page of this manuscript seems to have been compressed for reasons of space and has more abbreviations than usual and a few errors.

In the absence of a manuscript for the remainder of the book, we also consulted the 1497 edition printed by Anton Koberger in Nuremberg, referred to as K, which allowed us to correct some dubious readings but also revealed more misprints there, not all of which are shown. The Preface Letter 20 shows variant forms found in the edition of Gentile, *Lettere*, vol. 1, referred to as G.

All the variant forms are given at the foot of each page with a letter in the vertical margin indicating the line where the amendment is required. This yields a reliable reader's edition of the text, even if not a full critical edition. Variations in spelling and punctuation have been recorded only if they affect the reading. Variations judged to be trivial, such as slight changes in the introductory greetings S.D. (*salutem dat*) and S.P.D. (*salutem plurimum dat*) have not been recorded.

Some variants are clearly erroneous and have been marked as such, but are included for the record.

Where a variant is too long to show in the normal way, its place has been indicated by an asterisk (*), and the variant is given below, at the foot of this note.

The last page of the Latin is the final page of the book and shows the colophon, giving publication details, followed by a list of page identifications to assist the binder, and the printer's mark. A translation of the colophon is provided in note 4 to Letter 42. The binder's instructions refer to the whole volume of twelve books. Only the last section, grouped under a reversed c, corresponds to the twelfth book, and the reversed c with numbering i, ii, iii, iiii and v can be seen at the bottom of folios 189, 190, 191, 192 and 193 recto. The other pages take their place naturally according to the way printed sheets were folded and sewn together.

For the letters and documents in the Appendix, Latin has not been provided, but the first note to each item indicates where the Latin may be found.

Abbreviations

As in previous volumes, the main abbreviations used by the printer of the Venice edition are as follows:

A slightly inclined line over what would be the penultimate letter of a word indicates omission of a final letter, usually an 'm'. Thus **quidẽ** for 'quidem'.

A similar line over a letter in the middle of a word indicates omission of one or more letters. The missing letters may be either side or both sides of the abbreviation mark. Thus **nũc** for 'nunc', **nr̃a** for 'nostra', **ur̃m** for 'vestrum'. Sometimes these abbreviations have been expanded in the amendments shown, especially where the marks are very faint. Other frequently used abbreviations include:

9 for 'us' as in **conat9** for 'conatus'

A flourish from a final 't' as in **morit̃** to indicate a passive, here for 'moritur'

q; as in **atq;** for 'atque'

ẽ for 'est'

q̃ for 'quam'

qñ for 'quando'

ẽt for 'etiam' | q for 'qui'
ꝓ for 'pro' as in ꝓcul for 'procul' | qđ for 'quod'
ꝑ for 'per' | ꝑꝑ for 'propter'.

Punctuation and Orthography

The Venice text uses punctuation in a somewhat fluid way. In general, colons are used in place of commas, but a full stop may also sometimes indicate a break between clauses rather than between sentences. Sometimes a capital letter follows a colon, but does not necessarily indicate the start of a new sentence. Brackets are used more frequently than in the other versions, especially the manuscript. Variations of punctuation found in the other texts have been omitted in this volume because they do not alter the reading.

Variations of spelling have been noted only where considered helpful to the reader. Common features to be noted in the Venice text are that 'u' is used for both 'u' and 'v'. The diphthong 'ae' is often printed simply as 'e'. Lower case 'f' and 's' may be difficult to distinguish. In general, a horizontal mark on the ascender indicates, usually but not always, that the letter is 'f': thus **infudiſſe** is 'infudisse'.

Variant spellings of proper names and some common words have not been recorded.

Longer Variants

p. clxxxvii	*a*	MS omits entire preface; B first title ***Marsilii Ficini Florentini Epistolarum, ad Hieronymum Rossium Dilectissimum suum Procemium.***
	b	B adds second title ***Marsilii Ficini Florentini Epistolarum, LIBER XII.***
p. clxxxxi v°	*n*	B adds ***ut*** after ***Atque.***
p. clxxxxiii	*q*	Dur deletes ***familiaria*** but indicates its insertion on next line before ***sint.*** B adds ***nota*** after ***sint.***
p. clxxxxiii v°	*y*	B ***scribus*** (erron).
p. clxxxxvi v°	*f*	in place of ***incurabilia: mirabiliter.***
	h	B reads ***tantum*** as ***tamen*** and omits the next three words, ***petantur? Tunc divina.***
	j	B ***supplicitur*** erron.
	r	Dur corrects to ***expitiationes***, a rare word, but we have followed the original, expiationes.
p. clxxxxvii	*d*	B has ***ante*** (erron).

Prohœmium Marsilii Ficini in Duodecimum Epistolarum Librum ad Hie- a
ronymum Rossium Dilectissimū suum.

Marsilius Ficinus Hieronymo Rossio Dilectissimo suo. S. P. D.

Cum duodecimo epistolarū mearū Libro finē imposuissē: cogitarēq; cuinā i primis hunc inscriberē: rationi cōsentaneum fore censui: ut diuturni opis finē tibi singulariter dedicarē: ad quē sūmatim uniuersum opus iamdiu destinauerā ut ad finē. Præterea ut totū epistolarū mearū studiū in te dēiq; cōquiescat: ut in fine decreui. quotcūq; ēt posthac epistolas sum scripturus: ad librū hūc duodecimū uel lōgissimum pertinere: summatimque sub Rossio uel Roscio potius titulo contineri. Lege fœliciter: & fœlicissime uiue: certe fœliciter a nobis amate. b

Nullus mala pœnitus & curas extirpare potest.

Marsilius Ficinus Florentinus Ioanuictorio Soderino & Francisco Diaceto c
conphilosophis suis. S. P. D.

Quæritis quid sibi uelit euangelicum illud: Necesse est ut uēiant scandala. Idē profecto: quod & Platonicum il- d
lud: mala pœnitus extirpari non possunt. Sed circa mortalem hanc regionem: necessario reuoluuntur. Mitto eq e
dē nūc: quot mala nobis inferat fatum. Natura. Fortuna Elemēta. Homines. Aialia: Multo certe grauiora sunt: Quæ ipsi nobis imprudenter inferimus. Iam uero mirū uideri nō debet hoies uel negociose uitæ deditos: uel li- f
bidinibus mācipatos: malis innumerabilibus opprimi. Quippe cū ipsi se fato passim & fortunę subiiciant & qua
si sponte ptnrbatiōibus freqūeter occurrant. Illud certe nimis est mirandum. Vi- gh
ros quin ēt qui uoluptuosa & actiua insup uita neglecta: se totos cōtemplatiue de
diderūt pturbationibus agitari. Causas. n. solicitudinū deuitauisse uident' Sæpe ij
tn̄ grauioribus curis q̄ uel uoluptuosi: uel actiui solicitantur. Contēplatores. n. spretis humanis: aut ad religionem: sanctimoniāq;: aut ad philosophiam sese conferunt. Vtrobiq; uero Incidunt in scyllam cupiētes uitare carybdim. Sancti. n. deliramenta nugasq; mortalium fugientes: in Demones incidunt tentatores. Nō enim his est certamen aduersus carnem & sanguinē: Paulus inquit apostolus: sed aduersus maleficos quosdā spiritus aeris caliginosi tyrannos. Quo fit ut sanctos dum deus exercitat Demonia uexent. Quid uero de philosophis dicam? Nonne
uel negocia Iouis uel oblectamenta Veneris respuētes: in Saturni tedia sæpe me- k
roresq; corruunt: & atrā bilem? Cui quidē ingenii malo: Democritus: Plato. Aristoteles ingeniosissimos quosque obnoxios arbitrantur: ut penas illas quodāmo
do quas furti cælestis Prometheus in monte Caucaso contemplator expendit: pē lm
dere uideantur. Tanto uero contemplatores utrique grauiores: sæpe subeunt cu
ras q̄ uel ingeniosi uel uoluptuosi: quanto inualidiores incidunt uexatores. nop
Quamobrem si eiusmodi uiri qui maxime omnium mala declamaturi putan- q
tur: in mala sæpius grauiora labuntur: nemo profecto cōfidere potest mala mor
talibus unq̄ posse uitari: Sed hoc forsitan interest: q̄ superiorum quidē illorū ma rs

a * b * c MS om. *Florentinus* d *veniant* e MS om. *hanc* f B *debitos* g *perturbationibus* h MS *admirandum* i MS *ediderint* B *dediderunt* Dur corr. illeg. j MS B *solicitudinum* k MS *moresque* (erron.) l MS *quarti* m B *expendis* n *quanto* o MS B *negociosi*, Dur illeg. p B *validiores* q MS B *declinaturi* (corr.) r MS *inquam* s *quod*

a la paulatim in pessima conuertuntur. Hi uero si prouidenter professionem suam
constanterque prosequantur: tandem auctore uidelicet & promittente deo: qui
bc seminant in lachrimis: in exultatione meṫtent. Euntes ibant & flebāt: mittentes
semina sua: uenientes autem ueniēt cum exultatione: portantes maīpulos suos.
d Hæc uero commemorate uobis dilectissimi conphilosophi mei. Operepræcium
e fore censui: ut neque confidatis uos dulces philosophiæ sapores absque amarore
quodam degustaturos. Neq; rursum desperetis uel amaritudinem ipsam: auctore
deo: quandoq; quod & in pomis sæpe natura facit: in dulcedinem posse conuerti.
Valete fœlices: & in contēplatiōe uestra (quēadmodum cœpistis) prudenter cō
f stanterque perseuerate. Die. xxvii. Septembris. Mcccclxxxxii.

Solem non esse adorandum tanq̄ rerum omnium auctorem.

Marsilius Ficinus Eberardo inclyto comiti Virtembergensi & montis peligar
di Seniori. S. D.

g SOcrates in castris sæpe sub diuo solem suspiciens orientem stetit attoni-
hi tus in eisdem uestigiis: inmotis membris inconiuentibus oculis statue
more: quousque solem salutaret iterum resurgentem. His ergo platonici
similibusque signis adducti socratem forte dicent phœbeo quodam Demone sta-
tim ab ipsa pueritia ductum: phœbum ipsum uenerari summopere consueuisse.
eademque ratione sapientissimum græcorum omnium: appollinis oraculo iudi-
catum. Ego uero quid de Socratis demone: seu genio siue angelo: affirmandū ma
j xime uideatur in p̄sentia prætermittam. Id certe ausim affirmare socratē in eo mē
k tis excessu nō solem quidem hunc admiratū fuisse: sed alterū. Cū n. admirationē
sola nouitas afferre soleat: quid tantū stupeat hūc admirabūdus socrates: quē &
quottidie uidet: Cuius & motus omnes uiresq; iandiu: mathematica simul: & phi
sica ratione compræhenderat. Quem (teste platone) nō deum primū: Sed dei fi-
liū appellauit. Non filium inq̄ dei primum: Sed secundum iamque uisibilem. Pri
l mum nāq; dei filiū nō solem hunc oculis manifestum: sed alterū: hoc longe supio
rē: intellectū. s. primū solo cōtēplabilem intellectu. Socrates igit̄ sole cœlesti non-
nūq̄ admonitus: solemq; inde supcœlestem auguratus: & illius maiestatē contem
plabatur attentior: & patris illius incōpræhensibilē bonitatem admirabatur atto
nitus. Hunc Iacobus Apostolus patrem luminum apellauit: Luminum inquā
plusq̄ cœlestium: atq; cœlestium. Apud quem non sit transmutatio: neque uicissi
tudinis obumbratio. Nam & supercœlestia illa facta putat naturaliter mutabilia:
m & cœlestia quottidie per noctium uices obumbrari nō dubitat. Quamobrem oē
l datum optimum. s. menti naturaliter insitum: & omne donū perfectum uidelicet
post naturales dotes adhibitum: non a sole hoc stellisq; mundanis: Sed altius ab
n ipso patre luminum descendere censet. Nam intelligentie uiribus. q. gradibus qui
busdam nonquidem cœlitus: sed desup acceptis freti: sup cœlos ascendimus: ibi-
que multa cœlis præstantiora: cognoscimus: amamus: & colimus: ipsumque cœ-
li fabrum ante omnia ueneramur. Neq; tamen possemus intelligētia incorporeū
aliquid cœloque melius intelligere: uel amare: si cœlitus tantum intelligentiā ha
o beremus. Iam uero ne quis solem lūam stellas nimium admiratus: & adoraret: &
p tāq̄ intellectualium munerum auctores: & patres uenerarentur: prudenter admo-
nuit solem hunc non esse uniuersi principium. Missas in presentia faciam rationes:

a MS *prudenter* b MS *seminat* c *metent* d MS B *commemorare*
e B *amatore* (erron.) f MS adds *Floren.* g MS *stet* h MS B *immotis*
i MS B *inconniventibus* j *praesentia* k B *Cui* l *scilicet* m MS *vires*
n *quasi* o B om. *admiratus* p B *numerum* (erron.)

quibus in theologia noſtra principium uniuerſi:nec corpus eſſe nec animam nec intellectum:Sed aliquid admodum excellſius affirmamus. A quo quidem ſol cœleſtis longiſſime diſtat:ut umbra quędam illius eſſe iudicętur:potiuſq̃ imago. Rationes autem quas Iacobus hic atringit breuiter:breuiter in præſentia perſtrigã. bcd
Cum ſtatus tanq̃ principium:& rector:finiſque motiõis:ſit omni motu pfectior: e
certe Deus ipſe principium & finis & rector omnium:mobilis eſſe non poteſt:ſol autem eſt aſſidue mobilis. Præterea principii uirtus tanq̃ immenſa: fortiter attingit omnia:nec uſq̃ cohiberi poteſt. Solis autem uirtus per radios agens præpedi f
tis paſſim radiis impeditur:defectum patitur obieta luna. Sæpe nubibus cohercetur. Terrena denſitate repellitur. Diſtãtia loci debilitatur Sol ipſe: quin etiam minima quædam eſt particula mundi. Anguſta quadam ſede tenetur: Trahitur a ſphæra rurſumque retrahitur. Contraque ſphęre proprie impetum a ſphera ſemp g
ſuperiore reuoluitur. Contrariis ſignis impeditur & ſtellis:& aſpectu malorũ nõ nunq̃ debilitatur. Denique principium uniuerſi omnia ubique & ſemper: & in omnibus operatur. Sol autem nec mundi globos ipſe facit:nec quæcunque frigida uel humida ſunt uel denſa ſimiliaque ipſe uirtute propria poteſt efficere. Neq; ſimiles in cœlo uirtutes ullam a ſole ducunt originem. Cæterumque q̃uis ſol ab h
auctore mundi longiſſime diſtet:cœleſtia tamen omnia ad ſolem unicum. q. re/ i
ctorem in cœlo menſuramque diuitus redacta uidentur. Vt hinc prorſus admo j
neremur:ut omnia quæ in cœlo ſunt & ſub cœlo & ſuper cœlum ad unum cũctorum principium ſimiliter referri conſiderantes:tandem hoc ipſum ea ſaltem obſeruantia uenerarerur qua cœleſtia Solem. k

Copula philoſophiæ cum legibus. q̃ fœlix & nobilis ſit philoſophus. l
Marſilius Ficinus Martino Vranio prænnygero Amico Vnico. S.D.

PHiloſophanti quidem mihi ſemper:nunq̃ uero legibus incumbenti. pfeſſores legum duo ſunt amiciſſimi. In italia quidem Ioanuictorius Soderinus. In Germania uero tu in primis optime mi Martine: & utrique cum inſigni facultate legum mirum ſapientiæ ſtudium coniunxiſtis. Dixerit ergo quiſpiam. Quæ nam legibus cum philoſophia cognatio? Quæ uidelicet Ioui legum auctori:cum ſaturno philoſophiæ duce:ideſt filio cũ patre neceſſitudo. Mitto nunc Aſtronomos aſſerentes Iouem quando cum ſaturno coniũgitur:nouas afferre leges. Præſertim quotiens in ipſis cœli cardinibus triplicitatumque capiti m
bus:coniunguntur. Nonne poetæ priſci. Vetereſque Theologi Saturnum in additis contemplatorem fingunt:legeſque & iura poſt diuturnam contemplationẽ n
excogitantem Quæ deinde Ioui filio actionum duci tradat obſeruanda ciuibus mandaturo. Homerus quoque Minoem inquit regem conditorem legum in Iouis antrum:annis nouem ſecedere ſolitum:ibique a Ioue leges accipere: Nemo uero antiquorum myſteriorum peritus proprium Ioui ſemper publico dedicauerit antrũ. Hoc igit̃ nihil aliud eſſe uidet̃ q̃ Saturni ipſius ſemp additũ domiciliũ o
uel ſacellũ. In quo qdẽ:& iuppiter cõſtitutus cũ ſaturno collega Regẽ Minoẽ legibus iſtruit:mox populũ formaturis:ſed miſſo iá officio legũ: ſapiẽtiæ ſtudium proſequamur. Multos equidẽ ad hoc totis uiribus capeſcendũ ſũ p meas epiſtolas

a DUODECIMUS   b B *quam*   c MS B *breviter* not repeated   d MS *praesenti*
e B *metionis*   f B *Solus*   g MS *prope* B *propriae*   h MS *Ceterum*
i MS *quasi* B *qua*   j *divinitus*   k B *venerarentur*   l B *quod*
m B *differe*   n MS *abditis*   o MS *abditum*

exortatus. Vos aūt iam in hoc ipō prouectos nō adhortabor equidē nūc: Sed po
tius cōfirmabo. Aut certe nos ipsos cōsideramus. Aut suspicimus Deum: aut cæ
teros homines circūspicimus. Si forte nos ipsos: sola sapiētia facit: ut & nos ipsos
deniq; cognoscamus. & soli nobis cum habitare possimus: propriis semp conten
ti diuitiis. Si uero deū: sola quin ēt sapiētia deo similes efficit: & amicos cōteplan
tes uidelicet assidue: quæ deus ipse fecerit cōtemplando: ipsumq; tanq̄ bonorum
oīum auctorem cognitum uenerantes: si aūt homines: sapientia quoq; sola sapiē
ab tem populis: regibusq; tandem constituit regē &. q. numen: deniq; uenerandum.
Cū igit̃ sapientiæ studiū fœlicē prsus efficiat animū. Nūquid præterea nobilem
c uel efficit: uel declarat? Si Platoni licet credere: nobilissimū ē pfecto philosopho
d rū genus. Nam & aureū esse inquit: & ab ipso Ioue mundi totius opifice reuera p
d fectum: si stoicis fidem adhibes: nobilitatem philosophorū ex posteritate cogno
sces: Solos. n. fore asserunt immortales. Prophetę dciq; Danieli nō credere nefas.
Fulgebūt (inquit ille) docti: sicut splēdor firmamēti. Et qui multos erudierint ad
iustitiam tanq̄ stelle in ppetuas æternitates. Firmamētum uero non octauū dūta
xat cœlum: Sed totā spherarum molem significare uidet̃: stellarū planetarumq;
oīum firmamētum. Hoc aūt etiā seorsum a stellis atq; Planetis quodāmodo sua
pte natura fulget: Sed rariore quadam & sparsa: & candida luce: ppea minus ocu
lis manifesta. Eiusmodi quadam luce fulgebūt: & hic & in patria docti reuera san
ef ctiq; uiri: ēt si nullos unq̄ ipsi docuerint. Qui uero nō solū sibi ipsis diuina cōtem
g plati fuerint: sed alios insup palam erudierint: legesq; dederint ad iustitiam obser
uandam: manifestiore præcæteris fulgore lucebūt: stellarum instar clarissime cor
h ruscantes. Neq; id quidem ad tempus certum: sed per omne tempus. Neque per
totum mundi tempus solum: sed p ipsum diuinioris æternitatis usum: nunq̄ ui
delicet interruptum: sed perpetuū pœnitus atq; continuum. Iustum enim esse ui
detur: ut qui publici diuiniq;: boni fuerint auctores sempq; sint hominibus pro
futuri. Lumenq; sibi diuinitus datum non absconderint: sed ad cōmune bonum
i prorsus ediderint: æterno quodam splendore diuinitus bonoq; donentur.

j Cur semper eadem & antiqua tractem.

Marsilius Ficinus Philippo Valori Oratori: apud pōtificem: Florētino. S. D.

k HEsterno uespere iā Franco nostro dixerām uale: tuq; mihi ad ualorē no
strū eris epistola. Mox aūt (nescio quomō) sum cōpulsus uespertinis lit
teris addere matutinas. Quodquidē & amātes factitare plerumq; solent
singulis epistolis non contenti. Francia igit̃ (ut ita dixerim) epistola nostrā tibi
l ualitudinem nūtiabit. Studiorū uero nostrorū rationē quā p negocia nō poterat
m frācus tunc accipere: epistoliū psens tibi reddet. Requiris (uideo) quid nūc agā.
n Quod equidē iādiu mi Valor agebā. Eodē sēp (nescio quo fato) reuoluor: signi
ficator nobis: ne dixeri ductor (ut scis) ab initio Saturnus sub Aquario ascendēs
extitit. Saturnia igit̃ & antiqua ppetuo retractam9. Cū primū oli rediit ad Aqua
riū prisca Platonis opa sub magno Cosmo semel iterpræetrati sumus. Iā Saturnus
iterū reuersus est ad idē. Ad idē nos quoq; reuertimur. Platonē iterū post Laurē
tianū plotinū interpretamur. Sed grande opus (ut par erat) grādioribus cōmēta
riis declaramus. Cōmētariolū i Timeū i agro maiāo apud te cōpositū: latius nūc
nobis excrescit: mox Parmēidē similiter aggressuris. Magnus ille patron9 noster

a *quasi* b B *generandum* c *est profecto* d *profectum* e B *etiamsi* f B *Quid* (erron.) g MS om. *sed alios insuper palam erudierint* h B *Nempe per* (erron.) i B *Vale.* j MS *eadem semper* k MS *Externo* in place of *Hesterno* l B *nuntiabat* m MS B *Francus* n B *revolutore* (erron.)

Petrus medices spem nobis firmam dedit se resurgenti platoni rursus aspiraturũ. Atq; iam ita prorsus inspirat ut plato noster hactenus errabundus: sit iam super hanc petram: suam achademiam fundaturus. huic igitur isthuc ad pontificem ac cedenti p ocium hac de re nostro nomine gratias q̃plurimas agito. Pœnes hunc. q. tuum Iouem: tuos agnosces dioscuros: bibienos: castorem: atque pollucẽ. his a
ergo post illum nos etiam commendabis. Finem uero faciã: Non inq̃ Epistolio b
sed iam æpistolæ: si tibi prius significauero: Martianam illam causam: immo iam tarditate saturniam: post medicam auctoritatem: tua insuper opera: iam esse con fectam. vii. Nouembris. Mcccclxxxxii. c

Similitudo Mercurii cum Saturno.

Marsilius Ficinus Philippo Carducio dilectissimo suo. S. D.

CVm epistolæ a me compositæ: iã oẽs tibi transcriptæ: propemodũ p ta- bellarium ad te pferende forent: decreui Mercuriale opus ad Mercuria d
lem amicũ nõ absque auspiciis mercurialibus aduehi. Vt siquid in nego ciis eiusmodi cœlestia ualent & ocius ad te perueniret: & cœlerius legeretur. Præ- e
terea ut diutissime relectum consideraretur: Mercurio Saturnum insuper addidi: Siue comitem: siue ducem. Legi hodie rursus in. x. de repu. mercurium Saturnũ q; colore. i. Luce cœlestium omniũ inter se simillimos esse: ut non mirũ sit intelli- f
gentiæ quoq; luce ita consimiles esse: ut alter quidem ad sapientiam exhortetur: alter uero Deo uidelicet altius aspirante perducat. Dei quidẽ imaginẽ esse solem uolũt. Deus ipse ẽ auctor sapientiæ primus: Sapiẽtiæ significatores: mercurius & saturnus: imaginis diuinæ comites: minime oium a sole discedũt: dũ uidelicet & mercurius sub solis splẽdore ferme semp incedit: & saturnus ab eclyptica solis uia g
minime oium præuaricari uidet. Hos Astronomi natura quadã similes eẽ putãt. mercuriũq; ædibus & finibus & aspectu saturni gaudere. Hic (ut opinor) efficit: h
ut ferme oẽs: qui a Mercurio suũ iter professionẽq; exordiunt: solũ desinant in sa i
turnũ. Vtinã tu mihi Carduci a Mercurio ad Iouem etiã quandoque peruenias. j
Vale. Die. xiiii. Nouembris. Mcccclxxxxii. k

Apologia in librum suum de Sole: & lumine.

M. F. Florẽtinus Philippo ualori Oratori apud põtificem florentino. S. P. D.

LIbrũ de sole clarissimo petro medici destinatũ domi iã diutius retinebã atq; cõtra præceptũ euangelicũ: sub modio lucernã: siue solẽ ferme iam impius abscõdebã. Sed petrus ille nerus: quẽ in æpistolis nr̃is frequẽter cãdidissimũ appellauimus: pium existimauit fore: ut lumẽ hoc q̃plurimis: ut de9 præcipit effulgeret: Itaq; cãdidissimo uiro ad quẽ potissimũ cura de lumine ptinet & cãdore libẽtissime parui. Atq; ultra mysteriũ magnanimo petro medici cõmen datũ pmisi librũ opera petri neri palã impressoribus exprimendum. Ecce igit mi Valor luce mihi carior: palã sol hic quãtuluscũq; meus iã exorit. Sed forte mox suborituris nebulis offendendus: uel etiam futurus noctuis quibusdam uesper tiliõibusq; molestus. Nebulas quidẽ aut uẽti ,ptinus dissipabunt: aut sol ipse cũ a l
scenderit altius: extẽuabit atq; dissoluet: Vesptiliõibus aũt sub lumie caligãtibus cecutiẽtibusq; cõsulito: si mõ cõsilii sint capaces: ne lucẽ quidẽ iciuset cæteris salu- tarẽ. Sed ipsi splendorem hũc effugiant: suo more potius: atq; (ut par est) indigni lumine assidue delitescant. Bona quidẽ spe ualorem meum ad hoc certamẽ pro

a *quasi* b MS om. *vero* c MS adds *Vale* before the date and *Florentiae* after.
d *perferendae* e B *pervenire* f *sit* g after *mercurius* MS adds *ferme semper est* underlined (perh. indicating error) h MS *hinc* i MS *ad* (erron.)
j MS *mi Carduci* k MS adds *Florentiae* l B *Nebule*

LIBER

uoco: ualorem inq̃ nõ solum cõtra bubões: sed aduersus etiã inania mõstra: Her
culis instar ualidissime pugnaturum. Soles. n. Boetianum illud pro Hercule dic-
tum in ore frequẽter habere: Superata tellus sydera donat. Herculem ueteres in
troducunt: uirum solis alunnũ: pro uera gloria: ꝓ ueritatis splendore: quæ solis 1
a ipius mũera ꝓpria & officia sũt. Labores duodeci. q. duodeci signa zodiaci subeũ
tẽ: Ito nũc alacer mi Valor in præliũ. propugnatores. n. illic (Scio quid loquar)
Tres saltem inuictos habebis: Pollitianum Herculem inquam: phœbeumq; Pi-
cum Amphionemque Landinum. Hi profecto q̃ strenue pro mea uita iam triẽ
bc nium certauerũt. tam fœliciter deinceps pro hoc meo (q̃tuscũque est) splẽdor
pugnabunt. Die. ii. Ianuarii. Mcccclxxxxiii.

Sepe in cœlestibus gemini sunt. Item Soles Duo.

d M. F. Martino Vranio Germano amico unico. S. D.

e Vuat una tecũ mi Vranie uir cœlestis cœlestia sæpe tractare. Non solum
In firmamẽto gemini sũt illi dioscuri. Sed inter plãetas sũt quoq; germãi
Mercurius. n. quasi minor frater ẽ Saturni. Cõsimili. n. (ut plato inqt)
luce fulgent: & igeniis utriq; præsũt. Germana Iouis est alma Venus: Phœbi quo
f q; Phœbę. Mars autem. q. superbior cõmunionis expers: solem ipsum non tã co
f mitatur q̃ emulatur. Preter. n. feruorem suum solis emulum. q. riualis: lumẽ (ne
scio quod) infundit Lunę paucis admodũ obseruatũ. Post hęc autẽ æternus aer.
f q. Iuppiter alter frater & maritus ẽ sequẽtis aeris. q. Iunõis: Sed ut reuertamur ad
Solẽ. Quid mirũ? siquidẽ in cœlo sũt gemini soles: geminos quoq; penes me qua
gh si soles eẽ natos: prio quidẽ maiorẽ deĩde minorẽ. Minorẽ igitur ipse orator ad põ
tificẽ proficiscens ꝑterita æstate apud nos uidisti florẽtiæ: qui & te hinc in germãi
am abeuntẽ: e uestigio sequutus est. clarissimũ principẽ tuum Eberardum saluta
turus: Alterũ uero solem: qui inter platonicas cõmentationes grandior iã coaluit
iure sibi uendicat petrus medices: qui & platonica iure sibi omnia uendicat lumẽ
similiter: o mi uranie mihi geminum inter lares eluxit. Minus atq; maius. Minus
quidẽ iãdiu Phœbo capelle fulxit. Maius uero nũc petro medici clarissimo lucet.
i Vtrumq; igitur uir cœlestis fœliciter cõtemplare. Contemplaberis uero fœliciter
si luminis huius similitudie platonicũ hoc quod sequitur de diuinitate mysteriũ
memorię cõmendaueris. Quę minimum lumen habent non aliter cernere con-
sueuimus q̃ passim quærendo ꝓprius accedentes. Solem uero uisuri: non tam
j quærere solem cogimur ultro nobis obuium atq; omnium patentissimumq̃ pur
gare oculos: aperire conuertere: proq; modo nostro hos ad illum accõmodare Si
militer cœterarum quidem rerum ueritates exiguas. q. scintillas argumentationi
bus perscrutari compellimur. Immensum uero dei lumen sic assequi nõ ualemus
sed & amatoria uolũtatis conuersione & serenitate mentis paramur ad illum: no
bis uidelicet præparatis ultro fœliciter corruscantem. Hinc platonicum illud. Di
k uina quidem uerbis rationibusq; doceri non possunt: quemadmodum cętera que
l discuntur. Sed assidua circa diuinum ipsum consuetudine uitęque cõmuniorem
subito tandem nobis uelut ab igne scintillante lumen effulget in animo: seque ip
sum iam alit.

m In librum de Sole: dono missum.

Marsilius Ficinus Laurentio cõphilosopho suo Laurentianæ ædis Antistiti.

a B om. *q[uasi] duodecim* b *quantuscumque* c *splendorem* (V B) corrected in K to *splendore* d B *Marsilius Ficinus* e K *unum* (erron.) f *quasi* g B *principio* h B *ipso* i *contemplare* j *quam* k B *caetera, quae* l B and Dur *communionem* m B om. *dono*

Vm ego supioribus diebus librum de sole & lumie: paruũ q̃dē: Sed ma
c gna cũ uoluptate cōponerem. Tu interim & si pręsentis mee lucubracio ab
nis inscius poportune admodũ astronomicis rationibus iuenisti nostrũ c
oē sapiētiæ studiũ: ad solem potissimũ ptinerę. Quoniā sors illa: quā ęgiptii sapiē
tię partē nominãt in genesi puenisset ad cor leonis. Sol uero Dominus eius nonā de
tenuisset cœli plagā: sapiētiæ destinatā: Oportũe rursus absoluto statim libro de
Sole & lumine heri ad nos cōputationē astronomicā attulisti. Eadē igitur opor
tunitate ego uicissim librũ ipsũ ad te hodie mitto: Vtinā nostrũ hoc lumē nō Lu-
nā uideatur proferre: sed Solē. Die: xviii. Februarii.. Mccccl xxxxiii.

Amor ipse Deus amantem redamari iubet.

Marsilius sicinns Florentinns Iuliano insigni theologie professori ordinis mino f
rum non minori. S.P.D.

NIhil est dilectissime mi Iuliane: q̃ silentiũ apud nos tuũ purges. Nā & si g
nobis quidem raro: frequenter tamē de nobis es locutus. Ac si quid uer
bis forte defuerit: id totũ ingēti erga nos amore cōpensas. Amoris equi
dē ardētis erga me tui: hinc argumētũ habeo proculdubio maximũ: q̃ ego te ab- g
sentem diu ardentiori quodam in dies amore complector. Prouerbiũ uero illud
si uis amari ama in libro de amore atque epistolis alicubi rationibus multis expo
sui. Sed omniũ maxima: quæ interscribēdũ modo mihi succurrit esse uidetur: ni
si repentina me fallit opinio. Sed ut fallat aliquanto leuius ita parũper confabule
mur. Apollinē & cupidinē Sagittarios antiqui fingebãt: hunc quidē flāmas: illũ
uero lumina iaculantem. Quēadmodũ igitur Apollo lumē simul in geminos ia
culatur: ut quo ego te lumine uiso: eodem & ipse me reuisas: ita cupido flāmas
ut qua iam ardet unus: eadem mox ardeat alter. Omnino uero amorē esse deũ: &
plato probat: & omnis testificatur antiquitas: & theologi nostri sanctũ quidē spi-
ritũ amorē primũ seraphicis. i. amatoriis angelis ãteponũt: & seraphicos angelos
ueris amoribus ubique pręficiũt. Amatoriũ ergo numen mutue caritatis & uni h
onis amicum. ubi aliquem accendit amore: statim ardentes ex hoc amore uelut
speculo radios: in amatum occulta quadam & mirifica uirtute reflectit: ut absens
uel inscius ille mirabiliter accensus: uicissim amet amantem. iustum nãq; numen i
non patitur amantem superno uidelicet instinctu cōcitũ non redamari. Sed iam j
de amore satis. Cōquerebaris p̄terea p epistolam plotin: libros ad uos minime p- kl
uenisse: meā propemodum tarditatem accusaturus. libri quidē ipsi p̄terito maio
sunt ab ipressoribus absoluti. Sed ~~in~~ hi quibus mãdatũ est a medicibus: ut eos saltē m
per italiam diuulgarent tardiores hactenus extiterunt: ac me etiā urgente: sũt tar n
di. Nouam platonis interp̄tationē nōdum edidi ultra dimidiũ iam productā. Ad
hanc tu me maxime omnium adhortatus es: forte interim cohortantibus angelis
in quorum ede id in cœna mihi persuasisti. Quo tempore post declamatiōes no
stras ibidem frequentibus contionibus tu orabas: libellum de Sole & lumine a o
me nup æditũ ad te mitto legendũ: ut ubi nr̄ iãdiu feruet calor: ibi lumē quoq; re
fulgeat. Die. xxi. Februarii. Mccccl xxxxiii. In librum de Sole.

Marsilius Ficinus mazingo Phisico insigni cōphilosopho suo. S.D.

OMnes (quod te non latet) Astronomi: Lunā quidem tertia ab ascēden
te cœli plaga gaudere putant; itineris illinc breuis religionis quę parue p

a B *componere* b B *praesenti* c *invenisti* d K *nominent* e K *novam* (erron.) f *Ficinus Florentinus* g *quod* h B *Iunonis* K *iunionis* i B *amat* j B *etiam* (for *iam*) k B om. *p[er]* l *Plotini* m Dur corr. *hi*; B K keep *in* n B om. *me* o B *frequentius* p B K *quae* (erron.)

ducem. Solem uero nona: longioris itineris: ac religiōis magne rectorem. Vt autem tutius loquamur saltem significatorem. Cum tu igitur longum religiosumq; ad Loretanam ędem iter sis propediem aggressurus: merito Solem quēdā nūc tibi trado mihi nup exortū: Futurū (ut opto) sereni aeris: facilisq; itineris auspiciū.

In librum de Sole.

Marsilius Ficinus Georgio Cyprio insigni Medico. S. D.

CVm phœbū oēs medicine auctorē medicorumq; patrē eē cōsentiāt: merito phœbeū de Sole & lumie librū a nobis nuper æditum ad te mitto legendum: Antiquū familię nostræ medicum. Phœbus igitur ppetui amoris erga te mei ueridic⁹ tibi testis erit. Sol tibi signa dabit (ut inquit Maro noster)

a Solem quis dicere falsum Audeat. Die. xiiii. Iunii. Mcccclxxxxiii

In librum De Sole missum.

Marsilius Ficinus Baccio Vgulino. S. D.

CVm fratres sint Phœbus atque Bacch⁹. Alter Merito salutat alterū. At uter utrū prior adit? nō appollinē qdē liber: metuēs forte ne uerba reportet. Sed Phœb⁹ ipse Bacchū: sperās referr mœrū. xv. Iunii. Mcccclxxxxiii bc

Fœlicia ad Philosophiam auspicia. a Mercurio & Saturno & Sole.

d Marsilius Ficinus Nicholao uolari dilectissimo suo. S. D.

e NVllus familiarium nostrorū fœlicioribus q̄ tu auspiciis Philosophari

f cœpit: Non cōmemorabo equidē latius in presentia: q̄tum ad phię studia conferre putetur: Cōiunctio illa Mercurii cū Saturno sub Aquario tunc imminēs quādo & ego librū de Sole & lumine cōponebā & tu Philosophie iam dabas exordia: atq; [hec] quidem ab ipso Sole sane tāquam orpheus alter ab Apol

g line potius q̄ a musis. Hūc ergo Solē quod quidē auspicia tāta decebat: aquilinis

h statim oculis suspexisti. A[b]d hoc uero deinceps: qui inter cœlestia dominatur: ad altiorē Solē cœlestiū auctorē mira quadā celeritate profectus: platonicā Theologiā

i fœliciter admodū es aggressus. In q̄[ua] quidē tā perspicue in dies ,pfūdissima queque

jk mysteria inspicis q̄ dilucide fas ē cū cernere: q nō sub Luna: sed sub ipso Sole singu ta cōtuet. Perge queso mi ualor: ea deinceps alacritate: qua cœpisti: & me passim socio & Apolline duce: sūmū ueritatis glorieq; splēdorē breui consequuturus.

Signa legitimi platonici: atque de ideis.

Marsilius Ficinus Francisco Diaceto cōplatonico suo .S. D.

l ERrāt oino: q pipateticā disciplinā platonice cōtrariā arbitrant: Via siq

m dē termino cōtraria eē nō pōt. Peripateticā uero doctrinā ad sapiētiam

m platonicā eē uiā cōperiet: quisquis recte cōsideraueri t: naturalia nos ad diuina pducere. hinc igit effectū ē: ut nullus unq̄ ad secretiora Platonis misteria sit admissus: nisi pipateticis disciplinis prius iniciatus. Absoluti uero Platonici

n tria sūt symbola: quibus sacerdos eius modi a ceteris phis septisq; discernit primū

o quidē ē mēs sublimis: ab inferioribus se ipsā sēp ad superiora cōuertēs. Secūdū ue

p ro religio. Tertiū eloquētia: & hæc q dē. q. poetica. Primū rursus ad Saturnū. Se

q cūdū ad Iouē. Tertiū ptinet ad Apollinē. Solus itaq; platonicus ē legitimus q illa

r quā diximus incedit uia. His ēdirus symbolis. His (ut ita dixeri) numinibus cō

s mēdatus. Q uāobrē cōphē mi frācisce tibi tāq̄ legitimo platonico gratulor & aca

t demię gaudeo. Vt aūt ad tuā illā de ideis questionē ,p epistolę mō respōdeā: ita

a B m.cccc.xciiii b K *Phoebens* c *referre* d B *Valori* e B *nostrum*
f *quantum ad philosophiae* g Dur adds *haec* h Dur *Ab* i Dur *qua* j *qui*
k *singula* l *omnino* m *esse* n *philosophis sapientibusque*
o *semper* p *quasi* q *qui* r *praeditus* s *conphilosophe* t *pro*

breuiter accipe. Nō putas ꝓprias singulorū ideas ī mēte pria īter se absolute qdē sed quadā relatione distingui. Ego semper similiter iudicaui. Neq; id quidē a ploti a
no iam tuo arbitror alienum. Quod sane in cōmentariis in eum breuiter explico Negat & in parmenide proculus ideas proprias singulorum: uidelicet absolute di stinctas. id proculdubio platoni maxime cōsonat in Timeo dicēti ideale exēplar æternum esse Quod ue ad ipsum exprimetur: atq; per ipsum: sempiternum fore significāti. Vnde colligitur naturalium species illinc pœnitus exprimi: tanq̄ uide b
licet sempiternas: singula uero nō æque: sed sequētibus deinceps causis ad extre/ mum inter se discerni. Quæ tamē distinctio intellectum primum non lateat uni/ uersi ordinis conditorē. Hinc in Timeo Iuniores dii: Demonesq; architecto man c
dante: atque disponente singulorum sub Luna fabricam prosequūtur: Ne igitur uel in eo quod summopere est unitum: extrema sit multitudo: uel eum q̄plurima lateant qui intelligētia facit & perficit omnia: singularium omnino mutabilium illic idee non sint re ipsa inter se naturaliter disiuncte: sed eiusdem intelligentiæ se d
ipsam aliter atq; aliter conferentis ratiōe distincte. Bene igitur excogitasti mi Frā/ cisce. Bene Vale. Die. xi. Iulii. Mcccclxxxxiii.

Purgatio silentii diuturni.

Marsilius ficinus philippo ualori oratori florētino ad sūmum pōtificē. S.P.D.

QVęres forsitan diuturni huius silentii causam. Hæc autem nihil aliud ē ut respondeam breuiter: q̄ incerta scribendi causa. Nā quid potissimum e
scribā? An forte quomodo ualeo? Qui male ne: an bene ualeam: semper ambigo. Nunquid significabo quid faciam: & de hoc hercle ambigo. Equidem quid uelim scio. Quid tentem. Quid autem efficiam adhuc ignoro. Ambigo qn f
etiam presentem ne te nobis putem: an absentem: q̄ quottidiana nicholai fratris tui mecum philosophantis consuetudo usq; adeo presentem reddit: ut esse opus æpistolis nō aduertem. Solent grati homines post diuturnum silentium æpistolas saltem mittere longiores. Ego autē adeo nunc ingratus fuero? ut breuissimo for/ sitan æpistolio: longissimum silentium compensare confidam. Nequaq̄. sed amor igēs potius: & fiduciā prestat & satis offō facit. Vale die. xv. Iuuii. Mcccclxxxxiii. ghij

In Librum de Sole

Marsilius Ficinus Antonio calderino. S.D.

SOl inter cœlestia Dominus i hoc uel maxime cæteras rerum naturaliū causas antecellit: q, calore quidem omnia facit: lumine uero demōstrat k
Mihi uero & si nihil opus est: ut calore Solis utar: ad calderinum calefa/ ciendum: quē in rebus meis expediendis atq; tuendis ubiq; feruentissimum sum expertus: lumine tamen solis utendum censui quo ardentem amorem nostrū ian diu testimoniis plurimis confirmatum: nunc insuper teste apolline palam oibus declararem. Die. xv. Iulii. Mcccclxxxxiii. l

Lumen est admirabile: quoniam est imago sapientię: Item q̄ mirabilis sit copu la sapientię cum potentia.

Marsilius Ficinus Ramberto Malatestæ: Illustri Sogliani Principi. S.D.

COmmūis omniū certaq; sententia est: & quasi uox ipsa naturæ: nihil as pectu pulchrius: nihil amabilius: nihil admirabilius esse q̄ lumen. Et si hoc omnes extra controuersiam confitentur: ubi tamen tante rei

a B om. *Ego semper similiter iudicaui.* b Dur corr. to *exprimitur* c B *seniores* d Dur *naturaliterve* e *quam* f *quin* g *ingens* h *officio* i *Iunii* j B *Mccccxciiii* k *quod* l B *declarem*

a tanque manifeste: causam queras non omnes iam inuenient rationem: Sed so
lus ille probabiliter respondebit: qui lumen hoc oculis manifestum animaduerte
b rit: nihil aliud esse q̃ occulte lucis .i. sapientiæ ipsius imaginem est enim reuera sa
pientia nihil aliud prẹter clarissimum intelligentiæ lumẽ. Quod quidem Plato
noster in phœdro uaticinatus est: siquando interioribus oculis cerni possit: amo/
res sui multo ardentiores excitaturum: q̃ lumen hoc patens in corporibus spe/
ciosis quottidie soleat amatoribus incitare. Quippe cum lumen hoc aspectu per
c spicuum non al~~umen~~ [unde] tantam apud nos gratiam admirationemq; nactum fuerit
q̃ ex illo secretiore cuius est imago: ex illo inquã diuinæ sapientiẹ lumine. Di/
uina igitur sapientia ubiq; dedit lumini tanquam suo cuidam uicario principatũ
d Corporis quidem nostri soli duces sunt oculi. Soli .n. inter membra sunt luminis
q. cuiusdam sapientiẹ compotes. Inter omnes quoq; animẹ uires regnat mens so
e la uidelicet munere sapientiẹ lucens. Elementorum prætęrea similiumq; corporũ
fg ignis est Dominus solus inter hæc. q. sapiens quidam lumine præditus. In cœlo si
militer Sol ipse solus fons luminis omnibus dominatur. Idemq; apud astrono/
mos potentiam significat atq; sapientiam: nona cœli plaga gaudens uelut æde mi
neruæ. Cuius etiam uicinitate Mercurius sapientis nomen obtinuisse uidetur.
h Quid plura? Ipsum deniq; totius mundi regnum non caloris ullius aut frigoris
uiolentia: aut motuum quorundam impetus: aut ulla corporum uel fluctuantiũ
i turba uel uastorum moles sibi uendicat. Sed sapientia prima: sicut omnia cernẽs
sic & omnia potẽs: sicut prouidens ubiq; singulis: ita rursus & domina singulorũ.
Hæc itaq; merito & nobis mandauisse uidetur ut ita sapientiam cum potentia p
uiribus coniungamus: sicut ipsa & in se & in uniuerso manifeste cõiunxit. Quã/
obrem diuinitus effectum arbitror: ut solis lumẽ idem: quod quidem efficit om
nia tanq̃ potens: similiter omnia demonstraret: uelut sapiens: imo & cuncta iuua
ret atq; delectaret tanq̃ bonum. Quo semper ammonemur cum potentia non so
jk lum sapientiam: sed bonitatem et copulare. Eiusnodi uero copulam uenerãdam
prorsus atq; beatam & poetẹ canunt extitisse quondam regnãte Saturno: & Pla/
to noster uidere præceteris exoptabat. Ac nos sectatores eius ante omnia cupi/
l mus Virum præceteris amaturi: qui singularæ sapientiæ studium morumq; pro/
m bitatem cum generosa stirpe sim̃ul & principatu coniunxerit. Hic iam adulatio
nis uanitatisq; suspitio a philosophis admodum aliena: prohibet latius explicare
quod sentio: fas uero sit id saltem breuiter eloqui. In Ramberto Malatesta Soglia
n ni Principæ: iam habeo tota quod mente petebam: tota hunc mente diligo. Atq;
lex amicitiæ iubet mea huic omnia communia facio.

o Quomodo Venus per cupidinem cõmiscet amãtes: Iuppiter amicabilis per
p Mercurium cõflat amicos.

M. F. Florentinus Ramberto Malatestæ Illustri Sogliani Principi. S. P. D.

ANtiqui gẽtium theologi amicitiam tanti fecerunt: ut inter cætera numi
na: immo & sæpe præceteris Iouem coluerint amicabilem: conciliandis
q ubiq; beniuolentiis amicitiisq; prefectũ. Apud hos ego quemadmodũ
r Alma Venus per cupidinem & accẽdebat amores & (ut ita dixerim) cõiugebat
amãtes: Ita Iuppiter amicabilis per Mercurium grauiores procreabat beniuolen
tias: amicitiasq; conflabat. Si nobis hodie liceat Iouem Mercuriumq; nominare

a B K *tamquam* b B om. *esse ... aliud* c Dur *non aliunde* B *non tam a lumine* d B om. *Soli n.*, adds *enim* after *membra* e B *munera* f B *quasi* g B *quidem* h B om. *Non* i K *fastorum* j *etiam* k *eiusmodi* l B *Utrum* m *simul* n * o B *cupiditatem* (err.) p B *constat* q B *ergo* r *coniungebat* profecto amicitiam hanc nostram non humana quadam causa dixerimus: sed Io uis amicabilis munere copulatam: siquidem ipsa Minerua beniuolétiæ nostræ cõ ciliatrix: fertur e summo Iouis capite nata. Sed nũquid per Mercurium id nobis effecisse dicemus. Per Mercurium certe: non solum per occultiorem illum atq; cœ lestem: sed etiam per notiorem nobis aliquem & humanum. Quandoquidem pe trus Martellus utriusq; nostrum amicissimus: qui & nos coniunxit in unum nõ solum Mercuriale fert ingenium: sed ipsam etiam effigiem indolemq; Mercurii p̃ se ferre uidetur. Quam equidem ut de meo quodam .q. uaticinio nonnihil dixe- rim nondum inspecta eius genesi auguratus sum: & inspecta: sum augurio cõfir- matus. Is igitur quemadmodum in amicitia inter nos uinciẽda: hactenus sub Io ue Mercurium egit: ita deinceps in mutuis consiliis inter nos significandis inter- prætandisq;: ultro citroq; Mercurius erit. iiii. augusti. Mcccclxxxxiii. a b

Sol imago Vicariusq; Dei.

Mar. F. Re. in Christo patri. D. Francisco soderino epõ Volaterrano. S. P. D. cd

LIbrum de Sole nuper magnaĩmo petro Medici dedicatum ad te quoq; necessariũ eius mitto legẽdũ. Sed ut tibi ẽt alteri patrono meo liber ipe totus uideat' i scriptus hãc totius sũmã tibi dedico: Tria thæologi Deo præcipua tribuunt: Potẽtiam: Sapientiam: Bonitatem. Sol igitur imago Dei ef- ficit apud nos omnia tanq̃ potens. Distinguit præterea quottidie: demonstratq; oculis singula uelut sapiẽs. Iuuat deniq; nos atq; delectat tanq̃ bonus. Dei solius proprium esse tradunt miracula facere. Sol itaq; dei Vicarius tria potissimum mi randa uidetur efficere. Sub cœlo quidem q̃plurima per hiemem quasi mortua in uere suscitat & æstate. In cœlo autem cœlestia omnia illumiat & moderatur & re git. Quæ uero super cœlum nõ oculis tantum: sed mentibus etiam nostris inui sibilia sunt. Sol ipse (ut ita dixerim) uisibilia reddit: dum admirandis cœlestium spectaculis nos admonet super cœlestia cõtemplari. Contemplare fœliciter sacer antistes Solem hunc nostrum atq; lumen: uero præceteris sole alma luce dignissi me. viii. Septembris. Mcccclxxxxiii. Florentiæ. e f g h

Prohœmium in æpistolas.

M. F. Florentinus cũctis semel æpistolis suis. Sal.

QVotiens ępistolæ meæ amicis meis (me iubẽte) Salutẽ dicitis: totiẽs amicissimo uestro Hieronymo rossio imortales salutes dicitis: Vos enĩ Ego mortales genueram: ac nescio qua fortuna propediem moribundas Hieronymus autem insignis pietate Vir regenerauit uos nuper (ut spero) iã im mortales. Latebatis. n. iandiu lucis cupide: nec quisq̃ adhuc e tenebris eruebat. Fato forsan uel genio nondum uolente. Rossius aũt noster: imo iã & uobis Ro- scius: qua pietate semper erga parentẽ uestrũ Marsilium se gessit: eadẽ nũc & uos caritate quadã hereditaria fœliciter est prosequutus: diligentia simul & opera cu ras: ut uestre facies iamiã oppressæ: prorsus exprimerẽtur: Hũc ergo doctũ piũq; restitutorem uestrum: hactenus quidẽ tristes: nunc hilares salutate: atq; p̃ ingẽti imortalitatis munere immortales gratias agite. xv. Decembris. Mcccclxxxxiii. Florentiæ. ij k l mn n o pq

Pro libro de Sole: item de Stella Magorum: in solennitate Epiphaniæ.

Marsilius Ficinus Angelo Nicholino ciui & Iurisconsulto præclaro. S. D.

a B *a summo* b *qui* c B *Marsilius Ficinus Reveren.* d *episcopo Volaterrano* e *etiam* f *inscriptus* g B om. *ipse* h B om. *Florentiae* i B *nostro* j G *dicite* k G *a tenebris* l B *vester* m G om. *quadam* n *curans* o K *salutaret* p B *immortalitatie* (erron.) q G *1494*

LIBER

HOdie magi (stellarum obseruatores stella miranda duce) Christũ stella
rum auctorem muneribus præcipue tribus salutauerunt: Auro: Mirra:
Thure. Hodie Christus sancto spiritu cœlitus corruscãte: fertur ab Ioã
ne Iordanis aqua perfusus. Hodie Christus aquarum procreator & Vini: nupti
ali conuiuio mirabiliter aquã cõmutauit in uinum. Hũc ergo diem tribus ingen
tibus miraculis celeberrimum: insignis pietate uir Angele: trino tu quoq; solen
niter quotannis honore concelebras: Cõuiuio: Musica: Lectione: Huic equidẽ
lectioni apud te sacræ: librum de Sole & lumine consecro: hac a me nuper ratiõe
a cõpositum: ut Solis luminisq; uisibilis cõparatione ad inuisibile diuinitatis lumẽ
pro uiribus cõtemplandũ lectorum mentes erigerentur. Vtinã sicut Stella mira-
bilis ad uidendum Christũ: Deum & Hominem: perduxit hodie magos: ita nos
ad Deum excogitandum hodie Sol perducat: Ianuarii. vi. Mcccclxxxxiiii.

Pro Bacchi dono. Item Euãgelicum illud: ex aqua uinum factum.

Marsilius Ficinus Mazingo insigni phisico. S. D.

MAtutinis infra octauam Epiphaniæ lectionibus: frequenter admonitus
Hodie mecum: euangelicum illud animo reputabam: Vinũ ex aqua
b factũ: An pter mysticã allegoriam: atq; moralẽ: phisicũ quoq; sẽsum ha
c beat: siquidem ~~nã~~ natura longo quodam tẽpore: aquam ferme: sicut momento Christus
permutet in uinum: Phisicus uero sensus: ad medicum præcipue ptinens: inuesti
gat. Cur nam hoc primum miraculorum suorũ Christus esse uoluerit? Forsitã ut
ostenderet: primum sũmumq; uitæ nostræ subsidium fore uinũ: Sed cur nã uinũ
d bonum i. ualidum: quale creticum & orientale merum seruatum est usq; adhuc.
ef Cur noluit ille uitæ magister in prima mensa uinum hoc afferre. Sed adeo distulit
g uoluit forsitan admonere: uinum uirtute uigẽs feruenti ~~iuuenti~~ iuventuti minime cõceden
dum: sed recreande potius frigidiori senectuti seruandum. Cur deniq; nõ partem
sed totam prorsus aquam permutauit in uinũ? ut uidelicet bonũ uinum in sene-
ctute presertim bibatur & merum. Itaq; cum hæc circa meridiem meditarer: ex-
optare cœpi atq; iam exquirere uinũ eiusmodi: quo & senecturem meam & ma
tris seniũ cõfouerem. Nam præterito autũno illa quidem octuaginta: ego autem
sexaginta iã ãnos impleuimus: Tu uero tãq̃ uates eadẽ hora uinum ad me misisti
diuinũ. Apollineũ certe medicum: qualis meus est mazigus & uaticinium decet
& bacchi munus: siquidẽ phœbus idẽ & primus medicus & uaticinii auctor apel-
latur: bacchi frater sacrisq; coniũctus. Quod deniq; multifacio: una cũ electissi-
mo liberi patris munere æpistolã dedisti galenicã: uitę salubriter cõsulentẽ: Vt cũ
auxilio cõsiliũ amice coniungeres. ego igitur quantũ cũ medicina pronosticum
& cũ Phœbo Bacchus: tantũ profecto sum atq; sẽper ero tecũ amore coniunctus.
Ianuarii. xiii. Mcccclxxxxiiii.

h Pro libro de Vita iterũ imprimẽdo. Itẽ auspicium de amicitia immortale.

i M. F. Florentinus Ioanni Menchen sacerdoti coloniensi præclaro iuris cãonici
professori magni colon: & antistitis secretario. S. P. D.

j QVintodecimo Kl'ndas Februarias prope solis ortum in somniis salutare
k uidebatur incognitum mihi antea uirum honesta specie prẽditum: ue
stibus comitibusq; ornatum. Qui post disputationẽ phisicã mihi pedẽ
l ostẽderet quasi curandum: eodem ipse die Florẽtiã accessisti: profecturus Romã

a K *visible* b *praeter* c Dur *natura* B *non* K *nam* d B *quare* e K *mense* f B *distulit?* g Dur *iuventuti* h B *rerum* (erron.) i B *Marsilius Ficinus* but om. *Ioanni* j B *Februarii* k Dur *videbar* l *Romam*

magni ãtiſtitis Hermãi legatus:q cũ pp cõtuſionẽ pedis ad noſ uẽire ñ poſſes deſi ab
deriũ uiſendi ſignificaſti:egoq; ad te : ut nõ oportebat ſolũ:Sed ẽt decebat:acceſ
ſi:itaq; cum primum te iam obuium ſum intuitus:agnoui ſtatim qualem in ſom
nis Heroicum uirum uideram: poſt ſalutationem primam in mentionem operis c
noſtri de uita mox incidimus:multaq; ad medicinam præcipue pertinentia inui
cem diſeruimus. Interloquendum: ut quicquid dormiens præſagiueram imple d
retur:pedem oſtendiſti contuſum. Itaq; non ſõnium quidem uidiſſe uideor: Sed e
oraculum diuinitus accepiſſe.Certũ (ut arbitror)auſpicium amicitiam noſtram f
fore diuinam. Quoniã uero Diuina ſunt etiam immortalia: immortalẽ:ego qui
dẽ(ut modo narraui)diuinitatẽ amicitiæ noſtræ præſenſi. Tu uero interim futu
ram eius immortalitatem excogitaſti. Decreuiſti.n.libros de uita noſtros curare
iterum exprimendos: Quos & noſtra hæc uita latius inde propagaretur:& poſte g
ri hoc tuo erga nos officio q̃tũ nos amaueris:pariter a nobis amatus:intelligant:
atq; ita diuia hæc amicitia noſtra apud poſteros imortalis euadat. Viue fœlix mi
Ioannes & noſtræ propagator uitæ:& uita digniſſime Vale fœliciter .xvii. Ianu
arii.Mcccclxxxxiiii.Florentiæ. h

Commendatio breuis in cauſa Iuſta.

M.F.Reue.in Chriſto patri dño Frãciſco Soderino epõ Volaterão . S.P.D. ij

MOnaſterium Septimi tibi cõmẽdaturus in cauſa Mutinẽſi paucis agam
Scio equidẽ q̃tũ monachos illos: uiros admodũ pios ames:Quos ego
quoq; nõ amo ſolũ Sed colo. Arbitror eos tanq̃ iuſtos iuſta etiã poſtula
re : tu iuris acerrimus es patrõus.Quicqd deniq; officii in hos cõtuleris in me ho
rũ obſeruatorẽ pariter collatũ eſſe putauero. Monachus iſtic huius cauſæ procu
rator:& re & nomine iuſtus diligẽter tibi referet oia. Me quoq; tibi cõmẽdo q̃ plu k
rimũ. Vale fœlix.xxv. Ianuarii.Mcccclxxxxiiii.Florentiæ. h

Plato multa Chriſtianis cõſentanea dixit. Platonici multi xpiana ſunt imitati. l

M.F.Florẽ.Reue.in Chriſto patri.D.Iacobo Rõdono epõ Ariminẽſi.S.P.D. ij

FRater ſanctes i ordine diui Dominici theologiæ profeſſor inſignis:tuo m
nomine me ſalutans:teſtimoniis profecto multis aſſeuerauit:me abſte
ardenter amari:quod quidẽ & ſi iãdiu mihi plane perſpectum erat:deſi
derabã tamẽ de proſpera ualitudine tua nuntiũ qualem nunc accepi diutius ex
optatũ.Philoſophia humanorũ omniũ bonorũ mater: amicitiã iandiu noſtrã pe
perit:omni(ut Plato inquit)neceſſitudini præponẽdã:nec tempore pituram. Sed
hæc profecto certiora ſunt:q̃ ut teſtibus uerbiſq; indigeant. Retulit præterea no n
bis fratrẽ (neſcio quẽ) in declamatiõe publica inſolenter aſſeuerauiſſe trinitatis
apud Chriſtiãos diuinę myſteriũ:apud platonẽ ipſũ extare: xpiãoſq; ~~familiaria~~ illic opq
primos accepiſſe. Vos autẽ a me ſuper hac re tanq̃ mihi Platonica ſint: iudicium
expectare. Ego igitur extra cõtrouerſiam aſſero:trinitatis Chriſtianæ ſecretũ in
ipſis platonis libris nunq̃ eſſe.Sed nonnulla uerbis quidẽ q̃uis nõ ſenſu quoquo
modo ſimilia. Similiora uero in ſectatoribus eius:qui floruere poſt Chriſtum:in r
numenio : Ammõio:Plotino:Amelio:Iamblico:Proclo. Qui cum & omnes Io
annis Euangelium egiſſent:Et quidam inſuper Dioniſii areopagitæ libros:non
nulla trinitati ſimilia libenter uſurpauerunt: ordineſq; angelorum & nomina
ſuſceperunt:tanquam platoni ſuo Moſis ſectatori plurimum conſentanea. Quã

a propter *b non posses* c B *mentem* *d disseruimus* *e somnium* *f* B om. *Certum* *g* Dur B *Quo* *h* B om. *Florentiae* *i* B *Marsilius Ficinus Florentinus Reverendissimo* *j episcopo* *k* K *refert* *l Christiana* *m* B *sanctus* *n* B *quae* *o* B *myijerium* (erron.) *p Christianosque* *q* * *r* B *vere*

obrem Aurelius Augustinus quondã Platonicus & iã de christiana pfessiõe deli'
a berãs: cũ i hos platonicorũ libros incidisset: cognouissetq; christiana p imitatio/
abc nẽ ab his pbata: deo grãs egit: redditusq; iã est ad christianã recipienda propẽsior.
Q uantũ uero platonica christianis similia sint: ex æpistola quã hac de re ad Brac/
d ciũ martellũ iãdiu scripsi: breuiter intelligere poteris. Hãc. n. nunc exscripta ad te
mitto. Vale fœlix: & me (ut soles) ama: te uehemẽter amãrem. Die. ii. Februãrii.
Mccccclxxxxiiii.

Semper aliquid agendum: & quoad fieri potest: in eodem perseuerandum.

Marsilius Ficinus Florẽtinus Callimacho doctissimo uiro: & amico opti/
mo. S.P.D. vagat

e CVm uniuersũ hoc cuius quodãmõ partes sumus: semper moueat: certe
f nos ab actione motuq; uocare: neq; possumus unq̃ neq; debemus: præ/
g sertim qm̃ primus ppetuusq; motus (ut placet platonicis) ẽ ipsi aiæ natu
h ralis: & uita nihil ẽ aliud q̃ aiæ mot9 & actus: ut q̃ uiuere: tã pfecto moueri & age
re necessariũ sit: & pariter exoptandũ. Sed nunquid ego interim sum ineptus?
ij Oportunius forte fuerat post diuturnũ silẽtiũ rõnes negociorũ nr̃orũ & ualitudi
nis nuntiũ: statim p epistolã tibi reddere: q̃ adeo repẽte philosophari. Certe fuerat
kl oportunius mi Callimache. Verũ qꝛ tã importune philosopher: i cã est: & diutur
nior iã nr̃ usus & Genius. Tu quoq; nobis cũ soles p epistolas sæpe: sed tempesti/
ue & apte sẽp philosophari. Pergamus ergo parũp (ut iã cœpimus) Vtinã nõ ine
pti. Tres pcipui sũt p locũ in uniuerso mot9. Alia qdẽ circa idẽ eodẽq; mõ ppetuo
reuoluunt. Alia uero cõtinue locũ situq; pmutãt: Alia partim quidẽ motũ illum
m circularẽ partim ẽt rectũ hũc imitant. Hoies quoq; alii motus alios psequunt.
Sed ut ego nũc de motu iã meo nõ alieno loquar: mihi certe datũ est: ut semp re/
uoluar eodẽ. Q uid nã hodie Marsilius agit? Q uod & heri. Q uid cras acturus?
Iterũ quod & hodie. Semp (ut uides) intra parietes achademiæ uoluor circa idẽ:
n iterũq; reuoluor. Q uid aũt hoc iãdiu circuitu fecerim: rursusq; refecerim: atq; rete/
xã: intelliges ex cathalogo librorũ meorũ: quẽ una cũ libro de Sole legendũ ad te
op mitto ut clarissimo phœbi muneris testimonio amicitia nr̃a præsentibus poste
risq; refulgeat. Mitto aũt triplicẽ de Sole & lumie codicẽ: ut nõ tibi solũ ego gra
tificer. Sed tu quoq; duobus tuis amicis gratificari possis. Q uæ igit componãt a
q nobis: ex his ipse pcipies. Ego uero te iã res tuas cõposuisse ex Octauiano tuo &
tedaldis accepi. Q uod quidẽ mihi cõtigit q̃ gratissimum. Vale fœliciter. Die. ii.
Aprilis. Mcccclxxxxiiii.

Sapientes filii sunt Mineruæ: Hæc philosophiam parit: Philosophia
philosophos.

M. F. Germano Ganaiensi dilectissimo fratri. S. D.

rm MInerua poetæ celebrãt ppetuo uirginẽ. Nulla tñ apud supos aut hoies fi
lios procreat grãdiores ppetua interim uirginitate seruata. Si quidẽ ipsa
s solo sũmi iouis capite nata: solo similiter capite generat: generat inq̃ pro
t extinctis gigantibus sapiẽtes. q. heroas gigantibus grandiores. Philosophia quo/
uv q; ppetua uirgo sophiæ. i. Mineruæ filia pro sapientibus phõs uertice parit. Salue
igit iterum dilectissime mi germane: quẽ mihi re uera germanũ cõmunis pepertit
wxy phia mater. Pia mater cũ nollet filios unq̃ iter se disiũctos & te (ut scribis) isthuc

a *imitationem* b *probata* c *gratias* d B *excsriptam* e Dur *vagat* f B *vacare*
g *animae* h *motus* i *rationes* j *nostrorum* k B *quod* l *causa* m *homines*
n Dur *iterumque* o Dur *Phoebe* p Dur B *amicitia nostra* q *percipies* r *superos*
s *inquam* t *quasi* u *id est* v *philosophos* w *philosophia* x B om. *Pia mater* y *

missa luce traxit in amorē mei:& me uicissim transmisso hucusq; ex ipsa luce ca-
lore rapuit in amorē tui. Q m̄ uero amicorū præcipue fratrū oīa debent esse cōia: ab
decreui mea omnia tibi ad uotū cōmunia fore. Itaq; mittā ad te primo quidē Dio
nysii platonicorūq; multorum libros tibi iam exscriptos: quos iādiu petisti. Dein c
de cōmentaria in Parmœnidē. Q uæ tui gratia quottidie exscribunt. Q uibus for d
te succedent cōmentaria in Timeum: atq; sophistam. Q uæ quidē in sophistā pro e
perant iā ad calcē transcribuntur: interea & æpistolæ recognoscunturq; ur cætera f
Plotinum enim habere te senseram: nuper autem non scribis habere. Si mitti uis g
significa. Vale.

Pro libro de Sole.

Marsilius Ficinus. D. Bernardo Bembo Veneto. S. D.

SOlet uulgaris amor sæpe propter absentiam longam diuturnumq; silen
tium refrigescere: prorsusue deleri. Amorem uero nostrum utpote singu
larem: propter hæc neq; deferuere unq̄: neq; oblitterari posse: Phœbus
ipse & calore sit pignus: & lumine testis. Die. xviiii.

Pro libro de Sole.

Marsilius Ficinus. D. Antonio Cronico Veneto. S. D.

IOuem quendam amicabilem antiqui colebant amicorum cōciliatorē:
amicitiæ seruatorem. Sed quasnam potissimum mundi plagas Iuppiter h
hic inhabitat. In Sole forsan posuit habitaculum suū. Si quidem amici-
tia ab amore dicitur atq; ducitur. Amor aūt calor quidam est. Amatorius uero ex i
notitia proficiscitur. A pulchritudine procreatur. Sed Apollo præcæteris caloris
ē & notitiæ: & pulchritudinis auctor. Iuppiter amicabilis: in hoc Appollieo mu
nere amicitiæ nostræ pignus esto. Die. xviiii. Augusti. Mcccclxxxxiiii.

Q uid sentiat de Astrologia.

Marsilius Ficinus Angelo politiano. S. D.

COntra multos Astrologos: qui more gigantum eripere cœlum Ioui tam j
frustra q̄ impie moliuntur: merito & Picus alumnus palladis: & tu miles
Herculeus sæpe fœliciterq; certatis. Nempe palladem Orpheus gigantū
expultricem canit: & ab Hercule poetæ multi gigantem Anteum a terra simul &
e uita sublatum ferūt. Ego autem quid? Profecto tanq̄ in omni uita uobis unani
mis: in hoc quoq; studio conspiro uobiscum: & si forte non decerto strenue: ta-
men ita plane decerno. Cæteri quidem platonici: cælestes imagines quas descri-
bunt Astronomi: pro oportunitate commemorant: neq; reprobant eas: neq; rur
sus comprobare student. Plotinus autem talia extra controuersiam ridet. Ego
quoq; in commentariis meis in eum: tanq̄ interpres æque derideo: partim quidē
eius auctoritate confisus: partim etiam quoniam nullam habeo certam eius-
modi rationem. Multas præterea ibidem Astrologorum regulas in controuersiā
simili ratione deduco. Sed in libro de uita: ubi profiteor medicinam: ac remedia
uitæ: utcunq; & qualiacunq; possū: undiq; diligenter exquiro: neq; despicio pr
sus imagines illas: neq; omnes respuo regulas: & si enim arbitror certam iis ratio
nem nullā inesse: tamen ut studiosissimus hūanæ medicinæ curator: remedia nō k
solū sapientibus certa: sed etiam multis probabilia sector: ut subsidia passim accu
mulē quomodolibet profutura. Nequid deniq; prætermiserim itētatū: qđ ad uitā lm

a *Quoniam* b *communia* c B om. *que* d *gratia* e B om. *in* f *quam ut* g Dur *olim* h B *servatoram* (erron.) i Dur adds *calor* before *ex* j B *multo* (erron.) k *humanae* l *intentatum* m *quod*

utcunq; cōductur ū cuiq̄ uideri possit: nonnulla tamē intersero firmiora: multa
quoq; passim cōgero: quæ & si forte minus spero: tamē opto prodesse. Quod autē
in principio libri tertii dicere uideor imagines ab antiquioribus Platonicis in cœ
lo dispositas esse: nō id eq̄uidē uolo Nō. n. consiliū ibi meū est: platonicos affirma
re cœlestiū imaginū assertores: de quibus aut nihil: aut parū quid loquūtur: Sed
platonicorū quorundā fuisse sentētiā: mundi animā cœlestia sibi corpora pepetis
se. Stellasq; cū cœlo: atq; ultra Stellas singulas: si mō ibi ulle sint imagines eius
modi quoq; imagines genuisse. Narro autem illic dispositiones signorū imaginū
a que non quales apud Platonicos: Sed quales apud Astrologos obseruaueri:
iam uero quantum imaginibus uel cœlestibus credā: uel arte factis confidam: pro
gressio libri declarat. Præterea in libro de Sole non tam Astronomica doceo
b q̄ per hæc morales allegorias affecto: anagogiasq; ad diuina perquiro: Denique
tā in libris de uita q̄ de Sole & lumine cū philosophicis poetica miscēs: liberius sū
c iterdū & forte licētius euagatus: cū Plotio parcius & seuerius ago: ut mihi tādem
nō igratū sit futurū: Astrologica portēta fuisse a Pico nr̄o mirādula singulariter
confutata. Quę. n. ego nusq̄ affirmo: imo & cū Plotino derideo: explodi a miran
dula gaudeo: superstitiosā præterea uanitatē ab illo tanq̄ a Phœbo pithōicū uirus
extingui tecū pollitiane cōgratulor. Tu. n. semper hac in causa (ut ubiq; soles)
Herculē præstitisti. Soles profecto iādiu hęc Astrologorū prodigia ut alia mōstra
d passim acriter insequi: ut nō in terris solū sed etiā in cœlo mōstra fortissimus Her
cules expugnaueris. Vtinā dēiq; sicut Herculi: sic & tibi: Supata tellus sydera do
net: interi in terris uiue diu. Vale fœliciter. Die. xx. Augusti. Mcccclxxxxiiii.

Pro libro de Sole.

M. F. Bernardo oricellario Marioti filio. S. D.

CVm & optans amicis lucem & cupiens eos lumine declarare: operā eq
dem iādiu dederim: ut libri de Sole & lumine mei apud omnes amicos
meos forēt: nimirū & tu dulcissime mi Bernarde nup hoc munere donādus acce
ef dis: mō uidelicet a nobis amatus: qa nup es cognitus: neq; tamē nūc solū sed & sē
g per amādus. q̄ autē te uehemēter amē: nō solū ingeniū tuū elegās probitasq; facit
h sed ēt qm̄ carus admodū sis Hieronymo rossio & oīum mihi carissimo: & p̄cęteris
ij luce dignissimo: sed ut aliqd tecū de lumie cōmētemur: Siqn̄ interlegēdū: illic es
j saueris: ubi solē uel lumē dicimus prio creatū: Animaduerte quęso ne forsā intel
ligas prio creatiōis momēto uel gradu solē uel solis lumē fuisse factū: cū moses ip
se dicat. In pricipio creauit Deus cœlū & terrā. Terra aūt &c. sed lumē angelicū
prio quodā ordinis gradu creatū: lum̄ uero solis: futurū primo die: Solis dēiq; ipi
k us globū atq; figurā q̄rto: oīno uero & lumen solis & globū: primo dignitatis in
ter cœlestia gradu. Vale iā & absq; hesitatione lege fœliciter.

Commēdatio cliētis apud Magistratū.

M. F. Nicholao Benino: litteris moribusq; prædito. S. D.

ERat profecto officii mei ab ipso tui magistratus initio pro beniuolentia
g nostra non mediocri: tecum non mediocriter gratulari: Nō solū q̄ hac
g dignitate ornatus fueris: sed etiam & multo magis q̄ magistratū fores
g pro dignitate gesturus. Congratulandum quoq; fuerat amicis cliētibusq; meis q̄
si uel insontes forent: Patrocinium abste consequuturi essent: uel si rei: Saltem

a V *observaverim* B *observaveris* b B om. *affecto: anagogiasque*
c B om. & d B *solem* e *modo* f *quia* g *quod* h *quoniam* i *Si
quando* j V *essaveris* B *haesitaveris* k *omnino*

índulgentíam quandam:atque clementíam.Nouí enim íngeníum tuum. Certo
ſcio te(qđ deus ipſe agendo præcipit)iuſtitiã rite cũ cleméria cõiũcturũ. Præte/
rea ſi qd hac i re circa ioué cõſabulari licet hũc hebrei ſedech.i. iuſtitiã nominãt: a
& Aſtronomi ioui ſuo iura legeſq; cõcedũt.Eũdẽ poetæ ioué canũt idulgẽtiæ ple
nũ:ut prætermittã poeticũ illud ad licẽtiã potiuſ declinãs q̃ idulgẽtiã:Iuppiter eẽ
piũ ſtatuit qđcũq; iuuaret:ſatis eſto apđ Aſtrologos:ioué cũ legibus afferre uel ſi b
gnificare clemẽtiã:in hoc ſane deus cœlitus hoíes admonuiſſe uidet̃:ut in magi
ſtratu pariter utrũq; miſcerent:ſed hæc tu pro ingenio tuo(ut arbitror)ſatis no
ſti. Vale fœliciter Florentiæ.xxxi.Auguſti. Mcccclxxxxiiii.

Gratiarum actio pro indulgentia in clientem impetrata.

Marſilius Ficinus Nicolao Benino Litteris Moribuſque Prædito. S.D.

CVm bonũ atq; malũ ſibi inuicẽ opponãt̃:atq; iccirco conditiões ſubeãt
inter ſe oppoſitas.Probabile nimirũ eẽ uidet̃.Si bonũ nã fœcundũ eſt: c
ut malũ:cõtra ſterile ſit futurũ.Quãtũ uero malũ crimen ẽ:tantũ clemẽ
tia bonũ ſit:ergo neceſſe ẽ:idulgentia clemens longe fœcũdior q̃ crimen atq; deli d
ctũ.Quãobrẽ ſi clientis mei delictũ æpiſtolã ad te noſtrã peperit:multo magis li/
beralis & clemens idulgentia tua parere rurſus debet æpiſtolã: ac multo meliorẽ e
atq; maiorẽ:pría quidẽ(ut ita dixerim)fuit Iouia:Iouis uidelicet cõparatiõe fre/
ta:ſecunda igitur nõ aliter ſupatura primã:uel ſaltẽ ẽ æquatura:q̃ ſi fuerit apolli/ f
nea.Solus.n.ſol põt ſuperare Iouem.Quapp ut apollineis auſpiciis hæc ſatis of/ g
ficio in meo tuo facere poſſit:mitto eã ad te phœbi comitẽ:ſoliſq; pediſſequã. Le h
ge libenter librum de ſole noſtrũ tibi dono datũ:ac uiue fœliciter.Die.iii.Septẽ/
bris.Mcccclxxxxiiii. De Ioue amicabili & Apolline Pro libro de Sole.

Oratio Marſilii Ficini Florẽtini ad Ioannem Matheronem magni Gallorum
Regis inclitum oratorem.

ANtiqui theologi primũ:deide poetæ iter cætera numia Iouẽ amicabilẽ
coluerũt:caſti amoris:ac firmioris amicitiæ patrẽ. Qui ppea & ab amo
re pariter atq; amicitia:nomẽ hoc amicabile reportauit.Cum igit̃ & pla
to nr̃ numinis huius nõnũq̃ faciat mẽtionẽ:ſæpe equidẽ itercõmentãdũ quæſiui
quo nam alio hũc deũ nomie clarius apellarẽ.Diu dẽiq; meditãti uenit in mẽtem
ut hũc præcipue deũ clariſſimũ.i.Apollinẽ nominarẽ.Lucis:caloris:harmoniæ:
notitiæ:fontẽ.Iã uero nec unq̃ amamus incognita:nec quicq̃ ſine luce cognoſci/ ij
mus:nec abſq; calore quodã ad amãdũ aliqñ puocamur.Præterea & harmonica k
quædã cõgruitas ẽ ad amorẽ & amicitiã neceſſaria.Rurſus ad amorẽ ſæpe deſide
rat̃ pulchritudo corpis.Ad amicitiã ſemp optat̃ ai pulchritudo: utraq; uero pul l
chritudo nihil aliud q̃ ſplẽdor qdã eẽ uidet̃.Splendoris aũt auctor ẽ apollo. Oẽs m
itaq; ratiões cogunt:amoris & amicitiæ fontẽ apollinẽ præcipue nominare. Nos
aũt ſi cõſabulatiõis gr̃a deorũ numerũ forte gentiliũ more recipimus:phœbũ eſſe n
dicemus:Deum quẽdam numenue ſoli præfectum inter cœleſtia regem:ſin ratio
ne potius ſeria:nitimur phœbum eſſe deum ſummum aſſeuerabimus:Cuius ſol
cœleſtis eſt imago.Itaq; phœbus ille honeſti amoris & amicitiæ firme auctor eſt
ſol uero ſignificator.Cum igitur ego phœbeo quodam ſapientiæ uirtutumq; tua o
rum ſplendore ſingulariter inflãmatus: te ardenter amem:affectemque amicitiã
ex amore conflare:nimirum & apollineis auſpiciis ad te uenio:Salue.

Multiſaciendum eſt Laudari a laudato uiro.

a quod *b quodcumque* c B *tam* Dur illegible. *d* B adds *sit* after *foecundior* e B *tuare* *f* B *quae* *g Quapropter* *h* B *in me* *i* Dur corr. to *incognito* *j quicquam* *k aliquando provocamur* *l animi* *m* B om. *pulchritudo* (deletion) *n gratia* o K *phoeba* (erron.)

LIBER

Marsilius Ficinus Germano Ganaiensi uiro Virtute præstanti. S.D.

QVæ de excellenti uirtute dignitateq; tua iampridem : e multis audiuerã:
nuper Cosmus saffectus:& Laurẽtius spinellus testimõiis apud me mul
a tis confirmauerant:uiri nobiles:atque testes hac in re profecto locuple
ctissimi. Narrauerunt præterea q̃ti me facias & q̃ ardenter ames. Ego uero pluri/
mi facio ꝓbari amariq; absteːlaude p̄cæteris & aore dignissimo . q̃ igit̃ tibi gratũ
sit: nr̃a uisere: tã nobis optabile:tibi prorsus gratificari. Videbis(ut spero) mox
nõnullos hinc ad te platonicos uenientes: Vidisses & Areopagitam simul platõi
b corũ culmẽ:si nũc eo habitu:qui & ipsum & te decebat accedere potuisset:ex scri
ptoris & librarii negligẽtia ĩpediuit accessũ:Paucos(ut spo)post dies:ueniet cũ
ꝑistolis. Exscriptũ iã tibi ẽ cõmẽtariũ in parmenidem. Q uottidie rescribit̃ in Ti
meum. Vale fœlix:atq;(ut cœpisti)carissime mi Germane:Marsiliũ germanum
sub platone tuũ ama p̄cor ardenter amãtem. Die. xvi. Octobris . Mccccxxxxiiii.

Pro libro de Religione Purgatio de tarda salutatione.

Marsililius. F. Ioanni stephão Equiti & Oratori Mediolanẽsi clarissimo. S.D.

ET si uirtus dignitasq; tua & amor ingẽs erga te meus iandiu postulabat:
ut te ultro frequẽterq; salutarẽ:tuorũ tamẽ negociorũ turba interpellare
c te nisi in re quadã necessaria ꝓhibebat. Nũc igit̃ cũ & mius tibi forte ne
d gocii fore putẽ:& nr̃a res exigat(ut iamp̃ridẽ par fuerat)te saluto:salue sẽp in ip̃o
sempiternæ salutis auctore Deo: uir oĩum salute dignissime. Nolui eqdẽ ad uirũ
uirtutis dignitatisq; plenũ accedere uacuus:ad inclitũ Illustrissimi ducis oratorẽ
sine duce uenire. Ducit itaq; me in presentia Christus ueritatis & gr̃æ plenus fe/
rẽtẽ mecũ librũ de christiana religiõe tractãtẽ. Neq; te offẽdat precor hũilis ac pau
p libri habitus:siquidẽ christiana religio & in primis humilitatẽ præcepit & liben
ef ter pauptatẽ tolerat. Oino uero liber de christiana pietate compositus te decet in
signẽ pietate uirum. Præterea duo potissimũ amor: ut sit pfectus: desiderare uide
ghi tur:ardorẽ iq atq; firmitatẽ. Profecto q̃ te ardẽter amẽ testimõio cẽ põt sol ille apđ
te noster: ut luminis: ita & caloris origo: q̃ uero firmus noster erga te amor sit fu/
turus argumentum pœnes te atq; pignus erit præsens de religiõe liber. Nihil . n.
religiosa pietate firmius:charitas nunq̃ excidit. Vale fœlix:meq; ama præcor ian
j diu ardenter amantem. Die. iiii. Nouembris. Mccccxxxxiiii.

Oratio Marsilii Ficini Florẽtini ad Carolum Magnum Gallorum Regem.

EXcelsa Maiestas tua: Rex Carole semper inuicte: solet nonnunq̃ (ut ple
k riq; ferũt)dicere: ad hãc expeditionẽ mitti diuinitus. Q đ qdẽ nos & uni
lm uersus hic ppl̃s florẽtinus tuus ꝓculdubio credit: firmiter spat:uehemẽ
ter cõgratulatur. Veri nãq; simile ẽ & christianissimũ Gallorũ Regẽ a christo mit
no ti:& carolũ p̄cæteris isignẽ pietate Regẽ:christiana pietate duci:pr̃ti cũ iter opus
p q; tñ ea mẽte sis aggressus: ut sanctã Ierusalẽ seuissimis barbaris occupatã : sũmo
hũani generis redẽptori: dẽiq; redimas. Regnũ ꝓfecto sanctũ spamus te facile re
q dẽpturũ: Recepto pri9 ob iter hereditario regno:siqdẽ hoc itiner̃ passim ꝓ uirib9
rs uestigia xp̃i leq̃ris : xp̃us rex pacificus pacẽ uolẽtib9 sæpe ꝓmittit: idẽ tu quoque
rex christianissimus singulari pietate præditus ꝓmittis(ut audimus: atq; ut spa/
mus)profecto præstabis: idq; reuera facies: quod pio quõdam Eneæ: Aeneadum
que generi mandatum est a patre. Parcere subiectis: & debellare superbos.
Quamobrem cum uolentibus pacem : omnibus pacis auctor sis futurus: tuis

a re b K potuisse c K in te d semper e Omnino f B om. de
g inquam h esse potest i apud j B ardentes k B has fuerunt for
ferunt (erron.) l populus m sperat o praesertim o inter p tantum
q itinere r Christi sequaris : Christus s volentibus

præſertim : ideſt nobis pacificum te præſtabis. Florentinam ciuitatem tuam miri
fica pietate uiſes. Florentiam a flore. i. a lilio dictã Liliorũ ubiq; plenã. In propria a
uenies & tui te tota mente recipient. Tu autem ducem tuũ imitatus chriſtũ cla-
mabis ad populũ. Venite ad me omnes qui laboratis & onerati eſtis: & ego refi-
ciã uos. Præſens itaq; populus & futurus in ęuũ gratioſũ regem carolũ a charitate
gratiiſq; nominatũ his ſemp uocibus celebrabit. Benedictus qui uenit in nomine
domini. Carolus carus nobis excelſus rex pacificus. Hæc ẽ dies quã fecit domius
exultemus & Lætemur in ea. Hæc inq̃ de tuo ſplendore populus Florentinus prę
ſens futuruſq; prædicabit. Totus aũt mundus: oiumq; cõmũis hiſtoria: quæ mox
dicam (ut arbitror) recenſebit: carolus gallorũ Rex inuictus Cæſarianũ illud: di
ctu magnũ: factu maximũ: Veni. Vidi. Vici. Adeo ſupauit: ut dicere iã iure poſ-
ſit. Nondum ueni: nec dum uidi: Iam uici: ſuperauit & celebratiſſimũ illum apud
omnes Herculẽ. Hercules. n. Manibus: Igne: Ferro: Claua: Laboribus dicit̃ pu-
gnauiſſe. Carolus autẽ magnus: non tot quidẽ machinis: Sed ferme Iouis inſtar:
ſolo (ut ita dixerim) nutu concutit orbem: ut iam nõ galliæ duntaxat: ſed ẽt orbis
dominus uideatur quando ꝙ uocandus. Q m̃ excelſus Carolus uidet̃ miſſus eſſe b
diuinitus ad domandos turcos: & ad ſanctã Ieruſalẽ ſic a mãifeſtis hoſtibꝰ uindi-
candam: ſicut ipſe Deus oipotens humanũ genus ab occultis hoſtibus liberauit.

Cur prouidentia permittat aduerſa. Item de uaticiniis remediiſque malorum.

Marſilius Ficinus Florentinus Ioanni Caualcanti Amico Vnico. S. D.

SAepe quæritur a Platonicis cur nam prouidentia diuina pmittat ſemp
homie ſmalis innumerabilibus agitari: Iuſtos pariter & iniuſtos. Sũma
tim ad hæc reſpõdere ſolẽt. Prio quidem a mortalibus ignorari: mala ne
iſta ſint an bona. Hũanas. n. res umbris: cogitationeſq; ſomniis eẽ cõſimiles. huc
tendit propheticũ illud: Oia uãitas: Ois homo mendax. Reſpõdẽt iterũ ẽt ſi cõſſi
terit: quæ mala uident̃: quodamõ ẽt eſſe mala. Denique malũ ab ipſo ſũmo bono
pmitti dũtaxat gr̃a boni. Res. n. difficiles & aduerſe uitiũ qdẽ curabile purgãt icu c
rabile uero puniũt. Illic igit̃ purgatiõis: hic iuſtitię lucet bonũ. Boni qnetiã hoies d
ĩ aduerſis diſcernũt̃ a malis & exercẽt̃ atq; pbãt̃. Probatio uero & pfectus & cõſtã e
tia bonũ. Opepciũ ẽ præterea diligẽter cõſiderare Platonicũ illud i Phœdro de ue f
neſica mali demonis aſtutia dictũ. Demon aliquis ſtatim ab initio uitiis q̃pluri- ghi
mis immiſcuit uoluptatẽ. Hæc quidẽ ibi ſocrates inquit admonens: malorum de
monũ pcipuũ eſſe ſtudiũ: animas ſeorſũ a cœleſti pr̃ia in hoc exilio diutius detine j
re ſupni patris oblitas: longaſq; machinari moras illecebris oblectamẽtiſq; terrẽis
quibus profecto quaſi poculis uenefice circes: ſoporiferiſq; ſyrenũ cantibus deli
nite: nũq̃ aut certe tardius in cœleſtem patriam reuertantur. Contra uero demõi-
cas inſidias benefica prouidentia dei ſtatuit: dulcibus quidẽ his lætiferiſq; ſapori-
bus: ſapores amaros interim cõmiſceri: ne ab eiuſmõi uoluptate: quã timeus ma-
lorum eſcam nomiat: capiamur ut piſces ab hamo. Hanc utiq; platonici præcipue
plotinus atque Syneſius magna ex parte cauſam eſſe putant: ut diuina prouiden
tia tot tantiſque perturbationibus aios i terris uexari uoluerit. Huc tendit Plato
nicum illud in libro de ſcientia: conſonũ euangelio: iãdiu dilectiſſime mi Ioãnes
ad te ſcriptũ: ac breuiter declaratũ. Impoſſibile inqt ẽ o theodore mala ſũditus ex kl
tirpari: Neceſſariũ. n. ẽ ſemp aliqd bono ſubcõtrariũ eſſe: apud ſupos qdẽ eẽ ma- m

a B *Florentinam* (erron.) b *Quoniam* c *gratia* d *homines* e *probantur* f *Operae pretium* g *aliquis statim* h B *initia* (erron.) i B *quae plurimis* (V *quamplurimis*) j *patria* k *inquit est* l B om. *o* m *superos*

la nō possunt. Per mortalem uero naturam locumque hunc inferiorem necessa-
rio reuoluūtᵣ. Quaobrē conādū ē: ut hinc illuc q̄celerime fugiamus. Fugere ue
a ro illuc: ē ꝓ uiribus se simile deo reddere: similes uero nos deo faciunt: iustitia: &
b sanctitas cū prudentia. Hæc ille. In his plato declarat nos ob eam maxie causā fu
gā hic ad deū aliq̄n meditari: ut mala quæ necessario nos hic affligūt: effugiamus
ex hoc uidelicet mortali malo: sempiternū illđ reportaturi bonū: iā uero nec ullus
nisi uexatus morbis cognoscit aditq; medicū: neq; nautæ: nisi fluctibus agitati gu
bernatoris prudētiā ammirantᵣ. Mortales profecto tā hæbetes sūt ut bonū nō aliū
de prorsus cognoscāt q̄ ex comparatione malorū: tā ingrati: ut deū bonorū oīum
largitorē nō facile colant: nisi malis oppressi. Quaobrē morbis ꝑturbatiōibusque
frequētibus cruciati: ad Deū ipsū tanq̄ ad medicū opitulatorēq; confugere cōpel-
c luntᵣ. Coguntᵣ quoq; cognoscere: nō terrenā quidē ꝓuinciā ubi anguntᵣ assidue:
d nūq̄ uero quiescūt: suā fore patriā sed cœlestē. Nulla uero potior assignari cā pōt:
e ob quā mala deus & aduersa ꝑmittat: q̄ rō euangelica Docens: cæcos mutilatosq;
nasci nōnūq̄ admirabilē dei potētiā bonitatēq; hoībus declarandā. Mala uidelicet
fg hoībus incurabilia: mirabiliter curaturā. Quemadmodū & morbi fluctusue non
quilibet: sed grauissimi: medicū gubernatorēue sūmū testificari solent. Sæpe igitᵣ
hoīes & priuati & publice: tā extremis undiq; cohercētᵣ angustiis ut nusq̄ pateat
hi exitus. Nulla iā speretᵣ hūana salus: sed tm̄ diuīa petātᵣ: Tūc diuīa bōitas & ptās fi
j liis suis pia mēte supplicitᵣ obsecrātib9 ꝓpitiā porrigēs ex alto manū declarat: deū
k solū eē in extremis calamitatibus suatorē. Idq; tūc quidē demōstrat aptius: qn̄ di
scrimia tāta diu prius q̄ ueniāt: p ꝓphetā quendā uētura ꝑdixerit. Medici quidē
l humāi officiū ē: & si minus sanitatē: saltē semp p̄stare pronosticon. Diuini uero pa
mn riter utrūq; cōplecti. Et si horū exēpla ex sacris lr̄is licet afferre q̄plurima: q̄ oībus
o sūt in promptu. Meū tn̄ cōsiliū ē in præsentia: qđ & semp fuit in lucē mīus nota ꝓ
ferre: mysteriaq; christiana quoad possē platonicis cōfirmare. Audi igitᵣ mi Ioan
nes tā diuinorū cultor: q̄ studiose platonicorū: quibus uerbis apud platonē socra
tes diuinū cōsiliū circa malorū humanorū remedia ꝓphetasq; cōfirmet: sic.n. loq
tur i symposio: sacerdos diotima fatidica mulier diuinorūq; ꝑita: pestē ꝑdixit athe
niēsibus iminētē. Itaq; sacris decennio āte pestē pactis: morbi dilationē dedit: itē
p sic in phœdro: si refferamus sibyllā: & alios quicunq; usi sūt uaticinio q̄ multa ꝑdi
centes in futurū profuerint: prolixum nimis extendemus sermonem: ac rē mani
festam oībus proferemus. Et Paulopost inquit. Antiqui testificantᵣ uaticiniū diui
no quodā furore ꝑfectum: cōiectura prudentiaq; hūana supra modū præstantius
eē. Atqui aduersū morbos laboresq; grauissimos ob antiqua delicta quādoq; diui
q na indignatiōe mortalibus iminentes: diuinus gētibus quibusdā aliūde furor
aduenīes: & futura prædicens: quibus opus erat: remedia mirabiliter adinuenit:
r cōfugiens ad uota cultusq; diuinos. Vnde expiatiōes ꝓpiciationesque consequ-
tus incolumen reddidit possidentem: & in præsens tempus & in futurum absolu
tionem præsentium malorum recte furenti occupatoque adeptus. Hæc ibi præte
rea in libro legum primo: Plato sic inquit. Epimenides cretensis: uir diuinus de
s cē ānos ante psicū bellū: dei oraculo mōitus: ꝑuenit athēas: & sacrificia quædam
dei oraculo ædita fecit: atheniēsibusq; psicā formidātib9 classē: ꝑdixit decēnio per
t sas non uenturos: & postq̄ uenerit infecta re discessuros. Eiusmodi sane uirum

a K *illud* (erron.) b B *Haec in Plato declarat* (erron.) c K *eguntur* d *causa* e *ratio* f B *incurabiliter* * g *curatura* h *tantum* * i *potestas* j Dur *suppliciter* * k *servatorem* l *praestare* m *litteris* n *quae* o *quid* p *sibyllam* q Dur *alicunde* r * s *annos* t *venerint*

Plato oium sapiētissimū eē cēset: quis sæpe uulgo stultissimus habeat. Itaq; ī phœ
dro scribit mirabile qddā hūc imodū. Diuinis meditatióibus: q recte utit: pfectis
q; mysteriis sēp imbuit: pfectus reuera solus euadit: ab humāis aūt studiis segre/
gatus: diuinoq; inherens carpit a multitudie. q. extra se positus. Sed ipse deo ple/ a
nus multitudinē latet. Posthæc plato cū pphetā & sacerdotē diuinis occupatū: b
sapiētiæ humāæ lōge admodū iteruallo præposuisset: describit mētē quandā diui/
no prius āore flagrātē: exstasimq; amatoria patientē: atq; furorē alienationēq; hu c
iusmōi: nō solū humane prudētiæ: sed diuinis ēt mūeribus oibus anteponit. Vbi
plāe cōprobat apostolicū illud. Maior horū charitas. Mitti āt pphetas a deo: & q̄ d
ratióe mittāt: Auicēna ēt in libro diuinorū multis ratióibus cū platone cōsentit. e
Sed longioribus iā digressióibus ptermissis: ad institutū breuiter redeamus. A iad
uersióe pfecto nō mediocri dignū ē: qd ī supiobus iqt plato: pp ātiqua delicta idi
gnatū deū calamitates hoibus quodāmō destinasse: Hinc asseuerat oraculū il/
lud: pp peccata ueniūt aduersa. illud quoq; mosaycū: ex primorū delicto parētū:
aduersa nobis oia contigisse. Vbi præterea subdit plato deū tanq̄ misericordia qua
dā affectū: frequēter afflare pphetas: futura nobis flagella prænūtiaturos: ut hic
admoniti ad uota expiatióesq; sacras cōfugiamus. Quibus rite pactis: incolumes
frequenter euadimus: ibi pfecto: oia uidet ecclesiæ nræ mysteria cōprobare. Pro f
inde ne forte rei tātæ lōgius exēpla petāt: Nōne pp multa delicta prostremū huic g
urbi hoc autumo exitiū iminebat? Nulla prius hominū uirtute uitandū? Nonne
diuia clemētia Florentinis indulgētissima: itegro ante hūc autūnū quadriēnio no
bis istud prænūtiauit? Per uirū sanctimonia sapiētiaq; pstātē Hieronymū ex ordi
ne prædicatorū: diuinitus ad hoc electū. Nōne præsagiis monitisq; diuinis p hūc
ipletis: certissimū iāiā supra nostrū caput iminens exitiū: nulla prius uirtute nra: h
Sed præter spem opinionēq; nostrā mirabiliter euitauimus? A domino factum est
istud: & ē mirabile i oculis nris. Reliquū ē optie mi Ioānes: ut deiceps salutarib9
tāti uiri cōsiliis obsequētes: nō solū ego atq; tu: sed oēs ēt Florentini: deo nobis
clementissimo: grati simus: & publica uoce clamemus: Cōfirma opus hoc deus
quod operatus es in nobis. Die. xii. Decembris. Mcccclxxxxiiii.

Gratulatio pro litteris diu expectatis.

Marsilius Ficinus Germano Ganaiensi dilectissimo suo. S. D.

EAdem tempestatis huius iniquitas: & tua ad me & meas ad te sæpe lras i
itercepit. Heri tādē uicit iter durū picas: expectatāq; diu tuā mihi cōces jk
sit epistolā: surge mea nūc epistola præsens: I nūc ad decus nostrū: melio l
ribus utere fatis: sed quid nā prio scribā? Certe qd in primis cōtigit mihi gratissi/
mū: me uidelicet & commēdatū eē p epistolā tuā fratri tuo Ioāni: acati regio pari
sii psidenti. Id quidā opeprætiū nobis fuit & erit. Nā Italia ferme tota: certe tuscia mno
ois pserti Florētia externis pariter & internis quottidie tumultibus agitat. Cōuēi p
equidē hic apud excelsū Regē uestrū supioribus diebus Ioānē nostrū: uirū frequē
ti salutatione dignissimū: eiusq; cōspectu nō solū ob splēdorē suū: gratulatus sū:
sed ēt ex hoc ualde cōgratulatus: q; in egregio frē tuo carissimū germanū meū ui qrs
dere uidebar. Me interim in psentibus angustiis consolātē. Proinde: & si pfessio
nostra est uacuæ mentis opus: pergo tamen inter hos strepitus in platonicis com
mētatióibus assidue quoad possū: eas ppediē (si deus aspirauerit) perfecturus.

Pia Platonis sententia: De amicis & inimicis dei.

a *quasi* b Dur *divinitus* c *amatoriam* d *autem** e B om. *cum*
f *nostrae* g *postremum* h B *exitum* (erron.) i *tuas* j *pietas* k B adds
tibi after *diu* l B om. *I* m B *praesenti* (erron.) for *praesidenti* n B *quidem*
o *certe* p *praesertim* q *quod* r *fratre* s B om. *germanum*

LIBER

Marſilius Ficinus Ioanni Caualcanti Amico Vnico.S.D.

COntuli heri tecum & cum genero tuo Gerardo Ianſilatio probo uiro:
quid in philebo plato de amicis dei ſentiat:uel inimicis. Placuit ergo ti
bi ut ipſa uerba platonis ad te ſcriberem:& quæ ibidem ſit expoſitio nõ
ſtra. Accipe igitur atque lege fœliciter. Verba platonis hæc ſunt:uir iuſtus & pius
a & probus nonne deo amicus eſt? Iniuſtus autem & improbuſ inimicus? Eſt pro-
fecto. Plurima quidem ſpe unus quiſque ducitur. Interiores enim ſermones qui-
dam ſunt in uno quoque noſtrum. Quos & opiniones & ſpes nominare ſolemus
ſunt quinetiam phãtaſmata picta. Nam cuique licet fingere ſe cumulum auri ma
ximum poſſidere:oblectamentiſque uariis abundantem omni ſuauitate perfun
b di. An non dicendum opiniones imaginationeſque eiuſmodi bonis uiris:qa deo
amici ſunt:ueras frequenter euadere? Malis autem ſæpe numero falſas? Dicendũ
certe:prauis utique uiris oblectationes quædam adſunt: ſæpe conficte:ac deniq;
falſe:falſis igitur uoluptatibus praui ſæpe numero geſtiunt. Homines autem bõi
gaudiis ſemper ueris aluntur. Hactenus Plato. Sequitur expoſitio noſtra:Bonus
uir a Platõe cẽſet᷑:qui i ſe quidẽ tẽperatus:ad deũ aũt pius ẽ:ad hoĩes uero iuſtus
cd Aĩus eiuſmõi pp ſimilitudinẽ deo p̃cæteris eſt ãicus:malus aũt pp diſſimilitudinẽ
inimicus:Itaq; cũ deus:& moueat intriſecus:& ubiq; p̃uideat:nimirũ opiniões
& imaginatiões ſpeſq; bonorũ uirorũ:uere frequẽter euadũt: malorũ uero falſe:
utriq; gaudia quædã. excogitant:optãt:ſperãt:hæc bõis uiris tãq̃ diuinis atq; ue
ridicis:uera ſæpe cõtigũt:malis uero falſa:mali.n. tanq̃ ſibi met mẽdaces:ſicut fre
quẽter opinione fallũtur:ita falſa ſæpius oblectamẽta cõfingunt:dẽiq; ſi prauis tã
e q̃ a diuĩa ueritate diſcordibus ſuccedere ſpes nõ debẽt:ſæpe tñ i externis ſucceſſũ
f hẽre uidẽt᷑:ſequit᷑ ſaltẽ:ut intriſecus nõ ſuccedãt. ſemp ergo ſolicitãt᷑ ĩtus atq; lan
guent:eorũq; uoluptates ſimiles ſũt falſis uoluptatibus egrotãtiũ: ſomniantiũ in
ſanorũ. Die.xx.decembris. Mcccclxxxxiiii. Pro Libro de Sole.

g Marſilius.F.Ioanni Ganaienſi Digniſſimo Pariſii præſidenti. S.P.D.

h CVm pp hoſpitũ domeſticorũ turbã:publicoſq; tumultus:tranquille iſt
i hic philoſophari nõ poſſẽ:philoſophicũ tamẽ officiũ mihi p̃petuũ inter
mittere nollẽ:in ruſticã ſolitudinẽ ex urbe ſeceſſi. Sed anteq̃ diſcederẽ:
j exoptatũ mihi diu ſplendorẽ tuũ ſæpe queſiui. Quẽ deniq; nõdũ ſalutaui p̃ſentẽ
hũc abſentẽ mũere quodã phœbeo ſaluto. Siquidẽ ipſe phœbus:q̃ forte nõ tangit
globo:radiis interi attingit ubiq;. ſplẽdor quin & tuus ſuis hucuſq; radiis: me cõ-
tingit. Per ipſũ luminis phœbei calorem te obſecro, ſplendidiſſime mi Ioãnes:ut
Marſilium ames ardenter amantem Vale. Pro Libro de Sole.

Marſilius Ficinus Paulo Veronenſi:inſigni doctrina Viro.S.D.

k VIdere te quidem Florentiæ licuit. Idque admodum mihi gratum conti-
git. Gratiſſimum quoque fuiſſet:præſidentem Pariſii uiſere:uirum aſpe
ctu digniſſimum. Quanq̃ ſi uos inuicem ea (ut arbitror) charitate de
l uincti eſtis ut ſit alter in altero:cum primum aſpexi Paulum in Paulo introſpe-
xi Ioannem:ita profecto phœbus dum ſplendore foris aſpicit:calore interim (ut
m ita loquar) introſpicit:deniq; p ipſũ phœbeũ munus:quod ad te quoq; mitto:te
uehementer obſecro:ut apollineo ioanni me ſæpe commendes. Vale.

n Finis Duodecimi & Vltimi Libri Epiſtolariũ Familiariũ Mariſilii Ficini Flo-
rentini Deo Gratias, Amen.

a B *Et* b *quia* c *Animus* d *amicus* e *tamen* f *habere* g B *Ficinus*
h B *hospitium* i *perpetuum* j *tuum* k *contigit* l B *Paulum in Paulo*
m B has *ut* in place of second *te* (erron.) n B *Epistolarum* (correct)

M.F.Florētini Eloquētissimi uiri Epistolę familiares fœliciter finiūt: Impēsa ꝓui di Hieronymi Blōdi Florētini: Venetiis cōmorātis: Opa uero & diligētia Mathei Capcasæ Parmēsis: impresse Venetiis: æquinoctiū Vernalę Phœbo introeunte: As. [lion] Dic & hora Mercurii: Vigilia Diui Gregorii. Anno salutis. Mcccclxxxxv. a

Registrū operis.

AA
Prima alba
prohœmium
rectius
nihil uel

a
Prohœmium
petenda. legi
men quia me
ris sensibus

b
me deus amet
has cantilenas
mas postulo.
auidiores

c
nūq̄ postulat
Carolus: Marsupi/
atq; diligit.
esse me dixero

d
præssit: mitto
ta mundus sit
mihi sit qđ hés
nem animæ

e
strinxit: sic.n.
uoto meo: &
aliud sit q̄ uera
& accende

f
uersales & sempiter/
ni repetendi
puriores ueriores
incūbūt

g
modi aūt
in corpore
bene esse
quidem horū

h
aliud est
quantum lux
intima eius
attentius pro

i
similitudine qua
cum singula
amisi: cum
iam saturni

k
turalis siue
suaue clarūq;
euadit pessimus
officiū est actio

l
lis appetitus
querenti mihi
uiribus semper
Athlāticis humeris

m
tunc morbo
gratus deo
or eni mihi
mortali animo

n
pellūtur auferunt
Quintus liber
frustra refugimus
consuetudine

o
sonans citharæ
num genus
Esto sane
la quidem

p
Sed ecce accusas
rima certe ad
lud mundi
cētū quiquaginta

q
animus noster
quot ue inde
præfecit. hinc
lium Bembo

r
noctu itidem
Marsilius Ficinus
tri tuo insigni
quasi aer inter

s
timeat ueneretur
ci tū ex Iouis
Locterium
Dolores oés

t
nē aut terminum
Marsilii Ficini
enim unicum
heroibus intus

u
dent illos horū
miliarē. Quāobrē
dio discrepat.
obscurū esse nō

x
Prohœmiū i librū
hos quandam
qui præcipit
ri pontificis

y
te ferendum
rum audiueris
cano deo. Et
serant si per

z
Aquileiā. s.ædē
respondeo uolu/
principiū Vndeci/
purgatio de lřis

&
cœli suspiciens
prętermisero non
aliis: unoquoq;:
secundū ordines

ↄ
Petrus medices
Cū ego supioribus
breuiter accipe
ꝑfecto amicitiā
magni antistitis

FINIS

a *As.* is followed by symbol of a lion, to be read as *Ascendente leone*

Biographical Notes

Gregorio Alessandrino: see **Gregorio Scuto**.

Pope Alexander VI: Rodrigo de Borgia or Borja (1431-1503) was elected pope on 11th August, 1492, in a fiercely contested election, with accusations of bribery on all sides. Advancing his own family's fortunes, he soon earned a reputation for nepotism, corruption, and political ambition, but he is also remembered for his legacy to the arts and his welcoming of the Jews expelled from Spain and Portugal, as well as a healthy respect for the traditions of the Church. During the period covered by the letters of this volume, Alexander was the pope to whom several correspondents made embassies.

Vincenzo Bandello or **Bandelli** (1435–1506): an outstanding student of philosophy and theology, by 1478 Bandello had been put in charge of educational matters at the Dominican *Studium Generale* in Bologna, and it was there that he taught Savonarola in 1478–79. In 1481–82, Bandello was serving as prior of San Marco in Florence, and initially welcomed Savonarola's arrival, but by 1487, back in Bologna as regent master of the *Studium*, he was responsible for the decision that Savonarola be dropped from the Order's programme of higher studies, and in the following spring Savonarola was duly re-assigned to Santa Maria degli Angeli, Ferrara.

The two men remained opposed to one another thereafter, especially on questions of austerity and communal property. In 1489 and again in 1493, Bandello was elected Vicar General of the Lombard Congregation of the Dominican Order; he was twice prior in Bologna and twice prior in Milan, where Leonardo's famous *Last Supper* was commissioned. In 1500, he was appointed Vicar General of the entire Order, and its Master General in 1501.

Bernardo Bembo (1433-1519): Venetian diplomat and close friend of Ficino, whose birth date he shared. It is not clear where Bembo was stationed at the time of Letter 28 in this volume, but he had been Mayor of Bergamo, 1489-90, and from 1497-1500 he represented Venetian interests in Ferrara. Bernardo had been ambassador to Florence for two terms of office in the 1470s. After he left the city, their friendship continued, with Ficino writing 31 letters to him in the course of several books. For details of Bernardo's career, see *Letters*, **6**, p. 96 and **9**, p. 120.

By the time of this volume, Bernardo's son Pietro was gaining fame as a poet, and was studying Greek in Messina and Naples. Pietro later became adviser to Pope Leo X and was made a cardinal in 1538. His love poetry and *Gli Asolani* are ranked among the finest Italian literature.

Niccolò del Benino (or del Benin, Albenino, del Venino) is the recipient of Letters 32 and 33, after his recent appointment to a judicial office of some kind. He belonged to a distinguished family of Florentine bankers, possibly a branch of the Del Bene, who had banking offices in Rome. They were Medici supporters. Vespasiano includes brief lives of two family members of a previous generation in his memoirs, noting their probity, virtue and commitment to education, but little is known of Niccolò's activities.

Girolamo Blondi or **Biondo**: it has been suggested that he may be a son of Flavio Biondo of Forlì (1392-1463), the famous historian, who published several major works: the first archaeological study of ancient Rome (*Roma instaurata*, 3 vols, 1444-1448), a history of ancient Rome as a model for contemporary government (*Roma triumphante*), and a geography and a history of Italy, both published posthumously, *Italia illustrata* (Rome, 1474) and *Historiarum ab inclinatione Romanorum imperii decades* (Venice, 1483). If he can be identified as Flavio's son, Girolamo was a churchman and a doctor of civil and canon law. Having been involved in the publication of his father's works, it is quite likely that he was also involved in the publication of other works, including Ficino's letters. See Appendix J, Appendix N and entry for Girolamo Rossi below.

Bibbiena: see **Dovizi**.

Filippo Buonaccorsi (1437-1496): usually known by his literary nickname, Callimachus. Following colourful escapades as a youth in the Roman Academy of Pomponio Leto, Filippo fled retribution and spent many years in the service of the Polish king. For his early career see *Letters*, **7**, pp. 195-6, and his correspondence there. In the unsettled times that followed the abortive Polish invasion of Hungary, he moved temporarily in 1492 to Vienna, but soon returned to Cracow, where he remained until his death in 1496. His letters to Ficino combine the personal with the philosophical. His other writings consisted mainly of poetry and political essays dressed as history. With Letter 26 Ficino sends him a copy of *De sole et lumine*, enclosing two additional copies for the Florentine friends whose company Filippo had so long relied upon in Poland, Ottaviano di Guccio de' Galvani and Filippo's kinsman Arnolfo Tedaldi, both originally from Florence but resident in Cracow. Arnolfo was the first to die, and Ottaviano arranged for Callimachus to be buried beside him in the Church of the Holy Trinity, just off Cracow's main square. The memorial inscription for Callimachus can still be seen in the choir, on a bas relief in bronze by Viet Stoss (Plate 2). In a letter back home to Lattanzio Tedaldi, Galvani lists the considerable wealth left by Buonaccorsi to his friends and benefactors. His description of the funeral, attended by all the local dignitaries, is reported in a collection of letters edited by Sebastiano Ciampi in 1834 (p. 32): see Bibliography.

Antonio Calderini (1445-1494): a close friend of Ficino's. Antonio had served the Medici until 1485, when he entered the service of Cardinal Marco Barbo in Rome, and eventually he took holy orders. After Barbo's death in March 1491, Antonio sought to return to S. Giovanni Val d'Arno, but it appears that he actually stayed in Rome. There are letters to Antonio in *Letters*, **1**, 106; **7**, 15, 31 and 45 (relating to the publication of *De vita* and the Plotinus commentaries); **9**, 19 and 23 (again related to these books) and a letter of consolation in *Letters*, **10**, 11. In this volume Ficino sends him a copy of his *De sole* (Letter 16).

Callimachus: see **Buonaccorsi**.

Giovanni Canacci: member of a leading patrician family, Canacci was a *priore* of the city in 1491, 1492 and 1497, and a close friend of Ficino, as witnessed in *Letters*, **10**, 27 and the 'Mammola' letters of *Letters*, **9**. In 1498 he played a leading role in bringing Savonarola to account, as mentioned in Ficino's *Apologia* (Appendix Q). In his *Life of Marsilio Ficino* (translated in *Letters*, **3**), Giovanni Corsi describes Canacci as 'serious in his ways, grave of speech, agreeably refined and very quick-witted', comparing him to famous models of simplicity and endurance in ancient Rome.

Matteo Capcasa of Parma, known also by several variants of his name, e.g. **Capodicasa** and **Codeca** and also as **Matteo da Parma** (d.1495): printer of Ficino's *Letters* in Florence. Little is known of his early career, but in 1485 he was working with Bernardo di Pino, and in 1489 he began collaboration with the Florentine publishing house of Giunta, which had recently moved to Venice and which would go on to become one of the main religious publishing houses of the 16th century. By 1493 Matteo was working again on his own account and published Luigi Pulci's *Morgante* (1489), a new edition of Dante (1491) and Landino's commentaries on Dante (1493) as well as several religious works. It was Matteo who undertook the printing of Ficino's Letters, in collaboration with Girolamo Biondo of Florence. The privilegium (Appendix J) was obtained in June 1494 and the volume appeared in the spring of 1495, followed shortly by the Letters of Filelfo and the *Comedies* of Plautus. Although later eclipsed by the much finer work of Aldus Manutius, Capcasa had run a successful commercial enterprise, using excellent type in a clear Roman style of lettering.

Febo (Phoebus) Capella (c.1420-1482): a humanist scribe in Venice, who began his career as secretary to Francesco Barbaro on a diplomatic mission to Milan, and was highly commended by him. With this recommendation he was able to embark on a successful political and diplomatic career in the service of the Venetian Republic, eventually as Secretary from 1442 and was appointed Grand Chancellor in 1480. His diplomatic missions included a prolonged visit to Florence in 1460, where he became a friend of Ficino's. Their friendship is attested by a number of letters addressed to him (*Letters*, **4**, 49; **6**, 19 and 20), and the dedication to him in 1476 of his treatise on Light (*Quid sit lumen*) included in the second book of Ficino's letters. In 1482 Ficino also sent him a copy of a long letter on astrology (*Letters*, **6**, 17). In Letter 7 of the current volume, Ficino refers to the treatise on light that has now been enlarged, rededicated to Piero de' Medici, and published with *De sole* in a joint volume, *De sole et lumine* (1493).

Filippo di Andrea Carducci (1449-c.1520): a member of the Florentine nobility, Carducci came into contact with Ficino during his education and soon became interested in Platonic philosophy. He remained a close friend through the rest of Ficino's life.

Filippo entered public life in 1484 as a member of the *Otto di Balìa*. He served as a *priore* in 1485, 1493 and 1497 and as *Gonfaloniere di Giustizia* in 1501 and 1512. Since he remained in close personal contact with Ficino, there are few letters between them but see *Letters*, **6**, 37, 44 and **10**, 26, 30 and its continuation in Appendix D of that volume. He was also a friend of Filippo Valori (*Letters*, **7**, 4). Letter 5 of the present volume accompanies a copy of all Ficino's letters to date that was copied out for Carducci. The first section of that manuscript, containing books I-VIII, was completed on 19th October, 1490 and has been referred to in the current edition of the *Letters* as L 28 (Laurenziana 90 sup. 43);

the second section, perhaps sent separately, and containing books IX to letter 5 of book XII, is now in Munich (MS Mo2). It constitutes the sole manuscript witness to the later books, and contains material not included in the printed edition, as indicated in the notes to Letter 5 and the introductory note to Appendix B.

Giovanni Caroli (1428-1503): a member of the Berlinghieri family, he entered the Cistercian order at San Salvatore a Settimo, but when the Benedictines from the Florentine Badia took it over in 1442, in a general reform of the orders, he was transferred to the Dominicans at Santa Maria Novella and was ordained as a priest by Archbishop Antoninus in 1448. He also taught at the *Studio* from 1453. In 1449 he was elected prior of Santa Maria Novella, but the years of his leadership were troubled ones, due to animosities on questions of reform. A period of exile beginning in 1461 allowed him to resume his outside teaching and literary activities. Returning to Florence, he became Dean of the College of Theology at the *Studio* in 1469. Though replaced by Domenico of Flanders in 1476, it gave him the opportunity to form a close friendship with Cristoforo Landino. In 1479, he was again elected prior at Santa Maria Novella. He continued to write prolifically, including commentaries on the political struggles of the time, generally supporting Medici policies. In 1483-4 he again held office in the theological college as well as his own monastic community, and enlarged its library collection. He continued to write, and from 1495 was actively engaged in opposing Savonarola, and indeed opposed the involvement of clergy in political affairs altogether. His writings all support a traditional Thomist approach of educated, rational argument against Savonarolan prophetic ideology, and, on Savonarola's execution, Caroli took the trouble to write in support of the Pope's decision to defend the Church against heresy. In 1499-1500 he was again prior of the monastery.

Gian Stefano Castiglioni: a nobleman from Lombardy who served as Milanese ambassador in Florence in 1491-2 or possibly longer, and was the recipient of Letter 36.

Giovanni Cavalcanti (1444-1509): the Cavalcanti family were originally feudal lords and merchants in Fiesole, supporters of the Guelf faction, though not inimical to the Ghibellines. Their ambivalence led to some problems, however, and they were debarred from holding public office in Florence during the 14th century. Cosimo de' Medici restored their political rights after 1434 on his own return from exile. They were also related by marriage: Cosimo's brother, Lorenzo di Giovanni, married Ginevra Cavalcanti (1397-1435) in 1416, and one of their two sons was Pierfrancesco de' Medici (father of Lorenzo di Pierfrancesco who became an important figure in the 1490s, and to whom Ficino wrote several letters).

The most celebrated member of the Cavalcanti family had been the poet Guido Cavalcanti (1255-1300), famous friend of Dante Alighieri. When Ficino composed his commentary on Plato's *Symposium*, *De amore*, Guido's love poetry is praised as Platonic, and Giovanni is credited with inheriting Guido's power to inspire important work.

Ficino's friendship with Giovanni dated back to 1452, but the first public information on Giovanni is a record of his presence at the joust held in honour of Lorenzo de' Medici in February 1469 (the year in which Ficino was writing *De amore*). Although Giovanni could not hold office for some years on account of disputed tax liabilities, he did start to serve in active posts during the 1480s. He was elected to the three main governing councils sixteen times, and serving twice as *priore* (1484 and 1495), twice as a member of the twelve *Buonomini*. He also took time to care for the business and domestic affairs of his wider family (possibly outside Florence). By 1494 he held a prominent place in the embassy that the *Signoria* sent to the young French King Charles VIII, encamped just outside Florence, to renegotiate the surrender of fortresses made by Piero de' Medici at a time of panic. At this time, Ficino, who was also involved in the embassies to the French king, writes a strikingly thoughtful letter about present misfortunes to Giovanni to give him the courage to face whatever would present itself (Letter 38), and gives Savonarola credit for averting the worst outcomes. Yet in Letter 40, written to Cavalcanti just eight days later, we read what may be something of a warning against the prophecies and intemperance of Savonarola, his fellow ambassador. In 1495, Cavalcanti was Florentine ambassador to Ludovico Sforza in Milan.

Besides inspiring Ficino to write *De amore* and being the recipient of some early philosophical works, Giovanni was the recipient of more letters than any other individual among Ficino's correspondents: there were 47 letters, 45 of them written in the years between 1473 and 1482, with these final two in 1494. Giovanni also wrote fourteen letters jointly with Ficino, between 1473 and 1480 (see earlier volumes of *Letters*, **1**, **2**, **3** and **6**). Documents have recently come to light that show the Cavalcanti family firm actively trading in England during the period 1521 to 1531, exporting English cloth and selling Florentine fabrics to the royal court.

Charles VIII, King of France (1470-1498): born at Amboise into the house of Valois, he succeeded his father, King Louis XI, at the age of thirteen. Until 1491, he was under the regency of his very able elder sister and her husband until his marriage in 1491 to Anne of Brittany, which temporarily brought the independent duchy of Brittany back into the kingdom of France. From 1489, Pope Innocent VIII tried to influence Charles to take up his claim to the kingdom of Naples. Innocent's successor, Pope Alexander VI, also had ambitions for expanding his own territories in central Italy. This caused Ludovico Sforza, Duke of Milan, to call upon Charles for military support. When King Ferrante of Naples died in 1494, Charles decided to assist Sforza and led an army over the Alps with the intention of moving on afterwards to assert his claim in Naples, and from there proceeding to Jerusalem on a new crusade.

He arrived in Pavia on 21st October 1494, and entered Pisa on 8th November. By this time Piero de' Medici had decided to cooperate with the French, but his surrender of key Tuscan forts and ports to the French led to his expulsion from Florence. The city still had to negotiate with the king for fair treatment, and Ficino's own address to the king (Letter 37) forms part of the appeals presented to the king during two formal embassies.

By February 1495, Charles had reached Naples and was crowned. However, his rule did not last long. On his way back to France in July of that year he was met by an army raised by the League of Venice (an alliance of several Italian states) at Fornovo near Parma. Although neither side won a clear victory, it effectively ended Charles's presence in Italy, and then Ferdinand II, Ferrante's son, resumed Aragonese rule in Naples. Charles was not able to raise a strong enough army to repeat the expedition the following year. Although many poets were attracted to his court, his reign in France left few distinguished achievements, as he died at the age of 28 after a fall, without surviving heirs. However, as a result of his diplomatic contacts and his expedition over the Alps the French court became far more aware of cultural developments within the Italian peninsula.

Giorgio Ciprio (George of Cyprus): George, who was born in Cyprus (see *Letters*, **5**, 18), was physician to Giovanni de' Medici but also cared for Ficino over a long period. In *Letters*, **5**, 34 he was amongst the physicians trying to help Ficino through a serious fever; he also cared for Ficino's mother (see *Timaeus* commentary, ch. 44). In *Letters*, **7**, 3 George is called a 'beloved fellow priest and best of physicians'. In *Letters*, **10**, 14, Ficino sent him a copy of *De vita* and referred to their close friendship. Letter 11 of this volume accompanies a copy of *De sole et lumine*.

John Colet (1467-1519): son of Sir Henry Colet, Lord Mayor of London in 1486 and 1495, John was educated at St Anthony's School and Magdalen College, Oxford. By 1490, when he obtained his Master of Arts degree, he had already joined the Church, holding various positions as rector. In 1493 he went to Paris, to study canon and civil law, theology and Greek, and from Paris he went on to Italy. In Paris he became a friend of Guillaume Budé and Erasmus. In Italy he heard Savonarola, but it is not clear whether he actually met Ficino. After his return to England in 1496, he settled in Oxford and wrote to Ficino from there.

He became a Doctor of Divinity, and held several benefices, being appointed Dean of St Paul's Cathedral in 1505. In 1508 his father died, and with the wealth he inherited he re-founded St Paul's School with a rigorous and forward-looking programme of education. His lectures on St Paul became famous, placing scripture firmly at the centre of daily life and earning Colet his reputation as a reformer. He drew from Ficino and Pico in his works, and Erasmus said of him 'When I listen to Colet it seems to me that I am listening to Plato himself.' (Letter to John Fisher, 5th December, 1499).

The letters Colet wrote to Ficino and Ficino's reply can still be seen inside Colet's copy of Ficino's letters in the library of All Souls' College, Oxford. See also Appendix P. Colet died in the epidemic of sweating sickness at the age of 52.

Leonardo of Colle (possibly to be identified with Ser Leonardo di Giovanni Tolosani da Colle, lawyer and scribe, b.1430). Before joining the monastery of San Marco, Leonardo of Colle had been a professor of law and a notary working for the city magistrature. He was a witness to Ficino's will (Appendix R), under the name given on becoming a monk. A letter to him from Ficino in 1479 had already proposed the religious life as the better path (*Letters*, **5**, 24). He also corresponded with Ficino's cousin, Sebastiano Salvini.

Antonio Cronico: see **Vinciguerra**.

Francesco Cattani da Diacceto (1466-1522): born into a patrician family in Florence, Francesco enjoyed an early education in humanist studies and at the age of eighteen, he married Lucrezia Capponi (d.1518). Despite his married status, in 1491, he was selected, together with Giovanni Vittorio Soderini, to be a companion of Giovanni de' Medici during his studies at the University of Pisa. There Francesco became a pupil of Oliviero Arduini for the years 1491-2, studying philosophy. Francesco did not complete a doctorate or hold a public disputation, but held various political offices from July 1498. However, his interest in philosophy continued and records show his use of volumes of Plato, Plotinus, Aristotle and Dionysius from the library of San Marco in 1499, and in 1501 he was offered the chair of Philosophy at the Florentine *Studio*. He declined this, but the following year accepted and lectured there, in 1502-4 and again in 1516-21, on

Aristotle's *De caelo, de mundo* and *Ethics,* and subsequently on Aristotle's *Physics* and *De anima*.

Francesco's connection with Ficino seems to have begun in 1492 with some kind of communication expressing unhappiness at Pisa, to which Ficino replied (Letter 1). In 1493, Francesco returned from Pisa to become a student of Ficino's. Letter 14 in this volume clarifies what it means to be a Platonic philosopher, and from what ensued it appears Francesco took this to heart. He remained with Ficino until Ficino's death in 1499, and was recognised as Ficino's successor. Alongside his Aristotelian lectures for the *Studio*, Diacceto taught Platonic philosophy, as part of his university courses, and perhaps also from his own home, and he was a leading participant in the discussions held in the *Orti Oricellari* (the Rucellai Gardens) and later in the Sacra Accademia Medicea. He also wrote a number of Platonic works, especially on the themes of Beauty and Love. His *De pulchro* was composed in 1496-9 and dedicated to Giovanni Vittorio Soderini, though not finalised and published until 1514. The preface includes acknowledgement of his immense debt to Ficino. Diacceto's *Three books on Love* were published in 1508 and were followed by a further *Panegyric on Love*, in both Latin and vernacular versions. He also wrote short paraphrases of some Platonic dialogues and Aristotelian works, and a few letters that show his continuing engagement in the teaching of Platonic philosophy. His concern was always to harmonise the two schools of philosophy, Platonic and Aristotelian, though he differed in some details of interpretation from both Ficino and Pico. His debt to Ficino is acknowledged in various of his writings. His biographer, Eufrosino Lapini, writing for the publication of Diacceto's work in 1563 (by Henricpetri and Perna in Basel, who both also published Ficino), writes of his love for philosophy and tells how once Diacceto came to study with Ficino, he never left his side and he calls Ficino 'that greatest philosopher who has never been praised enough. . . that holiest man, who was certainly a father of wisdom and a teacher of life's morals.' In Lapini's account, Diacceto, 'this most diligent student of Ficino not only avidly drank in all of Ficino's teachings regarding Platonic learning; he also, most precisely in his character and life, imitated everything exactly, so that you could truly recognise him as a Platonist, and at the same time as a student of Marsilio Ficino.'

Besides teaching philosophy, Diacceto remained politically active, serving in the electoral process in 1498, in the *Otto di Guardia* in 1510, as Captain of the Guelf party in 1515, as Ambassador to the Emperor in 1512 and *Gonfaloniere di Giustizia* in 1520. He and his wife Lucrezia had seven sons and six daughters.

Diacceto's name does not appear in the manuscript version of Ficino's list of his followers drawn up in the summer of 1492 (MS Mo2), but it was added by the time of the publication of his Letters in 1495 (*Letters*, **10**, 28). Diacceto is also mentioned in the *Parmenides* Commentary (ch. 84) with warm praise for his writings on Beauty and his commitment to Platonic wisdom; he is mentioned in Ficino's will (Appendix R) as a possible, and worthy, beneficiary, but the manuscript in question in fact reverted to the Benci family who had loaned it. Corsi speaks of Diacceto in his *Life of Ficino* (see *Letters*, **3**, pp. 146-7). For details of students of his who became prominent later, see Kristeller, 'Francesco da Diacceto' and Fellina, *Alla scuola di Marsilio Ficino* (see Bibliography for details of both).

Bernardo Dovizi (1470-1520): younger brother of Piero, became a close friend of Giovanni de' Medici from childhood. In 1488 Bernardo joined the Medici family's secretariat (or chancery); he travelled to Rome with Piero de' Medici to arrange Piero's marriage. In 1492 he represented Piero in Rome, together with his brother (see below, and Letter 4).

After the expulsion of the Medici in 1494, Bernardo travelled with Giovanni in exile, visiting Bavaria, France and the Low Countries. He then returned to Piero, still in exile in Venice, as a diplomat, but after Piero's death became Giovanni's secretary and trusted adviser. Giovanni made him a cardinal at the first opportunity in 1513.

Piero Dovizi of Bibbiena (1456-1514): educated with Piero de' Medici (Lorenzo's father) and then as a student of *humaniores litterae* at the *Studio*, he came as a tutor to Lorenzo de' Medici after Poliziano was dismissed in 1479. He stayed on as secretary, becoming eventually the head of Lorenzo's secretariat, a post he continued to hold under Lorenzo's son, Piero. He also undertook important diplomatic missions, including the one to Rome mentioned in Letter 4. After the expulsion of the Medici from Florence, Dovizi took refuge in Venice, from where he wrote to Ficino in 1495 (Appendix K). Some of his poetry survives, as do many letters to and from other poets.

Eberhard the Bearded (1445-1496): Ficino had corresponded directly with Eberhard V, Count of Württemberg since June 1492, as a result of his friendship with Martin Prenninger, who was in the Count's service. See *Letters*, **10**, 23 and 33. For his patronage of learning, see Biographical Note in *Letters*, **10**, p. 117. In 1495 the Emperor elevated his title to that of Duke, though Ficino had used that title earlier in addressing him. It was for Eberhard that Ficino wrote the first version, in 1492, of his book *De sole*, which is mentioned frequently in this volume. Letter 2 forms a final chapter to what he sent him. When Ficino published the enlarged version of this work, together with *De lumine*, in February 1493, he dedicated it to Piero de' Medici (see Letter 2, note 1 and Appendix B). Eberhard is also mentioned in Letter 7 to Martin Prenninger.

Paolo Emili of Verona (c.1455-1529): born into a patrician family in Verona, Paolo studied theology at the Curia in Rome. Cardinal Charles de Bourbon became his patron and introduced him to the French court in Paris in 1483. In 1487 Paolo wrote a history, now lost, but well received at the time. When his patron died in 1488, Paolo remained in Paris, teaching at the university and continuing a close connection with other humanist scholars, including Jacques Lefèvre d'Étaples, who had earlier been his pupil and who had visited Ficino and Pico della Mirandola in 1492. In 1489, Paolo was appointed official court historian, writing *De rebus gestis Francorum*, published in 1498.

From Letter 42 it would appear that he was in the company of the French delegation to Florence in 1494. In later years he retained close contact with the circle of humanist reformers in Paris (which included Guillaume Budé and Robert Gaguin), as well as with Erasmus.

Luca Fabiano (d.1520): Luca figured prominently in Ficino's life in these last years, although there are no letters to him from this period as he lived with Ficino. He had served him continuously as a scribe and amanuensis from 1476 or 1477. By 1491, he was also a notary, and by 1492 was serving as an assistant in the chancery, although continuing to live with Ficino. For more details, see note 12 to Appendix R.

Ficino Ficini (c.1470-1530): son of Marsilio's brother Cherubino, Ficini lived with his uncle Marsilio and served as his amanuensis during his later years. He was responsible, probably under Marsilio's direction, for the corrections in the Durham copy of the *Letters* which we have reproduced in our series. Marsilio provided generously for him in his will (Appendix R). After Marsilio's death he remained a student of Francesco Diacceto, joining a select group of pro-Medicean followers. In the troubled political times that followed the expulsion of the Medici, this support eventually cost several of them their lives. Ficini was subjected to torture on the order of a tribunal and was put to death for treason on 27th June, 1530. For other members of the Ficino family, see notes to Appendix R.

Matteo Franco (1448-1494) is the Franco referred to in Letter 4. He was born in Florence to a humble family in the leather trade but was a childhood friend of Lorenzo and received sufficient education to enter the priesthood and later become a member of the Medici household. At first, he held some kind of accounting and supervisory role there and had some involvement with the care of Lorenzo's children. He was rewarded with a number of minor benefices. In 1482 he was sent to accompany Maddalena de' Medici on her marriage to Franceschetto Cibo in Rome and he appears to have remained in her service thereafter. In 1492 Maddalena and her husband returned to Florence for the funeral of her father, Lorenzo, and took up residence in Pisa. Franco remained with them there, though he is also recorded as being a chaplain to the Medici 'court' (i.e. in Piero's household). Several letters were written by Franco in this period to seek aid for Franceschetto, who felt unable to return to Rome after his own father, Pope Innocent VIII, died on 26th July.

Franco was chosen to be a member of the party that set off for Rome on November 7th, 1492, with Piero de' Medici, to offer obedience to the new pope. This journey is well documented in letters between Dovizi and Giovanni de' Medici, and is the background to Letter 4 here. In 1493, Franco was given the position of canon in the cathedral of Florence, in recognition of his services to the family. This prompted a famously kind letter from Poliziano to Piero about Franco, which shows real friendship between them (Poliziano, *Epistolae*, X). Franco was also appointed administrator (*Spedalingo*) of the hospital in Pisa, where he took his duties seriously and died during an epidemic, on 6th September, 1494.

Other letters from Ficino which mention Franco include one to Poliziano, from 1474, in which Franco is credited with dispelling Ficino's gloom (*Letters*, **1**, 73). He is also mentioned (without forename, but there is no doubt of his identity) as a good friend around the time of Poliziano's dismissal from the Medici household (*Letters*, **5**, 25 to Poliziano.) During the mid-1470s, Franco's witty Tuscan poetry was well liked but led to a bitter rivalry with Luigi Pulci. Two sonnets Franco wrote to Ficino have survived (see Kristeller, *Sup. Fic.*, II, pp. 241-2).

Robert Gaguin (1423 or 1433-1501): a leading French humanist and philosopher, noted for his translation into French of Caesar's *Gallic Wars* (1485), some books of Livy, and one of Pico's letters to his nephew, *Profitable Advice against the Worries and the Tribulations of the World* (1498). His own writings were printed many times, especially his historical account of France, *De origine et gestis Francorum compendium* (also known as *Compendium historiae Francorum*) first published in 1495, and printed in Paris and Lyon in 1497. This had many subsequent printings, as did his earlier treatise on poetry, *Ars versificatoria*, of 1473.

Born near Béthune in the Duchy of Burgundy, Gaguin received his early education from the Trinitarian monks of Préavins, near St. Omer, not far from his home; he joined the Trinitarian Order and was sent to the University of Paris, first in the faculty of arts and later studying canon law. There he flourished under the teaching of Guillaume Fichet, a great orator, and when Fichet left for Rome in 1463, Robert was appointed to succeed him as Professor of Rhetoric. In 1475 he was elected Minister General of the Trinitarian Order. Due to his monastic and teaching responsibilities his own studies proceeded slowly, and he completed his doctorate in canon law only in 1480, though he served several terms as dean of the faculty of canon law and represented the university on ceremonial occasions and in legal conflicts. He was entrusted with important diplomatic missions abroad both for the Order and, in 1477, 1486 and 1491, for the French crown. During his mission to Rome in 1486 he visited Florence and may well have met Ficino. He had certainly befriended Pico in Paris in 1485, and in 1498, four years after Pico's death, he translated into French a letter Pico had written to his nephew, Gianfrancesco, in 1492, to console him against the tribulations of the world. (The same letter was also translated into English by Thomas More in 1503.) After the accession of King Louis XII in 1498, Gaguin was appointed a royal secretary.

He played an important part in the cultural life of Paris, through his own erudition and kindness to young scholars and through his efforts on behalf of the Royal Library collections. In September 1496 Gaguin wrote to Ficino expressing the appreciation for Ficino's work that was felt in Paris (Appendix M).

Ottaviano da Guccio **Galvani:** a Florentine patrician resident in Poland, perhaps as a diplomat, mentioned in Letter 26. See under **Filippo Buonaccorsi**.

Germain de Ganay (d.1520): brother of Jean de Ganay (see below), Germain served as a canon of the Cathedral of Paris, and was also a Counsel of the judicial body known as the *Parlement* of Paris from 1485. The title 'Royal Counsellor' is probably best compared with the English title of King's or Queen's Counsel, though there were differences in the structure of the courts. Germain subsequently became Dean of the Cathedral of Beauvais, then Bishop designate of Cahors (1509, confirmed in 1510) and Bishop of Orléans (1514). Throughout this time, he was a patron of humanist scholars, including Jacques Lefèvre d'Étaples, who visited Florence for a second time in 1492 and may have provided the initial link between de Ganay and Ficino. We have only Ficino's side of the correspondence with de Ganay, consisting of three letters included in the published collection (Letters 27, 35 and 39 in this volume), plus an additional two given here as Appendices F and H, both dating from 1494, and the dedication of a translation of Athenagoras, *On the Resurrection*, on which Ficino worked between 1490 and 1492 but which he probably sent to de Ganay in 1495 (Appendix G).

It was de Ganay's protégé Lefèvre who wrote a commentary for Ficino's Hermes translation and had them printed together in 1494. He also arranged for the Athenagoras to be printed in Paris in 1498.

Germain's interest in Ficino's work did not end with Ficino's death. An exquisitely written manuscript of the unfinished commentary on St Paul's epistles was prepared for him some time after Ficino's death and is now in the British Library, MS Harley 4695. For Germain's activities in promoting Ficino's ideas in France, see the articles by Sebastiano Gentile (1986) and Cesare Vasoli (2002) listed in the Bibliography.

Jean de Ganay (1455-1512): French nobleman, whose father had been Royal Advocate to King Louis XI and Advocate General of the *Parlement* of Paris. Jean followed in his footsteps, becoming an advocate (lawyer) at the Paris *Parlement* in 1478, a Counsel of the *Cour des Aides* (a court for matters relating to public finance and certain forms of taxation) in 1481 and later of the Paris *Parlement*, becoming its 'fourth president' in June 1490. He persuaded Charles VIII to pursue his claim to the kingdom of Naples, and was appointed ambassador to Pope Alexander VI. When the king invaded Italy, Jean de Ganay was at his side. He therefore arrived in Florence in November 1494, proceeded to Rome and reached Naples in February 1495, where he was appointed Chancellor. When it proved impossible to hold the southern kingdom, de Ganay was amongst those who negotiated a peace settlement.

After the death of Charles in 1498, de Ganay continued to serve his successor Louis XII, who appointed him 'first president' of the Paris *parlement* in 1505, Guard of the Seals, and in 1507 Chancellor of France, in which capacity he presided over important peace conferences. He died at Blois in May 1512.

Letter 41 is addressed to him. He is also mentioned in Letters 39 and 42.

Giacomo Gherardi, also known as **Jacopo of Volterra** (1434-1516): son of Niccolò Gherardi, Giacomo served as secretary to Cardinal Jacopo Ammannati, Bishop of Pavia, from 1463 until the cardinal's death in 1479. He collaborated with Ammannati on his *Commentaries* and also wrote his biography. He then became an Apostolic Secretary. Under Innocent VIII he was entrusted with important diplomatic missions to Naples and Milan, to broker peace between the two states, and to investigate the position of Florence in this regard. Lorenzo de' Medici was impressed with his abilities and appointed him tutor to his son Giovanni. He spent 1491-2 in Pisa with Giovanni de' Medici. Later he became Bishop of Segni (1512) and of Aquino (1513), both south-east of Rome. His diary of events in Rome, 1479-1484, (*Diarium Romanum*) and some of his correspondence survive. A letter to him from Ficino, written on 7th October, 1496 is translated as Appendix D. Appendix E is his reply.

G(h)erardo Gianfigliazzi: a member of one of the old noble families of Florence, and son-in-law of Giovanni Cavalcanti, he is recorded as meeting Ficino in December 1494 (Letter 40). He had been highly successful in business earlier with his brother, Bongianni, who was active in political life and diplomacy. Gherardo also travelled extensively.

Giuliano of Istria (c.1458-after 1509): born in Muggia near Trieste, Giuliano entered the Franciscan Order some time before 1488 and studied theology in Bologna, gaining his *laurea* (higher degree) in March 1491. He gained considerable fame as a Lenten preacher, first in Capodistria (1488 and 1489), then in Bologna (1491). In 1492, however, his Lenten sermons in Milan attracted the attention of the Minister General of his Order, Francesco Sansone (originally Nanni), on account of their reforming zeal, which included strong anti-Roman sentiment. He noted that Giuliano della Rovere (the future Pope Julius II) had demolished a Franciscan convent in Rome to build himself a new palace, leaving the monks in greatly straitened circumstances. He also voiced the opinion that the Church of St Ambrose (i.e. Milan) might do well to exert its independence from Rome, and that a Church Council should have greater authority than the pope. Sansone called him to account and started judicial proceedings against him in May 1492. Count Ludovico Moro, the regent of Milan (and later Duke), intervened to protect Giuliano, but wanting to maintain good relations with Rome confined him to a prison in his own castle at Vigevano. On 10th May, he ordered the Archibishop of Milan to conduct the hearing, using lay witnesses, all of whom were connected to the Milanese court and therefore sought to exonerate him. In a trial that was close to farce, Giuliano was acquitted but apologised publicly to the General in the cathedral square. Several poems record the event.

After this, Giuliano was free to resume his preaching, first in Pavia, close to Ludovico, then in February 1493 in the Church of the Angeli in Florence. On 16th May 1493, Giuliano was in trouble again with Sansone, but Ludovico called on the help of his brother Cardinal Ascanio Sforza to resolve it. In the summer of 1493, Giuliano visited his home town of Muggia, before going on to preach the Lenten sermon series in 1494 in Brescia, then in 1496 in Venice. Negotiations for him to be allowed to preach again in Milan fell through (although a very supportive reference can be found in Giorgio Benigno Salviati's *De natura angelica*, VI, 14, published in 1499). Sometime between 1495 and 1499 he preached again in Florence. Although he supported many of Savonarola's reforms, including, for example, the burning of carnival masks, he took up an opposite position on salvation: he argued the point taken up later by Erasmus that huge numbers of people are to be saved, and only a few are to be damned.

By 1505 he was preaching Lenten sermons in S. Petronio, Bologna and served as Vice-Deacon in the Theological College there, presiding over degree ceremonies in 1505 and 1506. At the end of 1506, the new Minister General of the Order, Egidio Delfin, sent him to Spain to settle the long-standing controversy between the Franciscan Conventuals and the Franciscan Observants. In Lent of 1509 he was preaching in San Marco, Venice. The place and date of his death are not known. Some of his poetry survives in manuscript, but his sermons and a treatise on the Immaculate Conception have been lost.

Giuliano has been called one of the 'forgotten humanists' of the Church but he re-emerges from the pages of Ficino's letters, with a keen interest in philosophy (Letter 9).

Guido di Lorenzo, see under **Lorenzi.**

Lorenzo di Guiducci also known as Lorenzo Cornius (d. 1496): the most likely recipient of Letter 8. A canon of the Medici church of San Lorenzo from 1473 and its Prior from 1482 until his death in 1496, he was interested in astronomy and mathematics, transcribing at least one work of the 10th-century Arab astronomer Alcabitius. He also compiled a treatise on God, Angels, the Soul and eternal happiness, preserved in MS Laur. Plut. LXXVI, cod. 55 (fols. 68^r-99^r). It ends with the question, 'What else is our end, if not to reach that kingdom which is without end?' He took care to note the date and hour on which he completed any work he wrote. He was buried in the chapter house of the church, his tomb decorated with an effigy of him looking up to the heavens and holding an armillary sphere.

Hermann of Hesse (1450-1508): mentioned in Letter 23, Hermann was born into the princely family of the Landgrave of Hesse and was trained for the Church, attending the Universities of Cologne and Prague. In 1480, after a period of turbulence in Church-State relations, he was appointed Archbishop-Elector of Cologne and in 1498 became also Prince-Bishop of Paderborn. He earned a favourable reputation as both spiritual guide and peacemaker.

Cristoforo Landino (1425-1498): Professor of Rhetoric and Poetry in the Florentine *Studio*, Landino was also famed for his commentaries on Dante and Virgil, his own poetry and his dialogues. His *Disputationes Camaldulenses*, published in 1480, feature Ficino as a participant. His relationship with Ficino began as teacher and mentor, but they became great friends and learned much from each other. Ficino refers in Letter 6 to Landino as Amphion (who could charm stones with his lyre), just as he had in 1489 when he called for Landino's help to defend his *De vita*. There are no letters extant between Landino and Ficino, perhaps because they were in regular personal contact. See *Letters*, **5**, p. 175 and **10**, p. 121 for further biographical detail.

Guido Lorenzi also known as Guido da Settimo (d.1500): Guido entered his monastic life as a Cistercian at the Badia of Settimo. Lorenzo de' Medici arranged his transfer to the Camaldolese monastery of Santa Maria degli Angeli in Florence, as prior, on 8th December, 1486. A close friend of Lorenzo de' Medici, he was also his confessor, and supported the use of the church for philosophical studies. However, there were strained relations with Pietro Delphin, the General of the Camaldolese order who resented the Cistercian takeover of his church, and disliked the changes being introduced. Guido appears to have undertaken a renovation programme at the monastery (see *Letters,* **7**, 53). In the early 1490s, Guido and his monks became dissatisfied with the growing influence of Savonarola. In 1498, after the Medici had been expelled, feeling embittered against his Vicar General, Pietro Delfin, Guido resigned his office and travelled to Rome, where he died. Appendix U is a letter from Ficino's cousin, Sebastiano Salvini, to Guido, written in 1487.

Ramberto Malatesta (1475-1532): illegitimate son of Carlo Malatesta, Lord of Rimini but subsequently legitimised, Ramberto was a member of a famous family of condottieri. The family was well known in the time of Dante, who immortalised the illicit lovers Paolo and Francesca. Ramberto came to Florence at the age of fifteen and joined Ficino's circle, remaining there for three years, until 1493. He also became a companion of the younger generation of the Medici family. Trying to distance himself from the reputation for treachery, violence and immorality acquired by earlier family members, he adopted the nickname Bonatesta. Later in life he was particularly interested in astronomy and made a collection of scientific books and instruments to be kept permanently in the fortress of Sogliano, but the collection was later dispersed.

Ficino writes two letters to him in this volume (Letters 17 and 18), expressing friendship with this eighteen-year old and sharing with him the essence of his teachings on light that were being published that year (1493). In 1494, when Girolamo Blondi applied for a *privilegium* (licence) to publish Ficino's letters in Venice, the Malatesta ambassador in that city, the physician, philosopher and acting governor of Rimini, Antonio Cauchorio, was instrumental in this being granted. Blondi and Matteo Capcasa published in Venice, the same year, a book on *The Heavenly Life*, written by a Franciscan, Johannes of Ferrara, with which Antonio de Cauchorio's name is also associated. It covered the nature of the soul and its immortality, as well as punishments and reward in the life to come. The actual ruler of Rimini at this time was still the much disliked Pandolfo Malatesta (1475-1538/9), Ramberto's uncle, though they were the same age.

In 1498 Ramberto was in Venice, with Lorenzo di Pierfrancesco de' Medici, both seeking support to win back their estates. In 1500 he married Maria de Foix but later abandoned her for a local girl, Angelina, by whom he went on to have ten children. In 1503, with Venetian aid, he regained control of Faenza and some other territories. However, he was driven out again in 1507, when his wife died in suspicious circumstances. He took refuge in Florence, and in 1512 succeeded in winning back most of his feudal domains with the help of French and Florentine forces. He continued to support the Medici family in Urbino and the papal states and was given care of Cesena by Pope Leo X.

Aldus Manutius, also known as **Aldo Romano** (1449-1515): Appendix N is a letter from Ficino to Aldus Manutius, who was preparing an edition of Ficino's translations of a number of Neoplatonic writers together with Ficino's own early work on Pleasure (*De voluptate*, 1457). They were published under the title of the first work, *De mysteriis*, in 1497. Manutius was born in Bassiano, some 60 miles south of Rome, and he received an excellent education under Gasparino da Verona in Rome and under Guarino da Verona in Ferrara, where he learned Greek. In 1482 he went to stay in Mirandola with his friend and fellow student, Giovanni Pico, where he continued his studies of Greek literature. Pico obtained for Manutius the post of tutor to his own nephews, Alberto and Leonello Pio in Carpi. They were able to help him later establish his printing press.

When Aldus moved to Venice, his press quickly achieved an outstanding reputation. He engaged the best typographers, including Francesco Griffo, and the best editors, including Pietro Bembo and Erasmus, and from 1490 started to publish the Greek classics in beautiful editions. From 1495 he was also publishing Latin classics, as well as more recent Latin works, including those of Poliziano, Erasmus and Sannazaro, and Bembo's vernacular *Asolani*. He was quick to include something of Ficino's, although most of Ficino's work was already with other publishers by this time. (Ficino's letters were published in Venice in 1495, but with Matteo Capcasa – see above.)

Aldus designed a new font, which became known as *italic*. in which the letters were inclined, designed to resemble cursive handwriting, He was also the first to use the semi-colon as a punctuation mark. Another innovation was the printing of relatively inexpensive, pocket-sized editions of important works, all beautifully set in a form resembling the finest manuscripts. The first of these appeared in 1501. In 1502, he founded an Academy for the study of Greek.

Later books from the Aldine press, including a second edition of Ficino's *De mysteriis* in 1516, carried the device of a dolphin wrapped round an anchor on the title page and also on the verso of the final leaf.

Braccio Martelli (1442-1513): a member of Lorenzo's close circle of friends from youth upwards, Braccio served Florence as ambassador on several occasions. In 1489 he was *Gonfaloniere di Giustizia*, and from 1486 to 1495 an official of the *Studio*. Braccio had been the recipient of two important letters from Ficino on the study of Plato and on Porphyry in *Letters*, **7**, 7 and 29. It is the first of these, *Concordia Mosis et Platonis*, that is mentioned in this volume, in Letter 25 to Jacopo Rondoni.

In *Letters*, **9**, 39, Braccio was mentioned as a supporter of the second edition of Ficino's Plato translations (Venice, 1491). The Martelli family were both wealthy and hospitable. Their wealth derived from the wool trade and banking, and by the 1470s they owned two palazzi near San Lorenzo. Pier Leone of Spoleto used to stay with them until his death in 1492. In 1508 Leonardo da Vinci was lodging there, and dedicated the Arundel codex of his notebooks to Braccio's son. For further details on Braccio's life, see *Letters*, **7**, pp. 202-3. For his son, Pietro, see below.

Pietro Martelli: mentioned in Letter 18 as being in the service of Ramberto Malatesta of Rimini, Pietro was the son of Ficino's close friend Braccio Martelli. Little is known of his early career, but in the early 1490s he seems to be part of the group who met with Matteo Bossi in the Abbey at Fiesole, including Pico della Mirandola, Poliziano and Roberto Salviati. By 1501 he was married, with a son whom he named after his own father, Braccio. In 1508, Leonardo da Vinci was living in his house, and he is mentioned in Leonardo's notebooks as a *commissario di signoria.* Pietro appears to have written four books on mathematics, which were lost during the Siege of Rome in 1529.

Jacopo di Martino Martini (active 1480-1519): the notary who drew up Ficino's will (Appendix R) and served as his executor. He was already a good friend by 1489, when Ficino sent him a copy of his *De vita (Letters*, **9**, 1).

Jean Matheron de Salignac (d. 1495): Matheron rose to prominence under René of Anjou, Duke of Lorraine, who also for a few years ruled Naples and Sicily. He appointed him Master of Requests, and sent him several times as ambassador to Pope Sixtus IV. The pope recognised his qualities and awarded him several honours, including a knighthood of St John Lateran, and the title of Count Palatine (1474). On the death of René in 1480, Matheron's career underwent a temporary eclipse: he had already opposed René's successor Louis XI on René's behalf over the succession in Provence. On Louis' death, Matheron was once again restored to grace and served Charles VIII in several capacities. In 1489 he was sent to Florence to negotiate free passage for the French army in the event of a reconquest of Naples. Ficino's letter of friendly overture to Matheron (Letter 34) suggests that Matheron was either in or approaching Florence in the autumn of 1494, prior to the arrival of the French troops in the city that November. Matheron died in 1495 while on another embassy to Rome.

Mazzingo di Paradiso Mazzinghi (b. 1451): member of an educated family originally from Signa, Mazzingo was a former student of Pier Leone da Spoleto. Like his teacher, he became a physician and served for a while as Professor of Medicine at the University of Pisa until he resigned from that post in 1479. Ficino and his family were among his patients. In his papers is preserved a translation of the Kabbalistic *Sefer Yetzirah* commissioned by Pier Leone. In *Letters*, **10**, 14, Ficino sent him a copy of his *De vita*. In Letter 10 of this volume, he sends *De sole et lumine*, and refers to Mazzingo's forthcoming pilgrimage to Loreto. In Letter 22, Ficino thanks Mazzingo for a gift of wine he had sent. Either Mazzingo or a younger relation of the same name was *priore* of Florence in 1523.

The Mazzinghi family is sometimes called Macinghi, and included Alessandra (1406-1470) who married Matteo Strozzi, leaving correspondence with her sons on the management of their family affairs that is of considerable interest (see Bibliography).

Cosimo de' Medici (1389-1464): the first of the Medici family to figure in Ficino's life. Cosimo, who was the major political force in the life of the city, supported Ficino's earliest studies in Greek and appointed him to translate the works of Plato, giving him the villa at Careggi. Ficino refers to this early work in Letter 4. See *Letters*, **8**, p. 125 for further details of his life.

Giovanni de' Medici (1475-1521): Piero's brother, and later Pope Leo X. There are no letters to Giovanni in this volume, and his influence on Florentine affairs during this period was slight. For more details, see *Letters*, **8**, pp. 125-6.

Giuliano de' Medici (1479-1516): Piero and Giovanni's younger brother. When the Medici were expelled in 1494, Giuliano, still a teenager, fled to Venice. He returned in 1512, ruling the city for four years. In 1515 he married Filiberta, daughter of the Duke of Savoy and was invested with the title Duc de Nemours by her nephew, François I, King of France. He died young, in 1516, leaving only an illegitimate heir, Ippolito.

Lorenzo de' Medici (1449-1492): a constant presence in Ficino's life from his boyhood until his death in 1492, Lorenzo is mentioned in this volume as the patron for Ficino's Plotinus commentaries (Letter 4). For eulogies of Lorenzo, see *Letters*, **10**, 8, 18 and 20; for biographical notes, see *Letters*, **8**, pp. 126-7 and **10**, p.123.

Piero de' Medici (1472-1503): when his father Lorenzo died, Piero was initially accorded authority over the city. However, lack of judgement and ability soon lost him the support of many citizens and his handling of the crisis attendant on the French invasion of Italy led directly to his expulsion from the city in 1494. Yet in the years before this, Piero was still important to Ficino and several works were dedicated to him, including his *De sole et lumine*, in the period covered by this volume (see Letters 4, 6, 7 and 19). Ficino had hoped Piero would support a new edition of his Plato commentaries, but this did not happen until after Piero's death. For further biographical details, see *Letters*, **9**, p. 126-7.

Johannes Menchen of Cologne (d.1504): a priest and Professor of canon law, Johannes became chancellor to Hermann of Hesse, Archbishop-Elector of Cologne, and served him for many years. Archbishop Hermann sent Johannes as an envoy to Rome, probably in 1493. He stopped off in Florence on the way and met Ficino. Ficino's letter to him (Letter 23) is dated 17th January 1494. It indicates that Menchen was supporting or subsidising a new printing of *De vita*; see note 4 to that letter for discussion of whether this printing took place.

Michele Mercati: mentioned in this volume in Appendix D (to Jacopo da Volterra), Mercati, together with Antonio Serafico, was one of the earliest and closest friends of Ficino. Mercati entered a monastery, but their friendship continued. Ficino sent him copies of his early works, and dedicated to him his *Theological dialogue between God and the Soul* (*Letters*, **1**, 4). For the story attending his death, see *Letters*, **1**, 2nd edition, p. 247.

Tommaso Minerbetti was a man for whom Ficino had immense respect, holding him up as an example of the quality of *humanitas* (*Letters*, **1**, 55) and as a model of kindness, generosity, authority and intelligence (*Letters*, **2**, 12). He was also an educated man, owner of several fine manuscripts. His wife was Bartolomea, daughter of Bernardo de' Medici, and they had at least three children. Ficino was chosen as godfather to their son in 1476 and in the same year, probably through Ficino's influence, his cousin Sebastiano

Salvini was appointed as tutor to Minerbetti's older children (*Letters*, **2**, 14), remaining with the family for four years. Tommaso was *Gonfaloniere di Giustizia* in 1486 and again in 1494; in 1491 he is recorded as Warden of the *Opera* of the Cathedral, leading discussions on the completion of its famous façade. In November-December 1492, he was one of the Florentine ambassadors to Pope Alexander VI, receiving a knighthood from him. He is buried at the church of Santa Maria Novella, near to his residence.

Piero del Nero (1440- 1512): a lawyer and statesman with roots in the cloth trade, Piero had played a part in the government of the city since the 1470s and continued to do so even after the expulsion of the Medici. He liked to attend Ficino's gatherings, and had been a close friend since the 1470s. In 1489 he helped to defend Ficino's *De vita*. In 1493 he financed the publication of Ficino's *De sole et lumine* (Letter 6). For further details of his career, see *Letters*, **6**, pp. 106-7.

Angelo (Agnolo) Niccolini: (1444 or 1445-1499): son of the Florentine nobleman Ottone di Lapo Niccolini. His younger brother, Giovanni, achieved eminence as the Archbishop of Amalfi. Both brothers were close friends of Ficino's. Angelo was educated as a lawyer, and served as *priore* in 1479, on the Council of 70 in 1489, and also as *Gonfaloniere* that year. Between 1484 and 1487 or possibly 1489, he was working at the Curia in Rome. From 1487 to 1493 he was a member of the *Otto di Practica*, and he was sent on numerous diplomatic missions, to Naples in 1492, to Milan in 1493, to Naples and Milan and to Charles VIII in 1494. Both he and his brother Giovanni decided to side with the French king, and were consequently exiled from Florence. Angelo was allowed later to return, but held no further office.

His first marriage to Luisa, daughter of Piero di Pazzi, produced no children. After her death he married Tommasa di F. Cambini and had 7 children.

At the time of Letter 21, Angelo was still held in high regard in the city. Ficino mentions the annual gathering held at Angelo's house, to celebrate Epiphany (6th January).

Paolo Orlandini (d.1519): a Camaldolese monk, theologian and poet. He entered the monastery of Santa Maria degli Angeli in 1488, around the time that Ficino gave a number of lectures on Platonic philosophy. After Guido Lorenzi's death in 1498, Orlandini became the prior, and was later twice Vicar General of the Camaldolese Order. During the 1490s he was at first a supporter of Savonarola, and played a part in the astrology controversy of these years, writing a *librum satyricum de notitia futurorum contra astrologos* (MS Laur. Ashburnham app. 1875). In 1496 he started to concern himself with the question of false prophets, at first leaning towards Savonarola's claims but later coming down against them. His work was mostly unpublished but was collected together in *Eptathicum*, a compilation on theology and morals, the principal manuscript for which is Florence BN II.1.158. By 1510, Orlandini was abbot of the Camaldolese monastery on Murano.

Despite his evident friendship with Ficino, there seem to be no letters to Paolo Orlandini within the published collection, nor is he mentioned in the list of Ficino's friends in *Letters*, **10**, 28. An earlier letter to 'Paolo of Florence' from around 1476 was thought to be addressed to Paolo Orlandini (*Letters,* **2**: 38), but later information led us to consider the Servite priest and preacher Paolo Attavanti as the more likely recipient. See notes to *Letters,* **7**, 72.

However, Ficino did write a preface to Paolo Orlandini which he attached to his commentary on the ninth book of Plato's *Republic* (*Opera omnia*, pp. 1425-6), which is presented here as Appendix L. It is dated 13th November, 1496, the year after the *Letters* were published.

This preface also mentions Guido di Lorenzo '*venerabili patri nostro*' to whom the General of the Order, Pietro Delfin, had written on 7th December, 1487, complaining about use of the Church of the Angeli for lay matters. See Allen, *Philebus*, pp. 8-9 and notes to Appendix U. This is certainly the prior, Guido Lorenzi (see above).

Giovanni Pico della Mirandola (1463-1494): this brilliant young nobleman from the duchy of Mirandola, whose wide-ranging views on philosophy and unpredictable behaviour caused controversy and censure, reached Florence in 1484, when he formed a warm friendship with Ficino. Their friendship persisted, despite several philosophical disagreements. Letter 30, to Pico and Ficino's mutual friend Poliziano, seeks to show that there is no disagreement between them on the limitations of astrology, against which Pico was writing a vehement attack, his unfinished *Disputationes adversus astrologiam divinatricem*. Pico is also mentioned as a defender of Ficino's work in Letter 6. By the time of this volume, Pico had moved into the circle of Savonarola at San Marco. See Letter 38 and Appendix F. Giovanni Pico died on 17th November 1494, the very day that King Charles VIII of France occupied Florence. For details of Pico's life and work, see *Letters*, **7**, pp. 142-147.

Giovanni Francesco (or Gianfancesco) **Pico della Mirandola** (1470-1533), nephew of Giovanni Pico (above): a letter from Ficino to Giovanni Francesco is given in Appendix I, expressing consolation on the death of his uncle, Giovanni Pico.

Giovanni Francesco was also a philosopher but with a strong interest in theology. He made himself responsible for the publication of his uncle's work, and he wrote a biography of him published in 1496. He also wrote a biography of Girolamo Savonarola, of whom he had become a dedicated follower. His own works are strongly influenced by Savonarola. The works for which he is best known include a treatise on *Imagination* (1501), writings against astrology and magic (1506-10) and one in defence of Christian teachings (1520). He was involved in controversies surrounding the witch trials of the 1520s.

In 1491 he married the Neapolitan noblewoman Giovanna Caraffa, with whom he had ten sons. With the aid of her dowry he managed to acquire from his uncle control of most of the family domains in Mirandola. This did not conduce to good relations with other family members and Giovanni Francesco was eventually murdered in the library of his own castle in 1533.

Angelo (or Agnolo) **Ambrogini Poliziano** (1454-1494): poet, scholar and close friend of both Pico della Mirandola and Ficino. In the 1480s, Poliziano taught poetry at the Florentine *Studio* and worked indefatigably to correct and restore defective Greek and Roman texts. In the early 1490s, he was permitted at last to lecture on philosophy, and wrote *Praelectio de dialectica* (an introduction to Aristotelian logic, (1491), *Lamia,* an introduction to Aristotle's *Prior analytics* (1492), and *Dialectica* (1493), an introduction to his course on Aristotelian philosophy. He is mentioned in this volume in Letter 6, is the addressee of Letter 30, Ficino's important letter on astrology, and is mentioned in Appendix F. For further details of his life, see *Letters*, **5**, pp. 181-2 and **8**, pp. 129-130.

Martin 'Uranius' Prenninger (c.1450-1501): several variants of his name are found, e.g. Praennyger, Brenninger, but we have kept the most usual form, Prenninger. By the time of this volume, he was an eminent lawyer and Counsellor to Count Eberhard V of Württemberg.

Prenninger had been a friend of Ficino's since he first visited Florence in 1476. In 1490 he had moved from his post as Chancellor in the Bishopric of Constance to the recently founded University of Tübingen, where he was Professor of Ecclesiastical Law until his death, and was soon taken into the service of the Count. He travelled with the Count to Italy in 1492, but had returned by 1493 when Letters 3 and 7 were sent to him, the first a philosophical reflection on law, the second a celebration of *De sole*. Ficino wrote twelve letters to him in previous books (*Letters*, **8**, **9** and **10**) and further biographical details can be found there.

Bindaccio da Ricasoli (c.1444-1524): a student of Ficino's from youth, named in Benedetto Colucci's *Declamationes* as one of the five noble youths studying with Ficino (c. 1474). Ricasoli remained a lifelong friend and follower, helping to maintain the Academy even after Ficino's death. He was the addressee of an important treatise on prayer (*Letters*, **9**, 33) which Ficino refers to in his commentary on Dionysius (*Mystical Theology*, ch. 3) and the recipient of four other letters (**9**, 42; **10**, 24, 27, 32). He is mentioned in five further letters (*Letters*, **1**, 52, 107; **8**, 2; **9**, Appendix D; **10**, 22) and in the *De sole* (Appendix B). Appendix C consists of a letter Bindaccio sent to Gregorio Scuto, accompanying a copy of the newly printed *De sole et lumine* and enclosing a list of all Ficino's works up to 1493. In 1493 Bindaccio was elected a *priore*.

After Ficino's death, Giovanni Corsi's *Life* of Ficino, written in 1506, was addressed to Ricasoli, and Diacceto's *Three Books on Love* were dedicated to him in 1508. For further details of Ricasoli's personal life and engagement in the government of the city, see the lengthier biographical note in *Letters*, **1** (revised edition), p. 255, or **9**, p. 129.

Jacopo Rondoni, also known as **Giacomo Passarella** (d.1495): a papal secretary from Cesena, some 20 miles from Rimini, who was appointed Bishop of Imola in 1479 and subsequently transferred to the bishopric of Rimini in 1488. He died in September 1495. Letter 25, to Rondoni, presents important points Ficino was keen to stress on consistencies between Platonic and Christian teachings.

Girolamo Rossi of Pistoia (c.1444-1517): this final book of Ficino's letters, as well as the collection of all twelve books, is dedicated with a Preface to his friend Girolamo Rossi. He had also been the dedicatee of a signed copy of Ficino's *De christiana religione*, in 1478.

Letter 20 of this volume also celebrates Rossi and was used as the preface to the first edition of all twelve books of the letters, printed in Venice in 1495. The printer was Matteo Capcasa of Parma. The 'privilege', obtained from the Venetian senate which allowed it to be printed, was issued in the name of Girolamo Blondi, or Biondo, citizen of Florence (see entry on Blondi above). Some older scholarship identified Biondo with Rossi (Francesco Puccinotti, *Storia della Medicina*, II, 1880, vol. II, p. 570, fn. 1, and Paul Oskar Kristeller, *Sup. Fic.*, I, pp. cvi-cvii) but Sebastiano Gentile maintains they are two different individuals (*Lettere*, 1990, pp. ccvii-ccxii). It was Biondo who paid for the cost of printing the letters, and Biondo may also have been involved in the second printing in 1497 by Anton Koberger in Nuremberg as well as the printing of the

Iamblichus and other translations of Ficino's by Aldus Manutius in the same year. Gentile proposed that Rossi served as intermediary between Ficino and Biondo.

Rossi certainly spent many years in Venice; we know he was there in March 1480 (*Letters*, **5**, 26); he made return trips to Florence to conduct business on behalf of Venetian citizens. On one of these trips he brought an antique bust to Lorenzo, that had been found in Athens and was commonly thought to have been a bust of Plato. This is related in Niccolò Valori's *Life of Lorenzo*.

By December 1497, Rossi was back in Florence, a follower of Savonarola and present at the siege of the Dominican monastery of San Marco in 1498, and was amongst the select few entrusted with the keys of the convent. In 1504 he became a Dominican monk, becoming prior in Lucca, then Pistoia and finally of San Marco in 1515. In May 1517 he was elected Vicar General of the Dominican Order. He died of a fever in September 1517.

Besides the dedications, Ficino mentions Rossi in Letter 31 to Bernardo Rucellai, in terms that are again highly complimentary.

Bernardo di Giovanni Rucellai (1448-1514): nobleman, diplomat and historian of some distinction, Bernardo was related to the Strozzi and married into the Medici family. He supported Medici rule and held high office in the city. In 1478, Bernardo had served as one of the *Officiales* of the Florentine *Studio*; in 1484, he was ambassador to Genoa. After Lorenzo de Medici's death in 1492, Bernardo allowed his gardens, the *Orti Oricellari*, to become the meeting place where Ficino's circle and others could continue their philosophic and literary discussions. Through his marriage to Lorenzo's sister Lucrezia (also known as Nannina) he was uncle to Piero and Giovanni (later Pope Leo X) and to Giulio (later Pope Clement VII), son of Lorenzo's murdered brother. Bernardo continued to hold high office after the expulsion of the Medici, serving as *Gonfaloniere di Giustizia* from 1497 to 1498. For further details of his career, see Biographical Notes to *Letters*, **1** (2nd edition). Bernardo was sufficiently close to Ficino to be selected by Giovanni Corsi as the dedicatee of his life of Ficino in 1506.

Bernardo di Mariotto Rucellai (b. 1464): a kinsman of the famous humanist and historian Bernardo di Giovanni Rucellai (see *Letters*, **9**, pp. 129-130). The younger Bernardo was a friend of Girolamo Rossi, as is recorded in Letter 31 when Ficino sent him a copy of *De sole*. He served for some time as an officer of the Mint. Two of his sisters appear to have been the first and second wife (in succession – both died young) of the merchant Francesco di Bartolomeo Gherardini, whose third wife is considered by most art historians to have been the subject of Leonardo da Vinci's *Mona Lisa*.

Sebastiano Salvini (c.1450-1511): Ficino's cousin. Sebastiano lived with Ficino after he was orphaned in 1462. He was educated under Ficino and Antonio degli Agli. He served as scribe to Ficino and as collaborator on his *De christiana religione*. He was ordained a priest in 1475 or 1476. By 1481 he had obtained a higher degree in theology and left Florence for a post at the papal Curia in Rome. In 1496, he returned from Rome, taking up the rectorship of a church in Fiesole. A letter from Salvini to Guido di Lorenzo is presented here as Appendix U. He was also a beneficiary of Ficino's will, Appendix R. For further details on Salvini's life, see Biographical Notes to *Letters*, **1** and **7**.

Cosimo Sassetti (1463-1527): son of Francesco, the General Director of the Medici bank, Cosimo was also employed in the bank. Some time before 1485 he was sent to investigate the losses of the Lyon branch, but he seems to have had little understanding of the situation, and Lorenzo Spinelli was sent too. If anything, Cosimo's presence exacerbated the bad relations between the branch and the main bank in Florence and it was left to his father to resolve matters and uncover the fraud that was going on. Cosimo's continuing role in the Lyon branch and at the French court drew criticism both at the time and from later historians, based on his lack of tact and personal skills, but it did provide the opportunity for him and his colleague Spinelli to facilitate contact between Ficino and Germain de Ganay. Cosimo was elected to serve as an official of the Florentine *Studio* in 1484-5 and again in 1485-6. He is portrayed with his brothers in the Ghirlandaio fresco entitled *Confirmation of the Rule*, commissioned by their father for the Sassetti chapel in the Church of Santa Trinità and painted between 1483 and 1486.

Girolamo Savonarola (1452-1498): born in Ferrara, Savonarola was first educated by his elderly grandfather, Michele Savonarola, a distinguished physician who had been brought from the university of Padua to the d'Este court. From the age of 20, Girolamo was writing poetry against the decadence of society and of the Church, and in 1475 he took the decisive step of abandoning the medical career planned for him and entering a Dominican Order in Bologna. There he took his vows and began his training in theology and as a preacher, returning to Ferrara in 1479 to teach logic, a branch of philosophy, to the novitiates at the Dominican house there.

In 1482, he took part in a public disputation within the Dominican order, attended also by Pico della Mirandola, who formed a very favourable impression of him. The same year, Savonarola was transferred to the monastery of San Marco in Florence as master of novices. As an outsider with a rather old-fashioned scholastic style of preaching, he struggled at first to establish himself. In the spring of 1488, he was transferred back to Santa Maria degli Angeli in Ferrara, with the recommendation that he be dropped from the Order's programme of higher studies. However, in 1490, largely through the intervention of Lorenzo de' Medici and Pico della Mirandola, and somewhat against the judgement of his Vicar-General, he was invited back to San Marco. He arrived in May or June of that year, to teach philosophy and biblical exegesis to the monks. His sermon style had changed during his time away, and he now delivered stirring addresses against sin and corruption, mixed with a radical social agenda. These attracted a growing audience and in May 1491, he was elected prior of the monastery and was invited to preach his sermons in the Cathedral, the largest and most prestigious church in the city. As prior, Savonarola proceeded to establish the independence of San Marco, both from Lorenzo and from the Lombard chapter of the Order. As a result, he was elected to continue as prior beyond the usual term of office.

By this time, he was increasingly given to prophecies and disturbing visions. During Lent of 1492, from the pulpit of the Medici church of San Lorenzo, he launched a strong attack on philosophers along with sodomites and corrupt churchmen. Though he avoided naming names, it was clear that Ficino was among his targets. Savonarola had made some study of Plato himself, but was now convinced that engaging with the philosophy of the ancients was one of the contributing factors that would unleash the coming apocalypse. At the end of 1492, he spoke of a repeated vision of the 'Sword of the Lord held by a hand in the sky', this time accompanied by divine voices warning of punishments to come. These warnings continued and his following grew, though opponents were also becoming more vociferous. The rise of numerous factions is discussed in the Introduction. When the French invasion occurred, in November 1494, it seemed to many of his followers that this was indeed the 'Sword of the Lord' and emotions reached fever pitch. In the absence of the Medici, who had been obliged to flee, Savonarola was chosen to act as intermediary with the French king.

From this time on, his hold over the newly constituted republic was unrivalled. In December 1495, he formed the notorious bands of *fanciulli*, youths who would patrol the city to monitor personal dress and behaviour. They took to their puritanical task with zeal and some excess. This, too, is the period of the 'bonfires of vanities', which were part of his plan to destroy offending works of art and literature and rid the city of its immoralities, making of it a new Jerusalem, with Christ as King.

What brought about Savonarola's downfall was his growing conflict with his superiors and with the papacy. He was summoned to Rome in 1495 but declined to attend, claiming ill health and fear of attack on the way. The papal response was to ban him from preaching. At first Savonarola obeyed, but, fearing his influence might wane, he returned with even more violent sermons, provoking a bull of excommunication in May 1497. In March 1498, the city government prevailed upon him to stop preaching. However, within a month talk had grown of his ability to perform miracles, and it was proposed to test his mission in a trial by fire. There was great excitement as the day approached – 7th April, 1498 – but a sudden thunderstorm drenched the prepared brushwood and the event was cancelled. Riots followed and Savonarola was imprisoned together with his two main supporters. Under torture he confessed to inventing his prophecies and visions, though he tried also to retract the confession. On 23rd May, the three friars were led before a tribunal of church and state officials and were condemned as heretics and schismatics. They were stripped of their Dominican robes and were condemned to death by hanging, while fires were lit below so that no relics could be gathered by their followers. Their ashes were thrown into the Arno.

Ficino's response to all this is discussed in the Introduction and in Appendix Q. After his death, Savonarola did become a revered figure, despite the government's efforts. His followers, the *Piagnoni,* were a potent political force in Florence until the ultimate re-establishment of Medici rule in 1530 and his numerous writings continued to inspire movements for religious, moral and social reform in Italy and beyond in the ensuing centuries.

Gregorio Scuto: a physician from Alessandria in Piedmont who formed a strong friendship with Ficino while in Florence. Ficino's letter on Gregorio's departure to Siena in October 1490 indicates that they held a great deal in common (*Letters*, **9**, 29). In 1493 Bindaccio Ricasoli sent Gregorio a copy of *De sole et lumine* together with a list of all Ficino's works (Appendix C).

Francesco Soderini (1453-1524): third of the four sons of Tommaso Soderini and Dianora Tornabuoni (whose sister became the wife of Piero de' Medici in 1444). Francesco had trained in law and was an Apostolic Secretary by the time of this volume. He had held the bishopric of Volterra since 1478, though he rarely visited it, being kept busy with curial matters and the pope's diplomatic, political and private correspondence. In 1495 he led an important diplomatic mission to the French King Charles VIII. He was made a Cardinal in 1503. For further details of his career, see *Letters*, **7**, pp. 212-3.

Over a period of 20 years, Ficino sent many letters to Francesco addressed to other people, over and above the ones addressed to him (of which there were eleven), relying on his advice on how to present them (e.g. to the young Cardinal Riario, to Cardinal Giovanni of Aragon and even King Matthias of Hungary). In this volume Letters 19 and 24 are addressed to him. In Letter 19, Ficino refers to Soderini's family connection with the Medici.

Giovanni Vittorio Soderini (1460-1528): Giovanni Vittorio trained in canon and civil law at the Florentine *Studio*, and started teaching there in 1485, specialising in civil law. He moved with the faculty, temporarily to Prato in 1486, and to Pisa from 1487 to 1492. In 1491 he married Dianora di Tanai Nerli, with whom he had four children.

In July 1492, he asked for a year of leave, perhaps associated with time spent with Giovanni de' Medici in Pisa, and Letter 1 was sent to him and to Francesco Diacceto at this time; he is also mentioned in Letter 3. By the beginning of the academic year in 1493 he was back in his teaching post. In 1494 he served with Ficino and others on the commission examining books in the Library of San Marco that had come from the collection of the Medici family. In 1495, he was elected to various posts in the new government, and seems to have resumed teaching law in January 1498, though he had to combine it with other political offices. From November 1502 until June 1503 he was a member of the embassy in Rome and in 1509 helped to negotiate with the Emperor Maximilian over the status and privileges of Florence, and was charged with several other diplomatic undertakings, involving travel to Carinthia and to some north Italian cities. However, when his brother Piero lost power in 1512, Giovanni found himself exiled to Perugia, until Pope Leo X's election as Pope, when the city allowed Soderini back, although he held no further important office until the last year of his life when he served on the Council of Ten for Liberty and Peace.

Lorenzo Spinelli (born 1452): member of a family prominent in the silk trade, Lorenzo Spinelli, son of Francesco, became manager of the Montpellier branch of the Medici bank in 1480 and of the important Lyon branch in 1486 or 1488. He was at the French court at least from 1492, and sent numerous letters to Lorenzo de' Medici, including one in March of that year, warning him that he, Lorenzo de' Medici, was being held largely responsible for the French decision to invade Italy. Lorenzo probably did not receive the letter as he died soon after. Spinelli, mentioned in Letter 35, had commended de Ganay to Ficino, even if he may not have provided the initial contact.

Francesco Strozzi: the Strozzi family had been rivals of the Medici as bankers and after a period in exile had succeeded in regaining some importance in the financial and political life of the city. There were several members of the Strozzi family who bore the name Francesco: one was the son of Benedetto; another was a son of Alessandro, who is mentioned in a letter of Alessandra Macinghi Strozzi as being with her son Filippo, a banker in Naples (in 1464). In this volume, Francesco is mentioned as a financial agent to Jacopo of Volterra (Appendix D).

Arnolfo Tedaldi (d. 1495): a relative of Callimachus on his mother's side, Arnolfo had been settled in Poland for a long time, as one of a small but important community of Italian merchants. He was director of the state monopoly of salt mines in Drohobycz (now in Ukraine), holding an influential position. He had been responsible for

Callimachus finding safe refuge in Poland back in 1470 and they remained closely associated, with Callimachus choosing to stay in Poland even after he could have returned to Italy from 1471. In 1472 Callimachus dedicated a collection of poems to Arnolfo. Arnolfo died in Cracow in 1495, a year before Callimachus. Other members of the Tedaldi family were within Ficino's circle (*Letters*, **1**, 2nd edition, p. 259.). See also Biographical note on Buonaccorsi and Plate 2.

Baccio, or Bartolomeo, **Ugolini** (d. 1494): Florentine poet and singer of great repute, renowned for his improvisations to the accompaniment of his 'lyre' (lute). He was chosen to sing the lead role in Poliziano's *Orfeo*, in Mantua in 1480. Baccio was a great friend of Poliziano and Lorenzo de' Medici. His role as a diplomat, however, is often overlooked. He carried out diplomatic missions for Lorenzo over a period of twenty years, including visits to Bruges, Basel, Paris, Rome and Naples. Lorenzo supported his ecclesiastical career, helping him to become parish priest of San Vicenzo di Valdambra, then prior of San Lorenzo a Campi in the diocese of Arezzo. He held a position in the court of Sixtus IV, and for several years he administered the Abbey of Monte Cassino for Lorenzo's son, Giovanni. In 1489 he became a canon of Florence cathedral and in August 1494, a few months before his death, he was appointed Bishop of Gaeta, in Lazio, south of Rome. The important abbey of Cassino lay within its territories. *Letters*, **1**, 52, on poetic frenzy, was addressed to Baccio and his friend Antonio Pelotti. In this volume, he was sent a copy of *De sole et lumine* with Letter 12.

Filippo Valori (1456-1494): member of one of the leading families of Florence, Filippo had been one of Ficino's principal patrons over many years, paying for the publication of his Plato translation in 1484 and his *De vita* in 1489. In 1492 Valori was the city's ambassador in Rome and Ficino writes to him there, adding a message for Piero de' Medici (Letter 4) and sending him a copy of *De sole et lumine*, which he asks him to defend if necessary (Letter 6). For further details of Filippo's career, see Biographical Note in *Letters*, **9**, p. 132. See also *Letters*, **10**, 17, 20, 22, 31 and Appendices A and B in that volume.

Francesco Valori (1439-1498): a leading statesman and strong supporter of Lorenzo de' Medici. He fulfilled many important roles in the government of the city and its diplomacy abroad, sometimes taking with him his nephews Filippo and Niccolò. In September 1492 he was appointed to the highest post in the government of Florence (*Gonfaloniere di Giustizia*). In November 1492 he accompanied Piero de' Medici to Rome, to greet the new pope, Alexander VI, and in 1494 he went with Piero to meet the French king. He subsequently withdrew his support from Piero, transferring it to Savonarola and becoming a leading republican figure. His opposition to the Medici and harsh treatment of their supporters in 1497 led to his assassination on 8th April, 1498.

Niccolò Valori (1464-c.1527): younger brother of Ficino's close friend, Filippo Valori, Niccolò is mentioned as being a student of Ficino's in 1492 in the famous list of his friends (*Letters*, **10**, 28). In this volume, he is the recipient of Letter 13 and is mentioned in Letter 15 as still studying with Ficino daily.

After 1494, Niccolò followed his uncle Francesco in transferring allegiance from the Medici to Savonarola's party. Yet this did not prevent him from continuing to support Ficino, becoming in this period his principal patron and his most important political ally. Niccolò paid for the publication of the Letters in 1495, and the Platonic

Commentaries in 1496. In 1496 Ficino became godfather to Niccolò's son and acted on Niccolò's behalf in obtaining from the pope, in 1499, the right to a perpetual lease on a landholding belonging to the church of San Lorenzo. Ficino's assistance receives detailed record in the Valori family diary.

At the same time, the family were political supporters of Savonarola, and on 8th April, 1498, when an angry mob rampaged through the city after the cancellation of Savonarola's trial by fire, the Valori house was sacked. Niccolò escaped alive but both his parents were murdered. For a few years, he was excluded from any position in the city, but his abilities soon brought about a return, and in 1501 he was sent to quell an uprising in Pistoia. He held office as *priore* in 1502, 1506, and 1512, and on the Council of Ten of Liberty in 1505 and 1507. In 1502 he was among the officers of the University.

In 1503 he went with Machiavelli as ambassador to King Louis XII of France, who bestowed the title of Royal Chamberlain and Counsellor on him; in 1507 he led an embassy to King Ferdinand of Aragon in Naples. When a citizen militia was set up, under Machiavelli, Niccolò was appointed to the committee that oversaw it, and he was often called upon to play the role of peacemaker between Machiavelli and the Signoria. In 1509, Niccolò was rewarded with the gift of the castle of Montevecchio.

On the restoration of the Medici in 1512, Niccolò was excluded from office, and for a time was imprisoned on a charge of complicity in a conspiracy. Pope Leo X obtained his release. By 1518 he was once again being entrusted with commissions: in Arezzo (1518), Rome (1522), and at the Florence mint (1523).

His wife was Ginevra di Giovanni Lanfredini, and they had three sons.

Niccolò wrote a *Life of Lorenzo de' Medici* which he dedicated to Leo X. In it he defends Ficino's Platonism and his political views against the criticisms of Savonarola. Niccolò Machiavelli discusses various members of the Valori family in his *Histories*. The Valori also kept detailed records of their own in family diaries. Their palazzo in Florence, situated in the Borgo degli Albizi, was later decorated with busts, among which was one of Ficino.

Paolo of Verona, see above under **Paolo Emili**.

Giorgio Antonio Vespucci (1435-1514): a confidant of Ficino over many years, a fellow canon of the cathedral, Vespucci was witness to Ficino's will and one of his executors (Appendix R). He had joined the monastery of San Marco in 1497, after a distinguished career as a highly respected educator. For previous correspondence, see *Letters*, **2**, 21; **3**, 5; **4**, 47; **6**, 3 and for further details of his life, Biographical Notes to *Letters*, **6**, p.111.

Antonio Vinciguerra, also called **Cronico** (c.1440-1502): secretary to the Venetian Senate for over 30 years, Antonio was a close friend of Bernardo Bembo. He visited Florence with Bembo on his first embassy, serving as his secretary. He later cultivated a warm friendship with Poliziano and Pico when they were present in Venice, continuing to correspond with them after they left. Ficino sent him a copy of *De sole et lumine* on 19th August, 1494 (Letter 29). For earlier connections, see *Letters*, **6**, p. 112.

Giles (Egidio) of Viterbo (1469-1532): his family name was Antonini but his original first name is unknown. On entering the Augustinian Order of Hermits at the age of eighteen, in 1488, he was given the name Aegidius, which corresponds to the English Giles. He studied philosophy and theology at various Augustinian priories. At Padua, in 1493, he attended lectures on philosophy, but was repelled by the Averroistic interpretations of Aristotle then current. While there he struck up a friendship with Pico della Mirandola and particularly appreciated Pico's writings against astrology. After Padua, he passed through Florence on his way to taking up a teaching post in Capodistria, or else on his return in 1496. He certainly met Ficino, having already become interested in how Platonic philosophy, if not Aristotelian, could be harmonised with the Christian religion. He received a Master's degree in theology in Rome in the spring of 1497, defending a Platonic approach against Aristotelian ideas, as he recounted in a letter to Ficino (Appendix O).

For a few months, he taught at the monastery of Santo Spirito in Florence, but was summoned again to Rome in the autumn, and was kept in Rome by Pope Alexander VI, on account of the disturbances surrounding Savonarola, who was then attacking Giles's mentor Mariano da Genazzano, general of the Augustinian Order. In 1498 da Genazzano took him on an important mission to Naples. Edigio remained there as a preacher and took part in the intellectual life of the city, among the scholars who gathered round Giovanni Pontano.

In 1506 Giles became Vicar General of the Augustinian Order, and in 1507 Prior General. In 1517 he was made a cardinal. He enjoyed a considerable reputation as a keen reformer of the Church. In pursuit of biblical studies he became interested in the Hebrew language and can be counted among the early Christian Cabalists, with Johannes Reuchlin and Giovanni Pico della Mirandola, both of whom he knew and admired. He promoted the adoption of a strong statement on the immortality of the soul at the Lateran Council of 1512.

Jacopo of Volaterra: see **Jacopo Gherardi**

Bibliography

A select bibliography of works of particular use in compiling this volume

General Reference

P. O. Kristeller, *Supplementum Ficinianum: Marsilii Ficini Florentini Opuscula inedita et dispersa* (abbreviated as *Sup. Fic.*), 2 vols., Florence: Olschki, 1937; reprinted, 1973.

——, *Ficino and his Work after Five Hundred Years*, Florence: Olschki, 1987.

Accademia. Revue de la Société Marsile Ficin: see especially bibliographies compiled by T. Katinis, in II (2000), pp. 101–36; by T. Katinis and S. Toussaint in IV (2003), pp. 7–17, by T. Gilbhard and S. Toussaint in VIII (2006), pp. 7–21; XI (2009), pp. 9–26; XII (2010), pp. 7–12; XIX (2017) pp. 89–111.

Dizionario Biografico degli Italiani, Treccani, Rome, vols. 1–97 in print (1960–2020); also available on-line.

Marsilio Ficino. Index Nominum et Index Geographicus, ed. D. Gall, P. Riemer et al., Mainz: Georg Olms, 2003.

Marsilio Ficino. Index rerum, ed. C. Kugelmeier, P. Riemer and C. Zintzen, Hildesheim: Georg Olms, 2014.

Works by Ficino — Modern Texts and Translations

Ficino, Marsilio, *Opera omnia*, 2 vols, Basel, 1561, 1576, Paris 1641; 1576 edition repr. Turin: Bottega d'Erasmo, 1959, 1962, 1979, 1983; Paris: Phénix Editions, 2000.

——, *Commentaire sur le Banquet de Platon*, ed. and tr. by R. Marcel, Paris: Les Belles Lettres, 1956.

——, *Commentary on Plato's Symposium on Love*, tr. by S. R. Jayne, Columbia, MO, 1944; 2nd edn., Dallas, TX, 1985; repr. Woodstock, VT: Spring Publications, 1999.

——, *Commentaire sur le Banquet de Platon, de l'amour; Commentarium in convivium Platonis de amore*, ed. by Pierre Laurens, Paris: Les Belles Lettres, 2002.

——, *Commentaries on Plato*, vol 1, *Phaedrus* and *Ion*, tr. by by M. J. B. Allen (I Tatti Renaissance Library), Cambridge MA: Harvard University Press, 2008.

——, *Commentaries on Plato*, vol. 2, *Parmenides*, parts 1 and 2, tr. by Maude Vanhaelen (I Tatti Renaissance Library), Cambridge MA: Harvard University Press, 2012.

——, *Commentary on Plotinus*, ed. and tr. by Stephen Gersh (I Tatti Renaissance Library) Cambridge MA: Harvard University Press, vol. 4, 2017, vol. 5, 2018.

——, *Consiglio Contro la Pestilenza,* ed. by E. Musacchio, Bologna: Cappelli, 1983. (See also Katinis, in Selected Studies below).

——, *De christiana religione*, ed. by G. Bartolucci, Pisa: Edizioni della Normale, 2019.

——, *La religione cristiana*, modern Italian from Tuscan version, tr. by R. Zanzarri, Rome: Città Nuova, 2005.

——, *De sole et lumine* in *Margarita Facetiarum*, ed. by Johannes Adelphus, Strasbourg, 1508 and 1509.

——, *On Dionysius the Areopagite, Mystical Theology and The Divine Names,* ed. and tr. by Michael J.B. Allen, (I Tatti Renaissance Library), 2 vols., Cambridge MA: Harvard University Press, 2015.

——, *El Libro Dell' Amore,* ed. S. Niccoli, Florence: Olschki, 1987.

——, *Epistolae Libri XII,* Venice: Matteo Capcasa, 1495, reprinted Paris: Société Marsile Ficin, 2011.

——, *Correspondance*, I, ed. and tr. into French by J. Reynaud and S. Galland, Paris: Vrin, 2014; II, ed. and tr. by S. Galland, 2019.

——, *Lettere, I. Epistolarum familiarium liber I*, ed. by S. Gentile, Florence: Olschki 1990.

——, *Lettere, II. Epistolarum familiarium liber II*, ed. by S. Gentile, Florence: Olschki 2010.

——, *Le Divine Lettere del Gran Marsilio Ficino*, tr. F. Figliucci, Venice, 1548, Italian translation. Facsimile reprint, ed. by S. Gentile, Rome: Edizioni di Storia e Letteratura, 2001.

——, *Meditations on the Soul*, Rochester, VT: Inner Traditions, 1996. A selection of letters from *The Letters of Marsilio Ficino*, vols. 1–5.

——, *Iamblichus: De Mysteriis Aegyptiorum*, Venice: Aldus Manutius, 1497, reprinted Paris: Les Editions du Miraval, 2006.

——, *Mercurii Trismegisti Liber de Potestate et Sapientia Dei,* Florence: S.P.E.S., 1989. facsimile reprint of the *editio princeps* of 1471.

——, *Mercurii Trismegisti Liber de Potestate et Sapientia Dei,* ed. by Maurizio Campanelli, Turin: Nino Aragno Editore, 2011.

——, *De sole*, tr. by G. Cornelius, D. Costello, G. Tobyn, A. Voss and V. Wells, *Sphinx. Journal of the London Convivium for Archetypal Studies*, 6 (1994), pp. 123–48.

——, *Marsilio Ficino and the Phaedran Charioteer*, text and translation by M. J. B. Allen, Berkeley & Los Angeles: University of California Press, 1981.

——, *Nuptial Arithmetic: Marsilio Ficino's Commentary on the Fatal Number in Book VIII of Plato's 'Republic'*, ed. and tr. by M. J. B. Allen, Berkeley & Los Angeles: University of California Press, 1994.

——, *The 'Philebus' Commentary*, ed. and tr. by M. J. B. Allen, Berkeley & Los Angeles: University of California Press, 1975; repr. Tempe, AZ: MRTS, 2000.

——, *Platonic Theology,* tr. and ed. by Michael J. B. Allen and James Hankins (I Tatti Renaissance Library, 6 vols., Cambridge MA: Harvard University Press, 2001–2006.

——, *Predicationes*, ed. by Daniele Conti, Turin: Nino Aragno Editore, 2014.

——, *Théologie platonicienne de l'immortalité des âmes*, ed. and tr. by R. Marcel, 3 vols, Paris: Les Belles Lettres, 1964–70.

——, Plato, *Opera omnia*, tr. by M. Ficino, 2 vols, Florence, 1484; Venice, 1491, repr. Paris: Société Marsile Ficin, 2020.

——, Plotinus, *Opera omnia*, tr. by M. Ficino, Florence, 1492, repr. Paris: Phénix Editions 2005.

——, 'De Raptu Pauli', in *Prosatori latini del Quattrocento, VII*, ed. by Eugenio Garin, Turin: Einaudi, 1977.

——, *Three Books on Life*, ed. and tr. by C. V. Kaske and J. R. Clark, Medieval and Renaissance Texts and Studies, vol. 57, Binghamton, NY: MRTS, 1989.

——, *Marsilio Ficino: The Book of Life*, English translation by C. Boer, Irving, TX: Spring Publications, 1980.

——, *De Vita,* ed. and tr. by A. Biondi and G. Pisani, text and Italian translation, Pordenone: Biblioteca dell'Immagine, 1991.

——, *De vita libri tres,* ed. by Felix Klein-Franke with notes by Martin Plessner (a facsimile of the second edition of 1498, Venice), Hildesheim: Georg Olms, 1978.

——, *Marsilio Ficino: Sulla Vita,* Italian translation by A. Tarabochia Canavero, Milan: Rusconi, 1995.

——, *Les Trois Livres de la Vie*, tr. into French by Guy Le Fèvre de la Boderie, Paris, 1582, reprinted Paris: Fayard, 2000, ed. by T. Gontier.

——, *Traktate zur Platonischen Philosophie*, ed. by E. Blum, P. R. Blum and T. Leinkauf, Berlin: Akademie Verlag, 1993.

——, *Supplementum Ficinianum: Marsilii Ficini Florentini Opuscula inedita et dispersa,* ed. by P. O. Kristeller, Florence: Olschki, 1937; reprinted, 1973.

Farndell, A., *Gardens of Philosophy: Ficino on Plato*, London: Shepheard-Walwyn, 2006.

——, *Ever More Shall Be So*: *Ficino on Plato's 'Parmenides',* London: Shepheard-Walwyn, 2008.

——, *When Philosophers Rule*: *Ficino on Plato's 'Republic', 'Laws' and 'Epinomis'*, London: Shepheard-Walwyn, 2009.

——, *All Things Natural. Ficino on Plato's Timaeus*, London: Shepheard-Walwyn, 2010.

——, *On the Nature of Love: Ficino on Plato's Symposium*, tr. from the Tuscan, London: Shepheard-Walwyn, 2016.

Kristeller, P.O., *Marsilio Ficino and his Work after Five Hundred Years*, Florence: Olschki, 1989. Contains some additional letters.

Kristeller, P. O., *Studies in Renaissance Thought and Letters,* 4 vols., Rome: Edizioni di Storia e Letteratura, 1956–1996. (vols. I and II contain some early writings of Ficino not published elsewhere).

Classical, Patristic, Medieval and Renaissance Sources Cited in this Volume

Abenragel, *Praeclarissimus liber completus in Judiciis astrorum*, Venice: Erhard Ratdolt, 1485.

Albumasar (Abū Ma'šar), *De magnis coniunctionibus,* Augsburg: Erhard Ratdolt, 1489.

Introductorium in astronomiam, Augsburg: Erhard Ratdolt, 1489.

Apollodorus, *The Library*, tr. and ed. by J.G. Frazer, (Loeb Classical Library), 2 vols, Cambridge, MA: Harvard University Press, 1921.

Apuleius, *On the God of Socrates*, ed. and tr. by C.P. Jones (Loeb Classical Library), Cambridge, MA: Harvard University Press, 1940, repr. 2017.

——, *The Golden Ass*, tr. by W. Adlington, rev. by S. Gaselee, London: Heinemann, 1915 and reprints.

Aquinas, St Thomas, *Summa contra gentiles*, tr. by J.F. Anderson et al., 4 vols., New York: Doubleday, 1956 repr. University of Notre Dame Press, 1975.

——, *Summa theologiae*, https://www.newadvent.org/summa/

Aristotle, *Complete Works*, ed. by J. Barnes, 2 vols., Princeton NJ: Princeton University Press, 1984.

St Augustine, *City of God*, tr. by H. Bettenson, intro. by J. O'Meara, London: Penguin Classics, 1972, new ed. 1984.

——, *Contra Faustum Manichaeum*, tr. by R.J. Teske and A.B. Ramsey, New York: New City Press, 2007.

——, *Confessions*, tr. Henry Chadwick, Oxford: Oxford University Press, 1991.

——, *De trinitate*, ed. by J. Rotelle, tr. by E. Hill, New York: New City Press; 2nd Revised edition (2015).

Aulus Gellius, *Attic Nights*, tr. by J. C.Rolfe, (Loeb Classical Library), 3 vols., Cambridge, MA: Harvard University Press, 1927.

St Basil, *Hexaemeron* and *Homilies on St John* can be read on the websites for New Advent: https://www.newadvent.org/fathers/3201.htm and Christian Classics Ethereal Library: https://ccel.org/ccel/schaff/npnf208/npnf208.ii.html

Boethius, *Consolation of Philosophy*, tr. by V. Watts, London: Penguin. 1976, revised 1999.

Bonatti, G., *De astronomia tractatus*, Augsburg: E. Ratdolt, 1491; repr. Venice, 1506, Basel, 1550.

Châtillon, Walter of, *Alexandreis*, tr. by D. Townsend, Philadelphia: University of Pennsylvania Press, 1996.

Dante, *Divine Comedy*, tr. by D. L. Sayers and B. Reynolds, Harmondsworth: Penguin, 1949–1962 and other versions.

Diacceto, F. Cattani da, 'Panegyric on Love' tr. by L. Dietz in *Cambridge Translations of Renaissance Philosophical Texts*, vol. 1, ed. by J. Kraye, Cambridge: Cambridge University Press, 1997, pp. 156–65.

——, *Opera omnia*, Basel: Henricus Petri and Pietro Perna, 1563, repr. in facsimile, ed. by S. Toussaint, Enghien-les-Bains: Miraval, 2009.

Diogenes Laertius, *Lives of Eminent Philosophers*, tr. and ed. by R.D. Hicks, (Loeb Classical Library), 2 vols., Cambridge, MA: Harvard University Press 1925.

Dionysius, *Pseudo-Dionysius. The Complete Works*, tr. by C. Luibheid, New York: Paulist Press, 1987.

Eusebius, *Chronicon*, Paris: Henricus Stephanus, 1518.

——, *Praeparatio Evangelica*, ed. by E. des Places, 8 vols., Paris: Editions du Cerf, 1974–1991.

——, *Praeparatio Evangelica* (*Preparation for the Gospel*) tr. by E.H. Gifford, vol. 3, Oxford: 1903.

Fulgentius, *Mythologiae*, in *Opera*, ed. by R.W.O. Helm, Lipsiae: Teubner, 1898 and on Internet Archive, https://archive.org/details/operafulgoofulguoft/page/xvi/mode/2up.

Giles of Viterbo, *Lettere Familiari*, ed. by A.M. Voci-Roth, Rome: Institutum Historicum Augustinianum, 1990.

Hermes, *Asclepius*, tr. by C. Salaman, London: Duckworth, 2007.

——, *Hermetica*, the Greek *Corpus Hermeticum* and the Latin *Asclepius* tr. by B. Copenhaver, Cambridge: Cambridge University Press, 1992.

Hesiod, *Works and Days*, tr. M. L. West, Oxford: Oxford University Press, 1978, repr. 1999.

——, *Theogony*, tr. by Glenn W. Most, (Loeb Classical Library), Cambridge MA, 2007.

Homer, *Iliad*, tr. by W. F. Wyatt, et al. (Loeb Classical Library), Cambridge, MA: Harvard University Press, 1924.

——, *Odyssey*, tr. by A. T. Murray, (Loeb Classical Library), Cambridge, MA: Harvard University Press, 1919, repr. 1995.

——, *The Homeric Hymns*, tr. by J. Cashford, London: Penguin, 2003.

Livy, *History of Rome*, tr. by A. de Sélincourt, London: Penguin, 1972, repr. 1980, 2002.

Ibn Ezra, Abraham, *The Beginning of Wisdom*, tr. by R. Levy, Baltimore: Johns Hopkins University Press, 1939.

——, *Sefer Ha-olam (The Book of the World*), ed. and tr. by S. Sela, Leiden: Brill, 2010.

——, *On Nativities,* ed. and tr. by S. Sela, Leiden: Brill, 2019.

Isidore of Seville, *On the Nature of Things*, tr. by C. B. Kendall and F. Wallis, Liverpool: Liverpool University Press, (Translated Texts for Historians, 66), 2016.

Julian, *Hymn to King Helios,* in *Orations*, tr. by W. C. Wright (Loeb Classical Library), Cambridge, MA: Harvard University Press, 1913.

Lactantius, *Institutes*, *Epitome*, tr. by A. Bowen and P. Garnsey, Liverpool: Liverpool University Press, 2003, 2006.

Landino, C., *Comento sopra la Comedia,* Florence 1481, Venice 1491, 1493; repr. Edizione Nazionale dei Commenti Danteschi, ed. by P. Procaccioli, 4 vols. Rome: Salerno Editrice, 2001.

Landucci, L, *Diario fiorentino dal 1450–1516*, Florence: Sansoni, 1883; translated by A. de R. Jervis as *A Florentine Diary from 1450 to 1516*, London: Dent, 1927.

Locatellus, B. (printer) and Scotus, A. (publisher), *Liber quadripartiti Ptholemei. Centiloquium eiusdem. Centiloquium hermetis. Eiusdem de stellis beibenijs et alia,* Venice: 1493.

Macrobius, *Commentary on the Dream of Scipio*, tr. by William H. Stahl, New York: Columbia University Press, 1952, repr. 1990.

Medici. L. de', *L'Altercazione*, also known as *De summo bono*, tr. in *Lorenzo de' Medici, Selected Poems and Prose*, ed. by Jon Thiem, University Park, PA: Pennsylvania State University Press, 1991, pp. 65–96.

Orphic Hymns, ed. by A. N. Athanassakis and B. M. Wolkow, Baltimore: Johns Hopkins University Press, 2013.

Orpheus, *Hymns of*, tr. by Thomas S. Taylor, London, 1792; second edition 1824; Prometheus Trust, 1995.

Ovid, *Metamorphoses*, tr. by F.J. Miller, revised by G.P. Goold, 2 vols. (Loeb Classical Library) Cambridge, MA: Harvard University Press, 1916 and several reprints.

——, *Heroides*, tr. by G. Showerman, revised by G.P. Goold, 2 vols. (Loeb Classical Library) Cambridge, MA: Harvard University Press, 1914.

Petrarch, *Africa*, tr. by E.Z.D. Ellis, Baylor University Theses and Dissertations, 2008.

Philostratus, *Life of Apollonius of Tyana*, ed. and tr. by C. P. Jones, 2 vols. (Loeb Classical Library) Cambridge, MA: Harvard University Press, 2005.

Pico della Mirandola, G.F., *Ioannis Pici Mirandulae Vita* (1496) in Giovanni Pico della Mirandola, *Omnia Opera*, Bologna, 1496.

Plato, *The Dialogues of Plato*, tr. Benjamin Jowett, 5 vols., Oxford: University Press, 1892. Repr. in 2 vols, New York: Random House, 1937 and reprints. See also Loeb editions and Oxford World Classics for individual dialogues.

Pliny, *Natural History*, 10 vols., tr. H. Rackham, London: Heinemann, 1938–63.

Pliny, *Letters*, at *Perseus Digital Library*, http://www.perseus.tufts.edu/

Plotinus, *Enneads*, tr. by A.H. Armstrong, 7 vols. (Loeb Classical Library), Cambridge, MA and London: Harvard University Press, 1966–88.

——, *Enneads*, tr. by S. MacKenna, London: Penguin, 1969.

——, *Enneads*, tr. by L.P. Gerson, Cambridge: Cambridge University Press, 2019.

Plutarch, *On the Daemon of Socrates (De genio Socratis)*, tr. by F.C. Babbitt, in *Moralia,* vol. VII (Loeb Classical Library), Cambridge, MA: Harvard University Press, 1994, pp. 361–509.

Poliziano, A., *Greek and Latin Poetry*, ed. by O.E. Knox, (I Tatti Renaissance Library), Cambridge, MA: Harvard University Press, 2018.

——, *Epistolae,* in *Opera omnia*, Venice, 1498.

——, *Letters*, tr. by S. Butler, (I Tatti Renaissance Library), Cambridge, MA: Harvard University Press, 2006.

Proclus, *On the Existence of Evils*, tr. by J. Opsomer and C. Steel, London: Bloomsbury, 2014.

Proclus, *Proclus: Commentary on the First Alcibiades*, ed. by L.G. Westerink and tr. by W. O'Neill, Leiden: Martinus Nijhoff, 1965; reprinted Westbury: Prometheus Trust, 2011.

——, *Commentary on Parmenides*, tr. by G. R. Morrow and J.M. Dillon, Princeton: Princeton University Press, 1987.

——, *Elements of Theology*, ed. and tr. by E. R. Dodds, 2nd edition, Oxford: Clarendon Press, 1962 and reprints.

——, *On Providence*, tr. by Carlos Steel, London: Duckworth, 2007.

——, *Ten Questions on Providence*, tr. by Jan Opsomer and Carlos Steel, London: Duckworth, 2012.

Ptolemy, *Almagest*, tr. by G.J. Toomer, London: Duckworth, 1984, repr. Princeton University Press, 1998.

——, *Tetrabiblos (Quadripartitum)*, tr. by F. E. Robbins (Loeb Classical Library) Cambridge, MA: Harvard University Press, 1940.

Savonarola, *A Guide to Righteous Living and other Works*, tr. by K. Eisenbichler, Toronto: Centre for Reformation and Renaissance Studies, 2003.

Seneca, *Hercules Furens*, tr. by N.W. Bernstein, London: Bloomsbury Academic, 2017.

——, *Epistles*, tr. by R.M. Gummere, 3 vols. (Loeb Classical Library), Cambridge, MA: Harvard University Press, 1917–1925.

——, *Dialogues and Letters*, tr. by C.D.N. Costa, London: Penguin Classics, 1997.

Strozzi, A., *Alessandra Macinghi Strozzi: Letters to Her Sons, 1447–1470*, ed. by J. Bryce, Toronto: Iter Academic Press, 2016.

Strozzi, A., *Selected Letters of Alessandra Strozzi*, Bilingual edition tr. by H. Gregory, University of California Press, 1997.

Suetonius, *Life of Julius Caesar*, in *The Twelve Caesars*, tr. by Robert Graves, London: Penguin, 2007.

Virgil, *Eclogues, Georgics, Aeneid*, tr. by H.R. Fairclough, revised by G.P. Goold, 2 vols, (Loeb Classical Library), Cambridge, MA: Harvard University Press and London: William Heinemann, 1978.

Zahel, *Introductorium*, see Locatellus above.

Selected Studies

Akopyan, O., '*Princeps aliorum* and his Followers: Giovanni Pico della Mirandola on the "Astrological Tradition" in the *Disputationes adversus astrologiam divinatricem*' in *Renaissance Studies,* 32/4 (2017), pp. 547–64.

Aldo Manuzio, Renaissance in Venice, Exhibition Catalogue, ed. by Guido Beltramini, Davide Gasparotto, Giulio Manieri Elia, Venice: Marsilio, 2016.

Allen, M.J.B, '*Homo ad zodiacum*: Marsilio Ficino and the Boethian Hercules,' in *Forma e parola: Studi in memoria di Fredi Chiappelli*, ed. by D. J. Dutschke et al., Rome, 1992, pp. 205–221, reprinted in *Plato's Third Eye: Studies in Marsilio Ficino's Metaphysics and its Sources*, Variorum Series, Aldershot: Ashgate, 1995.

——, '*In principio*: Marsilio Ficino on the Life of Text' in *Res et verba in der Renaissance*, ed. by E. Kessler and I. Maclean, Wiesbaden, 2002, pp. 11–28; reprinted in Allen, *Studies in the Platonism of Marsilio Ficino and Giovanni Pico*, Variorum Series, London: Routledge, 2017, pp. 67–84.

——, 'Marsilio Ficino on Plato, the Neoplatonists and the Christian doctrine of the Trinity,' *Renaissance Quarterly*, 37 (1984) pp. 555–84, reprinted in *Plato's Third Eye*, Aldershot: Ashgate, 1995.

——, 'Marsilio Ficino and the Language of the Past,' *Forme del Neoplatonismo*, ed. by Luisa Simonutti (Florence, 2007), pp. 35–50 at pp. 47–8, reprinted in *Studies in the Platonism of Marsilio Ficino and Giovanni Pico*, London: Routledge, 2017, pp. 135–50.

——, 'Marsilio Ficino on Saturn, the Plotinian Mind, and the Monster of Averroes,' *Bruniana & Campanelliana*, 16 (2010–11), pp. 11–29, reprinted in *Studies in the Platonism of Marsilio Ficino and Giovanni Pico*, London: Routledge, 2017, pp. 253–71.

——, *Synoptic Art, Marsilio Ficino on the History of Platonic Interpretation*, Florence: Olschki, 1998.

Andrews F. and Pincelli, A., *Churchmen and Urban Government in Late Medieval Italy*, Cambridge and New York: Cambridge University Press, 2013.

Bacchelli, F., *Giovanni Pico e Pier Leone da Spoleto: tra filosofia dell'amore e tradizione cabalistica*, Quaderni di *Rinascimento*, XXXIX, Florence: Olschki, 2001.

Baldini, N. and Bietti, M., *Nello Splendore Mediceo*, Livorno: Sillabe, 2013.

Bartlett, K., *Florence in the Age of the Medici and Savonarola, 1464–1498. A short history with documents*, Indianapolis: Hackett, 2018.

Bartolucci, G., *Vera religio. Marsilio Ficino e la tradizione ebraica*, Turin: Paideia, 2017.

Bertozzi, M. (ed.), *Nello Specchio del cielo,* Florence: Olschki, 2008.

Beiweis, S. and Ockenström, L., 'Memory, Mercury and Magic in Marsilio Ficino's *De Vita*', in *Rinascimento*, 2nd series, 59 (2019), pp. 271–96.

Black, C., *Pico's Heptaplus and Biblical Hermeneutics*, Leiden: Brill, 2006.

Black, R., *Education and Society in Florentine Tuscany: Teachers, Pupils and Schools, c. 1250-1500*, Leiden: Brill, 2007.

Brown, A., *Bartolommeo Scala 1430-1498, Chancellor of Florence. The Humanist as Bureaucrat*, Princeton: Princeton University Press, 1979.

Brown, A., *Medicean and Savonarolan Florence*, Turnhout: Brepols, 2011.

——, *The Medici in Florence. The exercise and language of power*, Florence, 1992.

——, 'Piero in Power, 1492–1494,' in *The Medici, Citizens and Masters*, ed. by R. Black and J.E. Law, Florence: Villa I Tatti, 2015, pp. 113–25.

——, 'The Revolution of 1494 in Florence and its Aftermath : A Reassessment' in *Italy in Crisis, 1494*, ed. by J. Everson and D. Zancani, Oxford : Legenda, 2000.

Caby, C., *De l'érémetisme rural au monachisme urbain. Les Camaldules en Italie à la fin du Moyen* Âge, Rome: École française de Rome, BEFAR-305, 2000.

Calzolai, C.C., *La storia della Badia a Settimo*, Florence: Libreria Editrice Fiorentina, 1958, revised edition, 1976.

Caroti, S and Perrone Compagni, V. (eds.), *Nuovi Maestri e Antichi Testi*, Florence: Olschki, 2012.

Castelli, P., *Il lume del Sole. Marsilio Ficino, medico dell'anima*, Florence: Opus Libri, 1984.

Catani, R., 'Astrological Polemics in the Crisis of the 1490s', in *Italy in Crisis, 1494*, ed. by J. Everson and D. Zancani, Oxford : Legenda, 2000.

Celenza, C., *The Lost Italian Renaissance. Humanists, Historians and Latin's Legacy*, Baltimore: Johns Hopkins University Press, 2004.

——, *The Intellectual World of the Italian Renaissance: Language, Philosophy, and the Search for Meaning*, Cambridge: Cambridge University Press 2018.

——, 'Francesco Cattani da Diacceto's *De Pulchro*, II, 4, and the Practice of Renaissance Platonism,' *Accademia*, IX (2007), pp. 87–98.

Charrier, S., *Recherches sur l'oeuvre latine en prose de Robert Gaguin* (1433–1501), Paris: Honoré Champion Éditeur, 1996.

Ciampi, S., *Notizie dei secoli XV. e XVI. sull'Italia, Polonia e Russia, raccolte e pubblicate da Sebastiano Ciampi colle vite di Bona Sforza e' Duchi di Milano Regina di Polonia e di Giovanni de' Medici, detto delle Bande Nere*, Florence, 1833.

Coleman, J. and Moudarres, A. (eds.), *Luigi Pulci in Renaissance Florence and Beyond: New Perspectives on his Poetry and Influence*, Turnhout: Brepols, 2017.

Collard, F., *Un historien au travail à la fin du XVe siècle: Robert Gaguin*, Geneva : Droz, 1996.

Copenhaver, B., *Magic and the Dignity of Man. Pico della Mirandola and His Oration in Modern Memory*, Cambridge, MA: Belknap Press, Harvard University Press, 2019.

Corrias, A., 'Ficino interprete di Plotino. Alcune considerazioni sull'uomo e sull'anima', *Interpres* 35 (2017): 98–120.

——, 'From Daemonic Reason to Daemonic Imagination: Plotinus and Marsilio Ficino on the Soul's Tutelary Spirit', *British Journal for the History of Philosophy*, 21, 3 (2013) pp. 443–62.

——, *The Renaissance of Plotinus: the Soul and Human Nature in Marsilio Ficino's Commentary on the Enneads*, London and New York: Routledge, 2020.

Davis, M., 'Plato's *Minos*: The Soul of the Law,' *The Review of Politics*, 78 (2016), pp. 343–63.

Della Torre, A., *Storia dell' Academia Platonica di Firenze*, Florence, 1902; repr., Turin: Bottega d'Erasmo, 1968.

de Roover, R., *The Rise and Decline of the Medici Bank 1397*-1494, Cambridge, MA: Harvard University Press, 1963, repr. 1999.

Dillon, J. 'The Theology of Julian's *Hymn to King Helios*', *Itaca*, 14–15, pp. 103–115, reprinted in J. Dillon, *The Platonic Heritage*, London: Routledge Variorum Series, 2018, essay XXIII.

Dooley, B., *A Companion to Astrology in the Renaissance*, Leiden: Brill, 2014.

Eastwood, B., *Ordering the Heavens: Roman Astronomy and Cosmology in the Carolingian Renaissance* (History of Science and Medicine Library), Leiden: Brill, 2007.

Faracovi, O.P., *Marsilio Ficino. Scritti sull'Astrologia*, Milan: Biblioteca Universale Rizzoli, 1999.

——, *Lo Specchio Alto. Astrologia e Filosofia fra Medioevo e Prima Età Moderna*, (Supplement 32, Study 11 of *Bruniana & Campanelliana*), Pisa: Fabrizio Serra, 2012.

Fellina, S., *Alla scuola di Marsilio Ficino. Il pensiero filosofico di Francesco Cattani da Diacceto*, Pisa: Edizioni della Normale, 2017.

Franco, M., *Lettere di Matteo Franco*, ed. by G. Frosini, Florence: Accademia della Crusca, 1990.

Garfagnini, G.C. (ed.), *Marsilio Ficino e il ritorno di Platone : studi e documenti*, Florence: Olschki, 1986.

Garin, E., *La cultura filosofica del Rinascimento italiano: ricerche e documenti,* Florence: Sansoni, 1961, repr. 1994.

——, *Lo Zodiaco della vita: la polemica sull'astrologia dal Trecento al Cinquecento,* Rome, 1976; tr. as *Astrology in the Renaissance: The Zodiac of Life,* tr. C. Jackson and J. Allen, revised with the author by C. Robertson, London: Routledge & Kegan Paul, 1983.

——, *Pico della Mirandola: Vita e Dottrina*. Florence: F. Le Monnier, 1937.

——, *Studi sul Platonismo Medievale*, Florence: F. Le Monnier, 1958.

Gentile, S., 'Giano Lascaris, Germain de Ganay e la *prisca theologia* in Francia', R*inascimento*, series II, XXVI (1986), pp.51–76.

——, 'Note sullo Scrittoio di Marsilio Ficino', in *Supplementum Festivum: Studies in Honor of Paul Oskar Kristeller*, ed. by J. Hankins, J. Monfasani and F. Purnell Jr., Binghamton, NY: Medieval and Renaissance Texts and Studies, 1987, pp. 339–97.

Gentile, S., Niccoli, S., and Viti, P., *Marsilio Ficino e il ritorno di Platone: Catalogo*, Florence: Le Lettere, 1984.

Gentile, S. and Toussaint, S., *Marsilio Ficino. Fonti, Testi, Fortuna*, Rome: Edizioni di Storia e Letteratura, 2006.

Gersh, S., *Interpreting Proclus. From Antiquity to the Renaissance*, Cambridge: Cambridge University Press, 2013.

Gianetto, N., *Bernardo Bembo Umanista e Politico Veneziano*, Florence: Olschki, 1985.

Goldthwaite, R.A., *The Economy of Renaissance Florence*, Baltimore: Johns Hopkins University Press, 2009.

Grant, E., *Planets, Stars, & Orbs. The Medieval Cosmos, 1200–1687*, Cambridge: Cambridge University Press. 1994, repr. 1996.

Greenbaum, D. G, *The daimon in Hellenistic astrology: origins and influence*, Leiden: Brill, 2016.

Hankins, J., 'Cosimo de' Medici and the "Platonic Academy"', *Journal of the Warburg and Courtauld Institutes*, 53 (1990), pp. 144–62.

——, *Plato in the Italian Renaissance*, 2 vols., Leiden: Brill, 1990.

——, *Humanism and Platonism in the Italian Renaissance*, Vol. II: *Platonism*, Rome, Edizioni di Storia e Letteratura, 2004.

Hankins, J. and Palmer, A., *The Recovery of Ancient Philosophy in the Renaissance: A Brief Guide,* Florence: Olschki, 2008.

Hankins, J. and Meroi, F. (eds.), *The Rebirth of Platonic Theology*, Florence: Olschki, 2013.

Hofmann, W. V., *Forschungen zur Geschichte der Kurialen Behörden vom Schisma bis zur Reformation,* Rome: Loescher, 1914; repr. Turin: Bottega d'Erasmo, 1971.

Jayne, S., *John Colet and Marsilio Ficino*, Oxford: Oxford University Press, 1963.

Jurdjevic, M., *Guardians of Republicanism: the Valori Family in the Florentine Renaissance*, Oxford: Oxford University Press, 2008.

Kaske, C.V., 'Ficino's Shifting Attitude Towards Astrology in the *de vita coelitus comparanda*, the Letter to Poliziano, and the *Apologia* to the Cardinals', in *Marsilio Ficino e il ritorno di Platone*, 2 vols, ed. by G. Garfagnini, Florence: Olschki, 1986, pp. 371–80.

Katinis, T., *Medicina e Filosofia in Marsilio Ficino: Il consilio contro la pestilentia*, ed. by T. Katinis, Rome: Edizioni di Storia e Letteratura, 2007.

Kristeller, P.O., 'Francesco da Diacceto and Florentine Platonism in the Sixteenth Century', in *Studies in Renaissance Thought and Letters*, I, Rome: Edizioni di Storia e Letteratura, 1969, pp. 287–336.

——, 'Sebastiano Salvini, A Florentine Humanist and Theologian and a member of Ficino's Platonic Academy', *Didascaliae, Studies in Honor of Anselm Albareda*, ed. by S. Prete, New York, 1961, pp. 205–43; reprinted in *Studies in Renaissance Thought and Letters*, III, Rome: Edizioni di Storia e Letteratura, 1993, pp. 173–206.

——, 'Marsilio Ficino e Venezia', *Studies in Renaissance Thought and Letters*, IV, Rome: Edizioni di Storia e Letteratura, 1996, pp. 245–63.

Lackner, D. F., 'The Camaldolese Academy: Ambrogio Traversari, Marsilio Ficino and the Christian Platonic Tradition', in *Marsilio Ficino: his Theology, his Philosophy, his Legacy*, ed. by M.J.B. Allen and V. Rees with M. Davies, Leiden: Brill, 2002, pp. 15–44.

Magnard, P. (ed.), *Marsile Ficin. Les Platonismes à la Renaissance*, Paris: Vrin, 2001.

Majercik, R. (ed.), The *Chaldaean Oracles,* Leiden: Brill, 1989, reprinted Westbury: Prometheus Trust, 2013.

Marcel, R., *Marsile Ficin*, Paris: Les Belles Lettres, 1958, repr. 2007.

Martin, F. X., *Friar, Reformer and Renaissance Scholar. The Life and Work of Giles of Viterbo,* Villanova, PA: Augustinian Press, 1992.

Maskell, D., 'Robert Gaguin and Thomas More, Translators of Pico Della Mirandola', *Bibliothèque d'Humanisme et Renaissance*, 37/1 (1975), pp. 63–8.

Matton, S., *Francisci Catanei Diacetii: De pulchro libri III*, Pisa: Scuola Normale, 1986.

Maxson, B.J., *The Humanist World of Renaissance Florence*, Cambridge: Cambridge University Press, 2014.

Mittarelli, J.B., and Costadoni, A. *Annales Camaldulenses,* VII (Venice, 1762).

Monfasani, J., 'Giles of Viterbo and the Errors of Aristotle,' in *Egidio da Viterbo: Cardinale Agostiniano tra Roma e l'Europa del Rinascimento*: Atti del Convegno, Viterbo-Roma 2012, ed. by M. Chiabo, R. Ronzani, and A-M. Vitale, Rome: Centro Cultúrale Agostiniano Roma nel Rinascimento, 2014.

Nauert, C.G., 'Rethinking "Christian Humanism"', in *Interpretations of Renaissance Humanism*, ed. by A. Mazzocco, Leiden: Brill, 2006, pp. 155–80.

Nodes, D., *Giles of Viterbo. The Commentary on the Sentences of Petrus Lombardus*, Leiden: Brill, 2010.

North, J., 'Types of Inconsistency in the Astrology of Ficino and others', in *Christian Humanism. Essays in honour of Arjo Vanderjagt*, ed. by A.A. MacDonald, J.R. Veenstra, Z. von Martels, Leiden: Brill, 2009, pp. 281–302.

O'Malley, J.W., 'Giles of Viterbo: A Reformer's Thought on Renaissance Rome,' *Renaissance Quarterly,* 20 (1967/1), pp. 1–11.

——, *Giles of Viterbo on Church and Reform: A Study in Renaissance Thought*, Leiden: Brill, 1968.

Overgaauw E. and Sanzotta, V., 'Una lettera sconosciuta di Marsilio Ficino a Lorenzo de' Medici nella Sammlung Darmstaedter della Staatsbibliothek zu Berlin,' in *Interpres*, XXIX (2010), pp. 171–182.

Pettegree, A. and Walsby, M., eds. *French Books, III & IV. Books published in France before 1601 in Latin and Languages other than French*, Leiden: Brill, 2011.

Pico della Mirandola, G., *Heptaplus,* tr. by D. Carmichael, in *Pico della Mirandola On the Dignity of Man*, Indianapolis: Hackett, 1965.

——, *On Being and the One,* tr. by P.J.W. Miller, as entry above, Indianapolis: Hackett, 1965.

Picotti, G. B., *La Giovinezza di Leone X, Il Papa del Rinascimento*, Milan: Ulrico Hoepli, 1927.

Polizzotto, L., *The elect Nation: the Savonarolan Movement in Florence 1494-1545*, Oxford: Clarendon Press, 1994.

Polizzotto. L. and Kovesi, C., *Memorie di casa Valori*, Florence: Nerbini, 2007.

Poncet, C., 'Un gioco tra profezia e filosofia: i tarocchi di Marsilio' in *Il linguaggio dei cieli: astri e simboli nel Rinascimento*, ed. by G. Ernst and G. Giglioni, Rome: Carocci, 2012.

Prescott, O. *Princes of the Renaissance*, New York: Random House, 1969 repr. Routledge, 2019.

Puccinotti, F., *Storia della Medicina*, Livorno, 1850–70, repr. 1880.

Rees, V., *From Gabriel to Lucifer: A Cultural History of Angels,* London: I.B. Tauris, 2013.

——, 'Celestial Bodies in the writings of Marsilio Ficino' in *Heavenly Discourses*. Proceedings of conference held at the University of Bristol, September 2011, ed. by N. Campion, Ceredigion: Sophia Centre Press, 2016, pp. 111–117.

Richardson, B, *Print Culture in Renaissance Italy: The Editor and the Vernacular Text, 1470-1600*, Cambridge: Cambridge University Press, 2004.

Robichaud, D. J.-J., 'Fragments of Marsilio Ficino's Translations and Use of Proclus' *Elements of Theology* and *Elements of Physics*: Evidence and Study' in *Vivarium*, 54/1 (2016) pp. 46–107.

——, *Plato's Persona: Marsilio Ficino, Renaissance Humanism, and Platonic Traditions*, Philadelphia: University of Pennsylvania Press, 2018.

Rochon, A., *La jeunesse de Laurent de Médicis: 1449–1478*, Paris: Les Belles Lettres, 1963.

Roscoe, W., *Life and Pontificate of Leo the Tenth*, 4 vols. Liverpool: Cadell and Davies, 1805, reprinted many times.

Rubinstein, N., *The Government of Florence under the Medici (1434–1494),* Oxford: Clarendon Press, 1997.

Rutkin, H. D., 'Mysteries of attraction: Giovanni Pico della Mirandola, astrology and desire,' in *Studies in History and Philosophy of Biological and Biomedical Sciences* 41 (2010) 117–124.

——, 'The Use and Abuse of Ptolemy's Tetrabiblos in Renaissance and Early Modern Europe: Two Case Studies (Giovanni Pico della Mirandola and Filippo Fantoni)' in *Ptolemy in Perspective*, ed. by A. Jones, New York: Springer, 2010, pp. 135–150.

Saffrey, H.D., 'Notes Platoniciennes de Marsile Ficin dans un Manuscrit de Proclus', *Bibliothèque d'Humanisme et Renaissance*, 21 (1959), pp. 161–84.

Sanesi, E., *Vicari e Canonici Fiorentini e il 'caso Savonarola'*, Florence: Libreria Editrice Fiorentina, 1932.

Scheller, R.W., 'Imperial themes in art and literature of the early French Renaissance: the period of Charles VIII', tr. from Dutch by M. Hoyle, *Simiolus: Netherlands Quarterly for the History of Art,* 12/1 (1981–1982), pp. 5–69.

Schnitzer, J., *Peter Delfin, General des Camaldulenserordens: (1444–1525)*, Munich: Ernst Reinhardt, 1926.

Soleymani Chaharfarsakhi, M., 'Avicenna and Ficino on Divine Prophets,' *Accademia*, XIV (2012), pp. 23–43.

Sorokina, M., 'Une source inconnue de la Disputatio contra iudicium astrologorum de Marsile Ficin: la Summa de astris de Gérard de Feltre,' *Bruniana & Campanelliana*, XXI, 1, 2015, p. 169–89.

Tambrun-Krasker, B., *Oracles Chaldaïques. Recension de Georges Gémiste Pléthon*, Athens: Academy of Athens, 1995.

Taylor, T., *Proclus: The Theology of Plato*, Frome: The Prometheus Trust, 1994.

Toussaint, S., 'Plotin chez les moines. En marge des *Ennéades*: Marsile Ficin dans une lettre de Pietro Delfino Camaldule?' in *Accademia*, VI (2004), pp. 47–57.

Tromboni, L., 'Girolamo Savonarola lettore di Platone: Edizione e Commento del *De doctrina Platonicorum*', *Rinascimento*, 46/2 (2006), 133–213.

——, 'La Discesa di Carlo VIII in Italia: L'Impatto culturale di un evento politico tra XV e XVI secolo', *Rinascimento*, 59 (2019), 297–333.

Vasoli, C., 'Sugli Inizi della Fortuna di Ficino in Francia: Germain e Jean de Ganay', in *Marsile Ficin ou les mystères Platoniciens*, ed. by S. Toussaint (Les Cahiers de l'Humanisme, II), Paris: Les Belles Lettres, 2002, pp. 299–312.

Viti, P., 'Documenti ignoti per la biografia di Marsilio Ficino, in *Marsilio Ficino e il ritorno di Platone: Studi e documenti*, ed. by G. C. Garfagnini, Florence: Olschki, 1986, pp. 251–86.

Weinstein, D., *Savonarola: The Rise and Fall of a Renaissance Prophet,* New Haven & London: Yale University Press, 2011.

——, *Savonarola and Florence: Prophecy and Patriotism in the Renaissance,* Princeton: Princeton University Press, 1970.

Wels, V., *The Antichrist Girolamo of Ferrara, Greatest of all Hypocrites*, Dallas: Perkins School of Theology, Southern Methodist University, 2006.

Witcombe, C.L.C.E., *Copyright in the Renaissance: Prints and the Privilegio in Sixteenth-Century Venice and Rome*, Leiden: Brill, 2004.

Zeller, W., *Der Jurist und Humanist Martin Prenninger gen. Uranius (1450–1501)*, Tübingen: Mohr, 1973.

Zoller, R., *Arabic Parts in Astrology: Lost Key to Prediction*, Rochester, VT: Inner Traditions, 1989.

Index

This index covers the Introduction, Letters, Appendices, Biographical Notes and Illustrations. To find relevant material in the Notes it is hoped that a letter reference will suffice.

Sepe magna est laus que brevis est. CXX[illegible]

Marsilius ficinus bartolomeo scale oratori.
Legi questiones christophori Landini camal-
dulenses. In iis libris maronis adyta pene-
trat. Ciceronis dialogos imitatur ad un-
guem. felicem virum fabricat felicissime.
Lege illos et tu. Scio mecum senties.
Vale. Sed quare in laudando christopho-
ro tam brevis es marsili? Quia ha-
bet nescio quid, quod exprimere nequeam.
Iterum vale.

hec et [illegible] manu [illegible] [illegible] [illegible] [illegible] etiam

Quam placeat bonis sibi [illegible]. CXX[illegible]

Marsilius ficinus laurentio medici viro
magnanimo. pax tibi. Si paci, docto
et bono sacerdoti favebis, favebis et
mihi. Cum enim viri boni et amici agitur
res, res agitur nostra: Vale.

[illegible] petitio et commendatio iusta. CXX[illegible]

Marsilius ficinus Laurentio medici viro
magnanimo. Multi alia te digniora se
petunt. Gregorius epiphanius longe dignior
est iis que postulat. Et si nobis amicissimus est,
tamen propter eius virtutem magis quam propter amicitiam
eum tibi commendo. Ita propter virtutem et amicus.